your
babycare
bible

your babycare bible

contributing editor
Dr A.J.R. Waterston
MD, FRCP, FRCPCH, DRCOG, DCH

VIKING
an imprint of
PENGUIN BOOKS

VIKING

Published by the Penguin Group
Penguin Group (Australia)
250 Camberwell Road, Camberwell,
Victoria 3124
Australia
(a division of Pearson Australia Group Pty Ltd)

Penguin Books Ltd, Registered Offices: 80 Strand,
London, WC2R 0RL, England

First published by
Carroll & Brown Publishers Limited
(United Kingdom), 2009
This edition published by Penguin Group
(Australia), 2009

1 3 5 7 9 10 8 6 4 2

Managing Art Editor: Emily Cook
Photography: Jules Selmes

Reproduced by RALI, Spain
Printed in China

A full CIP catalogue record for this book is available
from the National Library of Australia.

ISBN 9780670073726

penguin.com.au

Contents

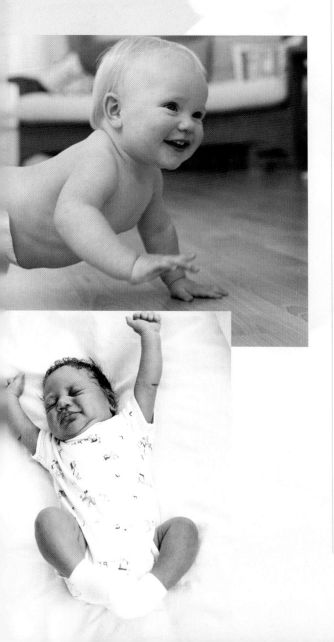

CONTRIBUTORS

A.J.R. Waterston MD, FRCP, FRCPCH, DRCOG,DCH
Consultant Paediatrician (Community Child Health) and Clinical Senior Lecturer, University of Newcastle upon Tyne

Penny Preston MD, ChB, MRCP
former GP specialising in child health and development; now writes full time on the subject

H.A. Raucher, MD
practising paediatrician and Associate Clinical Professor of Paediatrics at The Mount Sinai School of Medicine

Clare Meynell, RM
International Board of Certified Lactation Consultants

Alison Blenkinsop, RM, DipHE, IBCLC
Media Liaison, Lactation Consultants of Great Britain

June Thompson, RGN, RM, RHV
Maternal and Child Health Nurse and freelance health writer

Nicola Graimes
Nutritionist and author of healthy food books for children

Introduction

Raising a healthy infant and young toddler involves skills and information that parents need to access quickly and easily. Along with their newborns, parents are presented with the tasks of keeping their babies fed, clean and comforted, and safe from danger and ill health. These are enormous responsibilities in themselves, which can be made even greater if a baby is premature, a twin or is born with special needs. With little available free time, it's important that parents can readily find out what they need to know and be able to follow that advice accurately and effectively: in some cases, it may even make the difference between life and death.

Although you will be supported by a healthcare team – consisting, at least, of your GP and maternal and child health nurse – as a parent you are on the front line when it comes to managing your baby's and toddler's daily care, and recognising when there may be a problem that needs medical attention. Thus, looking after a baby can be filled with anxiety since most new parents are inexperienced and babies are quick to let you know they need attention. Moreover, there are many areas of care – from establishing feeding to ensuring a baby receives his or her vital immunisations – that are essential to a child's wellbeing and need to be initiated or done at certain times.

No parent, GP or even paediatrician has the wealth of knowledge that encompasses the entirety of contemporary paediatrics, and no book currently on the market offers sufficiently wide-ranging information. That is why *Your Babycare Bible* was created with a team of paediatric specialists and why it will prove an invaluable companion in raising your baby and toddler.

With the contributions of different experts, ranging from breastfeeding technicians to nutritionists and child behaviourists as well as top paediatricians, *Your Babycare Bible* will provide you with the most up-to-date and comprehensive information on all aspects of babycare for newborns to toddlers. Special fold-out pages make it easy to master the essentials of newborn care and emergency first-aid procedures, comprehensive chapters explain how to ensure your baby feeds and sleeps successfully and safely, and how you should interpret and respond to his or her crying. There is also in-depth coverage on keeping your baby safe and healthy and what to expect if your baby is born a twin, is premature or has special needs. A month-by-month guide will give you an overview of what to expect as your newborn grows into a baby and then toddler, and an entire chapter is dedicated to matters of growth and development and how you, as a parent, can promote these aspects. Finally, there is specific help given to new mums and dads – advice on how to prepare for your new arrival and how to manage all aspects of parenting.

Tony Waterston

Dr A.J.R. Waterston
MD, FRCP, FRCPCH, DRCOG, DCH

PREPARING FOR YOUR BABY

Readying your home

Having things ready at home will make the first hectic days of looking after your baby much easier. By getting all the little details taken care of ahead of time, you will be freeing up more time and energy later on to enjoy your baby.

If you are tempted, as many parents-to-be are, to paint, remodel or make repairs in your home, try to complete all these projects at least a month before your baby is due. Earlier is even better. Practically, you don't want to bring your baby home to a messy, unorganised and noisy scene if your birth comes earlier than expected or if the upgrading is running late. Pregnant women (and newborns) should not be exposed to the dust, commotion and smell of paint that arise with home improvements, so it would be best if work was carried out by a partner or professionals.

Expecting twins or more

Expecting twins is exciting but also somewhat terrifying. You will no doubt ask yourself, "How will I be able to care for them both?" But first, there are some more practical issues to face. Often, the birth of twins comes before your due date. Planning when you will go into labour is much more difficult, and the possibility of having the twins prematurely must be considered. Moreover, twins should only be delivered in a hospital. While twins may sometimes be born vaginally, there is a higher chance of needing a caesarean section than with single births. You must also put into your plans a slower post-partum recovery if a caesarean is needed.

If you plan on using a bassinet initially, you will need two and you will also need two of a lot of other items: two car seats, two infant swings, a double pram. When purchasing your baby clothes, however, it is not necessary to buy two complete sets of everything – your twins can share the vests and outfits. However, you may want to buy a few extra of items that are few in number. Additionally, if you know that your twins are of different sexes, you may either buy extra outfits, some designed for boys and others designed for girls, or buy unisex colours and designs.

With twins the expenses add up quickly. By the time you have purchased two of most things, you will have spent a great deal of money. If possible, borrow some equipment and clothes from friends or relatives or consider buying second hand.

Your baby's room

Whether you have a separate room for baby or make do with part of another room, and no matter your decorative style, it's important that furniture and storage spaces are arranged in ways that will be most convenient for you and will make it easier for you to get your baby into and out of her cot, change nappies, get your baby dressed or rock her to sleep.

Place the cot against the wall. From within the cot, your baby should not be able to reach a window, cord from a blind or curtain, or another piece of furniture. It is also common sense to avoid placing it against a wall shared with a noisy room or in a spot that permits direct sunlight to fall upon your baby in the early morning or during naps.

The change table should be placed squarely against the wall and away from a window. Have another piece of furniture immediately to the side of the table for storing nappies, wipes, nappy creams or ointments. This will allow access to all the supplies you need during a nappy change without the need for you to leave your baby unattended on the table, even for a moment.

The obvious place for a nappy bucket is right next to the changing table.

A comfortable rocking chair will come in handy in a baby's bedroom; you may end up spending hours at a time there. Place nearby a lamp with a low intensity setting that can be used to let you read and/or a small radio or CD player so you can listen to music while nursing or expressing; the lamp can function as a night light. A clock that you can see from the rocking chair is helpful for keeping track of how long you have been breastfeeding.

An expressing centre can be set up anywhere in the home, but is often planned next to the rocking chair. The pump, accessories and books or magazines to read while expressing milk all should be stored conveniently.

You will also need dressers, chests, crates or shelving to store clothing, toys and books.

What to buy

Every store and website selling infant clothing has a list of what they believe you need to buy. The specific number of each item will suit most families, but misses the boat for the rest. How much you need to buy depends really depends on how messy your baby is, how much of a stickler you are for cleanliness and how often you expect to do washing.

You won't know about messiness until your baby is born but it isn't necessary to put on fresh clothing for small amounts of sick or other unwelcome spills although you may feel more comfortable doing so. Obviously, if you will want to change outfits every time a little sick gets on her, you will need a bigger number of each item. However, if you plan to do a wash every day, buy less of each article and more if you think you'll wait three or four days between loads. To be on the safe side, add an extra day's supply.

So how may bibs should you buy? Assume for this exercise that you will do the washing every two days and you will change her outfit only when there is a moderate amount of sick on it. Times the average number of indoor garments or articles used daily (2) by the days between washes (2) by your "neatness" quotient (1) or 2 x 2 x 1 = 4. Then add 2 (one extra day's supply) so you will need 6. For outdoor clothes, buy no more than the recommended number no matter how often you wash.

INDOOR CLOTHES

Nappies at least 8–12
T-shirts or vests (wide-necked with front and back joined with press-studs between the thighs) 2–3
Socks or booties 1
Sleeping bags 1–2
Grow-suits 2
Bunny-rugs 2
Cot sheets 1–2
Bibs 2
Face washers 1–2
Hooded baby towel 1

OUTDOOR CLOTHES

Hats 2
Jumpers or cardigans 2
Blanket or sleeping bag (for use in the pram in cold weather) 1

Furnishing your baby's room

Whatever style of furniture and furnishings you choose, safety must be given a high priority (see Chapter 12). It also is important to look for products that are easy to keep clean.

Some items – chests of drawers and storage units – do not have to be baby-sized; full-size versions can cater to your child's needs for many years.

Where space is limited, think about using areas such as the top of a wardrobe for storing little used items of clothing or toys, or the back of a door for hanging nappy or toy bags. You also could install a peg rail around the room to provide hanging space for many items.

Nappy bucket

Most parents prefer to get a rubbish storage device that has a cover (to keep any aromas contained). Plastic rubbish bags inside can conveniently be removed and discarded. If you will be removing the used nappies frequently, you need only a small container and small-sized plastic bags. Small nappy buckets may be placed on a box or stool to decrease the amount of bending you must do, or simply get a bin with a foot pedal control for opening. If you will be emptying the bucket less often or are using fabric nappies, a larger container is more appropriate.

Change table

You will change an awful lot of nappies, so get a change table that is the right height for you – you shouldn't have to lean over to change your newborn. Safety is an important consideration: as your child gets older, she will squirm more and roll over with a potential for falls. Ideally, the surface of your change table should have raised sideboards on three sides. Your baby should lie on a soft mat or pad, which should be easily cleanable, which covers the entire top surface of the table. You may prefer buying a table with a removable, washable top. Your baby will need changing for at least 18 months, so choose a table that is large enough to accommodate a distracting book or toy, in addition to your child.

Some tables come with baths that slide in underneath or with shelves or cabinets for supplies and toys, which can be handy.

Accessories

Lights and lamps with low-intensity bulbs will throw sufficient light to let you check on your baby at night without awakening her. Position one near your feeding chair.

A room thermometer, either free standing or wall mounted will be necessary to ensure your baby's room is kept at a safe 18°C (65°F).

Mobiles will amuse your baby when she's older. These can be fixed to the side of the cot.

Cot

Safety issues involved when choosing a cot and mattress are discussed on page 156. Other things to consider are whether you want to choose a cot that converts to a bed or whether you want one that has storage drawers underneath.

Baby products

Below is a list of basic items you will want to have on hand in your baby's room at home when she first arrives.

- ◆ Waterless hand sanitiser
- ◆ Infant paracetamol (Panadol and others)
- ◆ Saline nasal spray
- ◆ Moisturising skin lotion
- ◆ Thermometer (a digital, rectal one is the most accurate)
- ◆ Nappy creams or ointments*
- ◆ Soap*
- ◆ Shampoo*
- ◆ Cotton balls or wipes (unscented, alcohol-free)*
- ◆ Rubbing alcohol (optional for umbilical cord care)*

*See Chapter 2 before buying these.

Storage

Although very small, babies can amass a surprising number of items that need to be carefully stored. Clothes, toys, toiletries and bulky equipment such as baths and nappy packs need to be easy to hand but still contained. Most of your baby's clothes can be stored in drawers although a trolley is a more versatile option. Stacking boxes or baskets are other options for everyday items. You also will need a laundry bag for dirty garments.

A nappy tidy can be fixed to the wall near your changing area to keep nappies within reach. Wipes, creams and disposable bags should be placed in a handy dispenser. Toys can be placed on shelves or in pocket tidies.

Rocking or nursing chair

You will spend many hours feeding your baby so choose something with good support. There are versions that recline as well as rock or glide and that have matching foot support. Make sure the fabric is spongeable or that there is a plastic covering.

Baby equipment

In addition to furnishing your baby's room, a number of other items are essential or handy to assist with her care. Again, the vital points are to check that equipment meets safety standards and is easy to keep clean.

Infant restraint

You will need an infant restraint suitable for newborns to take your baby home from the hospital or birthing centre. It should have a 5-point safety harness. The seat must be installed rearward facing and in a seat not fitted with an airbag. Don't leave installation until you are ready to bring your newborn home, as the set-up process may be tricky and time consuming. You can learn more about infant restraints on pages 97 and 321.

Swing

An infant swing is a wonderful invention. It is especially good at calming your baby during evening fussy spells and can keep her happy and quiet long enough for you to eat your dinner. Swings may be manual or battery operated. Make sure your swing has safety straps to keep your baby from sliding out; a washable, removable seat cover that is secured with strong stitching and heavy-duty snaps, and a padded reclining seat.

Portable chair/bouncer

This is useful when your baby is awake and you want to be sure she is safe next to you while you are busy doing something else. As well as reclining, some will support your infant in a more upright position; all will let you gently rock your baby. If your home is on two floors, consider buying an extra chair, so you can leave each in a different, convenient location. If you have one upstairs and another downstairs, you only have to carry your baby when you change floors. You don't also have to carry the chair.

Bassinet

This portable baby basket can be placed at your bedside so that you don't have to go far to get your baby for night-time feedings and is easy to transport if your baby will sleep outside your home. Some come with supporting stands and canopies. The downside of these little beds is their small size; your baby soon will outgrow hers.

Hospital checks on babies

If your baby is born in hospital, she will probably be first checked by a paediatrician. (If you have your baby at home, a GP may perform this first assessment.)

Apgar test

At 1- and 5-minute intervals after the birth, hospital staff will perform the Apgar test. Developed by Dr Virginia Apgar this test allows a quick assessment of a newborn's health. The word "Apgar" stands also for the signs that the staff are looking at – appearance, pulse, grimace, activity and respiration. For each of these, your baby will be given a score of 0, 1 or 2 (see box, below). Babies rarely receive a total score of 10, but a score above 6 is usually fine. A low score is not an indicator of a baby's future health; it simply means she needs some temporary medical help and monitoring.

Full physical examination

Within the first few days your baby's features, spine, anus, fingers and toes will be checked; his hips will be assessed for proper movement and placement. She'll be weighed, and her head size and length may be measured.

Heel prick test

After the first 24 hours, a blood sample may be taken taken from your baby's heel. This can be used to check her thyroid function and for a rare metabolic disorder called phenylketonuria. If there is a family history of any condition, a test may be done. The tests offered vary among healthcare providers, so it's important to discuss which ones your baby is being given.

Preventive treatments

At many hospitals, newborns receive an injection of Vitamin K because they often have low levels of this vitamin, which is necessary for the process of normal blood clotting.

With your consent, your baby will also be given a dose of the hepatitis B vaccine soon after birth. To be fully immunised, your baby will need three more doses of the vaccine given later on.

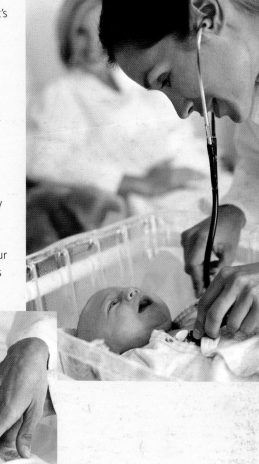

SIGN	POINTS		
	0	1	2
Appearance	Pale or blue	Body pink, extremities blue	Pink
Pulse	Not detectable	Below 100	Over 100
Grimace (reflexes)	No response to stimulation	Grimace	Lusty cry, cough, or sneeze
Activity (muscle tone)	Flaccid (no or weak activity)	Some movement of extremities	A lot of activity
Respiration	None	Slow, irregular	Good, crying

If you are having a planned caesarean – you are expecting twins or more, are carrying a baby lying in a position other than head down or who is very large or you have a medical condition or have had a previous caesarean (or if on reaching hospital some complication necessitates an emergency procedure) – you will undergo an invasive procedure (possibly under a general anaesthetic), require longer hospitalisation and be limited in your ability to hold and breastfeed your baby comfortably. Your baby may have breathing problems and be slow to feed.

If you have your baby at home with a supervising midwife, and there is a problem, you will need to be transported to the hospital for assessment. The time that it will take to get you from home to the hospital will be longer than is optimal, and the delay in starting treatment may have a negative impact on your health or that of your baby.

Circumcision

Removing the foreskin – the skin at the end of the shaft of the penis that covers the glans, or head of the penis – has been practised since Biblical times. Religious Jews traditionally have the procedure performed when a boy is eight days old. Many Muslims circumcise their boys at an older age.

There are many arguments both for and against circumcision, but there is no medical reason for having your baby boy circumcised, and many doctors will not undertake the procedure. Some studies indicate that a boy's chance of getting a urinary tract infection is slightly lower following circumcision, and that sexually transmitted diseases and penile cancer are also less likely in a circumcised male. However, urinary tract infections aren't very common in boys and this type of cancer is very rare. Some people believe that it is easier to clean a circumcised penis, but cleaning becomes much easier once a boy is two or three years old and the foreskin readily retracts, so this is not a good reason to carry out the procedure.

Circumcision has been found to lower the risk of acquiring HIV infection following intercourse with an unprotected HIV-positive partner. However, in developed countries like Australia where access to HIV testing and anti-retroviral therapy is almost universal, the number of HIV-infected individuals with undiagnosed infection is very low, and infant circumcision has little impact on HIV risk.

It is important to remember that circumcision removes complex nerve tissue and inevitably results in a loss of sexual sensitivity. Men circumcised as infants may be unaware of this, but many men circumcised as adults report a definite loss of feeling.

If there are religious reasons, it's a family custom or if you feel your son will otherwise be different from his peers, the procedure may seem a reasonable choice. On the other hand, if the discomfort and chance of remote but serious complications hold sway, then avoid it. You also may want to consider what your son will think about it when he is 15.

Storing cord blood

You may want to save your baby's cord blood. Cord blood contains stem cells made by your baby, which have the potential to differentiate into many kinds of blood cells or organ tissues (muscle, liver etc.). Should she ever need a bone marrow (or possibly other organ) transplant, your child's stem cells will be a perfect match; there is no risk of rejection by the body's immune system and medications given to suppress the immune system in hopes of preventing rejection would not be needed. Stem cells can be grown in cell culture artificially or can be stored in a frozen state for later use.

If your hospital allows the procedure, stem cells from cord blood can be obtained at the time of delivery. A kit from the storage facility with receptacles for the cord blood is required, but you can obtain this weeks before your delivery by contacting the cord blood bank you plan on using. They will charge a fee for their services. After the umbilical cord is cut, your doctor or midwife will insert a needle into the umbilical vein and withdraw blood for storage. The blood comes from the no-longer-attached umbilical cord and placenta; it is not taken from your baby. If you chose not to store cord blood, there is no use for this remaining placental blood and it is discarded.

Although growing in popularity, storing cord blood is not without problems; some children who go on to develop leukaemia already have pre-leukaemic cells in their cord blood, which can reinfect them. Donations to public institutions are regulated by AusCord, the national network of cord blood banks and collection centres. Private banks don't fall under the AusCord umbrella, but are regulated by the Therapeutic Goods Aministration (TGA).

Breast- or bottlefeeding

There are many advantages to breastfeeding (see box, page 20) and very few medical reasons not to do so. You can successfully breastfeed twins (see page 76) and a premature baby (see page 92). You will, however, be advised not to breastfeed: if you have an infection that may be transmitted to your baby in breastmilk such as HIV; shingles or herpes on your breast near the nipple; or if you are taking a medication that passes into breastmilk and it may be harmful to your baby such as sedatives (Valium and others), aspirin and amphetamines.

Choosing not to breastfeed

If you are unsure whether or not you want to breastfeed, try it for a week or so and then decide – you may like it! If you do not want to nurse, however, you may be feeling a little pressured to do so. Although you may regret that you are depriving your baby of the benefits that come with breastfeeding, formula is a very good alternative. Breastmilk may be the best nutritional food for your baby, but formula is a close second and is a perfectly adequate source of nourishment.

Carers

Although a maternal and child health nurse will be assigned to you (see page 21), you may have to choose a general practitioner with good baby-care facilities. You also may want a helping hand to assist with your baby and with chores around the house and a little time off. A trained nanny can provide you with professional, high-quality baby-care but a less expensive option is to consider hiring a babysitter.

Nanny

Although not trained nurses, nannies are usually experienced in taking care of newborns (and older babies). When hiring one, it is essential to check all qualifications and references thoroughly. Typically, a nanny arrives when you bring your newborn home and lives with your family for as little as one to two weeks or for months, according to your preference and purse. A nanny should be able to assist you with all aspects of daily care – including giving middle-of-the-night feedings if you are bottlefeeding or using expressed breastmilk – helping with chores such as doing your baby's washing, making up her cot, and aiding in calming her down if she is fussy.

Nannies can be quite good at saving you time and energy, and can take over at times you need to rest, but you may rely too much on one and not become confident in doing routines yourself. Ideally, a nanny should do less and less of the care of the baby as the days go by, so that when she leaves, you are comfortable and confident in your own ability to care for your baby.

Your baby's doctor

Choosing a general practitioner may be quite easy if you live in a small town and there are few choices. But if you do have more options, ask other mothers and fathers about their experiences with different GP practices. Besides finding out what they like about their doctors, also find out what they don't like. Be sure not only to ask about a doctor's competency and bedside manner; also inquire if his/her surgery runs smoothly; what coverage is available on weekends and holidays; and how easy is it to get your questions answered.

Many GPs offer antenatal checks. This is an opportunity for you and your partner to meet with your GP and find out about him/her and how the practice runs. Questions about his/her experience, hours and availability; about how he/she keeps up with new developments in the field; how emergencies or routine calls are handled; who covers on weekends and holidays – these are all fair game. If there are issues especially important to you, such as vaccines or antibiotics, ask about his/her opinion – see if you both agree on these, and if not, will your views be respected? Will you see a different doctor each time you come? How and by whom will your questions be answered?

While the number of questions you may ask is endless, two goals should be achieved by your visit. Firstly, find out about the day-to-day routines and procedures of the office. Secondly, and more importantly, discover whether or not you feel comfortable with this doctor and with bringing your baby to this surgery. Often, your instincts can guide on this subject.

Maternal and child health nurse

When your baby is born, the hospital notifies your local council of the birth details, and a maternal and

7 reasons to breastfeed your baby

1 Breastmilk is assumed to be the best nutritional milk for humans; formulas strive to be as close as possible to mother's milk, but will never be identical to it.

2 Breastmilk contains antibodies, immune system cells and antimicrobial factors to help protect your baby from infection.

3 Breastfeeding your baby will create a special bond between you and your baby.

4 Breastfeeding is much cheaper than formula and easily can be done wherever you and your baby go.

5 Breastfeeding may decrease your baby's chance of developing allergies or eczema.

6 Breastfeeding is said to increase your baby's IQ by 2–3 points.

7 Breastfed babies, on average, have a lower incidence of obesity.

child health nurse will contact you within a couple of weeks of delivery.

A maternal and child health nurse specialises in infants and young children up to school entry. She will visit you at home within the first ten days of your baby's life, and later you will see her at your local maternal and child health centre. The nurse is skilled in child development, infant feeding and common ailments, and you will find her a great source of information and advice. You may talk to her over the phone or request a home visit if you have a particular worry or concern.

She will have a schedule of regular visits over the first year, then with reduced frequency until your child reaches school age.

MORE **ABOUT** | the ideal general practitioner

The ideal general practitioner is kind and gentle, knowledgeable about the care of children, readily available and not in a rush. In addition he or she has an efficiently run surgery with friendly, helpful staff. Other doctors who cover when he or she is away are also nice as well as competent, and they will have access to your baby's records. You will be seen promptly when you go to the surgery and the doctor will form a personal relationship with you and your child. This GP is very thorough and conscientious, and offers anticipatory guidance (prepares you in advance for what you will face next). He/she is not afraid to say he/she doesn't know the answer to your question, but instead will find out and get back to you. His/her use of medications is judicious and appropriate. He/she takes time to talk about issues not strictly medical (such as sleeping problems, tantrums, sibling jealousy, etc.), will answer questions over the phone and respects your opinions when the two of you disagree.

Choosing a name

Coming up with a name for your baby is another important decision. Unless you are sure of your baby's sex, it is wise to have a name selected for both possibilities. There are so many names to consider! There are many books filled with lists of names to choose from, with the derivation and meaning of each.

Some families have customs or traditions for naming children, such as naming the baby after a deceased relative or a boy after his father.

You may be fortunate in that you and your partner quickly agree on a name or names; in other families it may be more of a challenge. Compromise may be necessary. Another method of arriving at the name is the matching list method. Each parent makes up a list of names desired for the baby, with the most favoured names highest on the list. If you are unsure of the sex, have separate lists of boy's and of girl's names. Remove any names from your lists to which a partner objects. Then find names that occur in both of your lists. The name on both lists that has the highest rating by you both is chosen. Unless you both consent, other relatives – prospective grandparents, for example – should not get a vote, though you may consider their preferences in making your choice. The latest list of the most popular names is set out, alongside.

GIRLS

1. Mia
2. Chloe
3. Olivia
4. Isabella
5. Emily
6. Charlotte
7. Ellie
8. Sienna
9. Ava
10. Sophie
11. Amelia
12. Grace
13. Lily
14. Ruby
15. Matilda
16. Zoe
17. Jessica
18. Hannah
19. Emma
20. Sarah
21. Georgia
22. Jasmine
23. Lucy
24. Madison
25. Isabelle
26. Sophia
27. Chelsea
28. Maddison
29. Zara
30. Holly
31. Elizabeth
32. Lara
33. Hayley
34. Eva
35. Abigail
36. Molly
37. Lilly
38. Amy
39. Scarlett
40. Imogen

BOYS

1. William
2. Jack
3. Joshua
4. Lachlan
5. Thomas
6. Cooper
7. James
8. Oliver
9. Riley
10. Ethan
11. Benjamin
12. Noah
13. Daniel
14. Samuel
15. Liam
16. Alexander
17. Ryan
18. Max
19. Lucas
20. Matthew
21. Jacob
22. Charlie
23. Jayden
24. Luke
25. Nicholas
26. Isaac
27. Harrison
28. Tyler
29. Jake
30. Jackson
31. Dylan
32. Angus
33. Harry
34. Oscar
35. Bailey
36. Michael
37. Nathan
38. Blake
39. Hayden
40. Adam

CARING FOR YOUR NEWBORN

First reactions

After months of waiting, your precious baby has arrived. You and your partner have been through a lot – an "easy" (vaginal) delivery is physically exhausting and longer labours and caesarean deliveries can be even more draining. But now that your baby is here, it all seems worth it. This chapter focuses on the first weeks after a healthy child's birth. If, however, your newborn is in the special or intensive care unit or has medical problems, skip to Chapters 4 (Caring for your premature infant) and 13 (Caring for your special needs baby).

Mums and Dads

Biology has "programed" mothers to care about and to want to nourish and protect their newborns; you may be astonished by just how powerful these sensations are. Most women also will feel tremendous joy and an immediate strong emotional attachment to their babies although for some women, this takes longer to manifest. In the days after delivery, your emotions may take you on a roller-coaster ride, with moments of unprecedented happiness and rapid swings to sadness and worry if something isn't right. And no matter what your usual demeanour is, you may find that feelings and innate passions hold sway over the more rational side of you. You may find yourself sad and crying when you try to feed your baby and he isn't very interested. It doesn't matter that your GP told you that babies are often very sleepy and not very hungry on the first day or two. While hearing this momentarily reassures you, very soon you may again feel that succeeding at feeding is urgently important.

Dads, too, will experience great happiness and excitement. You will sense the deep love you have for your partner and will feel closer to her and more connected than ever before. When you first hold your baby, any initial feelings of awkwardness will give way to thankfulness and wonder. You also will possess a powerful urge to protect your newborn and your partner, and thoughts about providing security and prosperity for your family will be uppermost in your mind.

At times, though, you may feel left out and pushed aside. It is assumed by all that your partner is in charge of feeding and calming your baby; they are the centres of attention. You may feel disregarded, relegated to making the going home arrangements and in competition with grandparents or other relatives for a chance to hold your baby. On the other hand, you may secretly be glad that it's your partner who is supposed to know how to care for your baby because you feel uncomfortable and inexperienced at the common duties of parenting.

You will both look at your baby with amazement, marvelling at how perfect he is and how wondrous the creation of another life. Before he was born, you had only a vague picture in your mind of what your baby would look like, but now he is a real human being. It may strike you suddenly that not only is he here, but that you are responsible for his wellbeing. You may feel terribly inadequate for the job. "How am I ever going to be able to take care of him? I hardly know anything about being a mother (or father)." Doubts that you won't be a good parent may creep in, leaving you feeling anxious and a bit scared of the task before you. But you will learn surprisingly quickly.

The baby

The psychological make-up of a newborn is quite basic. He knows only two states of mind – contentment or unhappiness. To be content, his fundamental needs must be met. If he feels secure, warm, sated and comfortable, life is good; but if any one of those wants is lacking, your baby screams loudly to protest.

Life on the outside is new and exciting. Tasting milk for the first time, taking a deep breath, and letting out a scream – they all seem to happen without much intention, but still what a change it is from laying confined in the dark womb.

Your newborn's appearance

When your child is first born, he will be wet and dirty, covered by a mixture of mother's blood and amniotic fluid. A thick white cream cheese-like substance, vernix caseosa, may remain in his groin creases or in his ears. His hair, if he has more than a little, will be matted against his scalp, and his head will be moulded into a cone-head (if delivered vaginally), or be fairly round if born by Caesarean, or be stretched a bit in the front to back direction if he was in a breech position.

Following a bath, he will start to look more like the baby you were expecting. He will have a nice pinkish-red colour to his skin although the bottom three-quarters of his fingernails will be purplish and from time to time his hands and feet will be cold and bluish. (Circulation in places furthest from the heart is sluggish.) Tiny white dots or milia will be on his face; these are clogged-up skin pores and will soon disappear.

Most of the time, your baby's eyes will be closed. His eyelids will be puffy and may be bruised. When your infant opens his eyes, it is normal in the first month or two for them to briefly cross or turn in.

MORE ABOUT

your baby's tummy button

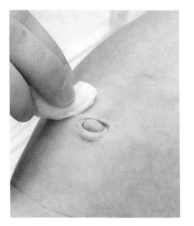

Depending upon the amount of force exerted by the pull of the cord while your baby was in utero, he will exhibit one of three configurations. If the cord was short or if a longer cord was twisted around him while in the womb, more tension would have been applied at the umbilicus and he will have a protruding tummy button or "outie". If very little cord tension was present before birth, the button will be recessed – an "innie"; and if the amount of pull was in-between, the tummy button will be at the level of the abdominal skin. Should your baby's umbilicus stick out, be patient; many outies eventually sink and become innies.

And, he may not yet have eyebrows or eyelashes. Don't worry, they will soon arrive.

The posture he assumes will reflect the way he was crammed into the small space of the uterus. His legs will be bowed and often both feet turn inward (but other poses of the feet, such as turned out, or bent fully back at the ankle, are also common). His hands will be tightly clenched, yet if you open one and place your finger across his palm, he will tightly hold onto it (the grasp reflex). The skin of the scrotal sack will appear a bit swollen and will have either a pink or darkly pigmented colour. (If you have a girl, the external labia [outer lips] of the vagina may also be swollen and pink.) Emerging from your nwborn's umbilicus is the remnant of the umbilical cord. In the hours after birth, this stump is yellowish-white and soft, with a clip at the end to prevent any of his blood from exiting his body via umbilical vessels. In another day or two, it will have shrunken, become dark in colour, and very hard to your touch. At this time the clip is no longer needed.

Your baby's skin

Your newborn has just spent months submerged in water, surrounded by amniotic fluid in the uterus. Often, shortly after birth, your baby's skin will start to peel and flake, especially at the wrists, ankles, and groin creases. It is as if he is shedding his underwater skin. When the next layer of skin arrives, it will be the soft, moist, smooth skin that is characteristic of older babies. Very often a baby's skin will exhibit one or more birthmarks. These come in many sizes, shapes and colors, and are rarely of major concern (see box, page 27).

Newborn rash

Known medically by the pretentious name of *erythema toxicum neonatorum*, these are red splotches the size of a five-cent coin with a small white- or yellow-headed pimple in the middle, which can resemble insect bites. Interestingly, the blotches and pimples are fleeting, with each individual spot going away in just a few minutes or hours. The cause of newborn rash is as yet undiscovered, but no treatment is necessary: in a week or two it will go away by itself.

Hormonal effects

Shortly before birth, your baby was exposed to high level of his mother's female hormones. This may lead to breast swellings in boys and girls. Hormonal stimulation of the breasts may also at times result in a small amount of milk production by your baby. Squeezing the breasts and expressing the milk from his breasts is not recommended. The swelling (and, if present, the milk production) peaks at about two to three weeks of age, and then goes away.

A mother's hormones may have a unique effect on girls. Your daughter may develop a small amount of thick, stringy white or yellow mucus discharge from her vagina. It is harmless and should be wiped away when you change her nappy. As the level of maternal hormones in her falls, a few drops of blood or even a clump or two of red blood cells may be seen coming from her vagina. This, too, is normal.

Coloured spots in the nappy

It is common to see a brownish or salmon pink stain in the nappy where urine has wet it. The brownish shading is from concentrated urine, while the pinkish-red stain is from the high levels of uric acid crystals excreted in newborn urine.

Birthmarks

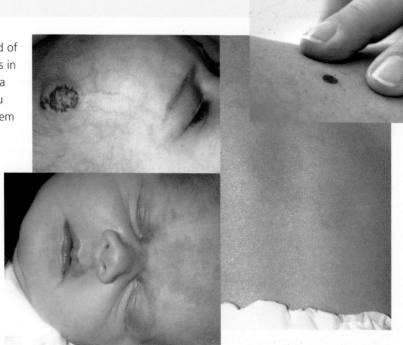

Haemangiomas are composed of many, many small blood vessels in a localised area. While the extra vessels are present at birth, you may not be able to visualise them as a birthmark until your baby (and the blood vessels) begins to grow. If noticed at birth, haemangiomas are flat, well defined and often pale-purplish in colour. As they grow (mostly up off the surface of the skin) in the first months of life, they become larger, redder and raised. At this stage, they are commonly called "strawberries", which they resemble. A haemangioma continues growing for the first six to nine months of life, and then slowly begins to shrink and lose its colour. The vast majority, even very large ones, are completely gone in a couple of years. Rarely, a large haemangioma is problematic due to its location near important structures (the eye, nose or mouth) or in areas that can be easily irritated (hand or nappy area). There are a number of treatments (injections of cortisone, laser treatments) that are successful in shrinking haemangiomas, but since they typically go away by themselves in time, treatment is limited to these "problematic" ones.

A naevus flammeus is also a localised area with extra blood vessels in the skin, but unlike a haemangioma, it is present at birth and does not grow. Flat and pinkish-red, common locations include the nape of the neck ("stork mark"), upper eyelids ("angel's kiss"), on the nose or just above it, and the forehead. Such birthmarks gradually lighten and usually disappear in time. However, when your baby cries or strains to have a bowel movement, a naevus flammeus will momentarily become redder in colour.

Pigmented spots are large, flat, greyish-black coloured spots that may be up to several centimetres across. Other than their colour, pigmented spots have no medical significance. Most commonly found over the low back and upper buttocks with a capsule-like shape, they are commonly called "Mongolian spots", since the shape resembles the map of that region. Pigmented spots can also be found in other areas: the back side of the hands and upper back and shoulders. Curiously, they are very common in black infants and those of Asian descent. Usually pigmented spots become much less noticeable with age.

Naevi A naevus (plural is naevi) is a black birthmark that may be flat or raised. Like haemangiomas, naevi also may not be present at birth, only to be seen later on. Many are small and look like what in older children and adults we call "moles". Occasionally larger ones are seen. They do not disappear or get larger, and only rarely are they a source of skin cancer (melanoma).

What your newborn can do

Now that your baby is here, you have a lot to do – holding, feeding, burping, bathing, comforting, changing and dressing him, for example – but what he does in a typical day is quite limited and driven by biological necessity and reflex. He will typically be very tired and will spend the majority of each day sleeping. When he is hungry or wants hugging, he automatically cries. When the breast or bottle is placed in his mouth, he starts sucking. And when he is full, he will stop feeding. Right after eating, his intestinal tract will increase activity and often,

reflexively, a bowel movement will result. A sudden movement or noise will make him startle. And when you hold him in your arms, he will enjoy hearing your heartbeat and being close to you.

He is also very good at getting your attention and becoming the focus of your new life. Although this fact doesn't change, within a few weeks he will prefer your face to that of others, track you briefly with his eyes, and smile at you. And from there, it keeps getting better!

surprisingly normal behaviours

There are a number of things that are common and normal in newborns but often unexpected by parents.

1 **Hiccups** Your baby may spend minutes at a time hiccuping. Usually, he is completely unbothered by it, and you do not need to do anything to try to stop them.

2 **Snorting and sneezing** At times your baby may breathe loudly with a snorting noise coming from the back of his nose. Sneezing is common; it is a reflex to help him clean out his nose.

3 **Tremors** From time to time, your infant's arm or leg may repetitively and rhythmically shake, resembling the shuddering of an older person with a chill. This is a sign of neurological immaturity. Unlike a seizure, which they vaguely resemble, the tremors are easily stopped by simply grabbing hold of the arm or leg and they have an even, back and forth quivering motion; in a convulsion, the arm or leg moves with much sharper, jerky motions.

4 **Startle reaction** Following a sudden noise, vibration or movement, your newborn may wrinkle his forehead, squeeze his eyes shut, and quickly move his arms upwards and outwards until they are straight at the elbow. This series of motions is called a Moro reflex and will be present for weeks or months.

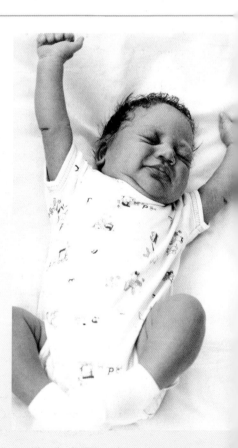

Sleeping

After a few hours of being awake and alert right after birth, your newborn will characteristically go into a sleepy phase for the next two to three days. Being asleep 18 hours a day or more is typical.

Preventing a misshapen head

In the past decade, much emphasis has been given to placing babies on their backs when sleeping. Research has shown that this position decreases the incidence of sudden infant death syndrome or SIDS (see page 63). SIDS is rare, but problems with an uneven shaping of your baby's head may commonly result from the supine sleep position. Many infants develop a strong preference for holding their heads to only one side while supine. For example, if your baby constantly holds his head turned to his right when lying down (which is much of his day and night), you may begin to see flattening of the rear of the skull on the right. This occurs because the weight of his head on this region of growing skull results in the skull conforming to the flat shape of the mattress or other surface he is laying on. If his head turning preference is allowed to continue, the flattening of the right side of the back of his head will be quite noticeable, and you may even notice that his right ear seems more forwardly placed than the left ear. To avoid this skull misshaping, called plagiocephaly (see page 331), encourage your baby to look to the side opposite his preference. This can be accomplished by making it necessary for him to turn to his non-preferred side to see objects of interest (your face, the window or light bulb). You may have to rotate him 180 degrees (his head is now where his feet just were) to make it necessary for him to turn to the non-preferred direction.

Feeding

During the first few days, it also is common for a baby to show few signs of hunger. As if by design, your breast milk will not appear in large amounts until the third or fourth day after delivery; this is exactly when your infant will become more awake and much more eager to nurse or take a bottle. There are some newborns who skip this sleepy phase

BLOCKED TEAR DUCT

A common, minor problem your infant may experience is a blocked tear duct. This may show up when your baby's eyes begin making tears at about two to three weeks of age. The eye with a blocked tear duct will tear more than the other eye, since instead of the tears draining to the back of the nose via an internal tear duct, they drain forward out of the eye. Another clue to a blocked tear duct is repeated bouts of conjunctivitis (see page 350), manifested as mucus in that eye. Babies with a blocked tear duct get mild infections in their eyes because the germs that are supposed to be washed away down the tear duct (along with tears) are able to persist in the eye. Blocked tear ducts almost always become unblocked; this may occur at any time within the first year of life.

While waiting for this spontaneous cure, wipe away the crusts and small amounts of mucus that accumulate due to low-grade conjunctivitis. If the amount of mucus gets very heavy and when wiped away recurs often during the day, your GP may prescribe a brief course of antibiotic eye drops. Some caregivers also suggest massaging the area over the tear duct with your finger to promote drainage, but do not do this without first being instructed in the correct method. In the rare case of a tear duct that doesn't self-repair, it can be opened by a paediatric surgeon with a thin wire probe passed from the inner corner of the eye down the length of the tear duct.

and are always eager to be fed, but most are uninterested in feedings during this interval. While the two- or three-day period is helpful in allowing you time to rest and recover from delivery, you may find yourself quite upset. Your innate maternal compulsion to successfully feed your baby leads you to worry unnecessarily. There is no need to feel you are starving your baby or that you are failing as a mother; however, since emotions trump rational thinking at this time of your life, you may find it difficult not to be troubled and very concerned.

Weight loss

Your baby was born overstocked with water, perhaps to cushion him during the hard journey of delivery or to provide fluids for him in the days of the sleepy period. He was also full of meconium (see below) at birth. In the next few days, he will urinate and pass meconium often, and since he will be eating little, he will lose weight. This weight loss is not from poor nutrition and starvation, but is simply a mathematical event, for more is going out (urine and stool) than is going in (milk). It is normal for your newborn to lose up to 10 per cent of his initial weight, but he will soon begin gaining weight when the equation is reversed and more goes in than comes out! Regrettably, the normal, physiologic loss of weight in the first days may only increase the emotion-driven worries of a mother who fears her child is starving. Frequent reassurance and support from dad and others will help greatly.

Meconium and bowel movements

Before birth, faeces are present already in your baby's intestines in the form of meconium. Quite a large amount of this passes out in the first two to three days after birth. Meconium is blackish-green in colour and is thick and sticky. Once the meconium has all been excreted, bowel movements become yellow, green or brown, and will be soft and mushy. If you are breastfeeding, your baby's stools will be very watery with small solid specks mixed throughout – and they will occur frequently. It is common for a newborn to have six, eight or even ten bowel movements a day. Sometimes the stool will be squirted out forcefully.

MORE **ABOUT** | the colour of your baby's bowel movements

Formula is white and breast milk is typically whitish-grey. But bowel movements are seldom these colours. Where determines the colour? After leaving the stomach, the milk enters the small intestine, where bile from the liver and bile duct is added. Bile is green and this becomes the colour of the intestinal contents. Bacteria that live in your baby's intestine, especially the colon, or lower intestine, are capable of metabolising components of the bile. Initial steps in the breakdown of bile result in molecules with a yellow colour. Further digestion by the bacteria may then leave products with a brown colour. However, the faster the intestine propels its contents along the many feet of the alimentary tract, the less time there is for the bacteria to metabolise the green fluid to other colours. When, at an older age, you introduce solid foods into your baby's diet, the colour of a food and its breakdown products also may contribute to a bowel movement's colour. Green stools, therefore, will be produced when transit time through the intestines is rapid and there is little breaking down of bile components. If transit time is a little slower and the bacteria do a better job of breaking down bile, the stool will appear yellow. And if the passage through the intestines is even slower and bacteria more fully metabolise bile, brown bowel movements result.

Bonding

As you spend time together – holding, feeding, soothing or changing your baby – your love and desire to protect this little person will grow and become a very powerful emotion. The growth of a strong attachment between you and your newborn is known as bonding, and most parents experience these strong feelings from the moment of birth, and some even earlier.

Shortly after birth, your newborn is alert and ready to nurse. His eyes will be open when you hold him and the two of you can gaze at each other. Interestingly, this initial state lasts on average about an hour (see page 73), but it allows both mother and father to experience the first joys of parenting. Interacting with your newborn triggers a loving response in you.

At birth, however, your infant is not yet experiencing this same attachment to you. He is totally dependent on you, and his early behaviour is designed to provoke in you the deep feelings just described. As he gets older, though, he will get to know you, become attached to you, and prefer you to all others. The bond he feels with his mother is especially intense, and when he reaches the age of nine to ten months, he will be very upset to be away from you (known as separation anxiety).

Bonds are also important between your newborn and any older siblings (if present). While an older brother or sister may at times ignore or be jealous of the attention your newborn receives, there is also an innate mechanism to encourage attachment. When your newborn is only a few months old, your older son or daughter will discover that he or she has a unique ability to calm and entertain his or her younger sibling. Your infant will find his older sibling amusing and will reciprocate with laughter and howls of delight. This certainly allows the older child to feel good about the younger one. In a few more months, your baby will seem to worship his brother or sister, no matter how nicely or badly he is treated. A baby's behaviour seems to be designed to gain favour with a sibling.

Your interactions with your newborn should trigger warm feelings of attachment in you. If you feel that this is missing, speak to your own GP or maternal and child health nurse. You may be suffering post-natal depression or another ailment.

1 Slide one hand under your baby's neck, supporting his head, and the other hand beneath his bottom. Take his weight in your hands and slowly raise him from the surface.If he's awake, talking quietly to your baby will help keep him calm as you lift.

2 Keep your baby's head slightly above the level of the rest of his body. Draw him into your body. If he's awake, look into his eyes as you move him.

HOLDING AND CARRYING

Resting against your shoulder
This is the most intimate and comfortable way to hold your baby. As with lifting, you need to support his bottom and upper back and neck – one part with each hand.Your baby is able to nestle close against the skin of your neck and may be comforted by the sound of your heartbeat.

Face down in your arms
This hold can provide a welcome rest for tired arms and a change of view for your infant. It also may be good for colic. Support your baby along one arm with his head near the crook of your elbow. Your other arm slides through his legs until your hand is resting on his stomach.

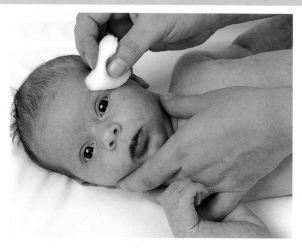

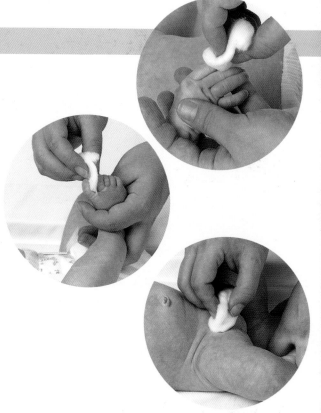

Eyes and ears Wet some cotton wool with cooled boiled water and wipe each eye, above and below, from the inner to the outer corner. Use a different piece for each wipe and each eye, to reduce the chances of spreading infection. Use more cotton wool to clean around and behind the ears. Do not clean inside the ear.

Neck Wipe clean with wet cotton wool and pat dry with a soft cloth.

Hands Unclench your baby's hands to check for dirt between the fingers and underneath the nails. Wipe and pat dry as before.

Feet Clean the top and bottom of your baby's feet, and his toes, gently easing them apart, where necessary. Pat dry with a towel.

Stomach and legs Wipe his tummy with more wet cotton wool, then use new cotton to start on the folds where his legs meet his torso. Wipe down along the creases and away from his body to avoid transmitting infections to the genital area (this is particularly important for a girl). Pat dry with a soft cloth or towel, checking that no moisture is trapped in the folds.

Care of the umbilical cord

Expose the stump to the air
The stump will dry and heal much faster if you expose it to air as much as possible. In particular, don't cover it with plastic pants and nappies and, if it does get wet, make sure it is thoroughly dried.

Cleaning the stump
Use clean cotton wool, moistened with rubbing alcohol if your caregiver advises, to gently wipe the stump, the area around it, and the crevices of the navel. Make sure you dry the area gently.

After the stump has fallen off
There may be a few spots of blood as the wound continues to heal. You should clean and dry it daily until the area is completely healed.

CHANGING A NAPPY

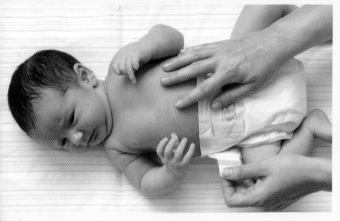

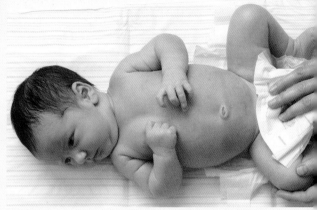

1 Have all your supplies – nappies, cotton wool, water and nappy bag – by the change mat. Now pick up your baby and place him, face up, on the mat. If he's dressed, strip him down to his vest or just his nappy. Unfasten the tabs or fasteners.

2 Slide the nappy away, using an unsoiled area to give a first wipe. If your baby is a boy, the cooler air may make him urinate as his nappy is removed. Drop a tissue on the penis to deflect the flow, or, if the nappy is only wet, hold it over the genital area until the danger time has passed.

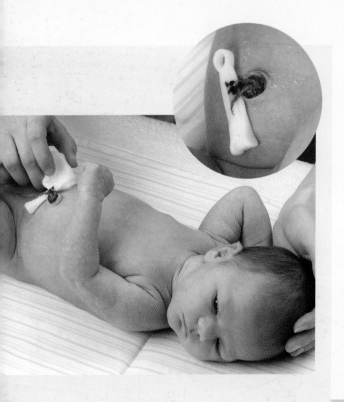

Cleaning a girl

Using fresh cotton wool moistened with water, clean the outer lips of her vulva – but don't clean inside. Always wipe downward, using a fresh piece of cotton wool for each wipe. Raise both her ankles gently with one hand and clean her buttocks using fresh cotton. Clean the backs of her thighs and up her back, if necessary. Pat the whole area thoroughly dry.

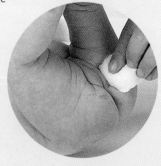

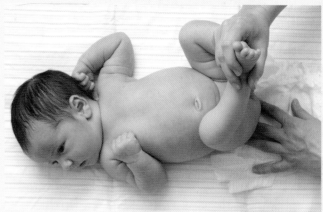

3 Roll up the nappy with one hand and place it where your baby can't kick it. Now clean carefully within all the skin folds, see below. Pat dry, particularly in the folds where soreness can develop.

4 Spread out a fresh nappy. Lift your baby's legs and slide it underneath his bottom. Bring the nappy up between his legs. If your baby is a boy, make sure his penis points downwards so he doesn't urinate into the waistband.

Cleaning a boy

Using fresh cotton wool moistened with water, wipe his penis using a downward motion – don't pull the foreskin back. Clean around the scrotum as well. Use fresh cotton for each wipe. Holding both your baby's ankles, lift his bottom gently and clean his anal area, buttocks and the backs of his thighs. Pat the whole area thoroughly dry.

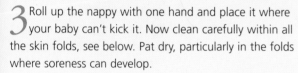

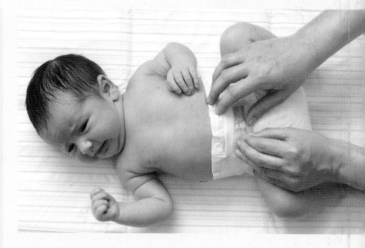

5 Secure the nappy at the sides and tuck in the top edge neatly. Once your baby is dressed, place the disposable into a bag and throw it away or place a soiled fabric nappy into a holding bucket.

BATHING

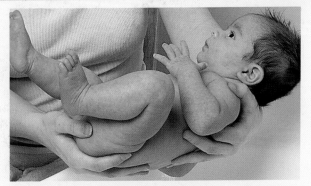

Lower your baby into the water Kneel close to the bath and supporting his bottom with one hand and his back and head with the other, place his bottom and then his back into the water.

Wash his chest and stomach Keeping his head and shoulders supported, grip him gently under the arm to prevent him from slipping down into the water or rolling over. Use your hand to gently wash water over his torso.

Wash his upper back and neck Next, sit your baby up, supporting his chest against your arm. Gently pour water over his back and down his neck.

Wash his lower back Tip your baby further forward, taking care to keep his face out of the water, and rinse his lower back and bottom.

Lift him out Lean your baby back into the starting position. Using the same supporting grip as you used to lower him in, remove him from the water and onto a clean towel.

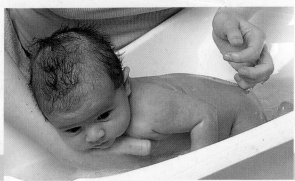

Drying

Your towel should be laid out ready on a change mat near the tub. Use it to pat your baby dry – especially in the skin creases. If you like, wrap him up to keep warm, but avoid covering his face.

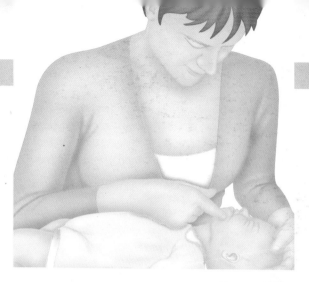

Under one year old

1 If your baby isn't responsive – doesn't react to your calling his name and gently tapping his foot – place one hand on his forehead and gently tilt his head back and lift his chin. Remove any visible obstructions from his mouth and nose with a finger.

2 Check if he's breathing by looking, listening and feeling for breathing on your cheek for up to ten seconds. If he is not breathing normally, follow steps 3 and 4 for one minute then call 000. If another person is present, ask him to call an ambulance straightaway.

3 Fill your cheeks with air and place your mouth over your baby's mouth and nose and blow gently and steadily two times. Look along the chest and stop blowing when your baby's chest rises; allow it to fall.

4 Place two fingers in the middle of his chest and press down one-third of the depth of the chest. After 30 chest compressions (at the rate of 100 per minute) give two breaths (as in step 3). Continue with cycles of 30 chest compressions and two breaths until emergency help arrives.

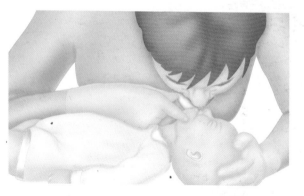

Recovery position for babies

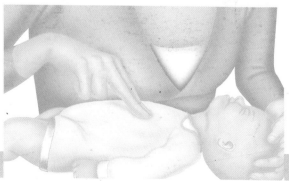

If your baby is unconscious but breathing, hold him on his side, head tilted, as if you were giving him a cuddle, with his head lower than his tummy.

Over one year old to puberty

1 Place one hand on your toddler's forehead and gently tilt back his head and lift his chin. Remove any visible obstructions from his mouth and nose.

2 Pinch your toddler's nose. Place your mouth over his mouth and blow gently into the lungs two times, looking along his chest as you breathe. Take shallow breaths and do not empty your lungs completely. As his chest rises, stop blowing and allow it to fall.

3 With your arm held straight, place your hand on the centre of his chest and using the heel of your hand, press down one-third of the depth of his chest 30 times (at the rate of 100 compressions per minute). Depending on his size, you might need two hands. After every 30 chest compressions give two breaths (as in step 2).

4 Continue with cycles of 30 chest compressions and two breaths until emergency help arrives.

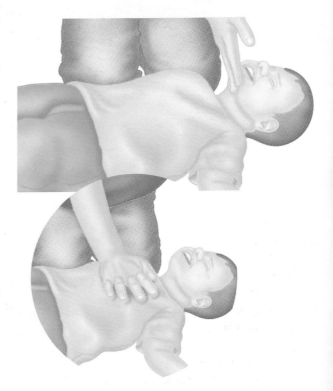

Recovery position for toddlers

If your toddler is unconscious but breathing, place her on her side in the recovery position (bottom picture). Place the arm nearest you at a right angle. Move the other arm, as shown in top picture, so that the back of her hand is against her cheek. Then get hold of the knee furthest from you and pull it up until foot is flat on the floor. Pull the knee towards you, keeping your toddler's hand pressed against her cheek, and position the leg at a

right angle. Make sure that her airway remains open by lifting her chin. Keep checking she is breathing until help arrives.

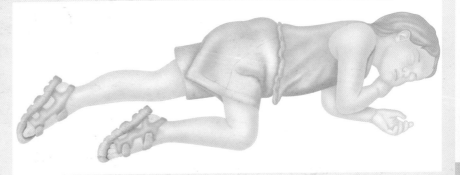

CHOKING

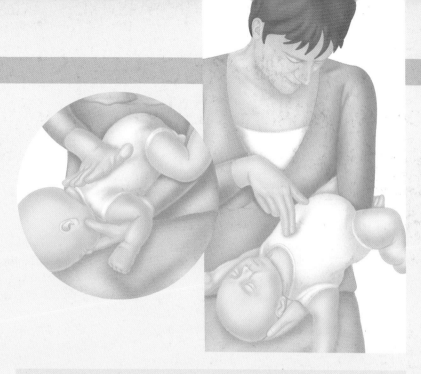

Up to one year old

If your baby is able to breathe, cry or cough, this is a mild case and the obstruction will probably clear on its own. Keep an eye on your baby and make sure his condition doesn't deteriorate. If it does, or if he's not breathing initially, you should:

1 Lay your baby face down along your forearm, with his head held low. With the heel of your hand, give up to five back blows (as shown) between his shoulder blades. Check his mouth quickly after each one and remove any obvious obstruction. If the obstruction is still present:

2 Turn your baby onto his back and give up to five chest thrusts. Using two fingers, push inwards and upwards in the middle of his chest. Check his mouth quickly after each thrust. If the obstruction does not clear after three cycles of back blows and chest thrusts, call for an ambulance. Continue cycles of back blows and chest thrusts until help arrives and resuscitate if necessary.

You must seek medical advice for any child who has been given abdominal thrusts.

Child aged over one

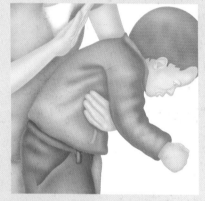

1 Using the heel of your hand, give up to five back blows between your child's shoulder blades. Check his mouth quickly after each blow and remove any obvious obstruction. If the obstruction is still present:

2 Give up to five abdominal thrusts. Place your clenched fist between his navel and the bottom of his breast bone and pull inwards and upwards. Check his mouth quickly after each one. If the obstruction does not clear after three cycles of back blows and abdominal thrusts, dial 000 for an ambulance. Continue cycles of back blows and abdominal thrusts until help arrives and resuscitate if necessary.

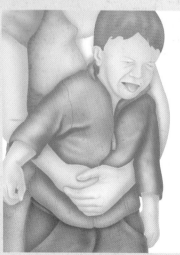

Holding and handling

You'll be handling your baby a lot – picking him up to feed, putting him down to sleep and holding him when he cries – so it's important to do it right. A young baby's head will flop backwards or forwards if not supported, so one of your hands should support his neck while your other supports his bottom until he is securely in your arms or has his head on your shoulder (see pages 32-4). Maintaining eye contact will help build attachment.

Your baby will enjoy being held close to your body – particularly if he can hear your heartbeat. Swaddling (see page 34) or otherwise wrapping him in a blanket so that his limbs are held close to his body can reassure him as this closely imitates the confined space in which he was held in the uterus. Many babies also are unhappy when naked, so when bathing or dressing your baby, expose him to the air as little as possible. On the other hand, skin-to-skin contact, as when breastfeeding, can be delicious for both parent and baby.

It's easy to spot the parent who is new to picking up a baby. With a tense look on his face, he or she puts both hands underneath the supine baby, one hand supporting the head, the other under the buttocks. The elbows are bent ninety degrees and when the baby is tentatively lifted up, the rigid position of the elbows is maintained. All movements are slow and tentative. On the other hand, when your baby's grandmother takes him from his cot, she quickly picks him up without a trace of fear that he may break. With a little practice, you, too, will feel at ease with your baby, being able to lift and carry him as you would a kitten, puppy or football.

Getting into the right position now for lifting your baby will prevent backache later on when he is much heavier. It is easier to lift a baby who is lying face up, so if he is lying prone, gently roll him over onto his back and have his feet pointing towards you. Stand with your legs slightly apart, bend your knees and keep your back straight as you lift him close to you. Keep the same stance when you lay him back down.

When holding your baby in your arms, it's important to be aware of the position of his head in relation to your own body. Make sure his head is tucked into your body or keep a protective hand over the back of his head when walking with him in your arms, particularly as you move through hallways or doorways or close to objects at the level of his head.

Carriers and slings

If you are the type of person who likes to do two things at once, in this case holding your baby and being able to move around or use your hands, then a baby carrier or sling is for you. Of course, this assumes that both you and your baby enjoy the feel of these items.

Carriers are backpack-like, but with the load to be carried in front of you. Two holes for your baby's legs at the bottom of the pouch allow him to remain upright against your chest. Straps over each shoulder and one going around your midsection, fastening in the rear, hold your baby in the carrying sack close against you. A newborn and young baby should be positioned facing you, while an older infant (one

CARRIERS

Advantages
♦ Distribute your baby's weight on both your shoulders, which is more comfortable for longer outings.

Disadvantages
♦ Adjusting the shoulder and waist straps is time consuming. If you and your partner are differently sized and both of you plan to use the same carrier, you will have to re-adjust the straps each time the other one uses it. An alternative is to buy two carriers and have one adjusted to fit you and the other to fit your partner.
♦ The size of the leg holes must be adjusted so they are small enough to prevent your baby from falling through.

SLINGS

Advantages
♦ Are easy to put on and adjust.
♦ They come in many colours and patterns.
♦ Most slings can be worn in a way that allows your baby to nurse while in the sling. A few models have extra material left over after you have secured your baby. This material can be used to cover you and your baby while nursing or to shield him from the sun.
♦ Slings, when folded, can easily fit within a nappy bag.

Disadvantages
♦ The weight of your infant is born by only one shoulder. This can be tiring if you plan on having him in the sling a long time. To solve this problem, you can remove the sling and switch shoulders. Or you can buy a wrap instead.
♦ A wrap resembles a sling but uses both shoulders for weight bearing.

who can support his head) may face away from you, which allows him to better see what is going on.

Slings go over one shoulder and around your waist, and allow your baby to rest in any position from laying flat to being upright in what resembles a hammock. Most parents choose to carry their babies between these two extremes. Your baby can lay facing in towards you, facing upward or facing outward. There are many brands and styles of both devices available.

Don't forget to count the carrier or sling as a layer of clothing when you're calculating how many clothes your baby needs (see also page 57). It can get quite warm in the sack of the carrier.

Choosing

Whichever you choose, you must follow the manufacturer's instructions carefully – your baby's safety depends upon it. Most importantly, check your product's guidelines for weight. Many slings and carriers are not intended for newborns or premmie babies, although there are models for babies as small as 1.5 kilos (3.5 pounds). (There also are models of carriers for holding twins, but the extra weight will soon become too much for you to support.)

Do not use the item if, while he is in it, you cannot see your baby's face. This is especially true for smaller babies in carriers: do not place your newborn in a carrier if his head does not rise above the uppermost part of the carrying compartment.

When your baby is in either contraption, his weight will pull you forward. You will have to compensate for this by leaning backwards. As your baby grows, you will eventually feel the strain in your back and shoulder muscles. This is when it is a good time to give up that particular device. A good alternative at this point, assuming your baby can hold his head well in the sitting position, is to use a strap-on backpack seat, with your child sitting behind you, facing forward (see page 213).

Comforting

Your role as parent is to care for and soothe your baby. How and when to respond to your infant's cries is covered in detail in Chapter 8 but feel free to soothe your newborn whenever he needs you. Holding, gentle rocking and swaddling are all time-tested methods, which can be accompanied by music, singing or gentle speech.

Changing

You will spend a lot time changing your infant's nappies, since he will urinate and defecate on numerous occasions throughout the day and night. It's been estimated that the average baby needs around 6,000 nappy changes between birth and being toilet trained.

Nappies

Washable fabric and disposable versions are available and since nappies will play a big role in your life for the next couple of years, it's important to choose the type that best fits your lifestyle. Disposables have greater absorptive capacity, will keep your baby drier and are more convenient, but they also are more expensive than fabric nappies in the long term. Disposables need to be disposed of carefully but fabric nappies, while reusable, need to be rinsed, sterilised, washed and dried. The latter also may need plastic pants and optional liners, though there are some versions with a plasticised outer layer. Some parents like to use a combination of fabric nappies and disposables. Generally, a newborn may need as many as 12 nappies a day, although this will drop to around seven during the first year and around five as he gets still older.

If you are going to use fabric nappies, it is a good idea to pre-wash them beffore putting them on your baby. Don't use fabric softeners as these may make the nappies less absorbent. You can, however, add half a cup of white vinegar to the final rinse.

Changing a nappy

A step-by-step sequence using a disposable is demonstrated on pages 36-7 and for a fabric nappy on pages 50-1.

Cleaning the nappy area is the same in both cases. Use cotton balls, a soft, moist facecloth or commercially available wipes to remove any remaining stool or dried urine from the skin. If you choose to use a bottom cream or ointment (see page 48), apply it to surfaces that will directly come into contact with the nappy, for these are the areas most likely to be affected with nappy rash.

Special attention to hygiene is necessary when changing a girl's nappy. Wiping "front to back," starting in the genital area and proceeding toward the anus, is recommended. Once a cotton ball, cloth or wipe has faeces on it or has been in the vicinity of the anus, it should not be used to clean the area near

WHICH IS GREENER?

In the 1990s a debate raged between those favouring the convenience of paper nappies and those believing it was more beneficial to the environment to use fabric nappies. The effect of disposables and fabric nappies on energy use and environmental waste was finally compared in a scientific fashion. It was concluded that using disposables resulted in large heaps of garbage; yet the environmental impact was about the same as using fabric nappies if the energy consumed by washing machines, the effects of laundry soaps on the environment and the water and petrol usage (by nappy delivery vehicles) were all considered. That, plus excellent advertising by the manufacturers of disposables, has led to their widespread uses.

The argument for and against commercial wipes for cleaning the nappy area is quite similar. Here again, wipes are much easier to use. Although a baby occasionally reacts to the cleaning chemicals – alcohol in wipes can irritate the skin – or any perfume included, this is uncommon. A number of products are available with only "natural ingredients" and without alcohol or perfume.

the vagina. The goal here is to keep faecal bacteria away from the vaginal region. In older girls, improper wiping technique has been shown to increase the risk of urinary tract infections (which are usually caused by germs originating in faeces). Logically, the same principle is applied to newborns and infants. But be aware that even with all your efforts to wipe properly, many times a week your daughter will soil her nappy and lay there with faeces all over the vaginal area.

A difference in anatomy, with a greater distance between the anus and the urethral opening, where urine exits the penis, allows you to be less cautious when changing a boy's nappy. The "front to back" technique is not necessary. However, there is still cause for caution: on exposure to air when his nappy is removed, he may squirt you!

Bottom creams, ointments, powders

When changing your baby's nappy, should you apply a bottom cream or ointment? In theory, applying either to the skin in the nappy area creates a barrier against irritants that cause nappy rash. While this makes sense, evidence that a particular product works well or is better than another similar product is lacking. It is clear, however, that baby powders do not provide a barrier and are not an effective way to remove moisture from the nappy area. For these reasons and the fact that inhaling powder aerosolised during application is potentially harmful, baby powders are not recommended.

Tradition and custom are the prime factors determining most advice about using creams and ointments. Two schools of thought have emerged. About half of families regularly apply an ointment or cream in hopes of preventing rashes. When a rash does occur, switching to a different ointment or cream is suggested to treat the rash (returning to the original formulation when the rash has healed). In other families, no bottom cream or ointment is used routinely and when rash appears, a favourite product is used to treat it (returning to no cream or ointment following healing). So, in the absence of any compelling evidence that one technique is superior to the other, try one way according to your preference. If it works, great! If it doesn't, try the other method (see also nappy rashes, below).

Nappy rashes

Although nappy rashes are quite common, what is more miraculous is how often your baby will sit in a wet or dirty nappy without a rash resulting! No doubt this is a tribute to the innate properties of an infant's skin. Nappy rashes occur primarily due to irritation by urine and faeces. More precisely, several factors go into making a nappy rash.

Wetness from urine macerates the skin, breaking down the skin's barrier to other irritants. Highly absorbent disposable nappies are much better at keeping the wetness off the skin's surface than fabric ones. Studies have shown that fewer nappy rashes occur in babies in disposable than in fabric nappies.

Friction between the skin and the nappy also results in disruption of the skin's outer protective layer. An irritation rash may be caused only by the repeated rubbing of a clean nappy against the skin but rashes are much more likely if the skin is rubbed by a nappy that is also wet or dirty. The importance of friction in the creation of rashes is illustrated by the distribution of rashes in the nappy area. Rashes occur most frequently in the areas of skin that are in closest contact with the nappy, and are uncommon in the thigh creases.

Waste products from both urine and faeces can damage the skin as well. Faeces contain remaining bile elements (called bile salts) and digestive enzymes that can act upon the skin to cause local injury.

Skin barriers work best in an acid (low pH) environment. Urine, however, often has an alkaline (high pH) make-up. Diarrhoea, which commonly leads to rashes, also has an alkaline pH. To make matters worse, digestive enzymes in stools are activated at alkaline pH.

The role of bacteria and yeasts in causing irritant nappy rashes is poorly documented, but certainly may be a component in a rash's origin. Candida, a yeast, is well known to grow best in a moist environment and often infects already irritated skin. Preventing and treating nappy rashes involve minimising the above ingredients that go into making a nappy rash (see box).

Stubborn nappy rashes

There are two main reasons to explain why a nappy rash fails to improve after following the steps described in the box (right). First, the factors predisposing to rash may still be present. Exposing the skin to persisting diarrhoea is one such circumstance, another is irritation resulting when a baby sleeping through the night is exposed for long periods to urine. As long as the ongoing irritation is occurring, it will be difficult to cure the rash.

A second cause of persistent nappy rash is a Candida infection of the skin. This yeast, which lives in the intestinal tract, reaches the nappy area in faeces. It also is present in higher numbers when your baby takes an oral antibiotic, so resulting in an

HOW TO PREVENT NAPPY RASHES
- Change the nappies often.
- Use highly absorbent disposables. Avoid nappies that are too tight; they increase friction between the nappy and skin.
- Use an ointment or cream to act as a barrier to irritation and moisture. (The effectiveness of this is not well established.)

HOW TO TREAT NAPPY RASHES
- Change nappies often.
- Clean the skin gently with water and a soft facecloth or with a non-alcohol containing wipe.
- Expose the skin to air. Letting your baby go about with no nappy is optimal (but risky!). As an alternative, you may hold your baby sitting on your lap; open the nappy and have him sit on the nappy.
- Use a barrier ointment or cream (zinc oxide or petroleum jelly).
- If these measures are not successful, see *Stubborn Nappy Rashes* (left).

increased chance of a nappy rash developing. (The higher number of organisms, combined with diarrhoea that is likely to result from the antibiotic's effect on beneficial intestinal bacteria, make a rash more likely.) Usually, yeast infection occurs in skin already irritated. So initially you were dealing with an irritant nappy rash, but, in time, secondary infection with Candida occurs.

If you believe your child has a Candida rash, call your GP. Although treatment varies, an ointment effective against yeasts such as clotrimazole or terbinafine is typically used. Some GPs also recommend adding hydrocortisone cream to the regimen to treat the underlying irritant rash as well.

Fabric and pre-shaped nappies

In addition to fine muslin squares for a newborn and standard square cotton or terry-towelling ones for an older baby, plastic pants, nappy pins and optional liners also are needed as well as two plastic storage buckets, tongs, a plastic bowl and sterilising solution – as well as a washing machine – unless you use a nappy service who will supply the necessary items.

Pre-shaped nappies

These come already tailored to fit a baby's bottom, so you don't have to fold them or fiddle about with nappy pins. Most have elasticated legs and waist, as well as self-stick tabs or snap fastenings. Pre-shaped nappies usually have a separate waterproof cover. You also may want to use a nappy liner.

They wash and wear like ordinary fabric nappies, although you should check the care label before soaking them in sterilising solution as some brands may affect the elastic around the legs and waist.

Cleaning soiled nappies

Sterilising, washing and drying nappies is a labourious process, so you may prefer to use a nappy service. Moreover, incomplete cleaning can leave waste ammonia or bacteria on the nappy that can lead to nappy rash and infection. Using too much detergent on nappies, however, will irritate your baby's sensitive skin. Therefore, measure the amount of soap carefully and rinse everything twice.

To thoroughly sterilise nappies, leave them to soak for at least six hours in a bucketful of sterilising solution. Remember to use different buckets for soiled and urine-soaked nappies. A different colour for each bucket will help you tell them apart. The buckets should be big enough to hold at least six nappies but should not be too heavy to pick up when filled with water. Make sure they have sturdy handles and tightly fitting lids.

TO PUT ON AND TAKE OFF A FABRIC NAPPY

1 Fold the fabric in half to form a rectangle. Fold the short side of the rectangle a third of the way into the middle. Place the nappy on a changing mat and lower your baby on to the nappy. For a girl, the extra thickness should be under her bottom. For a boy, position the extra thickness at the front to give more protection over his penis.

2 Your baby's waist should be aligned with the top of the nappy. Now gather the corners of the nappy in your hands and pull the fabric up between her legs, smoothing the front over her stomach.

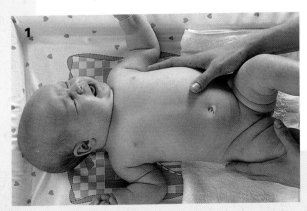

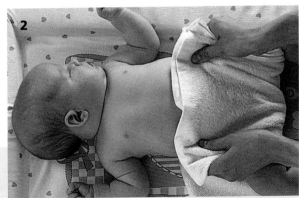

With soiled nappies, scrape as much excrement into the toilet bowl as possible, then rinse them. If you are using biodegradable nappy liners simply remove the liner with the stool and flush down the toilet. Then place the soiled nappy to soak in the bucket with the lid tightly sealed. Rinse urine-soaked nappies under a tap then wring out the moisture. Wash plastic pants with some washing-up liquid in water that is neither too hot nor too cold, otherwise they will go hard. If they do stiffen, soften them by tumble drying on a low setting for 10 minutes.

3 Keeping your hand between the fabric and your baby's skin, pin one side. Adjust the fit, then fasten another pin on the other side. Slip the open plastic pants under your baby's bottom and take the front of the pants up between her legs. Making sure the nappy is well tucked inside the plastic pants, pin one side and then the other.

4 To remove, place your hand between the fabric and your baby's skin and carefully unpin each side; place pins out of baby's reach. If there is any mess, hold your baby's ankles with one hand to raise her bottom, and wipe away any excrement with the front edge of the fabric. Fold the sides of the nappy into the middle and slide the nappy out from underneath her bottom, rolling it up as you remove it.

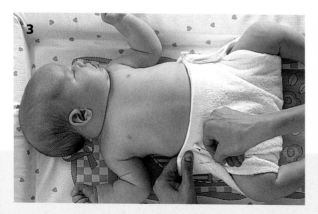

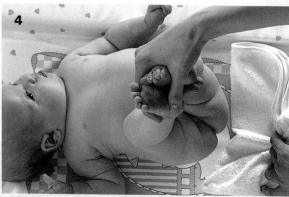

Care of the umbilical cord

Shortly after birth the umbilical cord is clamped and its attachment to the placenta is cut. Soon after, it will become hard and shrivelled. Usually this remnant of the cord separates from the body in a week or two, but up to a month is normal. Just before and for a few days after falling off, you may see a few spots of blood or clumps of thick yellow or green mucus arising from the base of the cord (where the cord remnant joins the body). This is a normal part of the healing process and does not constitute an infection.

Traditionally, paediatricians recommend keeping the umbilical area dry as a way of hastening the falling off and healing of the stump. This entails folding down the upper edge of a nappy so that a wet nappy doesn't overlie the umbilicus. Similarly, bathing is initially by sponge baths, with immersion in water postponed until the cord has completely healed.

Paediatricians also usually recommend cleaning the base of the umbilical stump daily with rubbing alcohol but additional research has shown that simply leaving the umbilicus alone and skipping the alcohol is approximately equivalent in regards to the incidence of infection. If your caregiver, however, recommends using rubbing alcohol, continue to do so until complete healing has occurred.

In the interval from separation to full healing, when bleeding, oozing of mucus and crusts are seen at the umbilicus, use a cotton ball soaked with alcohol or a commercially available alcohol pad to scrub within the navel. Be sure to remove any crust and debris while you perform your cleaning (see pages 35-6).

Umbilical granuloma

The mucus discharge and crusting seen following cord separation typically lasts two to three days. If this continues for several more days, an umbilical granuloma is likely the cause. A granuloma is a small bit of the umbilical cord that remained attached to the baby when the rest of the cord fell off. The oozing is likely coming from this small bit of cord tissue. You can do nothing (if you are following the method of dry care), continue to clean with rubbing alcohol, or your paediatrician can coat the granuloma with a grey chemical called silver nitrate.

Umbilical infection

As you now know, a mucus discharge and crusts and spots of blood coming from the healing umbilicus are not signs of infection. However, if the skin surrounding the tummy button becomes pinkish-red, this may indicate bacterial infection and you should call your GP promptly.

Umbilical hernia

All babies are born with a weakness or defect in the muscle layer of the abdominal wall. The muscles stretching from ribs to the pubic bones on each side of the midline form around the umbilical cord as it enters the body of the foetus. Thus there is no muscle layer beneath the tummy button. Gradually, beginning after birth, the muscles grow together and cover over the defect. Meanwhile, in some infants, the umbilicus will stick up or bulge when pressure within the abdominal cavity increases (i.e. crying or straining). Note: the size of the hernia is determined by the diameter of the area beneath the umbilicus lacking muscle. How high up the skin is pushed has nothing to do with the size of the defect. Umbilical hernias are rarely of any clinical consequence, slowly close by themselves, and almost never require surgical repair.

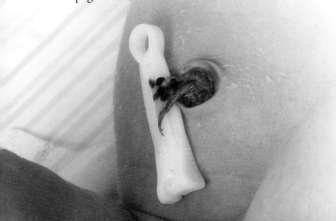

Care of the circumcision

If you chose to have your son circumcised (see page 18), the procedure was either done in the hospital or will be performed in the days following your arrival at home, most commonly on the eighth day of life.

A petroleum jelly-impregnated gauze may be wrapped around the penis upon completing the procedure, which can usually be removed the next day, but if you are instructed to wait longer, follow whatever instructions you are given. To remove the gauze, moisten it first and then slowly and gently unwind it. The gauze often will adhere to the skin of the penis and so taking it off may result in a little crying by your son. Don't be alarmed if you also see a few drops of blood resulting when the dressing is removed. Just take a clean gauze and hold it over the bleeding spot for a minute or two. If you see more than a few drops of blood, take a clean gauze square and put gentle but firm, continuous pressure on the bleeding spot. After two or three minutes, let go. Repeat this step again if bleeding persists, and if you are still unsuccessful in stopping the bleeding, continue applying direct pressure while you call your GP for further advice. Once the dressing is off, you can apply ointment to a single 5-cm gauze square or simply place some ointment on the head of the penis and use the nappy as gauze.

Antibiotic ointments or petroleum jelly products may be prescribed to provide a barrier between the sensitive skin of the head of the penis and irritants in the nappy.

After the circumcision, the entire head of the penis is fire-engine red, and as healing takes place, there may small patches of yellow or green crusts adherent to the skin. It is also common and normal to see a few spots of blood in the nappy adjacent to the penis or to see a few drops of blood resulting from your cleaning of the penis.

Once the original dressing has been taken off, you can clean the circumcised area at nappy changes. First, if you are using the square gauze, remove it. Using a clean cotton ball soaked in cooled-down boiled water, gently dab the head of the penis. Remove any attached crusty material if it comes off easily. Let the penis dry in the air. Then apply either the ointment-soaked gauze or the ointment with your finger. The rest of the nappy area can be cleaned with a facecloth or wipe, but until healed, do not use these on the circumcision. When reapplying the nappy, put it on so that it fits snugly against the penis. You may think that this will be uncomfortable for your son, but a snug nappy prevents the penis from moving around in the nappy (which is much more irritating).

Acute discomfort lasts only about a day, and even then babies seem to be very good at ignoring it. Keep in mind that in the day or so after the circumcision your son's cries may mean he is wet and uncomfortable, so change his nappy. The circumcised penis will not resemble its final appearance for quite a long time, but healing is essentially complete in about one to two weeks. The bright red colour of the head of the penis gradually becomes less red and, when healing is finished, ends up being a light purplish-blue.

It is good practice to clean the groove where the head of the penis meets the shaft. Thick white mucus secretions produced by skin glands there can, if not regularly removed when changing nappies or at bath time, cause adhesions (when the skin at the end of the shaft sticks to and grows together with the skin of the glands).

Infection following circumcision is rare, but if your newborn develops fever and is especially fussy, this could indicate infection. The shaft of the penis, which is not involved in the circumcision, should retain its normal colour; redness of the skin of the shaft closest to the head of the penis also may signify infection. Call your GP immediately if you are concerned that an infection is possible as this has potential to become quite serious.

Washing and bathing

A newborn has a limited potential for getting dirty outside of his bottom. He also has sensitive skin and a dislike of being immersed in water, so topping and tailing (see page 35) or a sponge bath (see below) is the best way to keep him clean and ensures the cord stays dry.

Sponge bath

There are many ways to give a sponge bath. The easiest is to place your baby on a dry towel on the counter next to the sink. Using a small basin of warm, soapy water, wipe your baby down with cotton balls or a wash cloth and promptly dry off with a second towel (see page 38).

Baby bath

Once you and your baby are "up" for a bath, you will need a baby bath with a textured nonslip base. Your baby should use this up until he can sit unsupported – around six months of age. Fill the bath with only 5–8cm of water. Always put cold water in first and then add hot water. The water should be pleasantly warm but not hot. Test the temperature with your elbow, but if you are not sure, use a bath thermometer. It should read 30°C (85°F). Water that is too hot can cause skin burns; water that is too cold will increase the likelihood your baby will become cold. Make sure the room is sufficiently warm, and the bath is well supported on a waterproof surface away from any draughts.

Have everything you will need ready to go before undressing your baby. You will need a soft, clean facecloth; a fresh, clean towel for drying him off; a nappy and clothes to put him in after the bath, plus all the supplies you will need for the bath itself.

Follow the procedure on page 38 and be quick – newborns and young infants can easily get cold, so the time your baby remains naked should be limited, and because he may cry for the entire bath so you'll want to get it done fast. You will need to wash his scalp but you can use soap and water instead of shampoo. It's a good idea to wash the cleanest parts of your baby first and the dirtiest parts last; this way you cut down on the risk of transferring germs from one body part to another.

As soon as you take your baby out of the bath, wrap him up in the towel but be careful not to cover his face. Gently pat him dry, paying particular attention to the skin creases around his legs, nappy area, under his arms and around his neck. Put on his nappy and clothes, keeping exposed parts covered with the towel.

Some parents feel they must bathe their babies daily, but there is no rational reason to do so. Other than dirty nappies, the only source for getting dirty is when your baby sicks up on himself. A number of babies sweat when they sleep, but this doesn't really cause a baby to become dirty. A bath every two or three days can suffice. However, if you would like to make the bath a part of your baby's going to bed routine or you simply just want to do it daily, that's fine, too.

BABY BATH FLOAT

If you need to use an adult bath for any reason, a float will help keep your baby close to the surface making it easier for you to handle him.

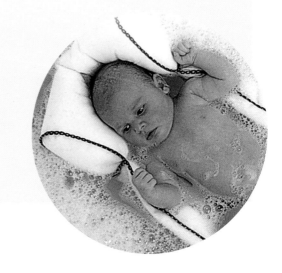

FONTANELLES

When your baby is born, the bones of his skull will not be entirely fused together, leaving small soft patches on the top of his head. These are known as the fontanelles. While you should obviously be careful around these, since they are spots where your baby's brain is vulnerable, they are covered with a tough membrane, so you don't have to avoid them altogether. Simply wash and dry over them gently, as you would the rest of your baby's skin. They won't knit together entirely until he is about two years old.

Washing the hair

You can wash your newborn's scalp while he's in the bath but some parents find it easier to do so once a baby has been taken out of the tub and dried.

Holding him wrapped in his towel and under your arm with his head supported, place his head over the baby bath and first wet his head then apply the soap or shampoo. Rinse off with more water (see box, below). To dry his hair, gently pat, rather than rub it with a towel. Use a corner of the towel as covering his face may frighten him.

Cradle cap

Otherwise known as seborrhoea, cradle cap is a condition marked by excessive flakiness of the scalp (see also *Seborrhoeic dermatitis*, page 357). When flakes fall on the forehead, face, ears and neck and irritate the skin, small pimples result. This rash is often incorrectly assumed to be neonatal acne.

Treatment is optional, since the pimples and scalp flakes cause no harm. But if desired, getting rid of the scalp flakes will lead to the facial rash disappearing. Rub baby oil into the scalp and allow it to remain there a few minutes. Then, shampoo and scrub the scalp. Shampoo daily to prevent the accumulation of flakes. Replace the baby shampoo with an (adult) dandruff shampoo if flakes persist. Beware that on the first day or two of treatment, the rash on the face will actually get worse before getting much better.

Eczema is the name of the rough, dry patches of skin some babies get (see page 357).

MORE **ABOUT**   shampoos and soaps

Most parents wash their infants' skin with a baby soap and use a baby shampoo on their hair. It is commonly said that infant products should be used because they are "milder" or "gentler". Is this true? Actually…no. There is no advantage to using baby soaps over adult soaps when cleaning the skin. In point of fact, many doctors recommend adult soaps with moisturisers, such as Dove, for bathing babies. Additionally, the only advantage of a baby shampoo is that it is formulated with ingredients that sting less if accidently allowed in the eye. Baby shampoos still sting the eye, only less so than adult shampoos. There really isn't any good reason to think that an adult shampoo would be harmful or "rough."

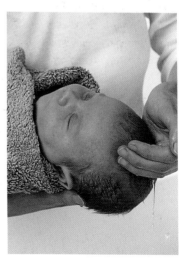

Care of the hair and nails

Some babies are born with a full head of hair, others have a sparse covering. Thick or thin, newborn hair is invariably shed after a couple of weeks – often a cause of concern for parents, but perfectly normal. Your baby may also have a covering of downy body hair, known as lanugo – this, too, will rub off within a couple of weeks.

Your baby's hair will need only simple care at first – wipe it down with a damp cloth or sponge, and brush it through with a soft brush. Do not use a comb as it could catch on the scalp and cause your baby harm. Your young baby's head is particularly sensitive due to the soft areas known as the fontanelles (see box, page 55). Don't be afraid of handling your baby's head though: simply ensure that any contact with it is carried out with the utmost care.

Gentle washing and brushing of your baby's hair should also guard against cradle cap (see page 55).

INFANTS' NAILS

You can cover your young baby's hands with a pair of soft mittens to prevent him scratching himself or irritating any dry skin condition he may have.

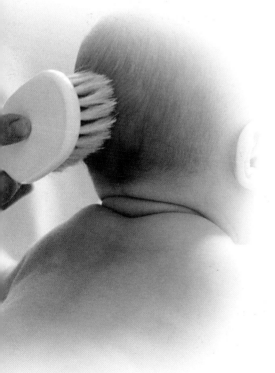

Nails

A newborn's nails are often quite long and you should trim them to stop him scratching himself. You will know it is time to cut them when your baby starts scratching himself (or you) with his nails. In a newborn, this occurs every three or four days; Use an emery board to do this. Cutting with scissors can risk tearing the skin, which is not only uncomfortable for your baby but could also lead to infection. Alternatively, you can gently nibble off the nails – your mouth is more sensitive than a pair of scissors. Soft mittens on your baby's hands will prevent him scratching himself or irritating a dry skin condition.

Toenails tend to grow more slowly than fingernails but often excess skin encroaches on to the nail bed, making toenails difficult to trim. To avoid catching your baby's skin, file toenails straight across. If you do draw some blood, blot with a tissue then dab some antiseptic ointment onto the area.

Dressing

Dressing your newborn can be fun and there are many ways to make him look extremely cute but remember that spending a lot on expensive baby clothes is for your benefit only; your baby has no idea about what his clothes look like and couldn't care less.

Getting your newborn dressed

As a rule, babies don't like being dressed or undressed; they dislike the feeling of air on their skin and garments being placed over their head. Make it easy on yourself and your baby by having everything within reach – and never leaving your baby alone on a raised surface, whether or not he can turn over.

You can make dressing fun by nuzzling and kissing your newborn, but be careful to be gentle.

What to put on

When dressing your infant, avoid either too much or too little clothing. He shouldn't be too hot or too cold, but should remain "just right". Your baby can withstand cold weather – recall that Eskimos also have babies – or warm weather, if dressed appropriately. As a guide, count how many layers of clothing you need to wear to be comfortable in your environment. Your baby will need about the same number of layers of clothing as you do. Premature infants who are still small (less than 2.75 kilos) should have one more layer. If using an infant carrier, count the carrier as a layer of clothing.

It is customary to put an extra layer on when outside in very cold weather, but avoid over bundling. If you are unsure if your baby is warm enough, place your (warm) hand under his shirt and touch his chest or back – he should feel just warmer than your hand. In hot weather, he may only need a vest and a nappy, or perhaps just a nappy. For how to put on and take off a vest and bodysuit, see pages 39-40.

Clothes

Choose clothes that also are gentle on your baby's skin. Natural fabrics like cotton and soft wools will be warm and allow your baby's skin to breathe. Avoid synthetic fabrics that feel scratchy. Check all

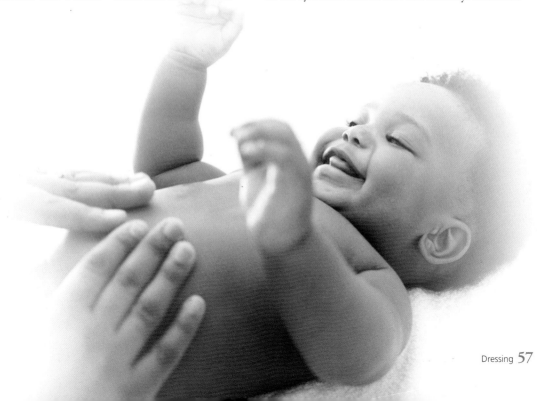

garments for raised seams and scratchy labels. The latter can be cut out but raised seams will annoy your baby.

Because clothes can become dirty or stained very quickly, particularly in the nappy area and neckline, they will need to be changed and washed frequently. Buy colourfast, machine-washable clothes that are suitable for tumble-drying. Avoid anything that needs hand washing or ironing.

Short-sleeved cotton vests with press-studs at the crotch don't ride up like bottomless shirts and keep your baby warmer. Choose ones with envelope necks; these are easier to put over your newborn's head. Long-sleeved all-in-ones or babygros are warm and easy to wear without restricting your baby's movement. Make sure there's always plenty of growing room in the legs. For advice on sleepwear, see page 157.

Hats

Other than in the first hours after birth, your baby does not need to wear a hat indoors unless it is quite cold inside (less than 20°C [68°F]). When outdoors, your baby needs a hat whenever your head feels a little cold, too. In the summer, a sun hat is essential if you spend a lot of time outdoors in the sunshine.

Washing clothes

Common wisdom dictates that special care should be taken when washing your baby's clothing: a mild soap should be used and his clothes should be laundered separately from the rest of the family's clothes. Both of these beliefs are illogical. While it is true that occasionally a baby will get a rash from sensitivity to the laundry soap used, this is uncommon and may occur with any brand of soap or detergent. No comparative study has ever demonstrated that one brand of laundry soap is better for babies than another. Washing your child's clothes separately from your own clothes also makes very little sense. There is certainly no medical advantage to this practice. However, it is recommended to wash baby clothes before putting them on your baby for the first time.

Visitors and going out

Shortly after your delivery, relatives and friends may begin arriving at your hospital room with well wishes, hoping to get to see and perhaps hold your newborn. (And this will continue once you are at home.) You, too, will want to see your close friends and family. Keep visits short and don't be afraid to say you are tired or uncomfortable, so guests will leave you to relax. Dad can be most helpful by keeping close tabs on mum's energy level and advising guests and would-be-visitors that there is a need for Mum to rest. Also, if you are nursing your baby, you may be hesitant to breastfeed when others are present. But do not let visitors interfere with feeding your baby: ask for privacy or cover yourself to maintain your modesty.

Germ prevention

Visitors also are a source of germs that may be spread to your newborn. No one wants his or her baby to become sick, but there are additional concerns about preventing your newborn from becoming ill. Young babies are more susceptible to severe bacterial infections than older children and adults, and if such an illness occurs, it can progress rapidly. Additionally, it is harder to distinguish milder illnesses from the start of a potentially serious one in newborns and young infants (see box, page 60). However, most illnesses that occur in young infants are not bacterial infections, but are colds and viruses. In fact, germs spread from visitors to your baby will almost always result in a viral illness. But such illnesses can resemble the beginning of a bacterial infection and may prompt the tests and treatment described below. Thus your efforts to prevent your baby from getting ill or febrile are worthwhile. Not only will you be preventing him from the discomfort of an illness, more importantly, you may be able to avert the worry and invasive procedures that result if your child needs to be hospitalised.

3 ways to limit infection

1 **Postpone visits from anyone under the weather** Tell people with coughs and colds to put off visiting until they are well.

2 **Limit the privilege of holding your baby** to just a few close family and friends, and only after they have washed their hands. Other visitors are allowed to look at, but not touch or kiss, your baby.

3 **Have hand sanitisers close by** Place alcohol-based hand soaps or sanitisers that do not require a sink or towel near your baby.

exposure to germs. While it is true that in the first hours after birth your newborn may not yet be able to regulate his body temperature well, this is a short-lived problem (unless your child was born prematurely, see page 94). If dressed properly, your baby can withstand the same temperature variations that you can. A hat should be worn when outdoors in cold weather. And when you are getting uncomfortably cold or hot, assume your baby is feeling similarly, and go back inside or where there is cooler air.

Allowing yourself to rest and recover from your labour and delivery is important, and something that many mothers fail to appreciate. You should not take your baby out for long outings until you have first taken care of yourself but a brief walk outdoors can be therapeutic as well as enjoyable.

As you now know, the vast majority of infections are spread by face-to-face, close contact between a germ "donor" and your baby. For that reason, it is a good idea to avoid cramped, closed-in spaces (such as a busy store or crowded restaurant) but there is usually no danger in going to the park, walking along the road or in a shopping centre.

Most infections spread by close contact and touching, thus a number of precautions are in order (see box, page 59). While most adults are aware that you wish to keep exposure to germs to a minimum, there will always be some who think you are simply being too "neurotic". Feel free to place the blame for restrictions on your healthcare providers.

Going out

There is a long-standing tradition of keeping newborns in the home for at least two and sometimes until four weeks of age. Among the reasons commonly given are that staying indoors prevents the child from exposure to extremes of weather (hot and cold), gives you a chance to rest and recover from labour and delivery, and minimises your newborn's

MORE **ABOUT** | bacterial infections

In the first two to three months of your baby's life, any fever or illness with fussiness should be evaluated. If your doctor cannot exclude the possibility that the illness is a bacterial infection, he or she will admit your child to the hospital where blood tests and evaluation of urine and spinal fluid will be done to detect blood stream or urinary tract infection (see page 351) and meningitis (see page 348). Intravenous antibiotics are then started presumptively, for cultures for bacteria may not be ready for two or three days. If all tests are negative for bacterial infection, your baby will be discharged. But it is quite an experience for both you and your infant, one you would have liked to avoid.

becoming and remaining a good sleeper, there are a number of reasons not to insist on these habits initially. Newborns have erratic sleep rhythms; their longest periods of sleep come during the afternoon. Better day-night differentiation begins to appear at about two to three months of age, when, thankfully, your baby will begin sleeping longer intervals at night. Your newborn also will need to wake for feedings several times a night. In addition, if he has fussy spells (colic) in the evening, helping him through these difficult periods certainly takes precedence over emphasising sleep habits.

The first months are among the hardest for parents, primarily because you will be chronically exhausted. Because your baby lacks the appropriate day-night rhythms, he will be up often during the night and you will soon become very tired. Getting sleep whenever possible should be given a high priority. So while trying to create good sleep habits is desirable if your baby readily goes along with them, do not pursue them if he does not cooperate. Do whatever it takes to get some sleep, even if bad sleep habits are formed. (They can be changed to good ones later when your infant is ready to sleep all night.) So if your baby falls asleep best while being rocked, do it. If he sleeps best in the swing or car seat, that is also fine. Have him sleep in a bassinet next to you to make it easier to pick him up when he cries at night. This will also facilitate breastfeeding. If you bottlefeed, use ready-prepared formula so that preparation time during the middle of the night is kept to a minimum.

It cannot be emphasised enough how important it is for you to get your sleep. You will feel worse, be grouchier, and have much less patience for your partner and baby when you are overtired. Try to nap during the day while your baby naps. And while much of the burden for night-time feedings falls upon Mum, especially if your baby is breastfed, Dad also can help. He can bring the baby to his mum for feeding, change the nappy afterwards and be responsible for getting your baby back to sleep for at least one of the middle of the night feedings. Dads also like to feel included in the feedings and can give a bottle of expressed or formula milk during the night. And Mum can get some sleep.

When you do put your baby in the cot or bassinet to sleep, remember that the safest position for sleep is supine (on his back with his head up).

MORE ABOUT | sudden infant death syndrome

SIDS (sudden infant death syndrome) is the sudden and unexpected death of a baby aged less than one year where no specific cause can be found despite a detailed investigation. Babies who die from SIDS appear to die painlessly in their sleep. It usually happens when a baby is asleep in his cot, but also can happen during any other periods of sleep such as when in a pram or parent's arms. SIDS can happen to any baby, but premature babies, low birth-weight babies and boys are more at risk. SIDS is more likely in the night, between midnight and 9 a.m.

Although the exact cause isn't known, researchers think that a combination of factors play a role in SIDS. Breathing failures or problems in a part of the brain called the medulla oblongata that controls breathing, problems with the heart not beating regularly, allergy, bacterial toxins and genetic abnormalities are all claimed to contribute but none of these have been proven. Although little is known about the causes of SIDS, there is a great deal of proven information on the steps parents can take to help reduce the risk of it happening (see pages 156-8).

SIDS

A second troubling thought you may have recurrently is the fear that your child will be a victim of sudden infant death syndrome (see box). This is rare, but you may still find yourself going in to check on your sleeping infant frequently throughout the day and night when this irrational worry creeps into your consciousness. You can minimise factors that add extra risk for SIDS (such as stopping smoking and placing your baby on his back when sleeping) but since no one can guarantee that your baby will not have SIDS, the only remedy for your worries is to, with great effort, place these fears out of your mind whenever they arise.

Work commitments

Single mothers and most dads are subject to additional worries. They may find themselves dwelling on how they will be able to provide for their new babies and possibly a stay-at-home partner. They may feel torn between the wish to be home more to help out and spend time with their new babies and the desire to be more successful at work to better support their family. Even if part of a couple, some women may have the same pressures. It can take time to find a way to juggle these two competing desires and feel more comfortable about your role in the family. Today, some men choose to be the stay-at-home partner and provide the majority of baby care.

Twins

In recent years, the number of twin pregnancies has increased dramatically due to the success of in-vitro fertilisation and other techniques that improve a woman's chance of becoming pregnant. Twinning can occur by either of two mechanisms.

Identical twins arise when an embryo of only a handful of cells splits in two and each half becomes a separate foetus. When this occurs, the twins result from the same fertilised egg and thus both twins have the same genetic make-up. When the two identical embryos implant in the uterus, they are usually enclosed in a single amniotic sac.

If, on the other hand, two separate and unrelated fertilised eggs reach the uterus, fraternal twins result. The genetic code in the cells of one twin is different than that in the other. Fraternal twins are more alike than unrelated children, since they, like all brothers and sisters, do share a number of the same genes, but they do not resemble each other as much as identical twins do.

ARE YOUR TWINS IDENTICAL OR FRATERNAL?

Telling whether or not your twins are identical may be difficult in the newborn period. Identical twins can be born with different weights and sizes, and, due to different positions within the uterus, their heads may be shaped differently. Proof that your twins are identical or fraternal comes after careful study of the placenta. Genetic testing can also be done, but this is seldom necessary. Here are some clues to knowing if your twins are identical or not.

- If your twins are of different sexes, they cannot be identical. Same-sex twins, however, can be either identical or fraternal.
- If a single placenta was noted at delivery, the twins are likely identical. Fraternal twins typically have separate placentas, or if the two placentas are conjoined, the single placenta is much larger than usual.
- Twins occurring after in-vitro fertilisation are usually fraternal, since many fertilised eggs are placed in the uterus at one time to increase the chance of a single embryo implanting.
- Identical twins have the same blood type. This information is usually available while your babies are still in the hospital. Fraternal twins may have either the same or different blood types.

The biggest problem with twins is that there are two of them! A number of logistical problems arise. For example, you need to choose two names instead of just one, and you will need two car seats to get them home from the hospital. Furthermore, you will have to be able to tell them apart. This will be easier if you have fraternal twins, but more of a challenge if they are identical. As you get to know your babies well, the uniqueness of each will be obvious to you. But in the beginning it is better to rely on clues. A birthmark, a different head shape, more or less hair on the head, or a different umbilical cord position may allow you to distinguish them. For more certainty, you can leave the hospital identification bands on their wrists or ankles or you can put on a makeshift bracelet of your own.

There is also twice as much work to do when you have twins. You have twice as many nappies to change, twice as many baths to give, twice as much laundry to do and twice as much crying to comfort. When they are older, there will be two mischievous toddlers to chase after, twice as much cleaning up to do, and certainly squabbles between the twins to adjudicate. In short, as a parent you will be at least twice as exhausted as other parents. Getting help from your partner, family, friends or even a baby-sitter can be a blessing.

And it may be more difficult for you to feed both babies at the same time, especially if you are breastfeeding (see also page 76). Exclusively breastfeeding twins is achievable, but may be hard to do; you may need to breastfeed quite frequently, which can be exhausting. To get around this problem, you may look for relief by having your partner give a twin an occasional bottle of formula. This technique will relieve some stress, but risks one or both of your twins at some point coming to prefer the bottle to the breast.

Facing unexpected problems

Most problems you may experience with your newborn will be unexpected but even minor

difficulties can be very upsetting because you lack perspective. A birthmark (see page 27), some initial reluctance of your baby to feed, or a small amount of jaundice (see page 369) can seem like a monumental problem. Your GP, maternal and child health nurse or relatives can be very helpful in giving you the information you need to be able to place a problem in its proper context.

Rarely, a serious illness or malformation is found in a newborn (see Chapter 13). This will usually result in your child being sent to the special neonatal care unit (SNCU). You will, no doubt, feel shocked, distraught and helpless in a situation such as this. (For more about how you will be feeling and what you will experience in the SNCU, see Chapter 4.) Needless to say, you will desperately need two things: knowledge and support. Your paediatrician or other specialists involved in the care of your baby can be great sources of information for you. You will need to understand more about what the problem is, how it came to be, what can be done to treat it and how this will ultimately affect your baby. Although there is much you can learn through other sources, such as books and the Internet, you may be misled by the information contained therein (see box). In this book, great efforts have been made to avoid errors commonly encountered in other sources.

Having a sick newborn or one with serious problems will place an incredible strain on you as the parent. You and your partner may be overwhelmed and overwrought. Helping each other in getting through this difficult time will benefit you both. Other relatives and friends, just by being with you, can give you a great deal of comfort.

5 dangers of consulting books and the Internet

1 **Incorrect information** Books and websites can contain significant factual errors. You may not be aware whether a book has been critically assessed by an informed reviewer or that on the Internet, anyone can say anything he or she would like to without regard to the accuracy of the data presented.

2 **The facts you read may not applicable to your baby** Several medical conditions can resemble one another. You may find a disease that fits many of your child's symptoms, but which may be the wrong diagnosis or wrongly interpret likely outcomes. Another source of confusion is the error of over-inclusiveness.

3 **Information is probably nonspecific** Texts and websites offer information to a wide audience and any advice and information is directed at many different children; in order to cover the possibility of a more severe illness being present, extra precautions may be recommended. The case of each baby is best considered uniquely, however. In medicine, a one-size-fits-all policy doesn't work.

4 **Unreliable data** Many sources of information present data in a skewed manner. They include only selected facts and don't give a balanced presentation of them.

5 **Information overload** You may get more information than you wanted. Your doctor may have told you, "Your baby has an excellent chance of full recovery." Do you really want to know about the 0 1% of children with the same condition who have a much more serious outcome?

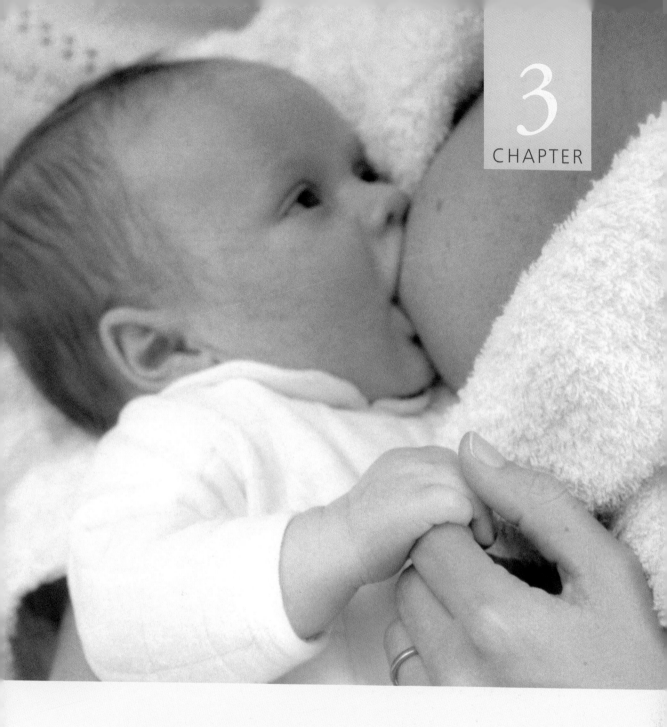

FEEDING YOUR
YOUNG BABY

Feeding basics

Whether you breastfeed or bottle-feed with expressed or artificial milk, you will find that most of your time initially with your new baby is taken up with feeding. Having someone else with you in the early weeks will make all the difference to your feeling "on top of things" as it can take a couple of weeks to settle into a pattern of feeding that makes you feel comfortable and reassured. If you are struggling, then it's worth getting help right at the start. If you're worried that your baby isn't "getting enough", discuss this with your health nurse or other new mothers, family or friends. You will soon be reassured when you see your baby growing well.

Breastfeeding will give your baby the best start in life, supplying him with vital nutrients and protecting him from infection. It also helps protect you from various diseases and enables you to create a strong physical and emotional bond with your baby.

Although women have always breastfed babies, nowadays many women in developed countries seem to have difficulty, and this may be because over the last four decades the knowledge about how breastfeeding "works" has been lost. Babies are just the same as they always were, and have the same natural instincts, but in industrialised countries, many of them are born with some intervention, and this can create problems in feeding for the first few days/ If, for example you were given pethidine or similar pain reliever in labour, this might have made your baby sleepy. If your baby was helped out by forceps or ventouse, he might have a sore head for a few days and if you had a caesarean, your baby's feeding reflexes might be delayed. If your baby was taken away perhaps because he needed extra support after some birth difficulty, his feeding reflexes may take time to return.

6 ways to tell your baby is thriving

1 **He is relaxed during feeding.** Your baby sucks and swallows fairly slowly, and pauses every now and then.

2 **He doesn't feed actively for more than half an hour at a time.** This indicates that he's latched on well. If it appears that your baby feeds for ages, something's not right and you may need help to improve the attachment.

3 **He is contented** or sleeps well between most feeds

4 **His poos change quickly from sticky black to golden yellow** in the first five days, and they are always soft (runny if breastfed, firmer if bottlefed).

5 **He has plenty of heavy, wet nappies.**

6 **He is alert and usually happy when he is awake,** is filling out and feels heavier.

Should you choose, however, to bottle-feed your baby – maybe because you have an existing medical condition, are taking medications or because you feel uncomfortable breastfeeding – the important thing is not to feel guilty about your decision. Your baby will still receive adequate nutrition and there are techniques for ensuring closeness. You are still going to be the best mother you can.

How often to feed

Adults have different eating habits: some are snackers, others grazers and still others, three-course diners. Babies differ, too. While they all need to eat frequently, especially initially, they can have different patterns. Some like feeding every couple of hours while others feed in a random fashion. Some are so regular that you could set your watch by them!

Whatever your baby's pattern – and whether breastfed or bottle-fed – nearly all health professionals have realised that most mothers know exactly when their babies are hungry, and recommend a flexible approach to mealtimes.

In the beginning your baby may seem to ask to be fed very frequently. His tummy is tiny and can't hold much more than 60–80 ml at a time. In the first few weeks, on average, a bottlefed baby may want feeding every three to four hours while a breastfed baby may want feeding every couple of hours, day and night. It can help to know that frequent breastfeeding helps to build up good amounts of breastmilk so that there will always be enough later on, when your baby will need more.

When you sit down to feed, remind yourself that this is a good opportunity to give your body a rest after the labour and to enjoy some calm relaxing time as you have probably been awake in the night. (Babies naturally wake to be fed in the night once or twice until they are about six months old.)

Breastmilk is low in protein and high in milk sugar, and babies need to have little and often to grow well. Bottlefeeding also needs to be baby led so you should feed your baby whenever he seems hungry. Most normal weight babies can go only about six hours without a meal. To begin with, this break usually occurs during the day, but it means your baby is learning to sleep longer and fairly soon he may well let the six hours pass at night.

During the first few days, some babies do not wake and ask to be fed. They may be sleepy from birth medications, or be uncomfortable from an assisted birth and want to be left alone. When your baby has had a long sleep, it may be worth gently waking him and offering him a feed right away.

How much to give

Babies have small meals and bigger meals just like adults. If you are breastfeeding, your baby will probably want to feed well from the first breast for as long as he can. Then you could offer a break for a burp or a nappy change, and bring him back to the other breast for a second helping. Babies love to be offered seconds, though more so if they are having a "three-course meal" rather than a "snack". Your first breast will refill while your baby is on the second side, so if your baby wants more, he can go back to the first side. Just as each baby has a different personality and a different suck, each breast has a different capacity and works individually but frequent feeding will help to build your milk supply in the first few weeks.

If you are bottle-feeding, your baby will need 60 to 75 ml of formula for each 0.5kg of body weight. For a 3.5kg baby, this would mean you need to give him 420 to 525 ml of formula in a 24-hour period. Until they weigh about 5 kg, most babies need at least six to eight bottlefeeds each day, as they only take in about 60 ml per feed.

Research tells us there is no need to give a breastfed baby water, even in hot countries, as he'll receive sufficient liquid by small frequent feeds. There is no nourishment in water and babies do not need it until they are older and taking solid food. Bottlefed babies may get thirsty in hot weather, or if too strong feeds are made up (which is dangerous!). If your baby seems thirsty, you can offer a little cooled boiled tap water after a milk feed.

If you have any worries about your baby's growth, taking him to a regular appointment with your maternal and child health nurse can help allay them. The weight charts for boys and girls in the back of this book and in your Child Health Record plot babies' weights against national averages. It isn't usually helpful to weigh babies every week, as they may not grow at a steady rate, and it can make mothers more anxious.

Growth spurts

Babies grow at different rates. Growth spurts may occur at around two weeks, four weeks, six weeks and three months. Just when you think everything is settled, your baby suddenly wants feeding more frequently. He has grown, and if you are breastfeeding, he is trying to program your milk supply to help him grow further. The only way he

can do this is to feed more often, which in turn bumps up your supply. When the supply is sufficient, he will settle to a more normal feeding pattern until the next growth spurt.

Growing can be uncomfortable for some babies who act as if in pain. If your baby seems affected, skin-to-skin contact, stroking, massaging, talking or singing softly will help him manage.

Days with a fretful baby can seem hard, but as long as you know they are only temporary you should find them easier to manage. These are days when you need to spend hours with your baby. You don't, however, have to suffer alone; invite a friend round. If you are breastfeeding and your baby seems

Helping to bring up wind

Several positions will help your baby get rid of painful wind in his tummy. Lift him up so that his head is over your shoulder, using one hand to support his bottom and the other to gently rub or pat his back. Or you can raise your baby into a sitting position on your lap. Support his head with one hand while you use the other hand to gently rub or pat around his shoulder blades. Another alternative is to lay your baby down so that his stomach rests on one knee and his chest on your crooked arm. His head should be facing away from you with nothing obstructing his mouth. Gently rub or pat his back.

fretful much of the time, don't hesitate to seek advice from someone knowledgeable before reaching for bottled milk top-ups. If it's a question of improving your milk supply, your midwife, health nurse, a lactation consultant, breastfeeding counsellor or peer supporter should be able to offer practical help (see page 80).

Wind

In the first few days of feeding most babies have very little wind. However, as your baby increases the amount of milk he takes in, he also ingests more sugar (a component of milk). This ferments and produces gas. Letting go of wind will make your baby feel better and he will release it from either his mouth or his bottom.

If your bottle-fed baby suffers from a lot of wind – you'll know because he'll seem upset and unsettled after his bottle – check that the holes of the teats are the right size (see box, below right). If the formula flow is slower than that illustrated, the hole is too small and your baby is having to suck hard to obtain the formula. This can mean that when your baby feeds he takes in too much air along with his formula. On the other hand, if your baby tends to gulp from the bottle, check that the holes of the teats aren't too large.

Make sure, too, that the bottle is always tilted enough when you feed your baby – the liquid should always completely cover the top of the bottle and fill the teat.

Most babies get very indignant if you try to stop and burp them in the middle of a steady flow of milk; imagine how you would feel if your drink was removed just when you were beginning to enjoy it. So if your baby is very windy, try a burping session when he takes a natural pause (see box opposite page). It is quite difficult for a baby to swallow air, but if your baby isn't fully attached to the breast or the bottle teat is too big, he may gulp and take in more air. In many cultures and countries where women breastfeed their babies for a long time, there

isn't a word for burping, yet in westernised countries it has become a sort of ritualised massage.

There is no need to spend more that a few minutes giving your baby the chance to burp. He can bring up wind just as well with a nice cuddle during or after the feed.

Possetting

Most babies have an excellent response to liquid in the back of their throats; they swallow! But the back of the throat and the top of the stomach are very close to each other, so some babies regurgitate a little milk alongside a big burp. Some babies posset a little after every feed. This is perfectly normal and nothing to worry about. True vomiting is much more noticeable, with more milk coming back.

CHECKING A TEAT

Fill a bottle with milk, add the teat and hold the bottle upside down. The formula should drip out at a steady flow of one drop per second. A small hole can be enlarged with a sterile needle.

Natural feeding

Whether you planned to breastfeed or bottlefeed, your body changed during pregnancy to prepare your breasts for feeding. You grew more mammary tissue and your breasts become larger.

Only a very small percentage of women are really unable to breastfeed fully; such women usually have had an injury to the breast tissue or breast surgery, or have hormonal or endocrine problems. But many women lack the confidence to breastfeed. Babies, however, do not have this problem. All babies are instinctively able to feed shortly after birth if they are given the right opportunity and environment. If during the "golden hour" (see box, page 73) you hold your baby skin-to-skin, he is most likely to show natural feeding responses.

Ensuring a good milk supply

Just as you nourished your baby in the womb throughout pregnancy, you can continue to nourish him naturally with your milk for many more months. Your breasts have developed a large network of special cells to make milk; when they release it for your baby to take, more is automatically made. In theory, this could go on indefinitely but at some stage your baby will begin to take less and less and eventually the supply will cease.

If you find that you don't seem to have enough milk for your baby, or the supply appears to be diminishing, you may be advised to introduce the bottle. But giving formula, especially in the early days, is likely to reduce your milk further. It's important, therefore, to take action or get good help quickly, as there are ways of boosting your own supply. Because of widespread formula promotion, many people believe that artificial milk is just as good as mother's milk. It's not! Only breastmilk contains all the nutrients and antibodies your baby requires. However, infant formulas are designed to give as many of the nutrients in breastmilk as possible, so if you don't have the option of breastfeeding don't be overly concerned.

As soon as your baby is born, colostrum (a highly nutritious early form of milk) already in your breasts starts to flow. To get the maximum supply, it's important to begin breastfeeding straight away, so that the colostrum starts to increase. If no milk is taken out, the supply will dry up within a few days.

By the third or fourth day post birth, your breasts will be producing much larger amounts of sweet milk.

4 ways of building up a good supply

1 **Encourage your baby to feed within the first few hours of birth** or start expressing your milk if he can't take it directly.

2 **Make sure your baby is fully attached to your breast at each feed;** get help quickly if this is difficult.

3 **Encourage frequent feeding,** day and night, for the first few weeks; use a sling to carry your baby around, and sleep close by to him.

4 **Get lots of help from family and friends** so that you can do the above.

You may find you have far more than you need for a few days, but this shows that your breasts can produce plenty for your baby – even if you have twins or triplets! Any milk left in your breasts after your baby has finished feeding will send a message to your brain to slow down the supply, so it begins to drop to what he needs. But if very little is taken out, perhaps due to problems with attachment, your supply may go down too much. This may explain why many mothers who find feeding difficult appear to have a low milk supply.

As breastfeeding continues, your supply depends on how much milk is taken out, not on what you eat, but it's important to get sufficient food, drink and rest. Looking after a young baby is very tiring and at stressful times, you may find your milk doesn't flow well; the let-down reflex works best when you feel relaxed. You may need extra support from family and friends so you can enjoy feeding, and the hormones released when you feed your baby will help you relax.

Your baby may seem to be very hungry and unsatisfied with your milk alone but he just may be fretting because he wants to be held close to you; if you put him down after a feed, he will probably object. Tucking him into a soft sling should help soothe him while leaving your hands free. Frequent feeding is good for young babies and helps you keep up a good supply.

Your breasts may start to feel very soft after a few weeks of feeding, and you may worry that your supply has gone down. However, this is normal and doesn't mean you aren't producing enough. If your baby seems to be thriving (see box page 68), you have plenty of milk.

Your baby may go through phases of feeding a lot. This might make you think that he's now needing more than you can supply. But this is normal behaviour, and not necessarily a sign of hunger. He may be asking for comfort as he's learning to deal with the world around him.

EXPRESSING MILK

If your baby is unable to breastfeed right away, or your partner is taking a turn at feeding, or you're going out for a while, you may want spare breastmilk. You can express milk using your hands or a pump. Many women find a pump quicker, more effective and easier than expressing milk by hand.

Your milk should be expressed straight into a sterile bottle or plastic container or breastmilk freezer bag and stored in the fridge up to 24 hours, or frozen and used within 3 months.

To use a syringe-style hand pump, simply place the funnel over your nipple, forming an airtight seal and then draw the cylinder in and out a few times to draw out the milk.

To express milk by hand, stimulate your milk flow by gently stroking downwards from the top of your breast toward the areola. Then place both your thumbs above the areola and your fingers below and begin rhythmically squeezing the lower part of your breast while pressing towards your breastbone.

Breastfeeding routine

Before starting to breastfeed your baby, try to make the atmosphere as calm as possible so that you can be as relaxed as you can. If necessary, take the phone off the hook or close the door so you won't be disturbed. Have a drink nearby to keep up your fluid intake. Make sure that both you and your baby are comfortable. If you're sitting upright you can either support his back and shoulders on your forearm or hold them with your free hand. His head should be at the same level as your nipple and he should be able to reach your breast without any effort.

Offering the breast

You may find it helpful to cup your breast with your hand or to support your breast by placing your fingers against your ribs just underneath it. Try not to place two fingers in a "scissors grip" around your nipple, as it can prevent your baby feeding properly. Nor do you need to press your breast away from his nose so he can breathe – his nostrils are flared to allow him to breathe and feed simultaneously.

Your baby may instinctively start to suck as soon as he feels your breast against his cheek, or you can brush his lips against your nipple to trigger his rooting reflex. Once he opens his mouth, draw him quickly to your breast.

Latching on

Your baby's mouth needs to be wide open so he can take in part of your breast as well as your nipple. His tongue needs to come

GETTING COMFORTABLE

A comfortable position can be the key to successful breastfeeding, so try out a few to see which work best. Whichever position you choose, firmly hold your baby close to you with his whole body facing your breast and his chest next to yours. You should be able to bring him easily to your breast.

Generally, most women feed sitting upright on a chair, often with their feet raised and a pillow supporting their arms, but other positions can be adopted in certain circumstances.

Lying on your side can be useful if you're tired or if you find it uncomfortable to sit – perhaps if you've had an episiotomy. Make sure that you have plenty of pillows to support you. Hold your baby close to you with his mouth in line with your breast. If you've had a caesarean or if your baby wriggles or arches his back, bend your knees and support your back with a pillow.

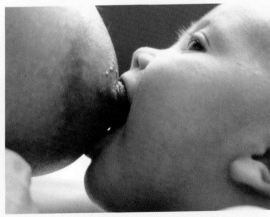

well forward so he can hold on to your breast comfortably while feeding, and press the milk from your breast behind your nipple. When he is fully on your breast, your nipple will be near the soft part at the back of his mouth, and every section of your breast will release the milk equally. When the milk flows, he will drink it slowly and steadily, and you may hear him swallowing.

If you need to reposition your baby, you can break the suction by inserting your little finger in the corner of his mouth.

Drinking his fill

Your baby's sucking pattern will alter while he feeds, from short sucks to longer bursts, with pauses in-between. He'll let you know when your breast is empty by playing with it, falling asleep, or letting your nipple slide out of his mouth. You can then offer the other breast. When you need to remove him from your breast, break the suction with your finger (as above). Don't worry if he refuses the second breast, but start with it the next time. When your breast is full, the milk is lower in fat, but as your milk is released, the fat level rises, and it's important for all sections of your breast to drain evenly, to prevent blockages.

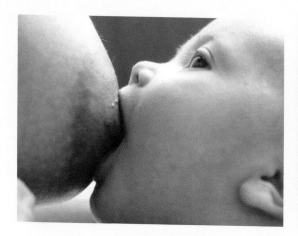

Breastfeeding twins

Breastmilk may be even more important for twin babies than it is for singletons. If born prematurely, breastmilk will provide twins with nutrients they would have received if they'd gone to term in the womb, including nutrients necessary for brain growth and protecting against infection.

The "mechanics" of milk supply and latching on (see page 74) are the same for twins as for a singleton but with twins, milk supply is maintained more easily since if one twin becomes ill or is a poor feeder, the other can keep the supply going.

Feeding together or separately

If you feed both babies together, it will be quicker and easier than bottlefeeding, and you will have two calmed and satisfied babies. However, it can take time and some experimenting to work out the best ways of doing so. You will probably be most successful with babies who are slower feeders.

Feeding your twins separately will enable you to get to know, and to spend time with, each baby as an individual and will be easier to manage if the babies have very different feeding patterns – one

wanting to feed more frequently or more vigorously than the other. Sometimes, twins have to feed separately – if there is a medical problem, for example – in which case you can express milk at the same time you feed the healthy one. However, breastfeeding separately is definitely more time consuming and the goal should be to try to set up a routine in which you can feed both babies together at least part of the time. This also ensures that you will get necessary and sufficient rest.

Creating a routine is easiest when twins are of a similar size and have similar feeding patterns. Even if you begin by feeding separately on demand, you can make things easier by feeding the first baby who wakes and settling him back down before waking his twin and then trying to modify this by waking the second when the first one awakes and feeding both together. This can take up to six weeks to establish but getting them on a routine will make it much easier for you to manage feeding.

Helpful positions

Whichever position you use, it is vital that each baby latches on correctly. You may prefer to start one baby off before you attempt to feed the other.

One useful way to position young babies is in a "V" position with both babies' feet towards each other (see picture). Other positions are the "football" hold – both babies are placed on pillows so their heads are level with your nipples. Their bodies lie under your arms and their legs are tucked behind you – and the cross-cradle hold – both babies are laid parallel across your chest in the same direction. Using pillows to support the babies' bodies, place one baby at your right breast, cupping his head with your right hand and hold the second one, tucked under your arm, at your left breast holding his head with your left hand (see page 93 for both positions). Whichever position you use, make sure you are sitting upright, your back is well supported and it feels comfortable.

Overcoming difficulties

Your baby was born to breastfeed, but feeding may take some time to get going well. Nature intends your baby to get all his food at your breast for around six months, then to carry on breastfeeding as he gets used to solid food. This will keep you both as healthy as possible. It will also give you a break from menstrual periods for several months, and can reduce the chance of an unwelcome pregnancy while your baby still needs a lot of attention.

Most mothers start breastfeeding, but many encounter problems and stop long before they had planned. The UK Government's five-yearly Infant Feeding Surveys show that nine out of 10 mothers who stop in the first six weeks would have liked to continue. The most common reasons given for stopping are:

◆ Baby rejected the breast;
◆ Breastfeeding was painful;
◆ The milk supply seemed low.

If you find yourself in any of these situations, don't despair. Extra support is available (see page 80). Breastfeeding is much easier when everyone is aware of why it is important, and it should help, too, if you understand how breastfeeding works.

If you and your baby had a normal birth, and you held him straightaway, breastfeeding is likely to get going well. If he appears to reject your breast, there'll be a good reason. You may feel that your baby is rejecting you, and that it might be better to switch to bottle-feeding. But your baby isn't saying "I don't want to breastfeed" but only "I can't manage to feed yet." Initial problems are generally a result of the birth. Anything that you found traumatic may have affected your baby, too.

Baby doesn't seem interested

Newborn babies feel safest when they are close to their mothers. Straight after the birth, if you held

4 ways to increase your baby's interest in breastfeeding

1 **Keep him in close contact** Hold your baby skin to skin or wear light clothing; he will be soothed by your familiar scent, your voice and your heartbeat.

2 **Maintain peace and quiet** Keep the room quiet and dimly lit and handle your baby gently. Hum or play music that you enjoyed in pregnancy – he will recognise it!

3 **Indirect feeding** Gve small feeds of expressed milk by syringe or cup every couple of hours but avoid bottle teats and dummies, as they might make breastfeeding harder.

4 **Co-bathe in a deep, warm bath** Put your baby face down on your chest with his tummy on your tummy as you scoop water over his back; have someone help you – wet babies are slippery!

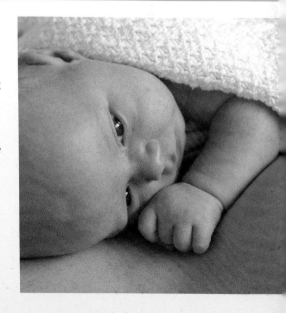

your baby close to you, skin to skin against your chest, this would have helped relax your baby and made him ready to feed within an hour or so. If this didn't happen for some reason, early feeds may be less easy, but you can correct it now. Help your baby to become more interested in breastfeeding by holding him close as often as you can. Soft slings make baby-carrying easy, or you could put your baby inside a low-cut stretchy top to hold him against your chest. Your partner can carry him, too.

Express your milk and give it to him in a little cup. (Ask your midwife to show you how to do this safely.) When you wash your top half, use plain water, so that your natural odour (which your baby recognises) won't be changed. Your breasts produce a scent to attract your baby, and he will start looking for the source of your delicious milk.

If your baby is finding feeding difficult, and if he seems fretful, it's best to keep him with you and your partner as much as possible until he settles down. Your family and friends will understand that it may be better for your baby to wait a bit before they give him a cuddle.

If your baby wants to feed but can't attach well — perhaps because your breast is swollen (see below) — he may become very frustrated and not want to try next time. Keep calm and offer expressed milk frequently, to help get your supply going until he's able to attach himself. If he can't breastfeed, you'll need to be very patient and gentle, and avoid pushing his head. If you give your milk in a bottle, it will help your baby if you hold him closely to your breast (with some skin contact if possible) while you feed him.

Painful breastfeeding

Breastfeeding should give mothers and babies pleasure for many months. It should NEVER hurt — any pain is a warning sign that something's not quite right. If it isn't comfy for you, it won't be right for your baby, so it's worth getting help quickly. With good support, the pain will go, and you will soon be able to enjoy breastfeeding.

You may be told that breastfeeding always hurts at first, and that your nipples need to toughen up.

REASONS FOR PAINFUL FEEDING

- **Swollen breasts** Temporary fluid retention developing at the end of pregnancy or in labour, or from engorgement as the milk increases a few days after birth, can make attachment difficult.

- **Enlarged or inverted nipples** Your nipple shape may be genetic or just caused by temporary swelling; you may need specialist help for a while until your baby can manage to attach.

- **Baby not opening wide** Your baby may not open his mouth well, so can't fully attach; this is common after a difficult birth.

- **Position of your baby** Your baby may not be close enough to your breast. His feeding reflexes may be reduced and he may then squeeze or pull on your nipple. Your nipple will then get rubbed by the hard part of your baby's mouth.

- **Blockages or mastitis** It's vital that all parts of your breast get well drained; any over-fullness can lead to painful feeding and lots of other problems.

- **Tongue-tie** If there's a restriction under his tongue, your baby may not be able to put it out far enough to attach well and a minor procedure to snip the tie may be needed; get a breastfeeding specialist's opinion.

There is no evidence for this, and it doesn't make sense either. Your nipples are meant to be sensitive so your brain can release the hormones, which operate your "let-down reflex", but they should not get damaged in the process.

You need to be comfortable, and your breast should be soft enough for your baby to attach well and get the milk to flow easily. When your baby is ready to feed, and lies closely to you, he can move himself around to find your breast. If he can't self-attach, you may need to help him a little, but no force should be used.

If your nipples are sore during feeding, your baby probably isn't fully attached to your breast. Check your nipples after your baby has finished feeding – they should look the same shape as before. If they're squashed, pulled out, grazed or blistered, your baby needs to get further on next time, or your nipples may then crack and bleed. It's important to get help quickly – see page 80.

see page 80.

MILK MYTHS

- Many mothers just don't make enough milk.
- Some babies are especially hungry and need top-ups.
- Feeding frequently means the breasts don't have time to refill.
- The milk supply can drop if mothers don't eat or drink enough.
- Mother's milk loses its value after several months so should be replaced with cows' milk.

5 ways to heal or prevent soreness

1 Make sure your breast is soft enough for your baby to grasp If your breast is very firm, press your fingers against your breast, about 4 cm behind your nipple, and push into your chest wall working all around the darker areola until it gets softer. This is called "reverse pressure softening". Pressing a little milk out first with your fingers may also help.

2 Hold your baby really close Lean back comfortably and let him lie face down on you – his feeding reflexes may improve so he can open his mouth wider. If you need to hold him, support his shoulders and bottom but don't hold his head; his chin should press into your breast so his nose is free. One layer of clothes is all he needs – your body will keep him warm.

3 Encourage frequent, short feeds Carry your baby around in a sling. Offer your breast as soon as he looks interested rather than waiting for him to cry – he won't attach so well when upset. Give him expressed milk to keep up your supply.

4 If your nipple starts to hurt a lot during a feed, slide your baby off carefully and try again, or offer the other side. If you can't get him on comfortably, get help as soon as you can. Dab your nipples with a little expressed milk to soothe and heal them. If your nipples are damaged, a tiny smear of pure lanolin may help them heal – avoid other creams as they may irritate and change the taste of your skin.

5 Keep your breasts well drained. Offer alternate breasts at each feed. Check your breasts for any lumps after a feed and gently massage them to prevent blockages. If you need to express some milk make sure your nipple fits the pump funnel well – some mothers need a larger funnel – and soften your breast first, if necessary.

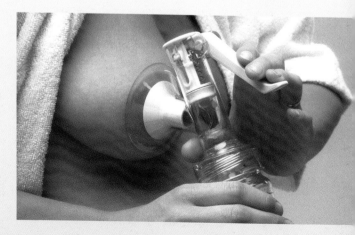

Support with feeding

Information on infant feeding is widely available from books, websites, professionals, and friends and relatives, but how can you judge the best advice? Babies are the same the world over, and have the same needs for safety and good food, but their parents may have different views of what babies need, based on their own upbringings and personal or cultural experiences. Such views may come from customs and beliefs rather than facts and evidence so that advice on feeding a young baby could be based on research into babies' biological and emotional needs, or it may be based on western expectations.

Considering advice

All babies have the same basic needs, but the way they are fed can make a big difference to how they behave and develop. Formula-fed babies may manage on four-hourly routines, and accept bottles from different people, but this isn't what they would choose. Babies are predisposed to stay close to their mothers and breastfeed frequently, so those who are bottlefed do best when they can choose how often to feed and how much to take, and get a close cuddle with Mum at the same time. So advice on formula feeding needs to reflect these facts.

When considering advice, look at who is giving it and ask yourself on what is the individual basing his or her guidance. Grandmothers, for example, are experienced in baby care, but may be advocating routines which are out of date and no longer recommended.

If a professional is giving advice, what qualifications does he or she have? Midwives have a grounding in infant feeding, but may recycle outdated knowledge. Maternal and child health nurses have training in infant feeding. Doctors often receive little if any teaching on this subject, but may have done their own studies into infant nutrition. All health professionals need regular training to keep updated. To ensure you get trustworthy information, check out the qualifications of those giving it.

Lactation specialists

Australian International Board Certified Lactation Consultants (AIBCLC) are breastfeeding specialists with a professional qualification, which is regularly updated. Many have midwifery, nursing or other health qualifications, and some specialise as infant feeding advisers in maternity units. Others are breastfeeding counsellors with voluntary organisations and a growing number are in private practice.

Australia's professional organisation is the Australian Lactation Consultants' Association or ALCA. Its website (alca.asn.au) lists practitioners around Australia who are available to support parents in various ways.

Australian Breastfeeding Association (ABA) counsellors or supporters have personal experience of breastfeeding, and take a course of training in listening skills and in helping to get breastfeeding going well and overcome any difficulties. The ABA offers many valuable services, including volunteers who have been through a short training program. They work in their own communities to encourage mothers by being alongside them. They refer mothers who have complex or unresolved conditions to health professionals or other breastfeeding specialists. They provide hospital and home visits, telephone counselling and support groups. For more information, visit their website at www.breastfeeding.asn.au.

Bottle-feeding

Whether you are feeding expressed breastmilk or formula milk from a bottle, you must maintain good hygiene as bottlefed babies are more prone to infections than breastfed babies and, if using formula, follow the manufacturer's instructions carefully so your baby receives the proper nutrients.

Types of formula

Until your baby is at least a year old, he should be given formula milk if you are not breastfeeding. All baby formulas are carefully produced under government guidelines to ensure that they replicate human milk as closely as possible and contain the correct amounts of fat, protein and vitamins that your baby needs. Ordinary cow's milk contains high levels of protein and minerals, which can put a strain on a young baby's immature kidneys and cause dehydration. Cow's milk also doesn't contain sufficient iron for young babies. Goat's milk and condensed milk are also unsuitable for young babies.

If you're unsure as to which formula is best for your baby, your health nurse will be able to give you guidance. You can buy formula in powder, liquid concentrate and ready-to-feed forms at most supermarkets and pharmacies. Powdered formulas are usually the cheapest of these, while ready-to-feed forms are the most expensive but can be useful in the first few weeks, while you're getting used to feeding or if you're short of time.

There are two basic types of formula: those based on modified cow's milk; and specialised formulas, which are usually based on soya milk.

Modified cow's milk

Most bottle-fed babies are fed with a formula based on modified cow's milk and if your baby has been fed on this while in the hospital without any problems, there's no reason to change when you get home. If you're concerned that your baby isn't

Continued on page 85 ▶

FORMULA MILK

- It is always better to feed your baby freshly made up formula milk. Stored milk may increase the chances of making your baby ill.
- The milk must be the correct temperature. Drop a little milk on the inside of your wrist; it should feel warm, not hot. If it is too hot, hold the bottle, with the cap covering the teat, under cold running water. Do not warm a bottle in the microwave as it will continue to heat when it's removed and can scald your baby.
- Give the correct amount. Too much powder can give your baby constipation and make him dehydrated; too little powder may not provide sufficient nourishment.

Sterilising bottles

Until your baby is at least six months old, feeding equipment needs to be sterilised whether you are feeding expressed breastmilk or infant formula.

If you do not want to buy a steriliser, you can boil your feeding equipment for at least five minutes. However, be sure to buy bottles and teats that can be boiled, as some cannot.

Always throw away any leftover milk not drunk within one hour. It's important to follow the manufacturer's directions.

WASH THE EQUIPMENT

Wash all bottles and teats in hot soapy water after using. A clean bottle brush should be used. Pay special attention to the screw thread at the top of the bottle and the inside of the neck; these are the areas where hardened milk can easily become lodged. Turn the teat inside out to finish the job and then rinse everything thoroughly using cold water.

STEAM STERILISERS

These can be either electrical or microwave versions. Add water to the unit (as per manufacturer's instructions). Place washed bottles upside down onto the locators on the base, screw rings onto the central stem and teats onto locators on the teat tray. Position the tray onto the central stem and place caps over locators on the cap tray and place this over the teat tray. Cover and plug the unit into the mains socket and switch on at the mains. Press power button to start. The unit will heat up for sterilising then cool down. After cooling is complete, your bottles are sterile and ready to use. Any equipment not used right away must be resterilised.

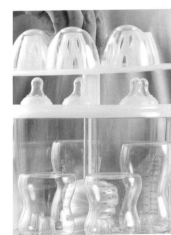

FITTING A TEAT

To fit a teat into the screw ring, hold it with sterilised tongs and pull it through.

COLD WATER STERILISER

Make up the sterilising solution (as per manufacturer's instructions). Place screw rings loosely over the neck of the bottles; do not screw on. Add the teats and caps ensuring that all the contents are submerged in the water and that there are no air bubbles trapped inside any of the products. Place the sinker on top of the items – this will ensure that they remain submerged in the solution. Place the lid on the steriliser. After 30 minutes your products will be sterilised and ready to use. Before use, rinse all your items in freshly boiled, cooled water. Do not leave the accessories in the sterilising solution for more than 24 hours. After 24 hours, the solution must be changed.

Making up formula routine

Fill a kettle with fresh or filtered tap water and boil. Do not use mineral water or softened water, because the level of mineral salts can be unsuitable for babies, or repeatedly boiled water. Let the water cool for no more than 30 minutes.

Meanwhile, make sure your work surface is clean and disinfected and thoroughly wash your hands.

Pour the correct amount of cooled, boiled water into the bottle (the water still needs to be hot, otherwise any bacteria in the milk powder won't be destroyed). Keep the teat and cap on the upturned lid of the steriliser; do not put them on the work surface.

Use the scoop provided to measure out the required amount of formula, then level off any excess powder with leveller or a knife – scraping across the scoop, not patting down. Double-check the amount of scoops you need and add them to the bottle.

Holding the edge of the teat, place it on the bottle then screw on the retaining ring. Cover with a cap. Shake the bottle hard so that the water and powder are thoroughly mixed.

Anti-reflux formulas are made up differently from other types. Ask your maternal and child health nurse for information.

OUT AND ABOUT

If you need to transport a feed, take some boiling water in a sealed flask and pre-measured formula in a sterile container. The one pictured here holds up to three feeds. Or, use ready-made formula cartons.

▶ Continued from page 81

Even when your baby gets older, don't leave him on his own to feed from a propped-up bottle – there's always the risk that he could choke. You should inspect bottle teats each time you wash them to ensure that they're not worn or damaged. If fragments break off in your baby's mouth it can be dangerous.

putting on enough weight or still seems hungry after you've given him his bottle, consider changing to another brand or type. However, always ask your health nurse's advice before you do this – the problem may not lie with the formula, but may be due to feeding techniques or an intolerance to a particular brand; or it may be caused by a medical condition that requires further investigation.

Specialised formula milk

For full-term, bottlefed babies who are diagnosed as intolerant to lactose or protein in cow's milk, or who have other feeding or medical problems, a range of specialised formulas is available. These formulas will be prescribed by your healthcare provider, if necessary. These include hypoallergenic formulas and soya milks, which have been formulated to provide babies with all the nutrients they need.

Feeding your baby

In the first few weeks, it can be useful to have ready-to-feed bottles on hand so you can feed your baby as soon as he's hungry. This will help prevent him getting upset while waiting and then refusing to feed. Also, avoid too many different people feeding him at first – let him get used to you and your partner. Feeding times should soon become a relaxing and enjoyable occasion and you can help this by holding him close to you and maintaining eye contact with him By the time your baby is three months old, you'll see him starting to get excited when he knows his bottle is on its way.

Twin feeding

It's easiest to feed both babies at the same time; choose times and stick to them.

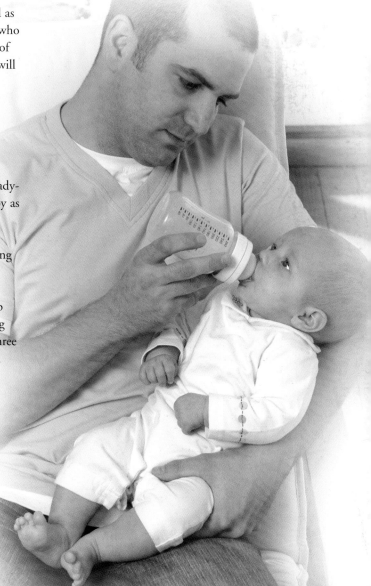

Bottle-feeding routine

Make yourself and your baby comfortable before you start and give him all your attention. Hold him securely in your lap with his head in the crook of your elbow and his back supported along your forearm. To help your baby relax, cuddle him close and talk or sing to him. Watch him all the time and respond to his demands. Some babies like to pause for air or to bring up some wind; others prefer to keep on feeding until all the formula has gone.

Check the temperature before giving the milk to your baby: shake a few drops onto the inside of your wrist. It should feel warm but not hot. If you want to cool it, hold the bottle with the cap covering the teat under running cold water.

Offering the bottle

Let your baby see the bottle then stroke his cheek to prompt the rooting reflex. He will automatically turn to you with his mouth open ready to suck.

Hold the bottle at an angle of about 45 degrees so that its neck is full of milk and there are no air bubbles. Offer the teat to your baby and allow him to take it deep into his mouth and begin sucking. Keep the bottle steady so that he can properly latch on.

Drinking his fill

You will feel him sucking on the bottle. Adjust the angle so that the top of the bottle is always full of milk.

Remove the bottle when your baby has finished feeding or you need to wind him: slip your little finger in to the corner of his mouth to break the suction. Once you have finished, throw away any unused milk and start the next feed with a freshly made-up bottle.

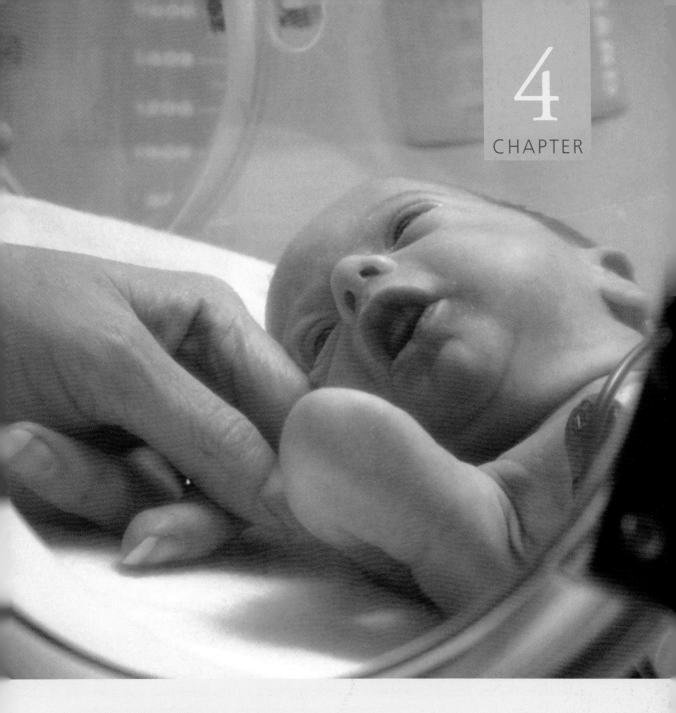

CARING FOR YOUR PREMATURE INFANT

In hospital

If your baby was born well before her due date, it is likely that the pregnancy and delivery you were expecting haven't occurred. Instead of a happy post-partum period, worries about your baby's health immediately dominate your thoughts. You even may not have had time to hold her, let alone feed her, right after the birth if she was whisked away to the special care nursery, or to the neonatal intensive care unit if she was very premature or had a health difficulty. Dreams of her sleeping in your arms and of you going home together from hospital are dashed. In fact, you feel somewhat helpless as you stand watching the special care nurses tend to your baby. Even if she isn't having any serious problems, your daughter is still so small and fragile!

Spending time with your newborn will be a priority (see page 89) but there are other goals you need to accomplish. If you had a vaginal delivery, you need to rest and recuperate after what may well have been a difficult and taxing process. It may be weeks until you feel like your old self.

If you had a Caesarean section, the time needed to heal properly is even longer. You may be tempted to neglect yourself in fulfilling your desire to help your newborn, but please resist this temptation.

Twins and more

Characteristically, pregnancies with twins (or more) end in earlier deliveries than singleton pregnancies. Although there may be other causes for this, it seems as if the enlarging uterus runs out of room for the multiple growing babies and has no choice but to deliver them. And as the number of foetuses increases, the chance of pre-term birth becomes greater and it is more likely that delivery will be earlier in gestation.

The biggest problem with twins and multiple birth siblings is a practical one: there are more of them! In the hospital, this may lead to minor difficulties such as two feedings for you to give at once or producing enough breastmilk for two. And now you have two (or more) children to worry about.

Another unique problem you may face is that one of the twins may be ready for discharge before the other. If the second twin will be discharged only a few days later, the first twin is often allowed to stay in the hospital so that both may go home at the same time. But practical issues once again dominate if you have one baby at home and one in the hospital: visiting one twin requires that

---

MORE **ABOUT** | multiple births

Although the vast majority of multiple births are twins, triplets, quadruplets, quintuplets and even sextuplets are becoming more common due to in-vitro fertilisation. Multiple siblings may be the result of the ovary releasing multiple eggs, or several eggs being implanted during fertility treatment. In such cases, each egg is fertilised separately and non-identical siblings, who can be of either sex, are conceived. Alternatively, a single fertilised egg can split, producing two, three or in some cases more identical embryos, always of the same gender.

Multiple births are extremely risky as the uterus is only capable of carrying, feeding and providing oxygen for a certain number of foetuses. In a multiple pregnancy, even a twin pregnancy, there is a greater likelihood of babies being born prematurely, developing health problems, such as blindness and cerebral palsy, or dying. To reduce the risks, doctors try to get mothers to have the babies one at a time, but this is not possible in all cases.

another adult be home watching the other. In addition, since you will likely be home more than in the hospital, you may feel guilty that the hospitalised twin is not getting enough of your attention. Or if your hospitalised twin remains ill, you may feel guilty for thinking of her too much of the time. There are still many organisational difficulties with twins once they are both home, but these were discussed in Chapter 2.

Visiting your baby in the hospital

Like all mothers who are recovering from their deliveries in the post-partum unit (and after discharge from the hospital), you will want to spend a great deal of time with your pre-term newborn. Being with her in the special or intensive care unit will allow you to get to know each other; your baby will certainly enjoy and be comforted by your voice and your touch and you will be able to learn how to care for her under the helpful tutelage of the nurses.

A balance must be struck between visiting your baby and resting enough to restore your health and energy. At the time of your own discharge, ask your caregiver how often and long you should make your visits. Initially, one visit a day (or perhaps less often if your own condition requires it), lasting two to three hours (if sitting down next to her incubator) or less (if standing up) is plenty. Later on, many mothers visit

once in the morning, arriving just before feeding time and staying until just after the next one. Then they go home and rest all afternoon, returning for a shorter visit in the evening. Premature infants sleep even more than full-term babies (who sleep about 16–20 hours a day) so your baby is certain to be asleep for much of your visit.

Fathers also want to spend time with their newborns, but have other pressing needs. They have to care for their partners – making sure they are resting – as well as doing the household chores to allow their partners time to relax, and taking them to and from the hospital. They also may need to continue to go to work. In fact, a dad's wish to amply provide for his now larger family may result in him feeling that he must work harder than ever. In some families, parents alternate trips to the hospital, with dad arriving in the evening after work. Fathers also can wear themselves out by trying to do too much, so be careful. Your baby will need two healthy, well-rested parents when she comes home because there will be much to do!

Having to leave your child in hospital when you are discharged is a great disappointment, often accompanied by sadness, but there is a silver lining to this dark cloud. Compared to mothers of full-term newborns (who have only a day or two in the hospital to get used to their infants and learn how to care for

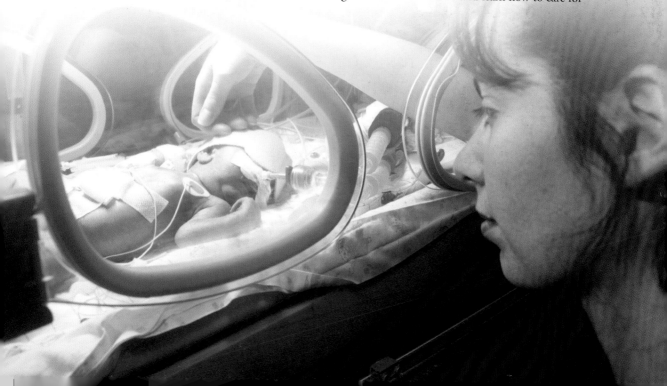

What is prematurity?

In humans the time from fertilisation of a mother's egg to delivery is normally 38 weeks. But we say pregnancy lasts 40 weeks, since historically it is timed from the beginning of a woman's last menstrual period (LMP), which generally occurs two weeks prior to ovulation and fertilisation. Although this method of counting is illogical, since according to it, for the first two weeks of your pregnancy you are not technically pregnant, it is used by medical specialists throughout the world. So, when doctors speak of the 36th week of pregnancy or that the foetus has a gestational age of 36 weeks, the counting begins at the LMP.

Instead of all pregnancies lasting exactly 40 weeks, there actually is a fairly wide range of what is considered normal. A newborn is said to be full term if she is born at 37 weeks or more (up to 42 weeks) of gestation. Prematurity occurs when the pregnancy ends before the 37th week of gestation.

Low birth weight and prematurity are not exactly the same. While both are often present in the same baby, occasionally babies born after 37 weeks of gestation, even though they are full term, weigh far less than expected. (They are termed small-for-gestational-age infants.) The concept of prematurity is really meant to describe the inability of a baby's body to function in the same ways that a full-term infant's body does. Using gestational age or birth weight to indicate immaturity of bodily function usually works, but not perfectly. Two children may be born at 35 weeks' gestation, but one's lungs or other body systems may perform much better than the other's. In other words, even though both were "in the oven" the same length of time, one came out "more cooked" than the other.

The age of a prematurely born infant may be expressed in either of two formats. The baby's chronological age is described in weeks or months since birth. The baby's corrected age, however, is her chronological age minus the number of weeks she was born prematurely. If your nine-week-old infant, for example, was born at 32 weeks of gestation, her corrected age is one week (40-32 = 8 weeks premature; then 9-8 =1). But this is only an approximation. It assumes that your infant now functions similarly as a one-week-old (full-term) newborn. Why do doctors use corrected ages? Because by using the corrected age, they can reasonably (but not exactly) compare infants born at different degrees of prematurity with each other and with corresponding full-term newborns.

TERMS USED IN TALKING ABOUT PREMATURE BABIES

Full-term/term pregnancy	Pregnancy lasted for 37–42 weeks
Prematurity	Pregnancy lasted less than 37 weeks
Pre-term Infant	An infant born less than or equal to 36 weeks of gestation
Gestation/gestational age	Number of weeks or months of pregnancy counted from the LMP.
Late Pre-term Infant	An infant born at or after 34 weeks, but before 37 weeks of gestation
Low Birth Weight	Birth weight is less than 2500 grams
Chronological Age	Age since the time of birth
Corrected Age	Chronological Age minus the number of weeks a child is born prematurely (example: an 8-week-old baby who was born 5 weeks prematurely has a chronological age of 8 weeks and a corrected age of 3 weeks). Another way to look at it is: the number of weeks since the LMP minus 40 weeks (i.e., if she had been full term).

them), you will have much more time to become expert in your baby's care. By spending time in the hospital and having the nurses show you how to perform the little tasks involved in daily routines, you will be more competent and confident in your skills by the time you bring your baby home. You will acquire proficiency in cleaning and changing her, and measuring and giving vitamins. Also, you will become comfortable picking her up and holding her, and will soon learn what her cries mean. In time, you will also become expert in how to feed her. Very premature infants are often quite ill initially due to immaturity of their lungs, intestines, circulatory system, etc., and being proactive and learning about your baby's medical conditions (and how to care for them) can be accomplished during the time she is in the hospital. Practice, under the watchful eye of a good neonatal nurse, will prepare you for what you will need to do once you and your baby are both home.

Life in an incubator

Very ill babies are treated on open infant beds kept warm by radiant heaters, but once medically stable, most premature infants live in an incubator. An incubator consists of a flat infant mattress enclosed in a box having clear plastic-like side walls and ceiling (roughly 75cm long, 50cm high and 50m wide). The incubator rests on a cabinet so that your newborn is about waist-high off the ground. Most models allow access into the "living quarters" via a rectangular door that comprises the lower half of one of the long sidewalls. On the upper half of the side wall there are also two "port holes" (round doors about 15cm in diameter and 30cm apart) which are big enough to admit your hands and forearms, but not requiring the larger door to remain open.

In the incubator, your newborn is shielded from the outside world in a heated environment, but at the same time, she can be seen and observed. She can be fed and procedures such as bathing, taking blood and starting intravenous therapy can be accomplished without removing her from her heated home. Via the port holes, you will be able to comfort her by touch until she is big enough to be allowed out of the incubator for hugging and holding. Incubators are far

from soundproof, so even though she is inside, you can talk or sing to her from outside her safe haven.

Keeping warm

Incubators are heated because premature infants are not yet capable of maintaining their own body temperature; inside, your newborn will stay warm. When your premmie baby is allowed outside the incubator, she will be well bundled, with a hat on.

Usually, when a newborn in an incubator is the equivalent of 35–36 weeks gestation, the temperature inside the incubator is gradually lowered to see if, dressed in clothes, she can maintain a normal body temperature. If successful, she will now move to a new home: an open cot.

Physical contact

Even if you can't yet hold your premmie baby in your arms, you can touch her and talk to her to show your love. Such activities will not only make you feel better but they will also benefit your baby: studies have shown that compared to other premmie babies, those who are regularly touched and talked to grow faster and get home sooner.

Feeding

Very small premmie babies are fed initially using a narrow diameter feeding tube that goes in through the nose (nasogastric or NG tube) or mouth (orogastric or OG tube) and ends in the stomach. Premature infants are usually incapable of strong sucking and the feeding tube bypasses the need for sucking. Expressed breastmilk or premature formula is measured in a syringe and dripped or pumped into the baby's stomach via the tube.

When your baby is older, bottle feedings can be given while she is in her incubator. Sit next to the incubator with each hand and forearm through one of the port holes. Using both hands, sit her up almost to 90 degrees, supporting the back of her neck and head with one hand. Hold the bottle in your other hand and place it in her mouth. Let her rest every minute or so until the prescribed volume is ingested.

The special care nurses can show you some of the tricks of the trade for getting slow or reluctant feeders to do better. For example, gently stroking her cheek near the mouth often induces a sucking reflex and can be used to get her to start feeding.

Breastfeeding in the hospital

Breastfeeding your pre-term infant is a lot of work for you, but valuable for your baby. The advantages of breastfeeding are many (see Chapter 3), but two are especially important for premature infants. Babies who receive breastmilk have fewer of the complications of prematurity, most notably a lower incidence of a serious intestinal disease called NEC (necrotising enterocolitis). In addition, the antibodies and immune system cells in breastmilk aid in preventing infections.

With the exception of some late pre-term infants, most premmie babies are not ready for breastfeeding after birth. They are too sick to be fed or are not yet able to produce a strong suck (or both). So your first experience with breastfeeding will likely be using milk expressed with a breast pump.

For breastfeeding to be successful, expressing must be started soon after your delivery and done several times a day. It is a substantial time commitment: even with the strongest pumps (and getting a very good one is best for saving you time), an expressing session often lasts 15–20 minutes. And if not done regularly, your milk supply will decrease. Two factors that also tend to reduce the amount of milk you will produce are stress and tiredness. Regrettably, mothers of premmie babies are typically full of anxieties and worries. Many spend all the time they can at their infants' bedsides, neglecting their own needs for rest and recuperation. So, again, please take care of yourself. Your infant will benefit from having a calmer, more rested mother in many ways, not the least of which is her mum's greater milk production.

Despite these obstacles, there is a very good chance that you will succeed at breastfeeding. Having a partner who shares your desire to provide breastmilk to your baby is very helpful and, almost universally, neonatal nurses will encourage and support your efforts, too.

Providing your premmie baby with breastmilk is good for her wellbeing and is something only you can do to keep her healthy. In doing so, along with the medical staff, you are aiding the process that will allow her to reach maturity. The expressing and all the efforts you have to make to nurse are a reflection of your love for your baby, and will, no doubt, make you feel good inside.

Giving the milk

In some nurseries, tiny feeds are given to premmie babies through an NG tube within a few days of birth. These are called trophic feeds, because there really isn't enough given to be a significant source of nutrition. Instead, these small amounts of milk are given to stimulate the intestinal tract, in hopes that in the future feedings will go more smoothly. If your newborn's doctor recommends trophic feedings, your expressed breastmilk (EBM) can be used for this. When more nutritious feedings are started later, your milk (often enhanced by the addition of a breastmilk fortifier) can be given via a feeding tube. Even though her sucking efforts are weak at this stage and she will not get much milk, some doctors and nurses suggest teaching your infant to associate breastfeeding with the positive feeling of satiety. This is done by placing her on the breast

MORE **ABOUT** | kangaroo care

Skin-to-skin contact with your premmie baby undressed (except for her nappy) and her exposed skin covered by a garment or blanket has many benefits. Both parents can engage in this to bond with their baby (see picture page 94) and breastfeeding done this way is often more successful, and has been shown to result in more weight gain and earlier hospital discharge than "standard" breastfeeding.

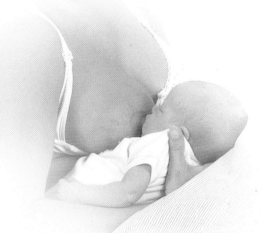

and encouraging her to suck while the milk is delivered via the feeding tube. Subsequently, when she does develop a more mature suck and swallow mechanism, feedings can be at the breast.

Producing and storing breastmilk

If you choose to feed breastmilk, begin expressing within a day of your delivery to stimulate milk production. You won't be able to express much at first, because your milk supply is not in yet. But express every three to four hours if possible, because more expressing results in a better supply of milk. Expressing can be done at home. Place the milk in sterile containers provided by the hospital. Bring to the hospital enough to meet expected demand and freeze the rest. Most hospitals also have a quiet room reserved for mothers while they express.

For the first days or weeks, you will have much more milk in bottles or bags than your infant will use. Extra expressed milk can be stored in your home freezer. When leaving milk at the hospital, label each bottle with your infant's name and the date the milk was collected. See also page 73 for more information about storing expressed milk.

Feeding at the breast

Getting milk from your breast is hard work for your premmie baby; strong, sustained sucking is required, resulting in great energy expenditure. Let the staff caring for your child guide you in how often to breastfeed her. Communication with the staff is important. If, for example, you call and say you are on your way to the hospital for a breastfeeding, the nurses will know not to give a bottle of expressed milk before you arrive. The nurses will also let you know if you are running low on stored milk.

Two breastfeeding positions that seem to work well are the "football hold" (see opposite) and the "cross-cradle hold" (see below). Both holds allow you to easily control your baby's head with one hand and hold your breast in the other. Many lactation specialists encourage "kangaroo care" or skin-to-skin contact (see box, page 92) and the use of a nipple shield when initiating feeds at the breast. Using a shield helps your baby to remove milk from the breast without having to generate as much negative pressure in sucking.

Monitoring success

The best indicator of breastfeeding success is if your newborn's weight continues to go up. But when you first start breastfeeding, you can approximate how much milk she gets at each feed by comparing her pre- and post-feeding weight. Since 1ml of milk weighs about 1 gram, an increase in weight of 25 grams with feeding suggests that she received 25ml of milk. If pre- and post-feeding weights are used in this fashion, your baby must be weighed both times with the same nappy on, the same clothing and the same amount of added materials, such as monitor leads. In addition, to minimise measuring error, the scale should not be moved or used between the two measurements. Even with all these precautions, there is a degree of imprecision based on the accuracy of infant scales (see page 99).

At home

Bringing your premature infant home will be exciting and perhaps a bit scary; you may feel overwhelmed initially by the responsibilities that go along with caring for her there. However, the skills you learned from the nurses in the hospital will stand you in very good stead. Almost all the information covered in Chapters 1 and 2 apply to premature infants as well as to full-term babies, but a premature baby needs extra attention in several areas.

In addition to the "routine" preparations for the arrival of full-term babies, there are some other issues to consider that are specific to premmie babies. Practically speaking, you will need to have on hand smaller nappies, vests, and outfits (easily found on the Internet if not in baby shops), but you may also need to adjust your "nursing skills" when dispensing medications and vitamins (see also pages 339–40), and be able to follow very specific instructions about feeding schedules or caring for ongoing medical conditions. While discharge instructions will be relatively short for a late pre-term infant whose only issue is slow feeding, there may be a great deal for you to do at home if your baby was much more premature or experienced complications.

Extra nursing care

Very premature infants often have continuing medical issues (see Chapter 13) so you will have to learn from the hospital staff the special care your baby will require at home. In addition to giving vitamins and perhaps other medications, your baby may require oxygen, or other special equipment or monitors with which you must become familiar. If your baby had major respiratory problems or apnoea (occasional long pauses in between breaths), you may be taught special resuscitation techniques (see pages 41–3) in the unlikely case that you will need to use them.

Maintaining body temperature

Nearly all premature infants (the exception being some late pre-term infants) are initially unable to regulate their body temperature adequately. Full-term newborns may need to be a few hours old to be able to generate the heat to keep themselves warm if clothed adequately, but it is a good idea, nevertheless, to avoid allowing them to become cold. Regulating temperature with a premmie baby, however, is much more of a problem. Because of her limited energy reserves and lack of insulation (body fat), even if wrapped in blankets, your baby's temperature quickly falls if she is not housed in a heated environment. By the time your baby comes home, though, she will have reached the point where she can keep herself warm if dressed properly. (One of the prerequisites for hospital discharge is the ability to maintain body temperature, which is typically mastered at 35–36 weeks of gestation.)

Generating heat, however, requires energy utilisation; the calories your baby uses up in keeping warm won't be used for growing and gaining weight. Thus you need to minimise the times she is cold or undressed. The rule of thumb for dressing a full-term baby is to put on her the same number of layers of clothing that you need to wear to be comfortable; for a premmie baby, add one more layer of clothing than you need for yourself. Hats

are commonly worn by premmie babies in the hospital to prevent heat loss from the head. However, once home, hats are not needed if the thermostat is set at typical living temperatures (above 20°C).

Germ control

The immune system of a full-term newborn is weaker than that of an older child or adult. Premature infants have even less resistance to infection while those of the lowest gestational age having the most immature immune mechanisms. In addition, if your baby was born before 34 weeks of gestation, she will be deficient in another component of immunity: maternal antibodies (see box). So the precautions you can read about in Chapter 2 – limiting holding, touching, and close contact with your baby to only a few close relatives or friends, and only after they have washed their hands; not allowing anyone with a contagious illness to visit; avoiding public places where people are in close proximity – are especially important to follow. Breastfeeding, however, will help protect your baby from infection, since breastmilk contains antibodies and immune cells active against many microbes.

Preventing infections

Your efforts to minimise your baby's exposure to germs are worthwhile and will often reduce the number and severity of infections. But do not assume that by making efforts to avoid exposure to microbes and breastfeeding you will prevent colds and infections. Infections such as head colds are inevitable. Here are some other ways you can help protect your child.

Beginning in the third trimester of pregnancy, antibodies present in the mother's circulation can cross the placenta and enter the foetus' bloodstream. At birth, a full-term baby is armed with a large repertoire of antibodies (pre-formed by mum) to bacteria, viruses and pathogens with which she has never yet had contact. But if born prematurely, maternal antibodies may be lacking, since the time for antibody transfer was missed. Maternal antibodies have a limited lifespan, and with time, each is removed from a baby's circulation and cleaved to small molecules for later use by the body. By six months of age, the level of antibodies in a baby falls low enough that protection is now limited; however, some of these antibodies can be detected even at a year of age.

Maternal antibodies may also play a role in certain cases of newborn jaundice (the yellow skin colouring that occurs in some newborns in the first few days of life, see page 369).

Bilirubin, the molecule that when present in high levels gives the skin a yellow colour, is a breakdown product of the haemoglobin in our red blood cells. Maternal antibodies may affect this process if the mother's and baby's blood types are different. Mothers, like everyone else, have circulating antibodies against foreign blood cells. If any maternal antibodies that cross the placenta are directed against the baby's red blood cells, more of the baby's red blood cells are destroyed than is usual, more bilirubin is produced, and the more jaundiced the baby becomes.

Immunisations

Vaccines are safe and valuable tools to prevent serious infectious diseases in infants born at term (see also page 336). They are also effective in premature infants. The schedule for giving immunisations is the same as for full-term infants. Be advised that when it comes to scheduling immunisations, chronological age, not corrected age, is used. If your baby reached two months of age in the hospital, she would have received her first immunisations while there.

Another way you can shield your baby from exposure to infection is to surround her with family members who are immune to certain viruses and bacteria. If you are immune, you cannot catch a disease, and thus can't spread it to your baby. Currently, immunisation against pertussis (whooping cough) and influenza (the "flu") is recommended for both parents and all other adults in your household including babysitters and frequent visitors as well as other children.

Palivizumab (Synagis)

Respiratory infections usually consist only of a stuffy nose and a cough. However, head colds are more likely to progress to wheezing, bronchiolitis (see page 345), and pneumonia (see *Lung infections*, page 347) in premature infants (especially those who required treatment for premature lungs and those whose lungs are still healing) than in other infants. Many viruses can cause respiratory illness, but two of them, the influenza virus and the respiratory syncytial virus (RSV) are notable for commonly infecting premature infants (and those born at term as well) and causing,

4 reasons for using palivizumab

1 Your baby is under 2 years of chronological age and required treatment (such as oxygen or medications) for chronic lung disease within 6 months of the start of RSV season.

2 She was born at or before 28 weeks of gestation and is under 12 months of chronological age at the start of RSV season.

3 She was born from 29 to 32 weeks of gestation and she is under 6 months of age at the start of RSV season.

4 She was born between 32 and 35 weeks of gestation and also has congenital heart disease.

on occasion, severe infections. Infants older than six months of age can be vaccinated against influenza, but whether or not your baby is vaccinated, the flu vaccine is recommended for parents, household members, sitters, and frequent visitors.

There is no vaccine for RSV, but there is a way to minimise its impact on your baby; many RSV infections are prevented or rendered mild by the use of palivizumab. This drug consists of antibodies against RSV made in cell culture and test tubes. It is very expensive and its use is limited to children who will benefit from it the most. During the winter months, when epidemics are most likely to occur, qualifying infants are given monthly injections of the antibodies.

Infants who were born most prematurely or had more severe lung disease are offered palivizumab while the healthiest and least premature infants are not. If you believe it will help your child, discuss this with your paediatrician.

Handling your baby

Prematurely born infants are smaller than full-term babies, but they can be picked up and held the same way (see pages 32–3). With experience, you will come to learn that your child is sturdy and only requires a little head support until she is strong enough to keep her head from flopping down, back or to the side.

Carrying your baby in a sling (see pages 45–6) or special premmie carrier, so she can hear your heartbeat and feel you breathing and moving, can help her to thrive as well as develop a stronger emotional bond with you. Premature babies grow faster while nestled in a sling (it mimics the womb). The transition from womb and incubator to the outside world is a lot easier, more secure and more comfortable. Once your baby has good head control (around 16–20 weeks), a carrier without head support can be used.

Car seats

You will probably be bringing your premmie baby home in an automobile, so you will need a car seat. Regrettably, most infant car seats are designed for full-term babies and infants who are even bigger. When placed in one of these car seats, some premmie babies' heads will slump forward, possibly resulting in the upper airway (in the throat and neck) being blocked so that insufficient oxygen reaches the lungs, and complications such as apnoea (cessation of breathing for many seconds), bradycardia (slowing of the heartbeat), and desaturation (low oxygen level in the tissues) may occur.

Car seat challenge

To be confident that your baby will not have these complications when going home, a "car seat challenge" is sometimes performed in the hospital before her discharge. While attached to monitors for heart rate, respiratory rate, and tissue oxygen level, your baby will be placed in a car seat (provided by you) as if she were in your car and observed for signs of airway compromise. If no apnoea, bradycardia or desaturation occurs in the next several minutes, she has passed the challenge, and you can safely take her home in the car seat. If your baby does not pass the test or you are recommended to use alternative means of transportation, a horizontal infant restraint may be recommended.

Baby capsules are available that enable your newborn to lie flat when travelling in a vehicle and may also be used as prams.

Using a car seat

The general principles of car seat use, as described in Chapters 9 and 13, are applicable to premature infants, but there are some further recommendations.

Only first-stage infant car seats (not those designed specifically for children weighing over 9kg) should be used. A few models designed to accommodate babies as small as 2kg are available. For information on brands and models, go to the *Choice* website and read the infant car seat reviews (choice.com.au).

Appropriate seats have a distance of 14cm or less from the crotch strap to the seat back and 25cm or less from the lower harness strap to the seat bottom. The car seat should be in the back seat of the car, with your baby facing the rear, and an adult should sit next to her to make sure that she remains in the proper position.

To avoid slumping, your infant's back and buttocks should be placed squarely against the back of the car seat. Special padded inserts are available or you can use rolled-up blankets or towels placed on each side – between your infant's head or shoulders and the side wall and between her legs and the lower side wall. If the crotch strap

cannot be pulled tight enough to securely hold her in, another rolled towel can be placed under the buckle. The retainer clip should lie over your baby's chest. It is important that your baby's head, buttocks and back remain flat against the back of the car seat so do not put any padding underneath her.

Seats that have shields, abdominal pads or arm rests should not be used, since your baby's head might strike these in an accident or if the car stops suddenly.

The car seat should recline 45 degrees backwards (since the seat is facing the rear, the top of the seat is tilted downward, towards the front of the car).

It is advisable to have your restraint fitted by an expert at a restraint fitting station; bring some towels in case the angle beneath the restraint needs to be adjusted.

Feeding and nutrition

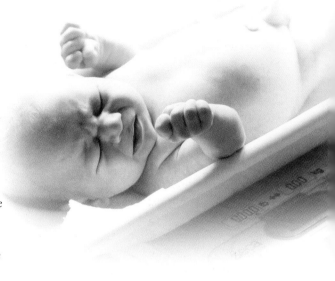

Premature infants are usually not discharged from the hospital until they can successfully be fed and are gaining weight steadily. But even those who are allowed home may not yet have perfected the skills required to feed easily. Premmie babies feed slowly and suck less strongly and efficiently than term babies. Weakness in the oral muscles, poor coordination of the tongue and pharynx, and the need to breathe frequently may further complicate feeding at first. Furthermore, the effort required to continuously suck at the breast or on a bottle can be exhausting for a small premmie baby. Having given many feedings in the hospital, you are probably quite good at feeding your baby but feedings will be slow and your baby may have to take several breaks to rest in the course of the "meal".

Premmie babies need proportionally more kilojoules, protein and fat than other newborns. In addition, large amounts of calcium, phosphorus and vitamin D are needed for building strong bones, while much iron is needed for the production of haemoglobin and new red blood cells. Part of the beauty of the way the human body works is that the breastmilk of mothers who deliver premature babies contains more of these nutrients than the breastmilk of mothers of full-term babies. However, to ensure that a premmie baby gets plenty of kilojoules, calcium, phosphorus, vitamins, etc., a powdered fortifier is often added to expressed breastmilk.

When premmie babies are bottle-fed, most are initially given a premature infant formula. Later on, a transitional formula (midway between a premature formula and a routine formula in kilojoules and nutrients) is used. Finally, once a baby has reached a target age and/or weight, a switch to infant formula intended for full-term infants is made.

There are different opinions on how to best feed a premature newborn, however, and while it is frequently done as described above, other ways are used as well. Some doctors, for example, send late pre-term infants home on regular formula. So when your formula-fed baby arrives home, she will most likely be getting a premature infant or transitional formula. Additional vitamins, as a multivitamin, and iron drops are also frequently recommended.

Your breastfed infant will also receive vitamin and iron supplements. If she gains sufficient weight with you breastfeeding her exclusively, no further supplementation may be needed; many breastfed babies, however, require some additional bottle feedings – either of fortified expressed milk or a high-kilojoule formula (premature or transitional).

As a rule, premature babies are not very good at knowing when they are hungry. The ability to sense hunger and let parents know (by crying) does arrive as your baby approaches the equivalent of full term (using corrected age); however, before then you must initiate the feeds at regular intervals, as directed by the caregivers in the hospital. Moreover, your newborn may not yet have developed the mechanism wherein her hunger is exactly proportional to the kilojoules she needs for proper growth. Thus to ensure appropriate growth, the volume of milk given at feeds, if bottles are used, will also be prescribed by her health providers. At this stage, obviously, a demand-feeding schedule, with the frequency and amount of feedings determined by the infant, is not recommended.

Weight gain

Most premmie babies leave the hospital weighing less than comparable full-term infants of similar corrected age. This is so for a number of reasons; for instance, oral feedings may have been delayed due to respiratory or gastrointestinal problems.

The best place for an infant to grow to term is in the womb. Even with the many advances in neonatal care and nutrition, including intravenous feedings (hyperalimentation) and high-kilojoule premature infant formulas, medical science has yet to match the natural method in which nutrients from the mother pass through the placenta and nourish the foetus.

When the barriers to adequate nutrition are overcome and full feedings are achieved, your infant will experience what is called "catch-up growth". Her rate of growth will surpass that of full-term infants of comparable corrected age. It is as if your baby is aware that her weight is too low for her age and she is trying to match the weight of those infants not born prematurely.

Once your baby is able to ingest sufficient kilojoules, she will grow remarkably quickly – typically, she will gain 20 to 30 grams or more per day. If you are like many parents, you will want to monitor your baby's weight gain frequently, but paediatricians and neonatologists, to prevent an excessive focus on weight, don't usually recommend having a baby scale at home.

MORE **ABOUT** | baby scales

You may have noticed when your baby was in hospital that at times she gained weight erratically; some days she gained a huge amount, while other days she gained practically nothing. Although the explanation for this may simply have been that your baby ingested more kilojoules on the days she had a bigger weight gain, this is not the typical reason for the daily variation. Instead, the problem is in the measuring. The scales used in the hospital are calibrated and accurate, but no measuring device is 100 per cent accurate. A good scale will give a weight measurement that is accurate to within one to two per cent of the true weight. So if your baby weighs 2000 grams, her true weight is actually 2000 grams plus or minus one per cent of 2000 grams, which is 20 grams, or somewhere between 1980 and 2020 grams. So in the case of your hospitalised newborn who, for instance, weighed 2000 grams yesterday, fed very well, but still weighs 2000 grams today, it is quite possible that she did gain weight but due to the small error inherent in each measurement, it wasn't detected. She actually may have weighed 1990 grams yesterday and 2010 grams today, but the scale only measured 2000 grams each day.

Another source of error inherent in weighing newborns relates to the fact that many variables, which would be relatively meaningless when weighing an older child or adult, are quite significant when weighing a much smaller infant. For example, if your baby had a big bowel movement or urinated shortly before being weighed, her weight would have been 20 to 40 grams lighter than if she had been weighed a few minutes earlier. With all the small inaccuracies involved in determining your baby's weight, you can see that it makes sense to follow the general trend in weight gain, viewing your baby's progress over several days, rather than focusing just on the change from one measurement to the next.

Health problems

Premmie babies are subject to all the same illnesses and medical problems suffered by babies born at term (see Chapter 13.) There are, in addition, some that deserve special mention due to their added significance in premature infants.

Reflux

Regurgitation of stomach contents to the mouth (or nose) and oesophagus is even more common in premature infants than in full-term ones (and it is very common in them as well!). Simple measures like holding your baby in an upright position for 20 minutes after each feed may help, as may smaller but more frequent feeds. Bear in mind that the amount brought up is usually far less than you would guess by the size of the spill. Also, posseting is no more than a nuisance and a mess with the majority of infants, as long as they are gaining weight well and are not uncomfortable during feeds.

Hearing loss

Loss of the ability to hear softer sounds is more common in premature infants than in other children. Diminished hearing ability may be the consequence of infection, the undesirable side effects of certain drugs used to treat medical problems in premmie babies, or may be due to prematurity itself. Typically, a hearing test is performed before hospital discharge, but many doctors recommend a follow-up test, especially for those most premature, when a baby is several months old. Early detection and intervention – hearing aids, speech and language therapy, programs designed for hearing-challenged children and perhaps cochlear implants – have greatly improved the speech and language outcomes of infants with hearing loss.

Retinopathy of prematurity (ROP)

This occurs when there is an excessive growth of blood vessels in the retina (the back wall of the eyeball, where sensors of the visual system are located). It is most often found in premmie babies born weighing less than 1000 grams, but may occasionally occur in larger pre-term infants. Periodic eye examinations, often started while still in the hospital, are necessary to determine if ROP has developed, and if present, whether it is healing or progressing. At-risk infants require follow-up visits to the ophthalmologist (eye doctor) until the retina matures sufficiently. Until that time, babies with mild, moderate or severe ROP require regular visits to watch for progression of disease and to monitor visual consequences (poor vision, nearsightedness or even amblyopia, retinal detachment, and glaucoma).

Dental problems

Infants who were helped to breathe by having an endotracheal tube put down their throats, usually because their lungs were premature, may have a variety of dental problems; these are thought to result from trauma to oral tissues caused by the tube. Problems include a high arched palate, deformities or defects in the enamel in the baby teeth when they erupt, or even missing teeth. Rarely, bilirubin (a normal waste product which is elevated in jaundiced newborns) or medications may stain the developing teeth. No specific treatment is needed, but routine preventive care and visits to the dentist, beginning when your baby is 12 months old, are recommended.

Inguinal (groin) hernia

When a foetal passageway from the abdominal cavity to the scrotal sac (males) or labia of the vagina (females) fails to properly close off, an inguinal hernia occurs. Early in foetal life, before the internal organs that distinguish males from females have developed, the testes or ovaries form in the abdominal cavity. In boys, each testis gradually travels to the scrotum, leaving the abdomen through a small round opening (the inguinal ring) beneath the skin and muscle and passing between the layers of muscles in the groin in a passageway called the inguinal canal. In girls, although the ovaries remain where they are formed, the inguinal ring and canal form as for boys. Later in foetal life, the inguinal ring and canal are completely sealed shut. But if this passageway remains intact, a piece of intestine can leave the abdomen and travel along that route. This will result in a bulge in the groin, scrotal sac in boys, or labia in girls that you can see, since it is typically the size of a ping-pong ball. Usually the protruding intestine makes a brief appearance outside the abdominal cavity but soon withdraws.

Inguinal hernias are more common in infants born prematurely in general, but most common in boys and infants who require a ventilator. If a hernia is discovered while your baby is in hospital, it will usually be surgically repaired before her discharge. If you notice a bulge in the groin, scrotum or labia at home, photograph it quickly (it may disappear within minutes), and report your findings (with the picture) to your baby's doctor. Surgery will be scheduled in the near future to sew shut the inguinal canal. If left intact, an uncommon but serious problem can ensue: intestinal strangulation. This occurs when a portion of intestine enters the canal, becomes caught there, and is injured when its blood supply is compromised.

Chronic lung disease

If your infant suffers from chronic lung disease, it will already be evident while she is in hospital; it does not appear for the first time at home. More formally called bronchopulmonary dysplasia (BPD), chronic lung disease most often develops in very premature infants who required mechanical ventilation. It is caused by a combination of premature lungs, the higher concentrations of oxygen needed, and trauma from the pressure at which the air is delivered to the lungs. BPD is diagnosed by characteristic clinical and radiographic findings (persistent rapid, laboured breathing; evidence of inadequate oxygen transfer in the lungs; multiple tiny round areas of hyperaeration (appearing black) surrounded by densities (appearing white) on x-ray) but practically speaking, your baby has BPD if she continues to require oxygen 30 days after birth. It may be necessary to continue giving her oxygen and/or oral medications at home until her lungs have healed further. Infants with BPD are more prone than other premature babies to having difficulty when a respiratory infection occurs. As noted, palivizumab (see page 96) is recommended for infants with BPD to prevent infection with RSV.

Rehospitalisation

Hopefully, this will not happen to your child, but a number of special care graduates require brief hospitalisation for treatment of respiratory infections. While the most premature infants and those with BPD are most susceptible, any premature infant can become quite ill when a head cold strikes. In them, the infection may spread to the lower respiratory tract, causing wheezing or pneumonia. It is worthwhile, therefore, to take measures (see page 95) to prevent the spread of infection to your baby.

Growth and development

Visits to the paediatrician will be scheduled frequently after hospital discharge. Initially, major areas to discuss will be your baby's, as well as your own, adjustment to her being at home; feeding and nutrition; status of any remaining medical problems; and her growth. While there are growth charts specifically for small premature infants (of greatest use for infants still in hospital), most of the time a standard growth chart is used. However, instead of your baby's chronological age, her corrected age is plotted against her weight, height and head circumference (see also Chapter 12 for a discussion of growth, development and growth charts). As already noted, even using corrected age, it is likely that your baby will start off in the lowest percentiles for height and weight. However, with catch-up growth, she will soon approach a level of growth more typical for full-term infants of similar corrected, and eventually chronological, age.

Although all infants have their developmental progress monitored, paediatricians pay particular attention to the developmental milestones of premature infants. And as is the case with physical growth, your baby's corrected age will be used when she is assessed for attainment of milestones. So if your baby was born two months prematurely, the expected time for her to start smiling would be at a chronological age of three and a half to four months (six to eight weeks of corrected age) since babies born at term normally start to smile at six to eight weeks of age.

There is great variation in when "catching up" is achieved. In both growth and the reaching of developmental skills, a healthy premature infant will usually have entered the range of normal without correction for prematurity by a chronological age of 12 to 18 months.

Certainly, it is a good sign if your baby reaches milestones at her corrected age initially and later catches up to other infants, appropriately attaining skills according to her chronological age. However, it is best to avoid putting too much emphasis on the timing of her achievements. What really is important is not when she reaches milestones, but that she does reach them.

MORE **ABOUT**   catching up

Catching up is the result of two forces. First, there is true compensation for prematurity, involving accelerated growth and development. But, in addition, the range of normal also widens with age, so that the development of an infant who is progressing regularly, but a few months behind average, will later fall within the normal range. If, using the example of the infant born two months prematurely (see above), she first begins to smile socially three and a half months after birth, she is clearly "behind" for her chronological age. But if she begins walking at 14 months (two months after the average time), she is well within the limits of "normal" for her chronological age, since the normal range for starting to walk, from 10 to 18 months of age, is broad.

Parenting issues

Being the parent of a premature baby will have a profound effect upon you as a person and as a parent. You are not the same mother (or father) you would have been had the delivery been at term. Your plans, hopes, and expectations will change dramatically. Instead of focusing on such mundane problems as learning to change a nappy or becoming comfortable with feedings, you will be forced to deal with more difficult issues. Concerns about your newborn's health and safety no doubt overwhelm you at first. You may wonder: "Will she survive? Will she be normal? Was this premature birth somehow my fault? What will I tell friends and relatives? How can I go home without her?".

You also at some level mourn the loss of the pregnancy, delivery and post-partum experience you had planned on but which never materialised. You lost much of the third trimester of your pregnancy and all the pleasant (and not so pleasant) experiences that go with it. And instead of holding your new full-term baby in your arms, surrounded by gifts and flowers, you are off to the hospital to visit your at-risk baby, whom you find attached to all sorts of machinery, getting fluids intravenously, and perhaps receiving oxygen or mechanical ventilation. While you counted on being the focal point of your newborn's life, you are relegated to the role of bystander, only allowed to watch as nurses and doctors render care to her.

Initially, you are fairly ignorant of what is being done and unable to participate or help. You have lots and lots of questions, but when you ask the most important ones, the answers often arrive as, "We'll have to see." Or else, "We can't answer that right now." You remain afraid that your baby might not do well, that she might not end up a perfect, whole child.

If you had intended on your baby being breastfed, she is not ready to be fed at the breast (due to prematurity and/or medical problems) and may not be ready for weeks. With time, effort and energy – for expressing is an everyday, around-the-clock chore – sufficient milk may be able to be expressed for her and the ability to breastfeed later will be preserved. If, however, breastfeeding is not an option, you may feel guilty that you are not doing everything possible to help your baby.

With time, you will feel more comfortable in the strange world of neonatal special care. You begin to know the nurses and doctors in charge of your baby; you may befriend the mother or father of another patient, and your newly acquired knowledge of what problems your baby faces and what the treatment will be enable you to feel a bit less shell-shocked. Yet your moods will rise and fall with her progress. When things go well, your spirits are elated and all is wonderful; when there are setbacks, a dark cloud falls over your world.

At times the stress and exhaustion strongly affect you. Perhaps you are cross with your partner. Or you may become critical of the care your baby is receiving, especially when something goes wrong. When the phone rings at your home, a momentary fear creeps in: "Is it the hospital calling? Is something wrong?" And always the questions to yourself: "Will she get better? Will she ever be ready to come home? Will she grow up to be a healthy, undamaged child?"

If you are fortunate, you have a partner, relatives, and friends who support you through the whirlwind of events. But others amongst this group may sometimes be unable to comprehend what you are going through. Those with healthy babies at home may feel uncomfortable talking to you; your partner, parents or in-laws, instead of being helpful, may add more turmoil to your already stressful life.

In a nutshell, you can become tired, stressed, and sometimes traumatised by the experience.

How this affects you

All parents, regardless of the size or health of their newborn, want only the best in life for their baby. If parents of infants who have never had a medical problem often worry that their children might not turn out healthy or developmentally normal, you can imagine how much more so parents of premature infants, especially sick premature infants, fear a less than perfect outcome. The trauma of your experience, the uncertainty of your baby's future, and your sometimes well-founded fears of a bad outcome, all have a profound effect on you and the way you will feel about your baby.

Compared to other parents, mothers of special-care babies are much more likely to have a high level of anxiety and to suffer from post-partum depression. Part of your heightened anxiety is quite realistic and expected. Your baby may have been very ill; she may still be recovering from some of the medical problems she experienced. If you have brought her home, you may have been given detailed instructions not only about how to take care of her, but also about what signs constitute danger, necessitating an immediate call to the doctor and possibly to begin resuscitation. No matter how it is phrased nor how often you are told an emergency is unlikely to occur, it is almost impossible to ignore the implication that your baby could experience a life-threatening event at home.

Another part of your anxiety is based on fears of what may come in the future. Sadly, at the time of hospital discharge, doctors can't give you a definitive answer as to whether or not your baby will have neurological problems, developmental delays or learning disabilities. The more premature and critically ill your baby is, the more reality-based are your fears. But some of these problems, if they do occur, will not be evident for months or years. "Will deficits occur? Which one or ones? How severe will they be?" No wonder you worry!

It's hard to be a calm, relaxed parent when your baby has ongoing medical problems and you know she is at risk for re-hospitalisation or other sudden medical emergencies. And certainly, worries about her future health and development, frequently creeping into your thoughts, won't help either. It is quite a challenge to strike an appropriate balance between worrying too much and not enough. You may receive the well-intentioned advice to "Treat her like a normal baby" and if your baby had few difficulties in the special care nursery and has no continuing medical issues, it may be appropriate and relatively easy to follow this advice. But if your infant had a stormy course in the intensive care unit, has enduring concerns, or you are just a worrier by nature, you will have difficulties silencing the doubts and anxieties you feel. Take it as a truth: it is hard to ignore what you and your infant have been through.

On the other hand, if you view your baby only as fragile or sickly, you may become an overprotective, fraught parent. If she has a runny nose, you may hurry to the doctor's office fearing she will develop pneumonia. You may have trouble being away from her or letting her do anything remotely risky (such as playing with other babies).

There is no simple solution to the difficulty of finding the middle road. With time, especially if your baby does well, you may be able to quell some of your anxieties. Even if your baby has "weak lungs" or faces disability, you will realise that being overprotective of her, while satisfying your own needs, is not the best approach.

All children need to assert some control over their world and show some independence. When they are permitted to do so, they feel proud of themselves. Stifling your baby's efforts to be more independent does not encourage her personal growth and sense of worth. So while it is easy to understand why you have many anxieties and tend to worry too much about your baby, your efforts to hold these tendencies in check will benefit her.

Finally, never lose sight of the fact that your baby, no matter how bright or how disabled, is a unique and wonderful human being. You will love her no matter what the future brings. She is your special, priceless, adorable, loving baby.

YOUR BABY
MONTH BY MONTH

Though it may seem to others that your wonderful newborn can only feed, cry, defecate and sleep, in reality he is capable of so much more. Even within the first week of life, your baby can recognise his mother's face (and his father's if he sees it often enough) and may imitate facial gestures (try making faces and see what happens). He can also distinguish his mother by smell and sometimes by voice.

Your newborn's main activity is sleep, and this can occupy up to 20 hours of his day. Many babies seem to wake for a feed then drop off soon after, but some babies are almost too sleepy to want to feed in the early days. While this doesn't matter very much in the first week or so, after that, if your baby is a sleepy one, he should be woken up for a feed.

Some babies do cry quite a lot! You will soon recognise your baby's cry – and whether it signifies hunger or something else (wetness, cold, too much handling, a desire for peace and quiet, etc.). Your newborn is also sensitive to loud noises, bright lights and strong smells and may cry if exposed to

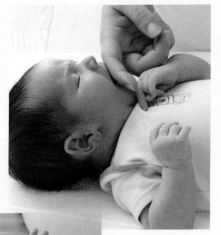

these. Rocking or singing in a quiet place may help if he is upset. If you are breastfeeding, putting your baby to the breast is wonderfully soothing. Some babies like to be carried around, and sometimes it helps to swaddle your baby to make him feel more secure (see page 34); after all, he was used to being held tightly in the womb before birth.

Your infant will not have much muscle power and you will notice that his head tends to fall back if you pull him to a sitting position (known as head lag). You must support his head well if you are lifting or holding him in a sitting position (see pages 33-4).

His arms will move in an uncontrolled way, and his hands will be more often closed than open – this gradually changes over the first few weeks. Your baby does have certain reflexes at birth, which slowly disappear. One is to grasp an object placed in his hand, another is to bring his arms round to the front (as if to grab hold of you) if his head is moved sharply back a short way. This is called the Moro or startle reflex, but it is not sensible to try it out too often!

Your baby will begin to fixate with his eyes over the first week or two but will not yet follow a face that moves across his field of vision. He can hear but does not turn to a sound; you may notice, however, that he quietens if there is a soft noise or a voice nearby.

Your newborn's bowel movements can be quite soft and particularly if he is breastfed, very frequent; it can also vary from dark brown to almost yellow in colour.

Before leaving hospital, your baby will have been given his first immunisation (Hepatitis B) and a dose of Vitamin K.

Now your baby seems much more alert as she is awake more of the time, is beginning to follow with her eyes and ears, recognises you more clearly, and takes an interest in the world. She may stare at you intently while being fed. You may notice a smile (though this is sometimes wind); the true smile comes in response to a smile of your own, and this usually happens around six weeks.

Sleeping is still her main activity and your baby may be starting to sleep for longer stretches at night although in most babies this won't occur for another month or two. Every baby is different when it comes to settling into a routine. Usually an infant of this age will be happy to last three to four hours between feeds but often not at night.

She still cries frequently, generally because she is hungry or uncomfortable. Some babies cry a lot and lustily, particularly late in the day. This is often called colic (see page 177) but the cause is not really known and there is no cure (though rocking often helps). It does get better though! She may also make little noises, but not true cooing, when content.

Your baby's muscles will be growing stronger and she can hold her head up for longer though it will still lag when she's in the sitting position. She will wave her arms and "bicycle" with her legs when excited (which is quite often). Her hands will be closed most of the time but she will open them and grasp a finger or other object placed in her palm.

She is starting to learn the connection between what her hands do and what happens when they move, and will enjoy it if you move them for her.

Your baby will need lots of cuddling and holding, and can never have too much of this. She will find pleasure in a mobile or other moving object placed in front of her face not too far away.

You can start to play games with her now. When she's on her change table, with her face about 20 to 30 cm away from yours, lean towards her and talk happily. Pause, and give her a chance to smile, gurgle, wriggle or move her mouth back at you. Try doing these things one at a time: smile, stick out your tongue, open and close your mouth widely, or giggle. She may start to imitate you! Your baby will also appreciate music and singing and gentle splashing games in the bath while you bathe her.

Your baby is growing rapidly although there is a lot of variation in weight and babies who were large at birth may not gain as much as lower birth-weight babies (see charts, page 380).

You should notice that your infant sleeps less during the day but (if you are lucky!) more at night. She may be aware of routines such as feeding and bathing, and gets excited when she recognises the signs. She is becoming more aware of the world, and of the special people around her.

Your baby will show recognition by becoming excited – gurgling, smiling and waving her hands – when she sees people or toys that she likes. If you talk to her, she should coo responsively and if crying, she will stop if you pick her up and speak to her. She enjoys company and if in a sociable mood, will become upset if left on her own.

Most babies of this age like to be cuddled, but all babies are different and at this age you will start to see her temperament appearing – that means how she reacts as an individual, and what kind of a personality she is going to have, whether outgoing and sociable or more reserved and thoughtful. You can help her by learning to respond in the way that suits her best.

She will watch objects more carefully if they are moved slowly across her line of vision. She will smile more frequently and may laugh and gurgle. She will also make more varied noises.

She should be able to focus on her face in a mirror, if it is held close enough. Move it slowly up and down and around and watch as she tries to keep her reflection in sight. She will love it when you talk to her, and it is through the constant interaction of language that she will learn her first words, though that is still a long way off.

Her hands hold more interest for her and she will look at them and grasp an object for a very short time. She will begin to notice her fingers and will curl them around objects placed in them. Try putting your fingers in hers and then gently rocking her from side to side. You can gently prop her up with cushions and place small colourful objects within view.

Physically your baby will be noticeably stronger. She will be able to hold her head erect for a few seconds if her chest is supported, and her back will be straighter when she is in the sitting position, though she is still some way off independent sitting. When she is on her front, she can lift her head up and arch her back; however, she may not yet be able to roll over, or to push up on her arms.

Routines become more and more important as she gets older and particularly so at night. A regular bedtime routine started at this age will help prevent problems later, and ease the time when she is able to move into her own bed.

Her rapid weight gain will continue.

Now is the time for your baby's first medical check-up and multiple batch of immunisations (see pages 325 and 337). Though this may be an anxious time for you, most infants are only briefly upset by baby jabs and they are over them in a few minutes.

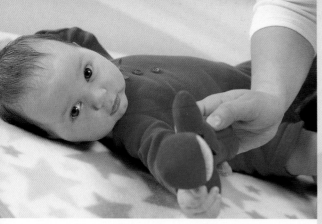

Your baby is becoming much more active and communicative. He will respond more to routines and be more sociable. He will smile more frequently, and at a variety of people in addition to his parents. He will also be making more sounds, including cooing and squealing. You should make sure you are talking constantly to your baby as talking engages his interest and helps familiarise him with the sounds of words. You can have a two-way conversation without using proper words. He will follow the expression in your voice and will learn to recognise words that are used all the time, for example if you talk about the parts of his body when he is in the bath.

Hearing and vision are becoming more accurate and your baby will be better at recognising people both visually and by their voices. He will distinguish people who are further away, and he can see several colours. He may show excitement when he hears a favourite song or music. At this age he is most interested in interaction – the interplay of action and reaction, the response that he gets from an adult in reply to his; DVDs and TV cannot interact, so it is best not to have them on when he is around. it may also interfere with his speech by offering a distracting "buzz" of sound in the background.

He is more familiar with cycles of day and night and as a result, he is becoming better at sleeping through the night.

His neck and back muscles will be strengthening and he will be able to support his head for a few minutes and sit (supported) for a longer period with his head and back straight – he will prefer sitting to lying down, and will take a keen interest in his surroundings. It is important that you encourage

your baby to spend some time on his stomach, under supervision, each day. By three months, when on his stomach, he may start to roll over – rolling from his stomach to his side then onto his stomach again. He will keep trying this manoeuvre until he rolls all the way over on to his back.

He will be using his hands much more and will put things in his mouth so you will have to be careful to check what he has picked up! In the bath, he will be starting to splash and will enjoy you letting water trickle down his body.

Crying is still common, and some babies continue to cry at night at this age. Usually "colic" will have ceased by three months but there are still many reasons for night crying – for a feed or company, for example – and for some babies it just becomes a habit. If crying is persistent, it is sensible to ask for advice to rule out any potentially treatable condition.

At three months, your baby starts to appreciate the feel of materials – and the difference between hard and soft, warm and cool, furry and smooth. Toys with different kinds of textures that he can grasp or feel, or just materials from around the house, are good for learning; stroking and massage can be very soothing.

Your baby will now spend lots of time awake although he'll still needs a couple of naps during the day. He gets excited when he sees the breast or bottle prior to a feed.

He is more and more interested in the outside world and in a greater variety of toys and other objects – those that can be touched, watched, banged and listened to. Praise has a great effect in helping him to learn; whenever he does something that is new or clever, praise him by smiling and telling him in a very positive tone of voice how wonderful he is.

Your baby will be moving his body more actively and he may begin rolling from his back to his front. If he spends time regularly on his stomach, he also is able to roll from his front to his back so be careful where you place him! He likes kicking his feet and occasionally may get hold of his toes and play with them. Either this month or next, he will be able

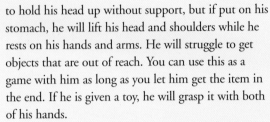

to hold his head up without support, but if put on his stomach, he will lift his head and shoulders while he rests on his hands and arms. He will struggle to get objects that are out of reach. You can use this as a game with him as long as you let him get the item in the end. If he is given a toy, he will grasp it with both of his hands.

Communication will improve, partly through facial expressions – he will learn to recognise yours as you can recognise his – which are becoming more varied. He will make a greater range of noises and will babble to himself. He will now perhaps be able to know his name – but babies are all different in their rates of development, and some will reach this stage sooner than others. He will look around to hear sounds, and will wave and gurgle in anticipation of feeding and other popular events. He can also indicate dislike by turning away from unwanted things.

You are beginning to understand your baby's temperament. His character is emerging and you will see whether he is a "slow to adapt" individual or one who readily accepts change. Whatever he is like, you can help him by seeing how he reacts to situations and doing what you think best to build his confidence.

Your baby is due for his second batch of immunisations to which he is less likely to have a reaction than after the first as these are a repeat. He is, however, more likely to contract infections as the immunity from his mother, which passed across the placenta at birth, is likely to be wearing off.

5

Physically your baby is growing much bigger and stronger. She is nearly ready to sit up on her own but will enjoy being propped up in a stroller, infant seat or highchair, where she can turn her head from side to side.

If she hasn't started rolling before, she will start to do so now; when lying on her front, she will roll onto her back and vice versa. She may be able to move about the floor by rolling or thrusting herself forward (centimetres at a time) but is a little young for crawling. She will push up on her arms, stand supported with your arms under her shoulders, and enjoy bouncing. If supported, she will jump up and down and push off the floor or table with her feet; her legs bend and extend on landing and lift-off.

Your baby will be much more adept with her hands and, if a rattle is placed in them, she will shake it. She will probably grasp her toes and start to put them as well as other things into her mouth so watch out!

She will enjoy more and more the pleasure of actively making noises and will be getting better at copying noises you make as well as facial expressions. She will use babbling to express both happiness and unhappiness.

Games will be a pleasure, and counting piggies will lead to squeals of pleasure. If you ring a bell or squeeze a squeaky toy then she will try to find out where the noise comes from. She will also enjoy being taken around the house and you can point out familiar items and let her touch flowers, cushions, rough surfaces and wooden tables to gain a sense of their differences.

Her vision and hearing will increase in accuracy and she will enjoy studying faces and objects. This is a good time to start introducing books (which at this age just means pointing to the pictures, but your baby will also love to hear your voice describing characters). She will become alert when someone enters the room, particularly if it's someone

she knows, although she will tolerate strangers well unless she is tired or hungry.

She will be very affectionate to you; she may pat you or get excited when she sees you approaching, and get upset when you walk away.

Your baby should be in a routine and have regular sleeping times (and probably will be sleeping through the night), so it should be easier to leave her for short spells with someone in whom you have confidence. She should be agreeable to being looked after by a stranger if she has developed confidence that her needs will be met when she cries. This is the time to start looking round the house for things that could be dangerous for her as she'll soon start moving around (see page 311).

Halfway through the first year is a big milestone. Most babies double their birth weights by five to six months and treble them by a year. Your baby is not only bigger but much more active and she is ready to start solid food.

Your baby may start to cut teeth and this may cause some pain (see page 200) so she may be irritable and cry more than usual in the day or so before a new tooth erupts.

Physically she will be moving around much more, either by rolling from side to side or beginning to crawl. She can support herself with straight arms and palms held flat on the floor. If you place her into a sitting position, leaning on her arms (held in

front of her) she can sit for a short period, but be sure there are some cushions to fall back on if she is propped in that position.

Her neck muscles are strong now, and when your baby is lying on her back, she can lift her head to look at her feet. She uses her hands more adeptly in finding objects to play with, and stretching out to reach them, and will start to transfer an object from one hand to another. Things usually go to her mouth so take care there are no small things lying around near her.

Your baby will enjoy being held in a supported standing position and can use a "jolly jumper". Jumping up and down can lead to endless joy – but limit time in this endeavour (to be sure she gets plenty of time to practise locomotion) and supervise her closely as accidents can happen. Be aware of the safety guidelines if you choose to use a jumper (the Children's Hospital at Westmead provides a useful fact sheet online).

Your baby will babble a lot and may make attention-seeking noises. She will begin to recognise words at this age and will listen intently when her name is used. Although she cannot make meaningful words, a conversational style is starting to develop and she will enjoy a response from you. Praise her when she seems to say something meaningful as this way she will go on trying.

Her hearing is becoming more accurate and she will like to play with things that make a noise. She will pick things up and shake them and will enjoy you making music and sounds of varied quality. She will also enjoy dancing – that is, dancing in your arms and moving her arms and legs to a rhythm. She may raise her arms to be picked up.

The next batch of immunisations is given at this age; if there were no serious reactions before it is very unlikely that there will be any now.

More settled in his habits and not quite ready to explore his mobility, your baby probably has a daily routine for napping, feeding, bathing and sleeping. However, because he's still having two naps a day, he may not be sleeping as long as you'd like him to at night and may prove troublesome at bedtime. It's important, therefore, to engage in night-time activities that will relax him and put him into the mood for sleeping – singing a lullaby, reading a story, massage or rocking – and to cut short his afternoon nap if it extends too close to bed time.

Your baby probably weighs about half a kilo more than he did last month and is a little taller. He's becoming stronger and can probably sit unsupported with his back straight. If he has not already done so, he will begin turning regularly from his back onto his stomach. He may also be able to bring himself into the crawling position. If he's very active, he may pull himself to standing – though he may not be able to sit back down and will cry until you "rescue" him.

His manipulative skills are growing, too. He is probably trying to hold his spoon by himself and can drink from a two-handled cup, if offered. He should be interested in finger foods, particularly as he's probably teething and these can be soothing to his gums. He'll also be grabbing and picking up lots of toys, trying to transfer them from hand to hand. When he has grasped something, he will examine it closely and may turn it over or "investigate" it in other ways.

Your baby continues to find ways to communicate, such as babbling to you and stopping to listen when you talk. He may even be able to imitate some of the sounds that you make and may raise his arms to be picked up. He may look intently at strangers, not sure whether he likes them or not.

Your baby's personality becomes more certain each day. If he seems strong-willed and highly strung, you will need extra patience. Talking to him frequently, giving him lots of cuddles and distracting him when he becomes irritable are good things to try. Or, he may be undemanding, and seem shy and sensitive. In this case, you'll need to spend time showing him how to play and tolerate people.

He'll enjoy playing with baby blocks and soft toys and being on the floor – preferably some of the time on his stomach while supervised. He also may like being around other babies – as long as you are near to give him confidence. Continue to read, sing and talk to him as much as possible.

Your baby will be starting to go places, though this may take the form of rolling and rocking, or scooting or slithering rather than crawling. He even may be able to pull himself up from a seated position and should be sitting without support. Once movement starts, there is a need to protect your baby from potential dangers. If not already accomplished, now's the time to ensure your home is safe (see chapter 13).

Your baby is growing rapidly, too. To feed his energy needs and to make eating more interesting, you can start to feed him a wider variety of coarser foods – many of which you eat yourself. However, another change will be the desire to dispense with

being fed in favour of self-feeding with foods he can pick up with his fingers. His grasp is becoming more refined and in addition to finger foods, he will be able to pick up very tiny objects.

Your baby may be using simple gestures, such as shaking his head when he means "No" and pointing at things when he wants you to give them to him. Sounds such as "na na na" or "ba ba ba" may be repeated. He may even say his first word – probably "mama" or "dada" or maybe "oh-oh".

Although he has a short attention span, your baby will enjoy manipulating toys that squeak and playing games with you, particularly "peek-a-boo". He may start looking for toys that he has dropped (known as object permanence). This development – the ability to track objects in space and time despite their momentary disappearance – is crucial to your baby's understanding of the way our social and physical worlds behave. Now when you leave the room, he's beginning to know you haven't disappeared forever and that if a ball rolls under a table out of sight, it sometimes reappears. Your baby is also learning a bit more about himself in the scheme of things. You may notice that he enjoys looking in mirrors and seems to recognise himself. While watching himself in a mirror, he may touch his nose or pull his ear.

This also is the time that your baby may display a dislike or fear of strangers. He may cry if you leave the room and may want more cuddles and kisses. The reason he does so is that new faces represent new experiences and he doesn't yet know whether these will be pleasurable ones. The same is true of other new situations – like being taken swimming – so don't force new activities on him. You may find he chooses a transitional object – one of his blankets or a soft toy – to comfort him at these times and when he goes to bed. If he hasn't done so, you might like to choose a suitable object and make it part of his bedtime ritual.

This is the age of active motion – crawling, pulling up and maybe cruising around the furniture, though the last is usually a bit later. However, it is important to remember that babies are different and some crawl later, so don't be anxious if your baby is not on her hands and knees by this age. Or she may be crawling backwards. This is because her arm muscles are stronger than her leg muscles so she finds it easier to push backwards. She should also sit happily on the floor amusing herself with nearby objects. She may be able to hold an object in each hand and bang them together.

You should encourage crawling by having a soft carpet and lots of interesting toys within reach. Your baby will like toys with interesting shapes and patterns, and holes that can be searched safely. She will also look for hidden objects so games such as "peek-a-boo" are great fun.

Your baby's communication skills are improving steadily. She responds to her own name and will repeat one or more sounds over and over and try to imitate what she hears, though there will not be much that sounds like real words. She will start to make simple noises like "ba" and "da" that at first are not used in context, but your response will help her to understand their meaning – she loves praise. She will show emotions more readily by being upset if a toy is taken away and sometimes by crying if

you have a cross face! She may also show sensitivity by crying when another baby cries. She may become more clingy and be afraid of things that didn't worry her before, such as loud noises or the big bath. Her personality will shine out more and more; she will probably be determined and may be stubborn, but this is most easily dealt with by distraction rather than by angry words, which she is too young to understand. She can demonstrate quite clearly what she likes and doesn't like.

Meals become times for serious enjoyment and this will be increased if she is able to participate.

Your baby has great curiosity and you can help her to learn through her senses. Stimulate her vision by bright colours and hanging objects; her hearing by music or singing; her touch by letting her feel different textures; her taste and smell through food.

This is the age when your baby will start to tease and test you. He is learning fast and beginning to see the things he can and can't do. He will drop things from his highchair and wait for you to pick them up, and will head off at speed for forbidden places, so you have to have eyes like a hawk and a great deal of energy!

Your baby will soon be able to crawl up (but not down) stairs, hence he will be at risk of a tumble; you will have to teach him repeatedly how to come down backwards rather than forwards. He may be able to walk if you hold his hands and may cruise around your furniture. Some babies become expert creepers and can get around really quickly. Whether your baby is trying to stand up or is content to creep, he loves pulling himself to standing and may be able to sit down from standing, which is quite an achievement.

His hands will be into everything and he will show increasing adeptness and perhaps laterality (whether he is right- or left-handed). He will be able to pick up small objects with his finger and thumb so you need to be careful as fluff and dirt of all kinds prove very attractive. He can feed himself with his fingers and at least help hold a cup. Whether now or in the near future, it is a good idea that he starts using a cup rather than a bottle to reduce the effect of sucking on his emerging teeth. He can begin to use a spoon, though most often the food will fall off when he lifts it to his mouth; if you feed him with a second spoon at the same time, this will make sure that plenty goes inside.

Your baby will vocalise more though not much in the way of understandable words will come out. He will communicate with gestures – such as holding out his arms to be picked up. He will wave bye-bye and pat a doll or stuffed toy. He may shake his head and say "No", though it doesn't always mean what it seems; he loves to copy what others do. He will be happy when you praise him and upset if you are cross; he may cry if another baby gets too much attention. He may show shyness of strangers by turning away and putting his head on your shoulder.

Your baby now knows where things belong, and that they don't disappear when out of sight. He will handle objects more appropriately, such as shaking a rattle. He will begin to imitate gestures and you can have fun with clapping and copying games.

Settling at night is not always easy and is helped by a routine, with things happening at the same time every night. When put down in his cot, he may pull himself up and protest loudly, for life is full of exciting events and he doesn't want to stop enjoying them.

giving you a present whilst cruising, waving whilst turning around. She can hold a crayon and may be able to use it though not to produce anything recognisable. She will hold her arm and foot out when getting dressed.

Her language is more apparent; she is likely to have a word or two that mean something and will vocalise a lot. Encourage her as much as possible by talking back. She will copy the expression on your face as well as more and more words that she hears. She will enjoy books and pictures and the stories that go with them, and will link sounds to pictures – for example, animals and their noises. She may even turn the pages though not in a logical way!

Your baby's personality is more to the fore and now that she knows much more about what she wants, she may get frustrated when she can't get it. This can develop in all sorts of situations – at home, at the supermarket or on the bus – and the best approach is distraction: point to something that is even more interesting, and go up close to have a look. Usually a baby's short memory span will not let her keep the original idea in mind for more than a minute or two. However, she's also more sensitive to your feelings. She will know when you are not pleased and may hide her face or turn away when this happens. Some babies enter a clingy phase, when they don't want to be set down – don't worry, it will pass, don't try to force it.

Your baby is now able to enjoy more sophisticated games, including water games in the bath; games involving music, rhythm and movement; stacking, tossing and rolling balls; using mirrors, etc. Involve her in these things and she will pay you back in laughter. She'll also enjoy new sensations – accompanying you to the shops, perhaps being taken to a restaurant and being introduced to new textures and tastes.

Your baby will now likely be underfoot for most of the time and will enjoy cruising around the furniture. If she stands, then she can sit down – usually by holding onto something. Some babies can walk on their own before a year while others take until a year and a half, so don't worry if your baby isn't up on her feet all the time. If she is not walking on her own, her ability is improving and she can probably do this with one hand held.

Even if she is walking, she'll still spend time crawling – especially if she wants to get somewhere fast. But she will prefer to be upright than on her back and may protest when you lay her down for a nappy change. She can also do more things at the same time – holding an object and climbing up,

Your baby has reached the magic age of one year and is becoming a toddler. By now she may be standing on her own or even walking; don't worry if she isn't, as most children do so later. If given the opportunity, she may start to crawl up and down stairs.

She will be able to hold something in one hand whilst using the other hand – a good example of multi-tasking – and can hold two objects in one hand. She will love banging spoons together or playing pat-a-cake. Although bath toys will be fun,

she's just as happy playing with soap suds. Her understanding will be considerably better; she may know some parts of her body (and may point to them when asked where they are), quite a few animals and their noises (which she may repeat), and the names of people with whom she is familiar. She may have several words as well as making up her own, but will quite often get them wrong (e.g. dog for cat). Even without words, she can clearly indicate her wants by pointing with her index finger. Her memory will be better and she will have favourite books that she loves coming back to – especially those with amusing actions or animal noises; she may point to named objects. She may even demonstrate that she has awareness of some cause-and-effect "operations". For example, if her toy is resting out of reach on a towel, she may pull the towel towards herself to reach the toy.

Your toddler will love giving and receiving hugs and kisses and can never have enough. She will also appreciate humour. This is a good time to introduce rules in a gentle way – for example no biting, no pulling hair, no throwing food on the floor – as she is starting to understand them; lavish praise on her when she does the right thing.

She will be attracted to the TV and will quickly pick up what the buttons are for, and will pound on your computer keys, if given the opportunity. She will particularly like toys that allow her to do things she sees you doing – a toy telephone, for example. Be careful of the TV; it does not interact. Talking and reading a book to her is much better for language development.

Don't limit your toddler's development or enjoyment by offering only gender-linked toys. Your boy can enjoy playing with a doll as well as a car, your girl will like to hammer pegs, and both sexes are happy to scribble.

Another batch of vaccinations is given at this age.

The pace of change is no longer as rapid as it was in the first twelve months but every month brings a new skill, and your toddler's personality will manifest itself more clearly.

She may well be able to walk now, though this depends on confidence; some toddlers are better at crawling than setting out on their own, so just wait for it to come. Give her the chance and don't push too hard. She is likely to be pretty fast at getting round without walking.

Her hand use will be improving and particularly the use of her finger and thumb to pick up small objects. She will watch objects that are dropped or thrown as they fall to the ground and will enjoy throwing things. She also likes finding things that are forbidden and especially things that are dirty! She will be more adept at using a spoon and managing a cup, because she can rotate her hand, though spills will be quite frequent. It is a good thing to let her practise as this is the only way she will get better.

With toys, she will be getting experimental, which means trying everything out with an innate sense of curiosity. If she's walking, she will like to pull things behind her or push things in front. If the toy also makes noise, she will find it particularly entertaining. Messy play will also be enjoyable for her and finger paints can be started at this age as can blocks and shape sorters. Your toddler may place one block on top of another.

She will demonstrate her desires more strongly and can be determined to get her own way. She doesn't understand about danger so be sure your home is well child-proofed. Try, however, to avoid too many restraints; it is much better to be allowed to play freely in a safe house than to be continually warned, "Don't, that's dangerous!".

Your toddler will enjoy hiding games – either you hiding behind something and popping your head out, or hiding a favourite toy and seeing if she can find it. She will be able to play on her own for a while, though she prefers it if you are around. Games involving instructions – "Show me the pony" – or ones where your toddler may anticipate actions – "The Incy Wincy Spider" – help build her communication skills and sense of trust, and form part of the social interaction between you.

She may give you a kiss if you ask her for one.

Your toddler will really be getting into words now, though as with walking, there is much variation as to when children reach this important milestone. He will understand quite a lot more than he can say – only having three or four words, but understanding up to 50. He will look in the right direction when you say "Where's Daddy?" and point, if asked, to parts of his body such as "nose". He will try hard to repeat words and sounds and more often get it right.

He will be using gestures more frequently, too – waving and clapping – and may wave bye-bye when you ask him to. Like all toddlers, he loves action words and songs, and will giggle loudly when the action is repeated. He will greatly enjoy looking at pictures in a book and particularly those that demonstrate action words, such as "up" – when you can both raise your arms. He won't yet understand a story although it is good to point to the pictures and describe them.

Your toddler will enjoy applying himself to a problem and will persevere in finding a solution by trial and error – for example, with a posting box or sorting toy, through learning to put the right object in the right hole. He will still need help, but try to find a way to let him work things out himself. He will love putting small things into and out of bigger things, such as blocks into kitchen canisters, and can open and close doors – so protect against trapped fingers. He may start to build and you can encourage this by using blocks and joining in at his level – constructing a tower and then knocking it down, or making a bridge or a train.

He is steadier on his feet and can stand for longer periods. He can bend over and stand back up again without losing his balance. Now, he won't like being restrained, and when he starts to walk, he will want to go off in all directions. When you are out and about, you may find it tricky to keep him within a safe distance without too much protest.

Your baby will now understand "No", and accept rules – such as not tearing books – but may not be able to control his urges. If you laugh when he does something he is not supposed to, he will take that as approval and do it again to gain another laugh. He may start to show a temper to which you should react calmly as he will soon get over it.

Mealtimes can be fun taken together. Serve foods he enjoys and don't be alarmed if he sometimes eats little. This is the best way to avoid food refusal, which some babies show at this age. Let him feed himself as much as possible.

Words are beginning to flow now, and understanding steadily increases. Your toddler will know the names of quite a few of the people with whom she comes into contact as well as those of common objects. If she doesn't know a word, she will indicate she wants something through a combination of vocalising and pointing. She may have up to a dozen words and be able to use a phrase, for example, "All gone" – even though to her it is a single word. You can help this by pointing out things in the house, street and in books, and by adding on to what she says as if you are having a conversation. If she says what sounds like a word (for example, cat), then say "Yes, that is a nice, friendly cat." She will like it if you copy her – both the sounds she makes and her movements.

Your toddler has a real sense of humour and will start to do funny things (and things she knows aren't allowed) to gain attention. She will be very affectionate and loving towards you and want you around for reassurance; she may be shy with babysitters and new people and may start to cry if someone she doesn't know picks her up or even smiles at her. Don't worry; some babies take longer to warm up to people than others. She may carry a security item such as a blanket or soft toy. Safety remains an issue, so it is fortunate for her wellbeing that she'll want to be near you most of the time.

But now your toddler may be testing her limits and may scream and shout to show how powerful she is. She may demand, by sustained finger pointing, objects that are out of reach. She may exhibit a temper, and this is still best dealt with calmly and quietly and using distraction.

Common household objects can be a source of much interest, and some are cheap and cheerful toys. Pots and pans are great for stacking or filling with smaller toys as well as for making noise.

Your toddler can begin to help with her daily care by holding her feet out for shoes and socks; by

understanding that a sponge is for wiping her face and hands; and so on. She will hold a cup and drink from it though she can still knock it over, so one with handles and a sucker base is an advantage.

She will stare at things for a long time to understand what they are, particularly if they move in an unusual way, such as a mobile in the wind. She will like using building blocks and can pick up small objects with great accuracy using either hand. She may carry her toys around, though not very carefully, and will regularly throw them to the floor.

Although she can get around pretty fast now, she's not completely steady on her feet and may bump into things frequently; she will probably walk with her feet kept wide apart. She may enjoy pushing a wagon or doll's pram and will start to play chasing games such as hide and seek.

Your toddler is becoming very curious so you will need to ensure that exploring is safe. If your home is danger-free then you won't need to tell him off frequently nor will you need to worry if he is out of view for a few seconds. However, silence is always a worry where a toddler is concerned; trouble is sure to be brewing!

This is a good age for learning how the world works. Your toddler will enjoy playing with different materials – sand, earth and water – and with things that have different textures – plastic, wood and metal. He will enjoy throwing a soft ball and may be able to retrieve a rolling ball but make sure he learns that throwing hard or heavy objects is not a good idea and may hurt. He will now start to run and this may well lead to falls but as long as the surface is

soft, then he is unlikely to do himself harm. He will enjoy pushing things – a little cart into which he can put toys is ideal and will teach him about wheels as well. He will climb better and can go upstairs on his hands and knees. He will like to carry things and turn the pages of a book, and wants, above all, to be independent to the extent of pushing your hand away if you try to help.

Switches have a fascination and in this hi-tech world he will quickly learn about the TV, radio and DVD player and want to keep switching them on. TV and video games remain unhelpful influences and should be kept turned off whilst he is up and about. Instead, show him lots of coloured pictures in books.

His understanding is growing by leaps and bounds and he will know about routines – holding out his hands to be cleaned when they are mucky, for example. He likes to mimic household activities, like sweeping and cooking, and may be able to identify and fetch a personal item – "Please bring me the book" may result in him carrying it over to you. At meal times he should be able to drink from a cup more safely and self-feed most of the time. He will still not be very adept at using a spoon, but will not want to have you feeding him, so there is an incentive to learn. Word use is expanding all the time and he will start to enjoy funny noise words such as "splat" and "boing" – particularly if you accompany them with actions.

You can begin to reason with him and use "reasoning control" (explaining in simple words) rather than "power control" (using force or coertion); the former promotes understanding whilst the latter suggests, unhelpfully, that might is right.

By now your toddler will be able to respond to simple commands and repeat words in the right context. He will follow simple instructions such as "Please get your shoes" or "Please give me the spoon", and when reading appropriate stories, he is quite clever at pointing to people and animals and may name them. He will understand about turning the pages and will bring a favourite book to read.

Your toddler will enjoy jokes of various kinds – talking in a funny voice, making animal noises, using made-up words which sound strange and mimicking a funny expression. Your toddler thinks he is the most important person in the world – and expects to get everything he asks for, so there will be a lot of disappointments when this does not happen. Therefore, he may become frustrated when unable to do what is wanted but if you distract him appropriately, he will quickly forget tears and retain his good humour.

This is the time to get into routines; toddlers thrive when things happen at the same time every day. Establishing routines doesn't mean you have to work by the clock, but if you do things in the same order, life will run more smoothly, particularly bedtime. Rules are important as well, as long as you don't have to keep saying "No;" the best way to enforce rules is by physical means – if you don't want your child to play with something, make sure it is out of his reach.

Safety will become a big issue at this age. Your toddler will very easily face threats of which he will not be aware, for example, standing up on a chair or the stroller, climbing downstairs standing up, missing a step going out the front door, and, of course, walking onto a busy road. It's important to teach him about potential hazards (see page 306), but your constant vigilance is always required.

He will love playing with toys now and good choices would be simple puzzles and an activity board with lots of different manipulative parts. He

will be able to throw a soft ball, build a small tower of bricks and copy a bridge or other simple construction. If you haven't introduced crayons before, this is a good time to give your toddler some chubby non-toxic crayons and some paper.

At this age he will often be hungry and snacks are a good thing; there are plenty that are both healthy and enjoyable.

Now your toddler is always on the go. Although her gait continues to be uncertain, she will try to run when she can and gets better at doing this without falling; walking will be steadier, too. Her climbing skills continue to improve; she will climb into and sit on chairs. She should be able to crawl downstairs backwards safely, though you still have to watch for a tumble, which can come from too much haste. This independence also means that she can entertain herself for a lot of the time, though she will rarely stick to one activity for more than a few minutes as her attention span is short.

She is starting to have strong feelings and you can help her by giving her feelings names so that she can understand and respond. "It is a bit scary coming to visit a house where there are lots of people you don't know, but you will feel better soon and I am always here for you." She will be cross if she doesn't get her own way so when she does get upset, just distract her or remove her from the situation.

This is a time to adhere to rules, and help your toddler to understand that some places are out of bounds, and that some things and possessions must be treated carefully.

Your toddler can easily make you aware of what she wants not only through an increasing vocabulary but also through sounds and gestures. She continues to point at objects that she wants and repeats what you say. She may vocalise to herself, particularly when playing, and may start singing now, too. She will use at least five words, but more likely 10–20, and may carry out simple tasks, such as "Please put the teddy down." Even if she is not talking a lot, which is not unusual, she understands a great deal more.

She will be much more accurate at stacking and sorting toys, at fitting puzzle pieces into their slots, and at using blocks for building, though she often fumbles and drops whatever she handles. She should be able to build a tower of three blocks and use a pencil to scribble back and forth and make dots. She also will begin to enjoy pretend games and imaginative play. She will like to push toys along the floor and use one toy to push another. You will notice that your toddler is developing a hand preference. She demonstrates her increased dexterity in taking off gloves and socks and unzipping things.

A vaccination against chickenpox is usually given at this stage.

New things are happening every day now and the pace of language development is particularly rapid. Your toddler can name pictures of common objects in books and shows sustained interest when you read to him. He has a good idea of what belongs to him but also where common household objects "live". Therefore, he can be more helpful if asked to help with chores. He likes to help, and should be given the chance to do so within his capability, and be praised strongly for doing well. He will enjoy taking a toy, usually a cuddly animal, on expeditions and will have a firm favourite. If he hasn't already, he may start to use a security blanket, too, and this is fine – he'll get over it in time.

Outdoor play will be more complex due to his improved manipulative and locomotive skills. It's a good idea to take him outdoors every day, even in the rain, so he stays fit and healthy. Not only will it help keep his boundless energy in check, but he'll be developing balance and coordination and a knowledge of distance, height and space by running, jumping, climbing and swinging.

He will also enjoy pretend play though most of his play is solitary. He will sometimes grab from other children; this must be controlled carefully, and ideas of sharing should be inculcated repeatedly as this virtue is not learned readily.

He will be able to use a stick to reach other toys and is developing an understanding of tools. Other advances are standing on one foot whilst holding on to something, kicking a ball, throwing a ball overhand and running without falling (sometimes). He will assist with getting dressed and undressed and will have a good go at washing his face and hands. He'll be able to feed himself more neatly now and is learning to brush his own teeth. He may be responding to early potty training or resisting it; if the latter, he may make a fuss during nappy changing and will require distraction. Or, he may let you know when he has soiled his nappy.

It will not be long before difficult behaviour will start to show up, particularly in a determined child. If you are strong-willed, your child probably will be, too. This will mean tantrums, screaming, shouts of "No, I won't!" and sometimes running away. A positive approach is best (see page 294).

Sleeping may give problems and is helped by a bedtime routine – doing the same thing every night, with a winding down period.

Your toddler will have a lot of words, on average 18–20 (although there is considerable variation in learning to speak, as for anything else). She will soon start to put words together reliably into short sentences and loves to name things and may ask for particular toys and food. She will follow more complicated instructions when so inclined and can name the parts of her body. She will enjoy being asked questions and is starting to learn about being polite – using you as a role model, so be sure to set a good example. Her sense of humour seems more apparent and she finds amusement in many of her activities.

Your toddler is going to enjoy music now so let her listen to all different kinds. If you play a musical instrument, let her look at it and investigate how it works, and play her a simple tune. Maybe she will sing along. She can certainly start to dance, and you can teach her about rhythm using two spoons, a drum, a keyboard, or your own voice and hands.

She will develop a much better understanding of what things are for, from dishwashers to mobile

phones, and may want to get involved if she sees you at the computer. She is also better at problem solving and may be able to fit puzzle pieces more accurately or attempt more difficult puzzles. Reading books is a great pleasure now and she will be able to turn the pages and join in with a story. She will have favourites and may want to read the same one every night. She may pull you to show you something interesting. Help her along with a simple explanation when something new appears.

She will enjoy dressing up and this is an entertaining activity for a wet afternoon. She will love to use play dough and face paints and generally anything that makes a mess. She is getting more sociable and will play alongside, but not with, other children.

As well as dressing up, she will be able to help with getting dressed in her ordinary clothes. It is a good thing to let her do this even though it takes longer. Everything she learns to do herself is a step towards her greater independence, and will relieve the burden on you in the future. She will also have a great feeling of pride for having "done it herself".

You may notice that your toddler has developed some awareness of concepts such as time – she may be able to wait quietly for something for a few minutes – or of notions such as up, down, big and small. She may be quite knowledgeable about what belongs to her and others, though she is chiefly concerned with what belongs to her. She may use this knowledge of things to be helpful occasionally and, when asked, she may put away her toys.

At meals, she may become rather fussy and not be prepared to try new items. Don't worry and don't get into battles over food as she is sure to win. Keep introducing new foods and praise her for trying them even if she doesn't eat much – "a no-thank-you bite" should be encouraged. She will start taking other things soon enough, particularly if she attends childcare or playgroup and copies other children.

Your toddler is turning into a little boy or girl and is reaching big milestones in language, social development, physical strength and personality. His language should be readily understandable and he will enjoy using it. His speaking is clearer, he refers to himself by name and is beginning to say "please" and "thank you" although reminders may be needed, as well as a good example from adults. He will understand quite complex sentences and requests and will like to answer questions. His vocabulary will be extensive; he uses many two-word and even perhaps three-word sentences. He can point to and name familiar objects.

Your toddler has mastered some new skills such as being able to climb onto and off furniture, running, and throwing a ball to be caught (though he won't manage to catch one that you throw quite yet). If he's on the stairs, he will climb up and down with two feet per step. He may be able to walk backwards and can jump with both feet off the ground. He may do a little dance to familiar music.

You may notice certain characteristics appearing such as a dislike of loud noises; odd fears, such as shrinking from dogs; or he may develop fussy eating habits. These won't last; just reassure him but refrain from applying too much pressure.

He can sit in a chair on his own and look at picture books for a short period, and will open boxes to discover what is inside. He will recognise his own image in a photograph.

He does not want to share yet. You can explain cooperation to him and set an example. It is very important for a toddler to learn that he is not the only one with needs and that others have them, too, but it takes time, patience and repetition. Your toddler may also hit or bite other children. This is best managed by taking him away with a firm "No" and then telling him why this is prohibited behaviour. If he does it again then this would justify the use of time out (see page 300).

He will now be able to build a tower of up to seven blocks and also build other shapes such as a bridge or steps, and will enjoy scribbling and drawing circles. Try to understand his feelings when he is frustrated, and help him to do things himself whenever it is appropriate.

He should be aware when his bladder is full and he needs to urinate; he may also know when he needs to pass a bowel movement so may be ready for toilet training. This is not something to push hard; he needs to go at his own pace. Girls tend to reach this milestone sooner than boys.

Physically, your toddler is getting strong and is proud of what he can do. Some children of this age can jump with both feet off the ground, balance on one foot (although not for long), and walk backwards as well as run fast. Most can stop to pick things up as they walk, push a cart, pull a toy or manoeuvre a ride-on toy.

His language is becoming exciting and more graphic. He will be able to use more complex words ("under" and "on top") to describe where things are and their properties ("round" or "hard") and will use sentences effectively. He also will be able to sing some words of songs, and will enjoy participating in group musical events. He may talk to himself quite a lot!

Drawing will also improve and he will be getting good at drawing a straight line, and much better at

more complex shapes such as circles. He will enjoy painting and making pictures using finger paint. Being able to screw and unscrew lids, turning handles and knobs and unwrapping objects are all new attainments. The former two mean you have to be on guard for possible safety risks but the latter provides opportunity for fun. You can make lots of pretend presents for him to rip open.

More and more your toddler will want to investigate – "What is in here? What's that? What is this button for?" The more he can understand, the more he will want to learn and you can never explain too much; just be sure that it is done in simple terms. Soon he will be able to tell the difference between one and two, but can't yet count any higher.

At this age, both boys and girls like to play house with dolls, particularly getting the doll ready for bed, but may also engage in other care-giving activities.

Socially, he will be more ready to be separated from you. This will depend on his confidence and feeling of security, which is partly related to his temperament and partly to the opportunities he has been given in the past. Don't push him to separate – this will make him upset; just take it gently and gradually and help to build up his confidence. When telling him to stop bad behaviour, don't put him down or criticise.

You may wonder about thumb-sucking. Does he still do this? Many children at this age still do and, of course, some still use a dummy. This can be thrown away any time, but a thumb can't! However, babies all round the world have used their thumbs for security for many years with the main harm being to the developing teeth. (A dummy, on the other hand, may occasionally interfere with speech development and can also affect the teeth.) There are ways of discouraging the thumb (for example, verbal discussion or smearing a nasty-tasting ointment on it) but don't make a big issue of it.

Now your toddler is developing imagination and you can use it for play and stories. Pretend games are great fun and can be endlessly developed. With stories, you can make them up – children love this – or put a twist into one that you are reading. You can ask questions about the story – "Why is the boy doing that? What is the dog thinking about? What kind of expression is on his face?"

Learning about emotions is as important as learning about numbers, and it is good for your toddler to recognise when he feels angry or anxious, and for you to put this into words. When he gets angry, you should point this out and help him to cope with the emotion rather than increasing the tension by getting angry yourself.

His language continues to expand; he will enjoy reading games – ask him to finish a word or sentence, or change it to something else as a joke. His memory is good and he will learn numbers and may begin to count. He is getting good at sorting objects by shape, size and perhaps colour. It is good to talk about colours; ask him to name the colours of the things you see: a ball, cat, car or flower, for example. He will know the difference between big and little, and probably between high and low.

Physically he will be strong and will enjoy active games; this is a good time to start working on ball skills – throwing, catching and kicking. Learning about coordination can take time so it is good to practise it; riding a bike with stabilisers is another way of helping this.

He will still enjoy making a mess and battles are inevitable. You can avoid this at mealtimes by eating as a family and just ignoring any refusal to eat certain items. It is also important to have rules about sweets, which can be such a temptation at this age. Bear in mind the possible effect of sweets – dental caries and obesity.

Your toddler also will enjoy outings but be sure to take along some favourite toys and also prepare him for new situations by explaining what will happen and who he will meet; some children are more wary than others. He may begin to play with some children rather than alongside.

Two and a half – your child is well into toddlerhood and is still affected by tantrums, rages and opposition although becoming more open to reason. This is the age when good management of emotional distress is all-important. Your child will want to test the limits and this is part of learning about the world, but if you have rules then he will get to know what they mean and accept them as long as all the family follow the same rules.

Daily routines will make life easier and traumas less likely. This means meals being at the same times and, if possible, everyone sitting down together. Children appreciate a social time and it is good practice for life as an older child and adult, to eat neatly, talk together and enjoy the food. He can be a real helper if you have another little one, he can give you a hand with his new sibling, or help with simple household chores, like putting dirty clothes into the laundry basket.

Your child is going to enjoy using words and language more and more and can have a prolonged conversation using more complex words. He will enjoy the different meanings of words and may start saying "Why?", so you need to be prepared with simple explanations for all sorts of complex questions from the difference between dogs and cats to why cars don't run on the pavement. Giving a good explanation is very important – even if it needs to be repeated again the next day. This requires patience, which can be in short supply in a busy household, but will be rewarded when your toddler uses the information months later. He should know some nursery rhymes.

Now he will be adept with his hands; he can hold a pencil in his preferred hand and use it to copy a circle as well as horizontal and vertical lines. He can also draw much more neatly and you can have games (and make interesting pictures) drawing around familiar objects and shapes such as jigsaw pieces, hands and feet, and stars and circles. He will be able to use switches and buttons and can have great fun with a torch as well as with battery-operated toys. At the seaside or sandpit, he will be more adept at getting sand into a bucket.

He is also much more coordinated and should be able to climb on simple play equipment with confidence, walk on tiptoe, and jump with both feet. He will understand time better now though may not readily wait when told, "It will only be 10 minutes".

Relationships become more interesting and more secure with others outside the immediate family, such as grandparents uncles, aunts, godparents, and cousins who may be the first close playmates.

Your toddler will be very interested in other children and is able to interact more with them and address requests and orders, particularly those concerning her toys, to them. She is likely to have a bossy tendency but may just begin to share – a valuable trait, which you need to nurture. Attendance at playgroup is beneficial in promoting pro-social characteristics such as this. She knows the differences between boys and girls.

Physically, your child is getting more coordinated when climbing and running. She can walk upstairs taking turns with her feet, will climb well on climbing frames and slides at the park, can balance on one foot for a significant time, and can kick a ball with reasonable accuracy.

She is learning up to 50 new words a month and can talk in quite long sentences. She is still interested in the sound of words and likes those that sound funny or rhyme. She is able to describe what she has done and can be clear but sometimes the words come out wrong. She is beginning to talk about "I" when describing herself and is more specific when answering questions.

She will be better at getting dressed and may manage buttons and press-studs. She will have her favourite clothes and there can be a tantrum if she is not allowed to wear what she wants.

She may enjoy constructional play using blocks or bricks and should be able to play meaningfully with toy cars and dolls' house furnishings. At this age, trial and error is very important so it is a good thing to offer toys that might belong to an older child and let her try them out. She will like to "read" books that

are concerned with things that she does – going to the shops, eating meals, playing with toys.

Your toddler is beginning to distinguish colours; she may be able to colour-match but naming may not come till later. She will be interested in drawing and painting, and making a mess with crayons and paint will be endlessly attractive. She may be able to draw more accurately and may draw part of a figure.

She should be able to control her bowels and bladder during the day and perhaps at night but don't push this too fast! She will be showing her own determined character and if pushed too much may decide to do the opposite. She needs guidance in doing the right thing and this is a more effective way of achieving what you want than punishment.

At this age it is essential to formulate good habits for meal times and access to TV, which should be controlled both in terms of what is watched and its duration.

Now your child is getting on for three, she is really becoming a little person who can have a conversation, understand an explanation, help you out, and knows a lot about the world. She can still be difficult, oppositional and resentful of being told what to do, and is likely to do something dangerous when left on her own. But much of her development now depends on the example you set her, and the discussions you have help her to become a more polite, helpful and considerate child and playmate.

She will enjoy playing with friends now and this is the chance to help her with sharing. Talk to her about taking turns and make sure that this is done fairly. Explain about saying "Please" and "Thank you" and make sure you do the same. Point out why some things are necessary (putting toys away after use) and why some things mustn't be done (tearing books or hitting other children). But explain it simply, don't take too long and don't use an angry voice, which will make it less likely your child will listen.

Children of this age prefer sameness in their activities and schedules – dressing to be done the same way and a book to be read without any changes – though this will moderate over the next few months. Some girls and most boys are aggressive at this age on some occasions; many are easily frustrated and they use the word "No" constantly. Your child is not able to modulate her behaviour easily and you can help her to understand what her feelings are at this time. Praise her whenever she does play nicely but be sure to take the same line whenever the same behaviour appears, then she will learn – as long as all those who care for her are consistent as well. Children of this age exhibit different levels of being able to control their emotions – some

are calmer but others still struggle. Some children are extremely confident, others fearful and insecure.

Your child now refines her motion by modulating her speed, dodging obstacles and being able to turn corners and make sudden stops. She is also more effective using her hands to string beads, to paint and to put puzzle pieces together.

She will enjoy doing more and more herself and this is something you can encourage by offering her jobs that are simple and easy. She can help you with cooking, and can carry some dirty laundry, bring a box from the pantry, or put the spoons away. She likes to know "Why?" and although this can be wearing, it is important always to give a reason, as this is how children learn. She will be able to talk in full sentences and most adults can understand what she says and what she means. Some children stammer or mix up words; if yours does this, it is best not to draw attention to the mistakes but just to use the correct words yourself.

Now your child will love playing games and there are plenty that can revolve around things in the house

including using the dressing-up box. It is also the time to introduce books with a proper story and you can allow her to choose the books that she likes to have read to her. A regular reading time is still very popular and if you can, make up some stories that will help to extend her imagination.

She will be better at eating and should be onto a greater variety of food. Try to make time for the family to eat together; this is good for conversation (as long as the TV is switched off) and helps to prevent faddy food habits, which are also quite common at this age.

From this time on, your child will increasingly spend time away from you, and although you as parents are still the most important people in his life, he will take enormous pleasure in his new experiences and the other people with whom he spends time. If your child begins preschool now, preparation will be needed – particularly in gaining confidence in being away from you. Getting to know the staff and the toys and where to find things, what kind of food is offered, what happens about the toilet, are all questions to sort out in advance. This time away from you may result in his picking up common childhood illnesses and having to learn more about potential dangers. He is beginning to understand danger but is not yet safe on his own – he may know about the source of danger but may forget. At this age you can start to help him to understand who to trust and of whom to be wary. Remember that the way to help him is to give him praise whenever he does what you expect, and explain to him when he doesn't why it was wrong.

Rules which are laid down now and enforced will be readily accepted and it is a good idea to think about how you expect him to behave socially and when out and about. If your child is upset about something, help him to talk about his feelings. Don't let him sulk or walk off in a huff, but make sure he explains what he feels and have a talk about it.

Playing in a group will be enjoyable and he will take part in make-believe, which can lead to endless fun with friends. Mechanical play or constructional toys should be encouraged, as well as the use of tools such as a hammer and screwdriver (this goes for both girls and boys). He should also enjoy playground visits as he will be physically agile.

Your child can take part in family activities much more now – maybe play simple board games, and join in with hobbies such as gardening. He will enjoy joining you for a bike ride and swimming at the pool, and may be ready for a movie or play.

He now boasts improved self-help skills; he should be adept with his fork, be able to dress and undress, wash and dry his hands, eat neatly (most of the time), and probably use the toilet and wipe his bottom. He can be a help to you by tidying away his toys and clothes, helping to lay the table, and maybe pouring out his cereal. Make chores fun and when he does well, praise him afterwards; if helping becomes routine at this age, there will be less resistance to continuing when he is older.

His understanding and speech are now very good; he uses longer sentences and complex prepositions such as "inside", "on top of" and "inside out". You can have a conversation with him. He will know his name and be able to repeat it, and it is a good thing for him also to learn to repeat his address. He will be able to use time concepts such as "yesterday" and also times of day, and can learn some numbers. He will also know the difference between large and small, singular and plural, and can identify colours and match shapes.

APPROACHES TO
PARENTHOOD

On being a parent

Every parent wants to be the best parent in the world, to get everything right, to make no mistakes and to raise children who are wonderful and who love them. While that's an admirable aspiration, achieving such a target is very challenging.

For a start, you quickly learn that your baby is a unique individual and what's deemed "best" for a child might not suit her – or you. There are fashions in parenting, just as there are in all other areas of life – for example, when you were young, you were probably encouraged to listen attentively, to follow strict guidelines, and to place school achievements above all else, whereas nowadays, children are encouraged to be independent thinkers, to make decisions for themselves and to develop their potential in non-academic areas such as music, art and drama. Because the way you plan to or actually bring up your baby is influenced by your own childhood, you may find you're constantly reassessing what you previously believed.

Despite these factors, you still have to make parenting choices every single day. You have, for instance, to decide how to manage your baby's feeding and sleeping, your toddler's tantrums, your

THE CHILD-ORIENTED PARENT

Description This type of parent considers that the best way to raise his/her baby is by responding to the baby's emotional and physical needs as they emerge. So when the baby cries, she is immediately given comfort; if she is hungry, she is immediately fed; if she is bored, she is immediately given stimulation. In this way, the baby drives the parenting. Of course, by the time she is three or four years old, life has evened out and she is expected to fit in with family routines and to recognise that other people have needs, too.

Impact On the plus side, the baby might never have to wait; her needs are satisfied instantly. Therefore, she might never feel alone, isolated or ignored. On the negative side, she may grow up to expect the world to totally revolve around her, and she may miss out on opportunities to develop resilience and coping skills of her own.

THE SCHEDULE-BASED PARENT

Description This type of parent works on the premise that routine is good for a child and that parents are the best people to decide that routine. Feeding and sleeping are delivered and encouraged according to a predetermined schedule, whether or not the infant appears to want to feed or sleep at that time. These parents aim to develop their babies' self-discipline through these methods and to ensure their growing children learn very quickly that they are part of a family, each member of which has his/her own psychological needs.

Impact On the plus side, the parent may have very clear ideas of what to do with his/her baby, right from the start; and the child can learn very quickly that her needs are not the only priority. On the negative side, she may resist the imposition of a fixed schedule that might not fit in with her changing emotional needs.

preschooler's progress in nursery and your child's friendships. You can't sit on the fence – your child needs a positive, confident parent with clear ideas.

The type of parent you are depends not only on such factors as how you were raised, the media and peer attitudes, but also on your personality, your baby's personality and the way the two of you interact with each other. You may, for example, seek to imitate your upbringing because you have happy memories, or opt for a totally different approach because you disapproved of the way you were brought up. The books and magazines you read and the television programs you watch will influence your approach as will the opinions and actions of your friends and family. And, as you get to know your baby better, you will intuitively change what

you do to match your baby's needs. In turn, your baby's behaviour and progress will be influenced by your actions. Your skills as a parent develop and change over time, matching your baby's growth and development.

Parenting choices

Although being a parent is an evolving process, you should decide what type of parent you want to be – given that there are as many styles of parenting as there are parents! One popular system of classifying parents is according to the extent to which they are led by their children's internal emotional needs and demands or the extent to which they require their children to adapt their needs to an external structure and routine. Looked at from this way, parenting can be divided into three common types (see boxes).

Most professionals would agree that a flexible parenting style is the most effective. Children dislike extremes; they thrive best in loving environments in which there are clear guidelines for behaviour but the occasional relaxation of the "rules."

Reaching consensus

No matter which type of parent you set out to be, in a two-parent family, agreement on parenting style is vital. That doesn't mean you and your partner have to be carbon copies of one another; on the contrary, your child benefits from your individual natures and personalities. But it is in her best interests for there to be a broad consensus on the main parenting concerns such as discipline, behaviour, relationships and routine.

Where differences in parenting attitudes and style arise between you and your partner – which is bound to happen in every family at times – try to resolve the disagreement privately, without your child having the opportunity to listen in. This will enable you to present a united front to your child so that she sees both of you support each other; this increases her psychological wellbeing, her confidence in you as parents and her sense of emotional security.

THE FLEXIBLE PARENT

Description This type of parent recognises that routine matters to a growing child and also that every child is an individual with her own particular blend of characteristics. While these parents have clear ideas about the expectations they have of their babies, they recognise that these can be realised in different ways. Their parenting has a common theme running through, but is adapted as circumstances change and as the child changes. This style tries to take what's best from the other two styles and blend them.

Impact On the plus side, parents may be able to be flexible depending on the child's age and stage of development; the needs of the child and her parents are both deemed to be important. On the negative side, ever-changing parenting can confuse a growing baby and can reduce a parent's confidence in him-/herself if he/she doesn't get the expected results.

The effect of temperament

From the moment your baby was born she started to show her temperament. She may have sucked well and enthusiastically during her first feed or seemed passive and only sucked slowly. Maybe she wriggled about when you first held her or snuggled close to you immediately. At birth, your baby had a wide range of responses to different situations, and this early temperament is the foundation for her later personality in childhood and adulthood.

Temperament profiles

Psychologists studying babies' temperaments have found that these components tend to cluster together in certain ways to form specific identifiable temperament profiles, and that most babies fall into one of three types. (You may find, however, that your own baby is one of these that can't be neatly categorised because she shares features from more than one type – this occurs in approximately a quarter of all babies under the age of one year.) The main temperament profiles are:

- *Easy* The easygoing baby is a pleasure to be with because she is very even-tempered and generally responds positively to anything that happens to her or around her. She is very adaptable to new experiences, welcoming them rather than avoiding them. Her mood and behaviour is regular and predictable.
- *Difficult* The hard-to-manage infant is very active for most of the time but is fractious and easily irritated. It doesn't take much to unsettle her; her moods vary and her behaviour does not follow a predicted pattern. She does not like change and she takes a long time to adapt to new situations or unfamiliar faces.
- *Slow-to-warm-up* The inactive child has mild reactions to most things. She will lack enthusiasm for new experiences, but her negative response will not be intense. If, for instance, she doesn't like a new toy she will simply turn her head away from it rather than actually physically reject it.

Although new personal characteristics can develop over the remaining childhood years, by the time the pre-school years are over, a major part of your child's personality has already been formed and stays with her for the rest of her life. One of the challenges you face is encouraging her to use her temperament in positive ways, even where characteristics may appear to be potentially negative. Take, as an example, determination to get what she wants. This trait can cause problems when your child confronts you but it can be useful when she wants to succeed in learning a new skill.

Sources of temperament

Nobody knows for sure why your infant has the temperament she does. Studies comparing the temperament of identical twins with that of non-identical (fraternal) twins have found that there is greater similarity between identical than non-identical twins, especially during the first year of life. This evidence strongly suggests there is a genetic component, that your baby inherits part of her temperament profile from you and your partner.

Yet there is no doubt that the environment also plays a part. Experimental evidence demonstrates that the more parents smile and show positive affection to their baby, then the more likely she is to be socially responsive, happy and smiling herself. The home environment clearly matters and can shape a baby's behaviour and feelings.

Even if your baby falls into a recognisable group, she will have unique aspects to her temperament. In a sense it really doesn't matter whether these traits are inherited or environmental – all that matters is that you respond to her in a way in which you are comfortable. For instance, if you are a loving, affectionate person with a relaxed manner, then stick to that approach even if your baby is fretful and hard to manage.

A lot depends on the way you manage your baby's temperamental profile. If your baby, say, dislikes change then you may be tempted to treat her very carefully, to avoid new experiences. While that strategy certainly reduces the number of difficult moments with her, it also reinforces her behaviour and does nothing to change it. But, if you decide to improve your baby's adaptability by deliberately introducing new experiences into her life, you may find that she gradually becomes less moody and more accustomed to change.

Matching parenting style to temperament

Before your child was born, you already had ideas about parenting. Possibly you thought the best way to bring up a baby is to have firm limits so that she quickly learns what she can and cannot do, or maybe you decided to let your baby learn for herself. Whatever your pre-baby thoughts on parenting were, you have had to transform these into reality.

Evidence suggests that the most effective form of parenting is one that is focused and based on a set of clear principles, but which also takes into account the individual emotional needs of the child herself. It's a case of you and your child meshing together.

If you child has a quiet and withdrawn temperament, you can't insist that she be the life and soul of the party but you can gently introduce her to a range of social experiences, which will help build her social confidence.

Nor can you squash the determination of a curious toddler, but you can channel that particular quality in a positive direction, for example, by encouraging her to complete a difficult task that she has already started.

Adapting your parenting strategies to take into account your child's temperament encourages her, in turn, to adapt her personality to meet your expectations – and that is usually a recipe for successful family life.

5 main components of temperament

1 **Activity level** Your baby's pace and vigour might be quick and energetic or she may be relaxed and sluggish, content to respond at her own steady pace.

2 **Irritability** Some infants cope with everyday experiences without becoming rattled or upset while others are easily upset, for instance, when feeding is slow.

3 **Soothability** This refers to the ease at which your baby calms down after she is upset; this varies greatly from baby to baby.

4 **Fearfulness** Stimulation can generate excitement or it can make a baby fearful; some babies are more easily frightened than others.

5 **Sociability** The sociable infant breaks out in a lovely smile when someone approaches while the unsociable baby responds with howls of anxiety.

Partner considerations

Raising your infant is not an exact science! Each parent has an opinion about the best way to manage bedtime routines, discipline, feeding and tantrums etc. And that's fine. After all, there is usually more than one way for everything. But problems can arise when serious differences of opinion occur between you and your partner over how to raise your child (although minor disagreements about infant-related issues are perfectly normal).

Some of the potential negative effects of sustained disagreements between you and your partner about bringing up your baby include:

- *Inconsistency* Your growing child needs a consistent structure at home, a predictable set of rules, which she is expected to follow. If you tell hier one thing and your partner tells her another, there is no consistency whatsoever. This confuses your child at first, and later on makes her feel anxious and insecure.
- *Tension* Serious disagreements – whatever their nature – will affect the atmosphere at home. You feel tense, your partner feels tense, and before you know it, your baby feels tense, too. In a strained environment like this, tempers become frayed. Soon adults and children in the house will have a higher level of irritability and bickering.
- *Manipulation* Even a young child can exploit differences of opinion. When your child doesn't get what she wants from you, she will immediately rush over to your partner in the expectation that he/she will be more obliging. Your baby is only interested in achieving her goal, and she'll approach the parent most likely to give in to her.
- *Resentment* Nobody likes to feel that his/her views are being ignored. If either you or your partner feels that your opinion is not valued, resentment will soon set in. In addition, your self-confidence as a parent will rapidly drop. If the situation persists over several months, these negative emotions will intensify.

Working together

Agree with each other that you won't fight about your growing child in front of her; always disagree in private. Aside from the fact that your child definitely doesn't want to watch you squabble with each other, she needs rules to be clearly set out. Witnessing the two of you having argument about, say, whether or not she should be allowed to have an extra biscuit during the afternoon, makes her feel miserable.

You may dislike what your partner has to say, but each of you is entitled to have an opportunity to speak. Your partner holds views just as strongly as you, and is as resistant to alternative suggestions as you. That's why you both need to express your ideas to each other. Letting each of you have your say helps reduce the tension and avoids a confrontation.

Set aside some time just for the purpose of talking about matters on which you may disagree. Once you have both had your turn to say what you think, and you've considered your partner's comments, spend time discussing the source of your differing opinions. Reflecting on your childhoods and the ways you were brought up by your own parents will help you understand each other's perspective.

You should consider the strengths and weakness of the various alternatives together. Be honest with each other – don't reject your partner's ideas just because you didn't think of them first yourself. Be prepared to accept that your way might not always be the only way. Talk through the pros and cons of each approach, trying to resolve the conflict without unnecessary confrontation.

Once you have reached an agreement on the preferred strategy, both of you should commit to carrying this out for a period of, say, two weeks, and then you will evaluate its success. If the strategy has worked, you can justifiably be pleased with yourselves. If it hasn't been effective, then make a further commitment to try the other suggestion for a couple of weeks. Don't be afraid to engage in some trial and error.

Single parenthood

As a single parent, you won't experience routine conflict with a partner over how to raise your child – there's nobody to disagree with you on a daily basis. Of course, you may have friends and relatives who have different opinions from you, but for most of the time, you make all the decisions on your own without anyone battling against you.

On the plus side, this means you don't have to resolve disagreements over baby care with someone else. You are the sole decision-maker. The downside, however, is that you need to have confidence in your judgements as a parent – and that's not always easy; you are bound to have self-doubts sometimes. It can help to bear the following in mind.

DO

Weigh up all the alternatives carefully There is no need to rush into things. Think about the implications of the different parenting issues, before choosing a particular strategy to use with your infant.

Follow through with commitment Once you have made up your mind what to do, stick with it for a few weeks before evaluating whether or not it has been successful. Your child may be resistant to change.

Be prepared to admit you have made a mistake Recognising that you need to do something differently is a sign of your emotional strength, not a sign of emotional weakness. There is no need to accept that your choice wasn't a good one.

DON'T

Assume you are wrong The chances are that the way you are raising your child is just what he needs. Just because your friends have a different approach doesn't mean they are right and that you are mistaken. Believe in yourself.

Always go for the easy option Raising a child sometimes involves hard decisions, especially when it comes to discipline. Resist the temptation to go for the soft option all the time, because you think that will be easier.

Chop and change too quickly You won't always get the results you hope for straightaway. Your child takes time to adapt as he grows. Once you have decided on a course of action, don't allow yourself to give up on it too quickly.

Putting your approach into practice

Most parents confirm that the three biggest challenges in raising a baby is managing her feeding, sleeping and crying. A baby who cries all the time, who refuses to sleep even when exhausted, and who constantly demands food, quickly exhausts even the most energetic parent.

Bear in mind, however, that no matter what style of parenting you adopt, the fact is that your baby's feeding and sleeping patterns change rapidly, especially during the first few months. For the first six to eight weeks, your baby physically requires feeding every few hours but by the time she is six months old, her feeding needs begin to resemble those of an older child. And while an infant needs to sleep up to 80 per cent of the day – she probably has at least seven or eight naps during a 24-hour cycle – by the time she is one year old, her total sleeping time drops to around 13 hours a day.

Adjusting your responses

How you respond to your baby depends on personal preference although most parents tend to use a mixture of the schedule-based and flexible approaches. It is a question of balance.

Take crying, as an example. In most instances, the best strategy is neither to rush to your baby the moment she cries nor to ignore her altogether. You should consider a more reasonable approach in which you don't set hard-and-fast rules about picking her up or leaving her. Sometimes your baby needs your cuddles and at other times she can manage without you by her side the moment she cries. Consider varying your response, depending on the circumstances. The same approach applies to feeding and sleeping.

SCHEDULE-BASED PARENT

Feed your baby at set times Once you have decided on the schedule for that day – perhaps, to feed her every three hours – you'll stick to that no matter what happens. If your baby hasn't finished her feed within 10 or 15 minutes, you'll stop anyway and you won't start again until the scheduled feeding slot. If she cries, you won't feed her earlier than you originally planned.

Encourage your baby to sleep at set times Once you have decided on the sleep schedule for that day – perhaps for her to sleep after her morning and afternoon feeds – you will tuck her up at those times whether or not she appears sleepy. You hope that by doing so her body will start to adjust to that routine so that her sleep patterns become predictable.

Deal firmly with crying episodes Once you have put your baby down for a sleep, you won't pick her up if she cries (assuming, of course, that you have checked there is no physical reason for her distress). You'll take the view that she needs to learn to manage her own crying and that if you pick her up every time she cries, she'll soon learn that crying is a good way to get your attention.

Effect on your baby She is more likely to adapt to routine when it is followed consistently and will learn self-discipline. However, the fixed schedule may not fit in with her biological clock and she may be very hungry because food is refused to her. She also may feel miserable when left to cry alone.

Effect on you You will be able to structure your day more effectively and probably will have more time to yourself. However, if your baby doesn't follow the schedule, you may have to battle with her.

FLEXIBLE PARENT

Feed your baby on demand You'll have a rough idea of how far apart the feeds should be, for instance, every three hours, but you'll be prepared to be flexible depending on your baby's needs. If she cries between feeds, is unable to settle and indicates with mouth movements that she is searching for food, you'll be willing to feed her out of schedule rather than allow her to continue to be upset.

Try to fit sleep times to your baby's natural sleep rhythm Although you have an idea of what times you would like your baby to sleep – and although you aim for these – you'll also identify the times that she actually wants to sleep. Then you will be willing to adapt your planned sleep schedule to suit. If she clearly doesn't want to go sleep at the desired time, you won't try to force the issue.

Pick your baby up when she cries You don't believe a young baby is manipulative and controlling but you think that a baby who cries is unhappy or distressed and needs attention in order to make her feel better. Whatever the cause of her discomfort, it may intensify if ignored.

Effect on your baby She may be happier because her needs are met immediately, she never experiences the distress of hunger or loneliness and she sleeps and eats according to her body's natural rhythms. However, she doesn't have any opportunity to learn how to control her urges.

Effect on you Confrontations are less frequent because your baby gets what she wants but because she's setting the schedule, you may not be able to plan your day with any degree of certainty.

Possible problems

Whether you opt for a schedule-based approach with your baby or try to be more flexible, you are likely to find that things don't always run smoothly. Below, you will find some very common problems and some suggested strategies for dealing with them.

Trying to feed your baby on schedule when he cries a lot in between feeds

Your baby might be crying because she simply isn't getting enough milk at each feed, or it may be that she isn't able to keep her hunger at bay for the full period between feeds. You also should consider the possibility that her crying has nothing to with hunger; it could be caused by boredom or even tiredness. Try doing the following:

- *Give her a longer time to complete each feed* In your determination to complete the schedule competently, you might not be giving her enough time to feed to her satisfaction. Make sure that you are relaxed when feeding her.
- *Have some flexibility with feeding* Every so often, try feeding in between the scheduled times or perhaps bringing the next feed forward by a few minutes. That way you'll find out if the scheduling is the root of the problem.
- *Distract your baby* If you know she is prone to tears before the next feed, try to plan how to fill her time, for instance, by playing with her, by taking her out in her buggy or by singing to her. You may find this settles her, without giving an extra feed.

Feeding your baby on demand but becoming worn out by frequent feeds

One of the challenges of demand-feeding – whether by breast or bottle – is determining when one feed is actually over and when the next begins. This is particularly important when a baby is slow feeder. Your own tiredness accumulates and then half the time you and your baby both drop off mid-feed! Try doing the following:

- *Start to introduce some structure into feeding* You don't have to switch to a rigid schedule, but you can start to aim for approximate feeding times.

Even if you hit within half an hour of these, on either side, you'll soon notice the difference.

- *When the feed is over, stop feeding* Decide on the way to judge when a feed is over, for instance, when your baby stops sucking for more than a minute, or when her eyes start to close. When you see that sign, end the feed there and then.
- *Get some rest* If possible, ask your partner (or a good friend) to give your baby a feed – breastmilk can be expressed. Once you feel a bit less tired, you'll be able to think more clearly.

Wanting to leave your baby to cry but not being able to bear his sobbing

You are probably not emotionally suited to a structured method of managing your baby's crying. Some parents are psychologically unable to ignore the sound of a crying baby. You are trying to follow a parenting strategy with which you are not comfortable – that's why you always want to pick your baby up. Try the following:

- *Consider a more flexible approach* There is no point in persisting with a parenting style that makes you unhappy. You could try a more flexible style of responding to his cries, at least for a couple of weeks, to assess its effectiveness.

- *Have a fixed time limit before responding* At the moment, you go to her when you can't stand any more tears and so there is no consistency. Pick a time, say, 10 minutes, and respond to her crying only after that time limit has passed.
- *Soothe him in other ways.* You don't need to pick your baby up every time in order to quiet her; you could, for instance, leave her in the cot and stroke her face, sing softly to hier, talk in a calming tone or provide a dummy.

Coping with an erratic sleep schedule

Your baby's need for sleep changes as she grows (see page 155) and it could be that you are trying to maintain a schedule that is no longer suitable. Another possibility is that you are giving up too quickly and not persisting with the one schedule for long enough. Try the following:

- *Keep a sleep diary* Do your best to detail the times your baby sleeps over a seven-day period, as that will give you a picture of her natural sleep rhythms. Then try to impose some structure around this basic pattern.
- *Be adaptable* If you see that she has outgrown the schedule that used to suit her, then change it. Remember that your baby needs less sleep as she

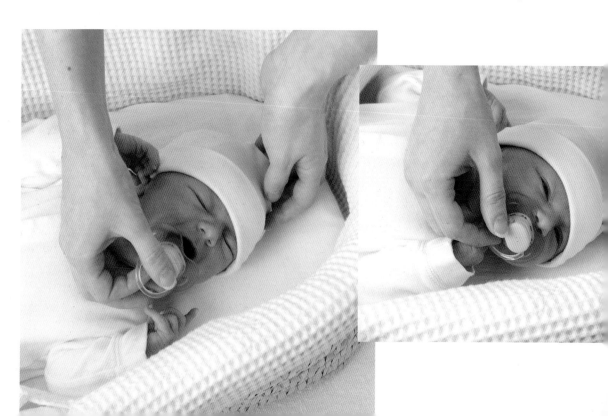

grows older and the gaps between each sleep episode become longer.

◆ *Don't give up too quickly* With every schedule-led approach, there will be times when a baby doesn't seem to fit in. But that doesn't mean you should give up. Perhaps if you persist for a few more days you'll find she sleeps more predictably.

Constant cuddling results in crying unless baby is held all the time

Although your baby is young, she is alert enough to learn the connection between his tears and physical comfort. You have taught her inadvertently that crying is an effective way to get your attention. She enjoys cuddles and is determined they will continue.Try the following:

◆ *Recognise the source of the difficulty* Admit to yourself that it's you who has to change your behaviour, not your baby – she's just doing what comes naturally to her. Make up your mind to alter the way you respond to her when he cries.

◆ *Soothe without holding* If you feel unable to leave your baby alone when she cries, soothe her

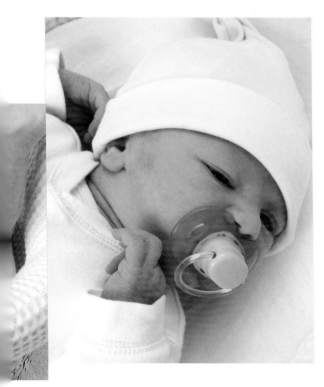

without taking her in your arms, without such close loving physical contact. Try to do this, no matter how tempted you are to lift her.

◆ *Pick her up when she isn't crying* As well as teaching her that crying won't always result in a cuddle, you should also teach her that she can get a hug from you without crying. Hold her at times when the tears aren't flowing down her face.

When success is elusive

There are bound to be times when your attempts to manage your baby are unsuccessful, despite your best efforts, and this can be very dispiriting. Before she came along, you probably viewed yourself as competent, caring and effective, and you may even have had responsibility for managing others. Yet now there are times when you are stunned by your infant's ability to thwart your every strategy!

And then there is the tiredness. Your baby's constantly changing sleeping and feeding needs turn night into day and day into night, as you search for the solution that will make her constantly contented and entirely predictable. You may feel that you are on an endless chase to find the "right" schedule for her and that just when you think you have achieved your target, she changes yet again. This is an inevitable consequence of normal development – virtually every parent has this same experience.

Don't panic; most other parents find that success sometimes is elusive when caring for their babies. Part of the solution usually involves adjusting your parenting philosophy and management strategies as your child grows and develops.

Instead of viewing these episodes as failures, look on them as learning experiences. It's not all about you. Your baby often cries for reasons, which are totally unknown to you (or to anyone else). This doesn't mean that you are doing something wrong. On the other hand, it does help to have clear, realistic targets. If, for example, you baby doesn't feed well, there is no point in setting the target of "feeds to only last 10 minutes", as that may be unrealistic. A more appropriate goal might be "a minimum of two hours break between each feed".

7 tips to restore yourself

1 **Be willing to change** Every so often step back and have a good look at the way you manage your child. Are these methods appropriate, and have you adapted them as she has grown and developed? Self-questioning can help keep your ideas fresh.

2 **Recognise others are like you** No one is perfect. Acknowledging that you are not alone in having self-doubts will help your confidence.

3 **Tell yourself you are doing a good job** Even if managing your baby is a struggle at times, you are probably achieving more than you realise. Don't expect to be successful all the time but don't lose sight of things that are going well.

4 **Look for change, don't apportion blame** Search for ways to change your behaviour so that your baby changes hers. Don't blame yourself or your baby.

5 **Get back in charge** A challenging infant can take over your life, leaving you with a feeling of passivity. Make clear decisions about the way you want to manage your baby and follow them through confidently.

6 **Give your baby lots of cuddles** No matter your parenting style, give your baby lots of hugs and cuddles. Loving, physical contact helps form an emotional attachment and makes you and your baby feel better about each other.

7 **Share the load if possible** Get your partner involved (or seek support from a friend if you are a single parent). With recharged emotional batteries, the challenges facing you won't seem so formidable.

Don't give up when the targets are not immediately achieved. You cannot reasonably expect your baby to change her behaviour quickly. That's why you should persist with a strategy for at least a couple of weeks before deciding whether or not to try something else instead.

Aim for gradual change. Your young child won't change suddenly; change is usually gradual and in small stages. If you feel she cries constantly, for example, set small, attainable targets, such as "settled for five minutes without crying" and then build up steadily in stages from there.

Understanding yourself

Faced with a challenging baby, coupled with incidents when you seem unable to achieve what you are aiming for with her, your own self-belief may start to drop. Here are some of the signs that your confidence is ebbing:

◆ You have doubts about the way you manage your baby, and you constantly wonder if there is a better way to do things with her.

◆ One day runs into the next, with no perceptible interval between them. You feel that each day is the same – dominated by your baby's routine.

◆ Time is at a premium and you never seem to have a moment to yourself. The daily demands of caring for your baby occupies every second that you have available.

◆ You constantly ask other people for advice before making a decision about your baby because you are sure they all know better than you.

◆ At night, you lie awake worrying about your relationship with your baby. You are especially worried that she may not love you.

If you find yourself experiencing these feelings, it's time to switch your perspective. Of course, every parent has moments of self-doubt – that's perfectly healthy – but when these moments become longer and longer, you need to turn things round so that you feel you are back in the driving seat.

Parenting twins

If you had thought that one baby would be challenging, you've probably discovered that twins can be twice the usual expense and work – but also twice the usual fun! And that makes family life very special for you. There are particular challenges for all parents who have twins, simply because of their closeness in age, their special relationship – which is often more intense than is normally found between siblings, and their underlying need to develop as distinct individuals despite being part of a twosome.

Although identical twins look the same to most other people who don't see them daily and therefore don't get to know them so well, you may notice some subtle physical differences. For instance, frequently one twin is left-handed while the other is right-handed, and the left-handed child is likely to be the smaller of the two; twins often develop different styles of handwriting, and often have significantly different personalities. Rates of development also vary.

Twins sometimes develop a secret language, one that adults may not understand. Make a point of having lots of language-based activities, particularly when your twins are toddlers. Your talking to them is especially important because research shows that twins often develop language at a slower rate than non-twins.

Similarities vs differences

Perhaps the biggest issue you have to face when raising twins – apart from the physical tasks of caring for two babies the exact same age at the exact same time – is to balance their similarities with their differences to ensure that each of your children is allowed to become a unique individual. The problem is that people like to see a matching set – they think it is cute for twins (especially identical twins) to be dressed in matching outfits, and to be regarded as one unit rather than as two separate individuals. While that's fine to begin with, eventually each child's distinctive skills and personality start to show through. And if each is not allowed to develop in her own unique way, they will feel stifled.

- The most common complaint of parents of twins during the first year is the physical strain of managing two sleeping and feeding schedules simultaneously.
- Identical twins have greater similarity in heartbeat, pulse and breathing rate than non-identical twins, suggesting these physical dimensions are inherited.

In family life, similarity between twins is easier to deal with. You can, for instance, buy them the same clothes, toys and even the same food. But its much more demanding if, say, one twin likes to play indoors while the other likes to play outdoors, or if one is easygoing while the other becomes upset at the slightest change in family routine. Yet managing such differences is part of the job when parenting twins.

Do your best to encourage each twin's individual interests and talents. One twin might enjoy stories while the other might prefer jigsaws. Provide opportunities to meet these different interests whenever you can, despite the practical difficulties you face. Don't worry about the possible impact this might have on their relationship with each other – rest assured they will remain close, even when their differences start to emerge. And they will quickly accept each other's distinctive strengths and weaknesses. You can help this process along the way by:

- *Taking an interest in everything each of your twins does*, whether both babies' interests coincide or not.
- *Giving individual time to both*; try to spend a few minutes alone with each twin every day; don't only spend time with them together.
- *Encouraging each twin to delight in her sibling's achievements*, as this helps engender respect for each other.

One-size doesn't fit all

Although it would be easier for you to treat both twins the same when it comes to setting rules and managing their behaviour, the reality is that you will need to match your preferred parenting style to each twin's individual developmental needs. Put simply, what works with one, might have no effect on the other. Take positive reinforcement, for example. One twin might glow with pride when you give her a smile for completing a small jigsaw, while her sister might not show any reaction at all unless she is given a large cuddle with lots of praise.

Make an effort to treat twins individually when it comes to misbehaviour, too. Just because you find them both getting up to mischief, doesn't mean that both are at fault. Instead of automatically assuming they are both guilty, find out the facts before attributing blame equally.

Being an individual

Each of your twins has to learn to gradually develop her independence, to stand on her own two feet, because at some stage a temporary separation from her sibling has to happen. At some point, your twins will form friendships with different children and their different personalities and abilities will take them into different aspects of life. That's why parents of twins often use the start of playgroup, kindergarten or school to specifically decide to encourage their twins' individual identities.

Bear in mind, however, that your twins may resist such a move. After all, they are used to each other's company day and night, and they may not have felt the need to develop the range of social skills necessary for socialising effectively with their peers. With your support, they will learn to mix confidently with other children their own age, even when their twin isn't alongside.

Listening to others

Life can be so hectic with your baby. You have to make so many decisions, some major, some minor. Parental decisions are required sometimes from the moment your baby is born and will be needed indefinitely. Like virtually every parent, you'll have occasional doubts about your skills and abilities. You want the best for your baby and you don't want to make any mistakes in raising him.

Hardly surprising, then, that you may want advice from other people you regard as more experienced than you. Advice from parents, grandparents, close friends, doctors and from anyone else whose opinion you might value can be very helpful, enabling you to make an informed choice about what to do. And, of course, there may be people who give an opinion without being asked!

Being open to advice is better than isolating yourself. When feeling uncertain about yourself as a parent, one strategy is to keep yourself away from other mums and dads. That protects you from any sort of challenge, but it won't help you advance your parenting skills in the long run.

3 reasons why it's good to listen

1   **You learn from others' mistakes** There is no point in making a mistake that someone else has made already.

2   **You learn from others' successes** Listening to the way in which someone else managed a problem means that you can try a similar strategy with your infant.

3   **You learn from others' uncertainty** It's always good to have confirmation that you are not the only parent who is unsure of her- or himself.

When there's too much advice

Yet problems can arise when too many people give you advice all at once. It's hard to know who to listen to, particularly when advice is conflicting, and particularly when each person giving the advice thinks he or she is the top expert! The fact that people's views are based on limited experience, and are influenced by their own and their children's personalities, doesn't stop them from expressing their firm opinions to you.

When confronted by a barrage of unsolicited – and conflicting – advice about how to raise your baby, remember there is no "right" way to raise a child. True, there are universal rules about parenting, such as the need to love your baby, the need to help him fulfil his potential, the need to stimulate him through play and so on. However, there are plenty of ways to meet these needs – not just one.

And what suits one baby might not suit another. The fact that your sister's baby liked a musical toy does not mean that your baby will do so as well. Every child is different, even if he or she is from the same family; what worked for your sister's baby might have no effect on your baby at all. And, of course, there is no point in listening to advice that runs counter to your basic beliefs because you won't be able to follow it.

In some instances, you may totally disagree with someone else's approach to parenting although it's not a bad idea to think about his or her approach. You don't have to do what this person does. Certainly, you shouldn't offer disapproval or negative remarks even though that might be what you really want to say. If in doubt, make a non-critical remark such as "That's interesting" or "I see what you are getting at".

5 things to consider when you receive advice

1 The giver Resist the temptation to reject a piece of advice simply because you find the person giving the opinion irritating. That individual's comments might raise your hackles, but carefully weigh up the advice anyway. You never know, the answer to your problem could lie there. Don't be offensive either to someone because you dislike the advice he or she offers. This person has given a suggestion based on good intentions, so there is no point in snapping at him or her. And you may discover that the advice is extremely helpful the next time.

2 Giver's experience Bear in mind that everybody's experience is limited. Even a parent who has raised five children might not have faced the same parenting challenges that you have to deal with. So an "old-timer" doesn't necessarily have all the answers, despite the fact he or she has been a parent longer than you.

3 Appropriateness You should never attempt to follow advice that makes you feel uncomfortable. For instance, a relative may suggest that you put your baby on to solids to help him settle at night, but you won't do this if you think he's too young to digest solid food. Only listen to advice that fits in with your own ideas.

4 Parenting trends Acknowledge that some parenting habits follow fashions. You may find it hard to imagine that decades ago child-care experts warned a mother not to let her husband play with the baby when he arrived home from work as the baby would become upset by this break in routine.

5 Ownership Never lose sight of the fact that you are the parent. You have the right to tactfully ask people to give you breathing space, to point out that you'd like to think about the difficulty on your own without discussing it with anyone else. Be prepared to say "thank you, but no thank you". It is often difficult to say "no", especially to someone you love and respect, yet that is your right as a parent. You may need to be assertive at times with those giving you advice.

Second-time parent

Just when you have reached the stage where you are confident about managing one child, along comes the second one! Of course you will become adept at being the parent of a two-child family in time, but your stamina, resolution and self-confidence as a parent may be greatly taxed in the early weeks and months. Managing two young children is much more demanding than managing one.

On the other hand, one of the benefits of having two children is that you have lots of experience to draw on, having already raised number one for a while already. Your parenting "L-plates" have long been consigned to the garbage bin, and you are no longer a complete novice. Many of the issues that used to worry you with your first child (for instance, whether she should be bathed every day) no longer bother you this time around (because you know that the occasional missed bath doesn't matter at all). So you are more practised, more knowledgeable and more familiar about raising young children than you were with your first baby. That helps you be a more effective parent. Below, you will find some common challenges and suggestions of how to meet them.

Your toddler insists on having her lunch while you are breastfeeding your new baby.

- Since she probably makes this demand just for the sake of attention, let your toddler sit with you and play a game while you breastfeed her younger sibling. As long as she feels she is getting some interest from you, she'll be happy

Your baby has fallen asleep and it's time to take your two-year-old to parent-and-toddler group.

- Either take your baby with you (hopefully she'll continue to sleep), or on this occasion ask another parent in the group to take your toddler with her or him. You need to be prepared to be flexible, especially when things don't go according to plan.

While shopping with your children in the supermarket, your toddler often runs away

- Leave your older child with a grandparent or other relative or friend while you shop, or else put "reins" on her just for the time you are in the supermarket. One way or another, you need to be able to control your toddler's movements.

Once you have dressed the children and got them ready for a family outing, your toddler wets herself as you close the front door.

- Stay calm; accept that you will arrive later than you originally intended (people expect young families to be late anyway), and change her wet clothes for dry ones. Accidents like this happen frequently with young children.

Your baby is fractious and won't sleep; your older child is moody and whining, and you are expected to visit someone that afternoon.

- You want your plans to go ahead but it is probably better to cancel the arrangement. There is no point in setting yourself and your children up for failure. You can visit another day when everyone is more settled.

Managing with more than one

Bear in mind that most other people know what it's like to have to look after children – they have faced the same challenges that you are facing right now and so they understand how you feel. So if you have to change your plans at the last minute, change them – nobody will be surprised. And if you have to ask for extra help in order to get through the day with two young infants, ask for it – people will be ready to help you out. Rest assured that you are not alone in struggling to meet the practical demands of more than one young child at the same time. The following should help you to cope.

Be adaptable. When it comes to household chores, for example, get rid of as many as you can.

You don't have to do them all. You'll find that the world continues even though your house is less tidy than it was when you had only one baby to look after. If possible, leave a share of domestic chores to your partner, postpone them until there is a more time available, or ignore some of the trivial tasks altogether. Adjusting your domestic routine to include only those tasks that are absolutely necessary enables you to concentrate on the more important business of raising your infant.

Do your best to plan your days, especially during the week, so that there is some sort of structure to your time. While it's true that children and babies are unpredictable – forming their own schedules independently of any hopes you have – some attempt at advanced planning is better than none. For instance, plan that trip to your friend's house, even if you need two days' organising to make it. This helps give you a feeling of control, a sense that you are in charge of your family, rather than your family being in charge of you.

Your confidence and self-esteem as a parent are vital, and it's only natural that you want to know you have the ability to be an effective parent. But you also should recognise you have limitations. Nobody has unlimited supplies of energy and enthusiasm. Take help when it is offered, and ask for help when it is needed. A little friendly assistance goes a long way. You'll be amazed how refreshed you feel after someone else has taken care of your children for an hour or so.

Don't let yourself become a slave to routine. One of the problems in caring for young children is that the routine of feeding, bathing and changing can quickly dominate, making every day seem the same. Don't lose sight of those terrific developmental changes that occur, as your new baby and young child steadily improve their skills. These are easily forgotten in the haze of tiredness, chores and other basic family pressures, so try to keep them in focus.

With the pressures of raising more than one young child, you may go through periods when you feel things are not going according to plan, and this can cause you to have a negative mindset. That's why it is important to concentrate on your achievements and your children's progress.

If you do decide to return to work – whether part time, job-sharing or full time – you need to identify and put in place high-quality, reliable child-care arrangements. That's not always easy to organise, and much depends on what is available locally or close to your place of intended employment. Consider all the options, such as day-care or child minding and calculate the likely cost of each. Check out the availability well before you intend to return to work so that you can make plans with some degree of confidence (see also page 304).

SLEEP MATTERS

Sleep and sleeping

There is much we don't understand about sleep, but one thing we do know is that everybody needs it to function. When we are short of sleep, we lack energy, become irritable and have problems concentrating. Having sufficient sleep at the right times is particularly important for babies. As they sleep, babies are thought to store the information they have encountered during the previous hours and form memories that are key to their learning and development.

The phases of sleep

There are two main types of sleep – light and deep. These can be further divided into a number of phases, which occur in a particular order. At first we enter a state of drowsiness, which is followed by light sleep. We then pass into dream sleep (also known as REM, or rapid eye movement, sleep). Deep sleep follows before we return to dream sleep, then to light sleep and back to drowsiness.

During the dream, or REM, sleep you will be able to see your baby's eyes moving under her eyelids; her body will twitch every so often and her breathing will be irregular. During periods of quiet sleep, her breathing will be regular with deep breaths. Occasionally her whole body will jerk before becoming still again.

All individuals go through the sleep cycle several times a night, waking up every so often. Unless we are disturbed when we wake, we simply turn over and go back to sleep. We don't remember waking and still get a good night's sleep. It is important that babies, too, can learn to settle themselves back to sleep, so that they do not rely on their parents to soothe them every time they wake up. This is encouraged by putting babies down in their cots to sleep when they are still awake rather than waiting until they are asleep.

Baby sleep patterns

Babies are individuals with their own sleep needs. Some babies will need more sleep than others and some will sleep through the night earlier than peers. It is important to remember this individuality and not to compare your baby's sleep routine to that of other babies.

For the first few weeks, babies sleep 16 hours a day on average, with around half of this sleep being at night. Your baby will wake up every few hours for a feed. With time, the duration and timing of your baby's sleeps will start to become more predictable; she will probably have her longest nap in the morning and then two shorter naps in the afternoon.

As your baby gets older, her sleep pattern will gradually change. Between three and six months she will sleep for about 15 hours in total, with most of the sleep being at night and probably three naps during the day. From six months, your baby may have only two daytime naps. By the time she is this age and possibly before, your baby may be able to sleep for up to eight hours in one go at night.

Your baby's sleep needs will continue to diminish. By 12 months, your baby will probably be sleeping for around 14 hours in total. She may sleep for about 10 hours at night, and will probably have two naps during the day, each for up to two hours. She may soon need only one nap a day.

Parents' needs

Most new parents experience sleep deprivation and it can have profound affects on energy levels, mood, concentration and ability to cope. Parents can become irritable and even feel resentful towards their beloved new baby.

It is important to seize opportunities for a nap, even if only for 15 minutes or so. It is tempting to stay up in the evening so you get some "you-time" after your baby has gone to bed but, in the early weeks in particular, it is worth going to bed early when you get the chance in preparation for the night ahead.

During your baby's first few months, it is a good idea to give your baby a feed just before you go to bed. There is then a good chance that you will get a few hours uninterrupted sleep rather than being woken by a hungry baby soon after you go to sleep.

You and your partner will develop a system that works well for you. If you are bottle-feeding, you may alternate nights on duty or feeds during the night. If you are breastfeeding, your partner may be able to give you opportunities to rest at other times or give expressed milk.

It is worth making things as easy for yourself as you can at night so that there is minimal disturbance to you and your baby. If she is due for a feed, try to feed her straightaway so that she doesn't have an opportunity to get really upset and then be more difficult to settle. If you are bottle-feeding, use ready-to-feed formula. Have everything you need for nappy changes close by.

Until your baby sleeps for longer at night, have her bassinet near your bed, which will make attending to her during the night easier.

Safe sleeping

Your baby will spend a lot of her time asleep so it's important that you take steps to protect her. You need to ensure her cot is a safe, secure place to be, and that you follow the recommendations for minimising the risk of SIDS set out below.

Where baby should sleep

For at least the first six months, some experts advise that the ideal is to have your baby sleep in your bedroom right next to your bed in order to reduce the risk of cot death. Whether you breast- or bottle feed, this makes it easy for you to put your baby back in her cot after night feeds.

If your baby was pre-term (before 37 weeks) and/or had a low birth weight (less than 2.5kg), it is much safer for her to sleep in her own cot for the first few months.

In the early weeks, you may wish to put your baby to sleep in something smaller and cosier than a cot, perhaps a bassinet – a newborn baby can look very small and lonely in the wide expanse of a cot. A bassinet also has the advantage of being portable, meaning your baby can feel at home wherever she sleeps. However, she will quite quickly outgrow a bassinet and be ready to move on to a cot.

The cot and mattress

It's not a good idea to use a second-hand cot as you won't know its history or whether it meets current safety standards. If you do, however, decide to use one from a relative or close friend, you must buy a new mattress. Ensure that any new (or used) cot carries a tag proving that it meets Australian safety standards. It should be stable with no sharp edges and the bars should be less than 45-65 mm apart. Ideally, cots should have a side that can be lowered – this means you can put your baby into bed and lift her out easily without putting strain on your back. When you leave your baby in her cot, always remember to secure the cot side in the up position. It is also a good idea to choose a cot with casters on the bottom so you can move it easily.

Cot mattresses come in foam, natural fibre, or with coiled springs, and there are hypoallergenic versions. As long as yours is firm, flat and fits well into the cot frame so that there is no risk of your baby becoming trapped, the choice will depend on how much you want to spend and what material you favour. Foam mattresses generally are the cheapest while natural fibre ones are the longest-lasting. Make sure there is no more than a 25mm gap between the mattress, the cot sides and the ends of the cot. The mattress should have a waterproof cover, which can be easily wiped after leakages.

Your cot should have a moveable mattress base that can be lowered as your baby grows and becomes more active. Once your baby can kneel and later stand, you need to start checking the height of the cot side to ensure it reaches her chest and there is no risk of her falling out. Once the cot side is below her chest, the mattress base needs to be lowered and when the cot side comes to below the level of her chest and the base is at its lowest level, your baby will need a bed. Babies can usually use their cots until they are at least two and sometimes three years old. Some cots can be converted into junior beds, which can often be used up to the age of six or so.

MONITORING YOUR BABY

There are a number of devices that can help you keep in contact with your baby while she's sleeping. Many are portable and can be used wherever your baby sleeps and will alert you to changes in breathing and movements. Some will stimulate a baby if her movements stop.

Never leave a toy in your baby's cot that could present a risk of choking or suffocating or leave your baby alone in her cot with a bottle as this presents a choking risk, too. Once your baby can stand or kneel, toys hanging over the cot, such as mobiles, should be moved so that they are out of reach.

Bedding and nightclothes

Your infant's cot should be free of bumpers, sheepskins, doonas and pillows; these can be overly insulating or potentially dangerous. Fitted cotton sheets are good, as they won't become creased up when your baby moves around. Cotton cellular blankets are ideal, their big advantage being that they can be taken off and put on easily to ensure your baby is kept warm but not too warm. After your baby is a year old, however, you may find a baby bedspread more convenient. As a minimum, you will need four sheets and two to three blankets. Smaller sheets and blankets are available to fit bassinets.

Another option is a baby sleeping bag; this cannot be kicked off by active babies like sheets and blankets can. Ensure that you have the right size bag for your baby; the best one to choose would be based on your baby's weight – not age. If the bag is too big, there is a risk of her slipping down inside. Sleeping bags usually have a tog measurement, or warmth rating; the higher the tog, the warmer the bag. A 2.5 tog bag is generally recommended for standard conditions (a room temperature of 16–20°C). As your baby becomes more active, she may want to move around more than a bag allows. If this is the case with your baby, it is time to change the bag for sheets and blankets.

Generally, your baby should wear a vest, nappy and grow-suit to bed. Her head should be left uncovered – so that heat can be lost as necessary to help prevent her from becoming overheated.

The right temperature

It is important to ensure your baby is warm enough when she sleeps, but it is also important that she is not overheated. The cot should not be placed too near heaters that may cause your baby to overheat.

The recommended temperature for a baby's room is 18°C. At this temperature, a single sheet and two cellular blankets (or a 2.5 tog sleeping bag) should provide enough warmth. The covers should reach no higher than your baby's shoulders.

You can remove a blanket if your baby feels too warm, or add one if she feels too cold. Remember, if the temperature is very warm, you will need to use a bag with a lower tog; in the very warm nights of summer your baby may need only a sheet.

Babies' hands and feet tend to feel colder than the rest of their bodies. To get a true idea of whether your baby is warm enough or not, feel her tummy. If she feels too warm, remove a layer of bedding and recheck her in a few minutes.

Sleep position

Your baby must be put into her cot (or pram) on her back. Research into SIDS has shown that this is the most effective way of reducing its risks. Position her so that her feet touch the foot of her cot; this will prevent her from wriggling down under the bed covers.

Once your baby begins to turn over, you should still put her to sleep on her back but there is no point in repeatedly returning to lay her on her back if she rolls over onto her tummy. By the time she can do this, she is at a lower risk of SIDS anyway and moving her will probably disturb her sleep.

Monitoring your baby

It is completely natural and normal to want to keep an eye on your sleeping baby. Most new parents – and more experienced ones too – feel the need to check every so often.

CO-SLEEPING CONSIDERATIONS

For safety reasons, experts advise that the ideal is to have your baby sleep next to your bed and that, particularly during the first three months even if breastfeeding, you should put your baby back in her cot after night feeds.Never co-sleep if you or your partner is a smoker (this increases the risk of SIDS).

If you are keen to co-sleep, you must bear the following in mind.

- Your mattress should be flat and firm.
- The bedding and clothing should be light (and the room not too warm).
- Your baby must not be able to fall out of bed or get trapped between the mattress and the bed frame or the wall. Also, you must make sure that she cannot be covered by a pillow or bed covers.
- Both parents must be aware that the baby is in bed with them.
- Once you have fed your baby you should place her on her back for sleep.
- Babies should not sleep next to other children or be left in a bed on their own.
- You should not sleep with your baby if you are very tired or if you have drunk alcohol or taken drugs or medication that may make you sleep heavily.
- You should never fall asleep with your baby on the sofa or in a chair, as this is associated with an increased risk of SIDS.

Using a baby monitor will keep you in constant contact with your baby and so help to reassure you. Baby monitors allow you to listen to your baby when she is in another room. They can be particularly reassuring if you have a large house and your baby's room is not nearby. The most basic monitors will allow you to simply listen to your baby; others have lights to represent the baby's sounds; some show the temperature in the baby's room. Various other features can be found and it is worth looking at the types available to ensure you find one that meets all your concerns and needs.

Breathing monitors are also available – a sound alarms if a baby stops breathing. However, these can cause additional anxiety if you are constantly listening out for the sound, particularly if there are false alarms.

As time passes, you will probably start to feel less anxious about your baby at night. Rest assured you are not alone in your concerns; most if not all parents share them.

Co-sleeping

There are benefits to sleeping with a baby – the closeness of being together and the convenience of having the baby close by for feeds during the night. In terms of feeding, it has been shown that breastfeeding mothers who sleep with their babies can get more sleep during the night and also feed for longer. In addition, many babies who co-sleep with their parents seem to sleep better, too.

Co-sleeping, however, is associated with a number of risks related to accidents and also to overheating (see box, left).

Other factors, too, may make you decide against it. You may find it difficult to sleep when your baby is in bed with you. Also, your baby may find it difficult to sleep when you are not there, which will present problems when you want to go out for an evening and again, later, when the time comes for sleeping in her own bed. Co-sleeping also can affect lovemaking.

Managing sleep

Babies differ in their needs for sleep; this is to some extent part of their individual make-ups. However, you can set the scene for your baby to sleep well and in a way that allows you to get the sleep you need, too. In the early weeks this will mean making the environment conducive to sleep, but soon there will be the opportunity to establish a routine that will hopefully provide the foundation for settled sleep in the months and years to come.

An individual approach

As with other aspects of baby care, your approach to bedtime may be more flexible or structured than your peers'. However, many parents find that their babies respond well to sleeping routines for day and night. While you may feel, particularly in the early months, that you do not wish to impose such a routine, it is worth bearing in mind that patterns set in the first year or so will set the pattern for the years to come. You may be quite happy when your baby is small for her to stay around until you go to bed but you may find later that you need to establish an earlier bedtime. This is to ensure that you get some time to yourself, and that your child gets enough sleep in preparation for all the activities in the day ahead. This is likely to prove difficult if your baby has never had a bedtime routine before.

Whether you start out being flexible or try to impose a strict schedule, your approach will evolve, not only as a result of your own attitudes but also in response to your baby's needs. Your baby's development relies in part on her getting enough sleep when she needs it. The habits that you establish early on will be key to setting a sleeping pattern that meets your own needs and those of your baby. You will probably be given plenty of advice by friends and family on how and when to get your baby to sleep; in the end you will find your own routine together. However, there are some points that may help you along the way.

The early weeks

Your newborn baby will sleep a good deal of the time; she will have frequent naps and wake often during the night for feeds. In these first few weeks, you will both be settling down and getting to know each other. At this stage it is a little early to try to establish a formal routine, but it is not too early to take the first steps to helping your baby sleep well.

Recognising sleepiness

It is important to look for signs that your baby is ready for sleep. Putting her to bed at the right time will give her the best chance of settling off to sleep peacefully. If she misses her sleep time, your baby may become alert and active again even though she is actually overtired.

In the early weeks your baby will tire quickly and easily. You will learn to recognise the signs of sleepiness – this can include rubbing the eyes, pulling on an ear or developing faint dark circles under her eyes – and you should act immediately. This ensures she gets the all-important sleep she needs for her development.

Allowing your baby to settle herself

Your newborn baby will wake frequently during the night, often because she needs a feed. Later, when she is older, she will still wake periodically although she will not need feeding. If she learns how, she will be able to settle herself back to sleep at these later times without becoming distressed or needing attention but if your baby becomes reliant on you to comfort her and settle her off to sleep in the early months, she will always need you to help her to get back to sleep when she wakes during the night.

A newborn needs a good deal of sleep, both in the day and during the night and your baby will easily drop off to sleep in your arms, often during a feed. Beyond the first few weeks or so, however, it is important to give your baby the opportunity to settle herself off to sleep. This means putting her in her cot

5 ways to help your baby unwind

1 **Talking** Tell your baby it is time for bed and talk to her soothingly as you get her ready. Although she will not yet understand your words, they will become familiar and pleasurable as part of her routine.

2 **Bath** Many babies find a bath pleasurable and relaxing although some babies are keener on baths than others. If your baby gets very excited or cries at bath-time, it is worth bathing her at another time and using other activities to calm her and prepare her for bed. After the bath, you can change your baby's nappy and put on her pyjamas.

3 **Stories** It is never too early to start sharing stories with your baby. Even before she can understand the words or pictures, she will love cuddling up to you and listening to your voice. She will also respond to the rhythm of nursery rhymes and enjoy their familiarity.

4 **Singing songs** Babies love music and lullabies. You may choose a particular song that means it is bedtime. Your baby will come to recognise it and associate it with sleep. You also can play some soothing music. Some babies like to go to the sleep to the sound of music playing softly.

5 **Cuddles** This is a lovely way to end this time together and make your baby feel reassured and loved before she goes to sleep.

for the night when she is sleepy but still awake rather than waiting until she is asleep. This also applies to nap times during the day. Your baby will sometimes need comfort, but from three months or so she will probably be able to drift off to sleep happily on her own. At the age of around six months, when she will probably be able to manage without feeds during the night, she will be more likely to sleep through if she is able to settle herself off.

Make night and day different
It is worth showing your baby the difference between night and day from early on (two weeks or so). In this way she will associate bedtime with peace and sleep and daytime with activity and wakefulness.

It is very important to make night feeds as quiet and peaceful as possible. No matter the room you are in, keep the lights low and talk to a minimum. Do not be tempted to turn on the television or radio. If you want to leave a light on for your baby, make sure the room is only dimly lit. If daylight causes a problem with early waking, you may wish to hang dark curtains to keep most of the light out.

During the day, don't be afraid to feed your baby in a lively and noisy environment.

Create a sleep-inducing environment
It is important that your baby feels safe and secure before she goes to sleep. Some babies feel cosier in a small space in the early weeks, so you may want to put your baby to sleep in a bassinet.

Your baby's room should be quiet, but don't feel the rest of the house must be silent. The normal background noise of a family home should soothe her. She may also like to hear the radio or music quietly playing as she settles down for sleep. Make sure your baby is clothed appropriately and her room kept at the correct temperature both for comfort and for safety reasons.

The use of comfort items
You may wish to give your baby something familiar to help her to settle to sleep – perhaps a favourite blanket or toy.

Or you may find a dummy soothes your baby. When she is disturbed during sleep she may start sucking the dummy again and drift back. Recent research has shown that use of a dummy seems to reduce the risk of SIDS and possibly reduces the influence of known risk factors in the sleep environment. This positive effect of dummies is postulated to result from the dummy keeping the infant's tongue from falling backwards, blocking the upper airway. However, if your baby is being breastfed, avoid giving her dummy until the age of one month so that she can get used to feeding.

There are drawbacks to using a dummy. It may fall out during the night, in which case your baby may become distressed when her sleep is disturbed and she cannot find the dummy. Also she will probably want the dummy in the daytime, too, which may affect her vocalising. And you may have problems in future years persuading her to give her dummy up.

The bedtime routine

From just a few weeks of age you can start to familiarise your baby with the concept of bedtime and start to develop your own night routine. Although you cannot determine how much sleep your baby needs, you can influence when she sleeps and how well she settles down to sleep.

By now, you will have discovered the ways your baby shows you she is sleepy. Be guided by this when you set her bedtime and times for daytime naps. Although you do not need to be absolutely rigid in keeping to these times, it is a good idea to stick to them as much as you can.

Making the routine

There are no rules about establishing a bedtime routine; what is important is to find one that suits your baby and your own lifestyle. Keep your routine simple so that it becomes familiar to your baby and also so that babysitters and other carers can easily replicate it.

It is important to set the scene for bed by making the period before it quiet and relaxing (see box, page 160). Prior to this time you may wish to encourage a burst of activity to ensure your baby has used up

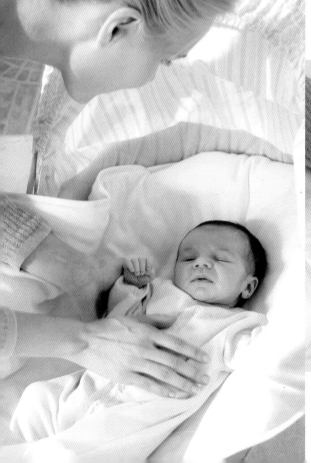

plenty of energy in preparation for sleep. After this playful session, the atmosphere should become quiet and calming.

The more you can stick to your own routine the better. Your baby will enjoy this special time you spend together and come to anticipate it with pleasure.

Other ways to settle your baby ready for bedtime:

◆ *A walk in the pram* This can be a calming and soothing way to prepare for bedtime. However, it is important that you do not use this as a means of getting your baby to sleep before bed. This will interfere with her learning how to settle herself.

◆ *Massage* A gentle massage before bed can relax and calm your baby. It can be done from the age of two weeks or so.

◆ *Swaddling* A successful strategy for getting many a baby to sleep, this involves wrapping your baby in a sheet or blanket to stop her from jerking herself awake (see page 34).

In the cot

As you put your baby in her cot talk to her gently to calm her. Reassure her that you are not far away. You may, like some parents, prefer to potter around in your baby's room while she goes to sleep. Over time, you should reduce the time spent doing this and then start to move around in the next room instead so that your baby is still reassured you are nearby but she is not dependent on you being in the room. However, you may, like many parents, choose to leave the room straightaway.

If your baby cries out for you, give her a few minutes to settle before you return and talk to her soothingly. Don't leave her too long – you don't want her to become distressed and to associate bedtime with being upset. Pat her on the back but, ideally, do not get her out of the cot. Keep the lights low and noise to a minimum. In this way, you will disturb her as little as possible and encourage her to drop off to sleep on her own.

From three months

You will probably have started to introduce your bedtime routine by now. Try to stick with it, even if you are away. Also, if you are keen for your baby to learn to settle herself, remember to keep putting her to bed when she is drowsy rather than being tempted to comfort her until she sleeps.

By now, you will have more idea when your baby is ready for bed and will be able to set a more fixed bedtime. Sometimes your baby may still be wide awake at this time but you will probably find she is ready for sleep once you start preparations for bed. If she stays up past her bedtime, she may become overtired and yet be alert again. Keeping to these times (with some flexibility) for both night sleep and daytime naps will ensure that she gets the sleep she needs when she needs it.

From six months

If you have a routine in place, stick to it. By now your baby will know what happens at bedtime and what these activities mean – that it is time for bed. Not only will your baby have a routine for bed, but you will also find her daytime activities of sleeping, eating and playing take on a predictable pattern.

Sleeping during the day

Babies continue to need naps until the age of one or so, and many for some time after that. Sleeping during the day helps your baby to make the most of her activities and, if timed right, will help her sleep well at night. Keeping her awake in the day in the hope that she will need more sleep at night won't work; an overtired baby sleeps less soundly than a well-rested one. The timing of the last nap is also important – it should not be too close to bedtime.

Setting a routine for naps during the day suits many babies. You will find over time at what points in the day your baby tends to become sleepy and will be able to time her naps accordingly. Some parents like to set up naps by having a quiet calming time before sleep. If your baby doesn't settle easily for naps during the day, set the scene as you do at bedtime by talking to her quietly or singing a lullaby and then dimming the lights to calm her.

Twins

It's tricky enough to settle any baby off to sleep, but it's often even harder with twins. It is a good idea to put your babies to sleep at the same time from the outset so that they establish a routine together. Imposing a sleeping timetable will ensure that your babies follow the same or similar body clock. While some twins may have very different metabolisms and/or personalities, which lead to different eating and sleeping habits, a routine will certainly add more structure and be an improvement than simply muddling through. And once your babies get into the habit of sleeping at certain set times, it will be easier to spot if they are sick. If they invariably sleep every afternoon for two hours and one day for just 20 minutes, you will be alerted to a possible problem that has kept them awake.

With two babies, it's difficult to get through the day without a rest period, especially if you are breastfeeding. If your babies regularly have a long afternoon nap, it should be possible to sleep yourself at the same time. It's important to prioritise sleep over household chores, since your health and well-being are more important.

Whether it is better to place twins in the same or separate cots from the start is really up to the individual parents; different solutions work for different couples. At least in the early weeks, twins usually settle more quickly and calm easily if they are placed side by side in the same cot. If you choose to put your twins to sleep in the same cot they will comfort each other and you'll also probably be able to keep them sleeping near to you longer, which is recommended. The twins should be positioned for sleep on their backs and with their feet touching the end of the bed (see also page 157). If you want to separate your babies, use a fixed cot divider (not a rolled up blanket).

As they get older, the twins may start to disturb each other, particularly if they have different sleep patterns and tend to wake at different times. At the age of three months or so you will probably find they need more space anyway, so this may be a good time to put them in their own cots. Keep the cots in view of each other so that the babies can still communicate and keep each other company.

If you are often disturbed by your two babies waking at different times during the night, it is worth waking the other twin when one wakes up for a feed. They will hopefully settle together afterwards and give you more time to sleep.

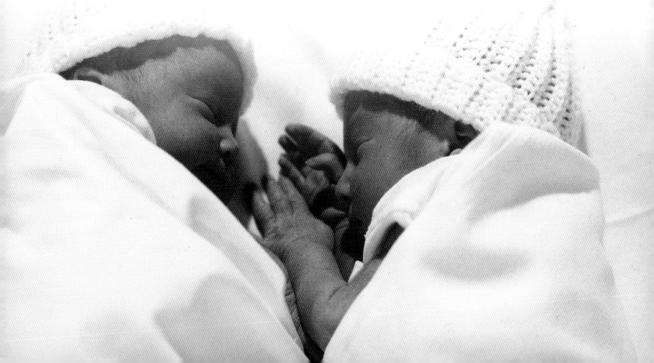

Sleep problems

All babies differ in their sleep needs and patterns and most babies will have a sleep-related problem at some time or another. A lack of sleep will interfere with your baby's enjoyment of life and with her learning. Sleep problems, particularly night and early morning waking, will also prevent you from getting the good night's sleep you need. So it is in everyone's interests to deal with sleep problems promptly and effectively.

Difficulty getting to sleep

As with all sleep issues, how quickly a child settles at night will rely to some extent on the individual child, but there are ways to help things along. If your baby is not settling easily it is worth revisiting your bedtime routine to ensure you are setting the scene for a good night's sleep (see page 161).

If you find your baby has problems getting off to sleep, it is important to leave her for a few minutes to settle by herself – you will probably need to let her cry for a while. Say goodnight and leave the room. If you return to her, avoid getting her out of the cot and try to disturb her as little as possible. Make the intervals between your checks a little longer each time. When you return talk to her for a minute or so and then leave again.

If your baby has become used to you being around when she goes to sleep and you want to change this, try moving a little further from her cot every night until you are outside the room when she goes to sleep. In this way she will become used to going to sleep on her own without feeling that she has been abandoned.

Many babies like to hear background noise elsewhere in the house, so don't worry about the TV or radio or other normal household sounds. Playing quiet music can soothe babies off to sleep. Story tapes can also be helpful – although a young baby will not understand the story, she may be lulled by the quiet voice.

Night waking

This is perfectly normal in the early months, as your baby will often be waking for a feed. Once she gets older and is physically able to sleep through without a feed, she may be waking as part of her normal sleep cycle. It is at such times, when you have ruled out the other reasons for waking (see below), that you can take steps to encourage her to go back to sleep on her own.

When your baby wakes during the night it is important to run through the checklist (see box, page 166). As your baby gets older, you will learn to recognise her different cries and will often have a good idea what is wrong.

To help your baby to sleep through, keep to your bedtime routine and remember to emphasise the difference between night and day – after a while it can be tempting to get your baby out of bed and lull her back to sleep while you watch night-time TV or a video. Remember, however, that night-time should be kept quiet and calm.

It may be better to avoid music as a soother for your baby during the night – if she comes to rely on

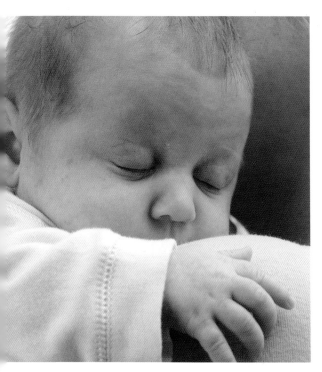

it to settle off to sleep she won't be able to manage without it. You will be called upon to get up and switch on the CD player every time she wakes during the night. However, some people advocate the use of familiar objects, such as a particular blanket, as soothers to comfort a child when the parents are not there during the night.

Three to six months

Once your baby can manage without a feed during the night, she will probably be able to sleep through. To do this she must learn to settle herself to sleep without your help. She may cry for a while when she wakes, but eventually she should go back to sleep. Most parents find leaving a baby to cry for long periods too distressing. However, there are other, less extreme, ways of dealing with night-time waking and you will find an approach that suits you.

Six months onwards

Sometimes, babies who have slept well in the past, start to wake at night. Separation anxiety is a normal feature of development, and can be noticed from six months or later. It may be reflected in night waking – your baby may wake as part of her normal sleep cycle, but then become anxious because you are not there. It is still important when your baby wakes to give her the chance to go back to sleep on her own, but it is also right that you should not wait too long to return to her. Left for too long, she may become distressed and then find it more difficult to settle.

From this age, babies also start to become more active and mobile. Sometimes, this means they have problems sleeping peacefully, because they wake up every so often to move around. It is important that you stick to your approach for night waking – being consistent is likely to be rewarded sooner or later.

Your baby may suffer discomfort with teething (see page 200), which may cause her to wake during the night. It is still worth leaving her for a while to settle down so she may get through teething without developing a habit of waking during the night. If your baby uses a dummy, leave several in the cot so that she may be able to find one if she wakes up. By now, you will usually know whether your baby

6 reasons for waking

1 Your baby needs a feed or is thirsty.

2 She has a dirty nappy.

3 She is too hot or too cold.

4 Your baby Is teething (from around the age of six months).

5 Your baby Is unwell (see box page 340 for what to look for).

6 Your baby simply misses you and wants your company.

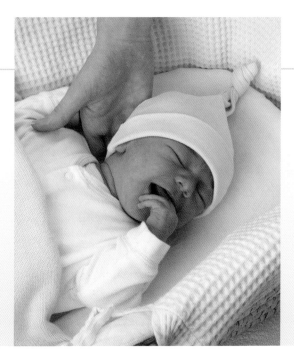

needs a feed. If she wakes and one is not due, don't feed her to help her settle; if you think she may be thirsty give her water only. She won't need much encouragement to develop a pattern of waking for feeds that she doesn't need. If your baby wakes during the night and cries for you, one option is controlled crying (see below).

Controlled crying
Appropriate from the age of about six months, this involves returning to your baby's cot when she cries, but leaving her in the cot and just talking to her soothingly. Do not pick her up or cuddle her. You should also avoid putting on the light so that you disturb her surroundings as little as possible. In this way you can reassure your baby that you are still around and can reassure yourself that she is well.

The first night she cries you should wait five minutes before going to see her; the next night ten minutes, and so on, until eventually she will, hopefully, go back to sleep on her own. This can be difficult to do, but it is very likely that, if you stick to your plan, the crying will stop in a week or two.

An alternative involves getting the baby out of the cot and rocking her to settle her. Some experts advocate this approach, as long as there is a routine in place for the baby's bedtime and she is able to get herself off to sleep when she first goes to bed. After a few weeks she should start to settle herself back to sleep during the night, too. However, this approach goes against the advice of minimal disturbance and there is a chance that the baby will become reliant on you being there when she wakes at night.

Early waking and other sleep problems
Some babies simply need less sleep than others and will always wake early no matter what you do, but there are some measures that may help you, and your baby, get more sleep. Gradually making the bedtime a little later (up to an hour later) may help older babies. However, some babies may wake just as early as they did previously but instead of being refreshed, may feel grumpy and tired.

As your baby gets older, you may find that she needs a little less sleep during the day and you can try shortening her naps or even eliminating one. However, it is important that she still has sufficient sleep during the day or she may become overtired. When your baby first wakes, it is worth leaving her for a few minutes to see whether she settles herself back to sleep. Alternatively, she may amuse herself happily in her cot for a while, giving you the opportunity for a little more much-needed sleep.

Try putting some music on for your baby – this may help to settle her back to sleep and in the light months of summer, when the sunlight wakes some babies before they are ready, it is worth hanging dark curtains or black-out blinds in your baby's room.

Rather than trying more tactics to change your baby's early waking habit, or continuing to go to bed late and denying yourself the sleep you need, you may just have to accept that your baby is an early riser. Going to bed earlier yourself will mean you are more able to cope with the early mornings.

When your child is older, she may start to wake during the night for different reasons. These include:

◆ *Disruption to the normal routine* Any change in her usual routine or circumstances, going on holiday or being moved to a new room, for example, can be reflected in disturbed sleeping patterns. Your child may not only awake early but may also have trouble falling asleep.

◆ *Teething* (see above)

◆ *Being afraid of the dark* This is quite common and can usually be helped by reassurance and some subdued lighting or a night light in the room.

◆ *Nightmares and night terrors* For toddlers, unpleasant dreams can be particularly distressing because they experience them as real more than we do and continue to remember bad dreams, remaining upset and afraid. Nightmares are usually brief and followed by a period of wakefulness when your toddler will need comforting. They usually occur during the second half of the night. If your toddler has come into your bedroom, take her back to her bed. Make sure everything is calm before she goes back. To help forestall bad dreams, it is a good idea to limit stimulation such as television viewing, loud music or noisy games before bedtime.

7 sleep promoters

1   Ensure your baby's last nap of the day is not too late and also that she is not sleeping for too long during her daytime naps.

2   Have a period of activity before the calm time of your bedtime routine begins.

3   Stick to your bedtime routine.

4   Set the bedtime for when your baby starts to become sleepy.

5   Give your baby the chance to settle down to sleep on her own – this means not feeding her or playing with her until she sleeps.

6   Make your baby's room a peaceful haven with dim lighting (try using a night light or leaving a light on outside the room).

7   Rock a fretful baby.

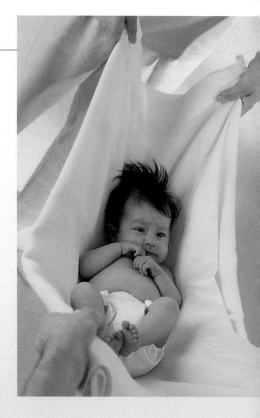

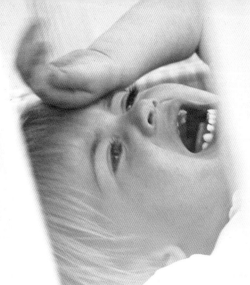

In contrast, night terrors usually occur during the first half of the night. Managing them is quite different to nightmares (see box, below). In most cases night terrors are part of normal sleep development; they will not harm your child. If, however, the terrors seem prolonged or violent, check with your maternal and child health nurse.

◆ *Feeling worried and anxious* Many things may make a toddler feel anxious, for example a new brother or sister, a parent being away from home or sleeping in a strange room. (If your child sleeps in a strange bed, say when you go on holiday or visit a relative, taking some favourite toys for the bed will be reassuring.) In such circumstances, it is important to make sure your child has plenty of attention to make her feel loved. And, if possible, try to find out what is worrying her. Stick to your routines, but be aware that she will need extra reassurance when she goes to bed and if she wakes at night.

Being consistent in your approach to bedtime and night waking is important to help your child settle back into a pattern. But do insist that she stays in her bed. Even if you need to go back into her room repeatedly to reassure her, you will avoid a subsequent sleep problem. After a couple nights of allowing your toddler to sleep with you, you may find that she quickly develops the habit of waking during the night and either visiting you or else crying until you take her into your bed. Besides interrupting your sleep, you will not sleep as well with your toddler in bed with you. The result: instead of being simply tired, you will be very tired.

It certainly helps to always make bedtime a positive experience. You should never send your child to bed feeling unhappy – for example, as a punishment or after a scolding. Don't insist either she goes to sleep straightaway.

Occasionally, sleep problems are related to medical conditions. If you have any concerns, seek advice from your family doctor.

MORE **ABOUT** | night terrors

These usually occur less frequently than nightmares, but many young children will have one at some time. They typically occur when your child is ill or overtired. Night terrors can cause children to sweat, scream and thrash about. Their eyes may be open and they may sit up and even talk, although they are still asleep. The scary part for your toddler is that she doesn't quite know where she is, who you are, or what's happening to her. If your toddler is having a night terror, it is important to sit beside her until she returns to peaceful sleep but not to hug or soothe her, as she may mistake who you are. In about a half-hour, she will generally fall back asleep.

CRYING AND RESPONDING

Purposeful crying

Since babies can't talk and explain what they want or what is upsetting them, crying is their way of communicating. Whether by design or evolutionary progress, crying serves the human species well. Your baby was born already knowing how to cry loudly and in a way that you will certainly find annoying. It is bothersome to you, no doubt, so you will refocus your attention on her. Crying surely prevents you from getting carried away with another task and forgetting about your baby.

Unfortunately, when your newborn cries – and newborns and young infants on average cry two to three hours a day – it is a general alarm that signals only that your baby requires your consideration. But it doesn't reveal exactly what it is that she wants or needs. In time, as you get to know her better, you will become quite good at deciphering your baby's meaning and will be able to make a very good guess as to the reason for her cries.

Likely causes

Crying that comes a long time (over two hours) after the last feeding should first be assumed to be hunger. So if you are feeding on demand, feed your baby. (If instead of demand feeding you prefer a fixed interval feeding schedule and it is not yet time for the next feed, try to stall your baby by using other methods to calm her (see pages 174–5). Try to make it until the time for the next feeding.) If hunger was the cause for her crying, your baby now will be calm. On the other hand, if your baby continues to cry after an attempt at feeding, look for another cause.

Crying that begins a short while (less than two hours) after your baby's last feeding is less likely to be due to hunger. Look first for another reason for her cries: Does she have a dirty or wet nappy? Does she simply want to be held by you? Is she overstimulated? Is she bored? Is she hot or otherwise uncomfortable? Perhaps she needs to be burped or

3 recognisable cries

Babies cry whenever they want something or when something bothers them and generally these are expressed by a repertoire of different cries.

1 **Hunger cries** are both braying and rhythmic and often are accompanied by kicking or other rhythmic movements.

2 **Pain cries** are louder and more intense than other cries.

3 **Boredom cries** are irregular and uncoordinated. Your baby will pause in between cries to see if you respond

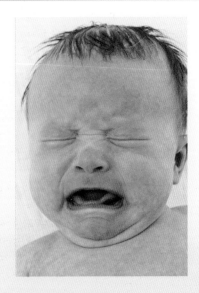

to satisfy her urge to suck. In succession, try checking her nappy, picking her up, winding her, eliminating unnecessary activity, initiating some play, removing or loosening some of her clothes and/or blankets, and letting her suck on your finger or a dummy. If one of these solutions stops her crying, you may now conclude that you have found the cause of her distress. But if you have tried them all with no relief, then try feeding her. Even though it may be sooner than you expected, her hunger, as you know, does not arrive only on an exact schedule.

Less likely causes of crying

Most of your newborn's crying will be readily solved by feeding her or providing one of these simple comforts discussed above. When these don't work, it may be a feeding problem such as GE (gastro-oesophageal reflux, see box), a milk allergy, a sign of illness, colic or chronic hunger.

A feeding problem

Crying babies who are hungry are typically quite content the moment they begin receiving milk. But what does it mean if your infant begins crying while you are in the process of feeding her? If her crying begins a few moments after starting sucking, it could be that your baby is having difficulty latching on to the breast (see pages 74–5) so in spite of her efforts to suck, she is getting little milk. Similarly, in the beginning days of breastfeeding, just as your milk supply arrives, your child may not be able to get much milk from your engorged breast. The pattern of crying will be the same as for the baby who is not latching on well.

If, however, your baby sucks strongly at the breast or bottle for a brief period (a minute or so) and then stops sucking and begins to cry, she may be "impatient". Many breastfed babies, once they reach a month or two of age, get quite upset when the milk comes slowly and steadily from the breast,

MORE **ABOUT** | gastro-oesophageal reflux

Babies with gastro-oesophageal (GE) reflux regurgitate stomach contents (stomach juices and partially digested milk) up to the oesophagus and mouth. While most babies with GE reflux have no discomfort from vomiting, a small group of such babies experience a burning pain in the oesophagus when reflux occurs. Reflux and crying occur during feeding or shortly thereafter.

instead of in larger amounts all at once. Your baby may be saying to you, "I want all my milk right away (not a little at a time)." Bottlefed babies may have the same type of impatient reaction if the hole of the nipple is too small or is clogged, so that the milk comes out more slowly than she desires. If you suspect this problem, buy a nipple with a larger hole or poke holes in the head of the nipple with a clean pin (see page 71).

You may think that it would be difficult to determine which of these causes is operating in your baby if she cries during feeding. However, it is not very hard to distinguish one from the others. The first two reasons for crying – poor latching on and breast engorgement – occur in the first days of breast feeding. Impatience, which usually doesn't show up until several weeks of age, is readily diagnosed. If it occurs in a breastfed baby, your efforts to calm her down (after briefly stopping the feeding) will ultimately succeed in her feeding well and happily. In a bottlefed baby, the cause becomes obvious if the crying is cured by a bigger nipple hole size.

Pain due to reflux is dramatic and is not easily solved by the measures that succeed well with impatience. GE reflux should be suspected if your infant possets often; if she does not, it is unlikely.

Discomfort due to milk allergy

It would seem logical that the intestinal pain experienced by your baby if she has a cow's milk intolerance would also occur soon after the start of a feeding. However, this is usually not the case. Only a small minority of infants who react to cow's milk have a true allergy, if one uses the strict medical definition of the word. An allergic reaction to cow's milk occurs soon after exposure to the allergen, usually taking place any time between a few minutes after starting the feeding and up to an hour afterwards. The reaction can consist of only crying, but usually there are other symptoms: vomiting, paleness and, less often, wheezing or signs of severe allergy (hives, shortness of breath, shock).

Interestingly, most children with reactions to cow's milk are not allergic but "intolerant" of cow's milk protein. This is not a true allergy because such children do not produce antibodies against cow's milk proteins of the IgE class (to satisfy the medical definition of allergy) and the reaction does not occur shortly after exposure. The crying from cow's milk intolerance is delayed so long (anywhere from one to twenty-four hours after exposure) that the temporal connection to drinking cow's milk proteins – in formula or in breastmilk after maternal cow's milk ingestion – is easily missed.

Fussy spells and colic

Babies with fussy spells and colic (see also page 194) feed very well and their crying does not occur during feeding. The fits of night-time crying are long and loud, but do not centre about feeding time. Rare causes of chronic fussiness in well-appearing babies include infant glaucoma (elevated pressure within the eyeball) and hair-tourniquet syndrome (a strand of hair or a fabric thread somehow ends up tightly encircling a toe or finger and by constriction, causes pain by reducing blood flow to the digit).

Illness

If your baby has a sore throat, stomach-ache or other aches and pains associated with illness, she will be whingy and perhaps cry excessively. Signs of being sick often will be present: fever, cough, runny nose and diarrhoea. Your sick baby will likely feed less well than usual, but her crying will be at times other than while feeding. And if your doctor recommends giving her paracetamol (Panadol and others), the medication will often stop the crying by relieving the pain.

Chronic hunger

While a breastfed baby may cry excessively when she is not getting enough milk to satisfy her, crying does not signal a baby who is not getting enough milk on a daily basis. Such babies are inactive, perhaps to conserve energy, and seem accustomed to their low-calorie diets. A reduced intake of milk is usually identified only at your baby's check-up, when it is discovered that she has not gained sufficient weight.

Responding to crying

Whatever the reason for her wailing, you will want to soothe your distressed baby. Responding to her when she is upset shows your baby that you love her and strengthens the bonds between you. Comforting her also gives you a good feeling inside. But if you pick her up and attend to her as soon as she cries, won't you "spoil" her?

Spoiling refers to the belief that it is wrong to quickly respond to all your baby's cries and that by doing so, your baby does not learn how to calm herself and thus becomes dependent on you to do so. Bear in mind that each baby is born with a unique temperament comprised of variations in how outgoing, fearful, upbeat, anxious, stubborn and sensitive she is (see page 139). Although not every aspect of your baby's basic make-up is obvious at birth, some personality traits are already evident. For example, she may be content to lie quietly in her cot for long periods or she may require a lot of your efforts to soothe her.

Believers in spoiling suggest that your constant attention to your baby's cries will lead her to depend on you for calming and to demand your presence continually. However, it is more likely that the opposite is true: your baby needs frequent tending to because, by nature and temperament, she is the type of child who requires more soothing. While it certainly is fine to give your crying baby a few moments in which she can try to calm herself, once it is clear that this is not working, feel free to pick her up. You are not spoiling her; you are merely giving more comfort to a baby who needs more comforting.

When to respond

Becoming skilled at how to best respond to your crying child comes with time. Obviously, the extremes should be avoided. Rushing to soothe her every time she cries will prevent her from learning how to self-calm. Yet if you seldom answer her cries she may suffer pain, illness, hunger or injury unnecessarily. The comfort you provide when she needs you confirms your love for her and forms the basis for her learning to love others. Part of the art of parenting involves finding the happy middle ground. If you are unsure about when to quickly go to your crying baby (or toddler), here is a guide:

Respond promptly when your baby:

- Is hungry. (This does not apply to toddlers who are stalling at bedtime by asking for food.)
- Is ill.
- Has an injury or is in pain.
- Is afraid or having difficulty in a social situation.

Respond only after waiting

(to see if your baby will calm herself) when:

- The cries don't signal anything urgent.
- You are imposing a feeding schedule and she is hungry.
- You are teaching your baby to soothe herself.
- You are in the middle of doing something and can't leave it immediately.
- You need some time to yourself (going to the toilet, showering etc.).
- You are teaching her good sleep habits (falling asleep by herself, not being fed during the night).

Try not to respond at all when:

- Your toddler is having a temper tantrum.
- Your baby is very overtired but refusing to sleep.
- Your baby (or toddler) is demanding your attention for a non-urgent matter and you decide you cannot or do not want to stop what you are doing to attend to her. Many situations involving separation anxiety fit into this category. For example, if you have to leave to go to work, she may begin crying immediately upon being put down. Picking her up only delays the inevitable if you still have to leave. Interestingly, when your older baby or toddler realises she will not get her way in such a situation, she will quickly calm down if you simply ignore her.

Ways of responding

By far the best way of calming your upset baby is to pick her up and hold her. Singing, talking in a soft, soothing voice, and for some newborns and young infants, swaddling – also help. Placing her in a dark, dimly lit, quiet room or going out for a walk also may be effective. See opposite page for more suggestions. You will come to know your baby best, and before long, will discover the most successful ways of calming her.

Dummies

Whether it is good or bad to give a baby a dummy to satisfy a strong sucking urge is not entirely clear-cut. Numerous studies have demonstrated that infants who use dummies do not continue to breastfeed as long as those who don't (see box) although there is also evidence that dummy use has a modest benefit in decreasing the chance a baby will suffer sudden infant death (see page 63).

On the negative side, though, dummy use has been related to a small increase in risk for recurrent ear infections. Also, if used past the age of two years, it may result in the forward splaying of the front teeth, possibly requiring orthodontic correction ("braces") at an older age.

Breastfeeding mothers can keep their babies calm by allowing extended breastfeeding sessions, the extra minutes of sucking being primarily non-nutritive. But this solution is not only time consuming, it can result in sore, cracked nipples. Another way to resolve the sucking urge problem is to let your baby suck on your finger. The pinky can be held palm side up, bent in the shape of a letter "C" and inserted into your baby's mouth until the tip of your finger rests against her hard palate. (It is a good idea to keep the pinky's nail short.) However, substituting your finger for the dummy doesn't prevent nipple confusion (if, in fact, it is a real phenomenon) and still requires you to hold your infant for long periods of time. With all the above considered, using a dummy may not seem so unreasonable thing for you to do in this particular type of baby.

MORE **ABOUT** | dummies and breastfeeding

Breastfeeding advocates believe that by sucking on a dummy, a baby sucks less at the breast and therefore the mother's milk supply can be affected. Additionally, they believe that infants may suffer from "nipple confusion", and may not suck properly at the breast because of their experience of sucking on a dummy. However, these conclusions may not be warranted. All the studies forming the basis for this negative view of dummies have a large flaw: in these observational studies, instead of investigators randomly assigning babies to one group or the other, the parents decided whether or not to use a dummy with their babies. This is problematic because babies vary in the intensity of their need to suck, and it is quite possible that the infants given dummies by their parents were those who had the most intense sucking urges. In other words, a baby who cried often because she needed to suck on something would be more likely to be given a dummy. So what the above trials may be showing is that babies with a strong urge to suck do not breastfeed for as long as those who have a less intense urge. These babies may be different from other babies and it may be their personal characteristics, not being given a dummy, that determines when weaning occurs. Moreover, a baby who is always eager to suck will breastfeed long and often. Perhaps her mother stops nursing sooner than other mothers because she finds it too time consuming. Furthermore, no evidence yet presented has documented that nipple confusion actually occurs in newborns.

Soothing techniques

Holding

Picking up your baby and holding her close to your body, preferably so she can hear your heartbeat or you singing, or carrying her in a sling or carrier will provide reassurance.

Bath

Some babies respond to being placed in a bath and having warm water gently splashed over their bodies. Alternatively, you could take your baby into a large bath with you and hold her close in the warm water.

Swaddling

Being snuggly wrapped replicates a baby's experience in the womb and can help to send a crying baby off to sleep. See page 34 for step-by-step guidance.

Stimulation

Some babies are easily bored! Showing your baby a brightly coloured toy or mobile or playing some music may help to distract her and stop the crying.

Rocking

Gentle motion such as being rocked in a bouncy chair, against your shoulder or in your lap; or swung in a hammock (see page 167) or being danced with in your arms may ease fretfulness.

Going out

Being taken for a walk in the open air seems to work with some babies.

Alternative communication

Starting when your child is about six to seven months old you can begin teaching your baby sign language, and by eight or nine months of age, she will be able to sign back to you. The baby in this picture is signing "Please."

Using standard hand signs devised for the deaf, known as Australian Sign Language (Auslan), you and your child can hold a silent conversation. There are signs for milk, hungry, tired/go to sleep, nappy, (give me) more, and just about everything you might need.

When the idea of teaching non-deaf infants signing was introduced, there was a concern that by using signs instead of language, speaking would be delayed. However, this has not been shown to be the case, and some studies even conclude that by starting to use language earlier with signing, your child will acquire spoken language sooner.

Recent research has revealed that pointing and gesturing at a toddler around the age of 14 months, has a significant effect on her ability to make conversation when she reaches school age.

Scientists believe that the non-verbal communication between parents and child gives the baby's brain a major head start in learning to talk. Previous studies have indicated that this effect is related to how the parents talk to the child. Now it is known that

how parents gesture to their children also appears to affect the children's vocabulary.

Auslan's website (auslan.org.au) has an online sign database, and websites such as australianbabyhands.com offer free charts and other products for sale. But once you know the signs you want to teach, how do you teach them to your baby?

Give the sign at the time the word is relevant. Use the sign for milk when you are about to breasfeed or bottle-feed; sign "time to sleep" when it's nap or bedtime. You might think that your baby would learn a sign quicker if you said the word or concept out loud at the time you are signing it, but many authorities on signing advise not to do this. They believe your baby

will learn sooner when only the signal is given.

It is hoped that by teaching your baby hand signing that you will both avoid the frustration that occurs when she cannot tell you what she desires and you can't figure it out. And with less frustration, your baby will cry less. Most children do not have a handful of words until 15 to 18 months of age, although this occurs a few months sooner in early talkers. In late bloomers, language develops at an even slower pace. In the interval between eight and nine months of age and the time your child acquires a vocabulary of words sufficient to express her needs, the two of you can "talk" to each other with signing.

Colic

Colic refers to long episodes of crying engaged in by healthy babies, which are unrelated to hunger or any of their other common needs. It is said that as many as 20 per cent of infants suffer from this condition, but this figure includes many babies with milder forms. During an attack of colic. a baby who has been acting fine all day suddenly brings her knees up to her abdomen, clenches her fists and begins screaming. The crying, despite your best efforts to remedy any need she might have, continues for hours. Typically these crying spells start at two to four weeks of age, gradually increase in duration and intensity, and peak at about six to eight weeks of age. Once the peak is reached, there is then a dramatic decrease in symptoms. Thereafter, episodes gradually become milder until they are gone, usually at about three months of age, but occasionally lasting up until six months. Colic most often occurs in the evening, ending somewhere between 11 p.m. and midnight. In the most severe cases, crying can be heard all day long.

Colic occurs equally in girls and boys, in breastfed and bottlefed infants, in rich and poor, in first born and subsequent family members, and in those born vaginally and by Caesarean section.

Most paediatricians regard colic as essentially a benign condition, which has no lasting effect on a child. But in some cases, colic has a pronounced effect on parents.

After many long nights of hearing their baby cry, often without being able to offer sufficient comfort, a couple's feelings towards their baby may change. They may begin to find being a parent less rewarding and fail to develop as close a bond with their baby as might otherwise have occurred. It is natural, at times, to feel anger at a baby for being so difficult. At moments when aggravation and annoyance are all that parents feel, expressions of love will be replaced by more negative emotions. And finally, when the weeks of colic are over, the way parents view their baby and how they respond to her may have been seriously altered. Colic can lead to child abuse at moments of intense parental frustration and anger.

Colic can also affect a baby. Some studies suggest that babies who suffered from colic are more prone to feeding and sleeping problems, have more difficult personalities, and may be at risk for behaviour problems in preschool. It is not difficult to imagine that such intense crying without relief can affect a child's emotional development. But do such changes result from having experienced colic or are they instead due to alternative reasons? For example, infants with colic may simply be born with more difficult temperaments that with or without the crying would have led to the same behavioural outcomes. Or perhaps it is the effect of the weeks of crying on the parents that, having tainted their style

RULE OF 3s

Dr M. Wessel, in 1954, gave colic a definition that has "stuck". He defined colic as:
Crying by an otherwise healthy and well-fed baby that lasts for at least

- 3 hours per day,
- 3 days a week,
- 3 weeks in a row.

In truth, you do not need this definition to tell you if your baby has colic; the wailing will certainly happen almost every evening. And certainly you don't have to wait three weeks to be sure it is colic. But having a widely accepted meaning of colic is useful for classifying patients in research studies.

A more practical definition of colic for parents is: daily episodes of loud, continuous crying with no apparent cause, that is difficult to relieve, and is very distressing to you.

7 common theories about what causes colic

1 **Intestinal immaturity and wind.** During attacks, infants look as if they are having abdominal pain and they often pass wind. This theory doesn't explain, however, why colic occurs mostly in the evening and is not immediately present at birth, and why babies display the same visual appearance when crying for other causes.

2 **A reaction to cow's milk proteins** in formula or transmitted via breastmilk after maternal ingestion of cow's milk. A small percentage of colicky infants get dramatically better when they are given a hypoallergic formula or their mothers omit milk (or another suspicious food) from their diets. However, this doesn't work for the majority of infants with colic and it doesn't account for the fact that colic occurs mostly in the evening.

3 **It is a baby's reaction when inexperienced parents miss her signals and are unresponsive to her needs.** A published study demonstrated that in one group of mothers and their babies, colic could be reduced by teaching mothers to better recognise cues from their babies and to react more immediately and effectively. However, most mothers and fathers of colicky babies have no problem with recognising and answering their baby's wants and needs.

4 **Being overtired.** It is well known that tired infants and children are fussy and grouchy. The timing of colic could be that tiredness is greatest at the end of the day. That colic resolves after six to eight weeks of age may relate to the fact that infants who do not have colic, have a greater sense of night-day cycles and longer night-time sleeping intervals between two and three months of age. But, despite seeming logical, there is yet no evidence that colic is a sleep problem.

5 **A very fussy temperament.** Like all personality traits, there is a continuum of colicky infants: some do not have fussy spells at all, many have mild cases of colic, and others have terrible colic. Many times, too, a parent of the colicky infant has a family history of suffering from the condition. (There is some inheritability to personality traits.)
A number of experts suspect that some babies with colic have a heightened sensitivity to sensory input. They are bothered much more than others by noises, bright lights and skin sensations. Colic, in these babies, is caused by what is perceived by them to be an environment full of such stimuli. However, there just isn't any solid evidence to confirm or deny this hypothesis.

6 **A result of "bad" bacteria outnumbering "good" bacteria in the intestines.** Infants with colic have been found to have significantly fewer non-pathogenic bacteria such as lactobacilli in their stools than other infants. When lactobacilli were fed to colicky infants in one study, the majority had some improvement in symptoms, while infants not given the probiotics did not improve; however, this does not explain why the symptoms are worse at night.

7 **A result of pressure on the back of an infant's head during delivery.** Such pressure may disrupt the normal function of the back of the skull and upper vertebrae (bones surrounding the spinal cord) in the neck.
This explanation is proposed by advocates of cranial osteopathy but there is no supporting evidence.

of parenting, leads children to behave thus. It is important, therefore, to bear in mind that in the experience of most paediatricians, nearly all babies and parents survive colic and go on to have loving and caring relationships.

Traditionally, colic has been thought to be caused by abdominal pain attributed to "wind" or to intestinal immaturity. In fact, the word "colic" comes from the Greek "kolikos", meaning "of the colon". However, this and other theories of the cause have not been satisfactorily proven (see page 178). Many scientists conceive of colic as a set of symptoms that result from not one, but multiple, possible causes. It is conceivable that several of the theories described are causes of colic in some infants. Alternatively, all these theories may be wrong and the true cause of colic remains to be discovered. What can be said with certainty is that there is still much to learn about colic.

Treatment of colic

Popular measures to treat colic can be divided into three categories: nonspecific, specific and ineffective. Although no measure has been shown to be completely effective (and certainly not the latter), if any of them seem to soothe your baby for even a few moments, it is worth continuing to use it. There certainly will be times when all your efforts will fail to relieve your baby's distress. When none of your attempts to calm her seem to work, lay her down in her cot, swaddled (see page 34), and turn the light off. Sometimes, just letting her cry for several minutes seems to help a great deal. Do not for a moment feel that her persistent crying is somehow related to your failure as a parent. The fact is that at certain times, no one will be able to calm her down.

Nonspecific measures

Remedies in this category clearly do not address the underlying cause of colic, but do sometimes and temporarily give relief. The emphasis should be on the word "sometimes".

Camomile or fennel tea

Given in a bottle, at room temperature, at the time of crying, herbal tea was shown in a research protocol to be more effective than a placebo in reducing the amount of crying. The remaining remedies in this group, illustrated on page 181, are not scientifically established as being effective, but they have withstood the test of time.

Specific treatments

According to which theory of causation is being subscribing to, treatments include: eliminating milk or "wind-causing" foods from the mother's diet for breastfed infants and switching to a hypoallergenic formula for formula-fed children (wind theory, milk or food allergy theory); teaching parents to pick up on clues to their baby's needs (parent-infant interaction theory); letting your crying baby scream until she tires of it and falls asleep (sleep problem theory); placing her, swaddled, in a quiet environment with minimal sensory stimulation (temperament theory); or giving probiotics (bacterial imbalance theory).

Specific treatments generally work dramatically in only a fraction of colicky infants, perhaps because there are many etiologies of this problem or because none of the theories is the correct one. The most recently proposed treatment, giving probiotics, is intriguing and shows much promise, but further studies are needed to confirm its effectiveness.

Ineffective treatments

Generations of parents have been recommended over-the-counter remedies such as Infacol and gripe water or used them and most will swear that they work. There is, however, no evidence that simethicone, the main ingredient in Infacol and other colic remedies, is helpful in treating colic; in fact, studies have found it only as effective as placebo in relieving colic symptoms. Gripe water also lacks any proof of therapeutic value. That symptoms improve when either is given is probably due to the natural course of colic (see box) rather than manufacturers' claims.

What to do about colic

Like most parents, you will have two reactions when the hours of crying initially arrive. First, you will worry that perhaps something is seriously wrong with your infant. (A visit to the GP is a good idea at this time to exclude the presence of any medical problem causing your infant such distress.) Second, you probably will feel at some level that the crying continues because you aren't a good enough parent.

Despite the fact that you are likely to be a very competent mother or father, the tendency to blame yourself for your baby's crying fits will compound the problem, since your frustration and anxiety may become apparent to her, increasing her sense of unease. Regrettably, when colic does arise, it comes at a time when you are quite new to parenting and may be insecure about your abilities to be a good one, and when you are most certainly exhausted from frequent night-time feedings. Mothers, particularly, due to hormonal changes, may experience post-partum mood swings and sadness. See page 182 for some ways to survive the experience.

MORE **ABOUT** | the natural course of colic

The severity of colic increases gradually and reaches its peak at six to eight weeks of age when, abruptly, there is a big improvement. This may explain why simethicone, gripe water, and other so-called remedies, which have no demonstrable value, are regarded by many parents as "miracle drugs". If, in a desperate search for relief, one of these remedies is started at the peak of colic, the dramatic improvement which follows may be attributed to the remedy when, in fact, the baby's crying was about to get better all by itself.

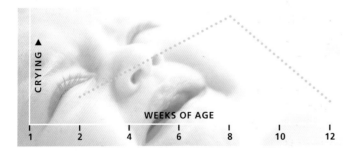

Things to try to ease colic

Motion
Examples of using motion to help calm your colicky baby include holding her in your arms and rhythmically rocking her back and forth, placing her in an infant swing or using a bouncer cradle, and laying her in her pram and rhythmically pushing it forwards and backwards. One of the most effective techniques is going for a ride in your car. Of course, your baby should be in her infant restraint while you journey.

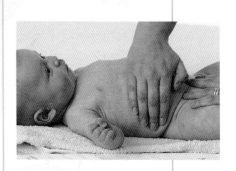

Massage
With cupped hand gently knead your baby's belly working from side to side and then clockwise. Only do this at times when your baby is not distressed.

Vibration
Remedies utilising vibration and noise also can be effective; some think that these techniques work by imitating the baby's uterine environment. To try this method, place your baby in her infant seat and hold the seat on top of an operating dishwasher, washing machine or dryer.

Alternatively, put her in her cot and lean a switched-on vacuum cleaner against the side of the cot.

Tummy-down
This holding position can be tried at times when your baby is relaxed or crying and when she is naked or dressed. Hold her so that she lies supported over both your hands and with fingers spread, try and gently knead both sides of her tummy. You can also walk around with her or lie her over your knee in the same position.

6 ways to survive the weeks of colic

1 **Bring your baby to your doctor's surgery** As soon as you become concerned about the long bouts of crying, have the diagnosis of colic confirmed. On a rational basis, this should give you confidence that there is nothing seriously wrong with her.

2 **Get support** Besides commiseration and empathy, let others in your inner circle help you by donating their time. Sharing the difficult evenings with another understanding person is very beneficial as is being able to walk away from the screaming for a short period to recompose yourself. If someone else gives you time to take a nap, exercise or get out of the house, you will be much better prepared for another evening of screaming.

3 **Bolster your rational side** Although you know intellectually that you are not to blame for the colic and that it will eventually go away, emotionally you are prone to momentarily disregard these facts, feeling hopelessly unable to deal with this seemingly never-ending torture. Tell yourself repeatedly or leave messages around your home to the effect that you did not cause the colic and that the episodes will end soon. Use the power of positive thinking; it will definitely help you to get through this unpleasant phase.

4 **Realise your role** Once you have convinced yourself that you are not a contributing factor, you can now focus on what you can do to help your baby. Use the nonspecific techniques on page 181. Also, decide with your partner, health nurse or doctor, which, if any, specific remedies are appropriate. Remind yourself often that, as the parent, you are here to help your baby get through this difficult period. The best way to help is to do your best to remain calm and be a source of love and comfort.

5 **Be wary of post-natal depression** Bear in mind that this is more likely to arise if your baby is demanding. Certainly the stressful evenings and days of crying, the exhaustion, and the sense that the crying will never go away can contribute to feelings of depression. If you are very sad, lacking energy, tearful or feeling hopeless, call your doctor.

6 **Recognise angry feelings** Unless you are superman or supermum, you will become frustrated at your inability to stop the crying. At times, you may even feel angry at your baby. This is quite normal. However, if these feelings occur repeatedly or if you are tempted to strike your baby or pick her up and shake her, stop and get help right away. You need a break from your baby, a chance to get some rest and relaxation. You must enlist your partner or other family members (or close friends) to assist you and relieve you. Of course you don't want to hurt your baby, but if you are sufficiently tired, isolated, frustrated and angry, you may lose control and lash out at her. Get help before you get to this point!

CARING FOR YOUR OLDER BABY

Anticipating change

Once the early weeks are over, your baby should be steadily putting on weight and sleeping more regularly so that you can finally begin to relax and really enjoy your baby. Each month will bring new abilities – and challenges (see Chapter Five) – but you also are much more confident about being able to interpret your baby's needs and look after her properly. Many of the tasks you performed for your newborn – care of the umbilical cord, for example – no longer need to be done and others – such as feeding and nappy changing – have almost certainly been mastered so they are like second nature to you. Just as the second trimester of pregnancy is

normally seen as the least problematic and most blissfully enjoyable part so, too, are the later months of babyhood (from three to 12).

Once your baby reaches 12 to 15 months, however, she will begin to have her own, often strong, opinions about what she will and will not do. And while you may envision that bathing your older baby, getting her dressed and brushing her teeth are relatively easy tasks, this is not necessarily the case. Your relationship is growing and once she begins to communicate, she will have more to say to you about what is happening to her. So in addition to the actual work before you (cutting

ways to help bring out your baby's best

1. **Help your baby feel confident** Expect your baby to achieve. You are an important influence on the way she views herself; if she believes you think she can, for example, learn to brush her teeth, then she will try a little harder because she will believe in herself, too. Take a positive view of your baby even when progress is slow. Tell yourself that there are always possibilities for change and advancement; low expectations may lead to underachievement.

2. **Treat your baby as special and unique** While your baby may inherit characteristics that are similar to yours, she remains an individual. You can help her develop her full potential by recognising her individual strengths and weaknesses and by supporting her according to her individual needs.

3. **Be a good role model** Given that your baby watches you, copies you and is heavily affected by you at all times, it is hardly surprising if she starts to behave like you. Therefore, make sure you act as you would like your baby to do so. Be aware of any behaviour that does not promote your baby's wellbeing and, if necessary, work to change it.

nails, brushing hair etc.), you also will have to contend with your baby's willingness (or unwillingness) to cooperate with your efforts.

Your baby's drive to assert herself has its roots in early infancy; it is this that enables her to gradually progress from reflex-driven behaviour (such as the startle reflex, see page 28) to increasingly controlled, voluntary actions (including moving her hands and fingers to point). By around 24 months, your baby will be driven to gain fuller independence. And although you may find her behaviour becomes difficult and tiresome, you should interpret any attempts to be assertive as a positive expression of your baby's growing independence and abilities rather than as defiance and naughtiness.

And there are ways in which you can help your baby learn to take care of herself that will make life less stressful for you as well as building her confidence and expertise. Bear in mind that what's easy for you may be much more difficult for your baby to master. Your goal throughout should be to promote your baby's resilience and self-esteem, and the best way to do this is to ensure you have a loving relationship.

EQUILIBRIUM/DISEQUILIBRIUM

Childhood experts have identified that emotional development invariably proceeds by having periods of calm and contentment (equilibrium) followed by periods of turbulence (disequilibrium) – generally at six-month intervals. In fact, experts believe that for further development to take place, some of the "good" that was previously learned has to be forsaken. Two and three year olds are relatively positive, for example, but two-and-a-half year olds can be very difficult – "the terrible twos".

Building your relationship

As your baby grows and develops, you will find that rather than your being a caregiver to a helpless infant – attempting to understand and meet her needs – that your baby becomes an eager participant in the relationship, better able to communicate her wants and desires and more able to have you respond to her the way she wants.

Two-way communication

In a matter of weeks, your baby will attempt to communicate by a wider range of responses than crying. For example, she may indicate dislike of something by beginning to "fuss", turning her head away, arching or stiffening her back, sucking her thumb or fingers or refusing to establish eye contact. This last is important as eye contact is one of the main ways that babies communicate before they can speak (other means outside of crying include combining gestures with sounds, facial expressions and gazing), which is why you should always look into your baby's eyes when you feed her, change her and comfort her. If you talk to your baby at the same time (see box), your baby will start to learn the basics of language. She will begin to gurgle in response to your vocalisations and will soon develop a repertoire of imitative vocal sounds.

When you talk to your baby, you'll notice that she will make agitated movements, gurgle, smile or simply gaze intently into your eyes. Of course, she doesn't understand what you are saying, but she is capable of following your intonation patterns, the rhythm of your speech, and any accompanying hand gestures and eye contact. In time, the sounds of frequently occurring specific words will become familiar, and they will often be her first words.

Within a few months after birth, your baby will start to play a more active role in your relationship. She may stretch out her arms towards your face as you approach her cot, indicating that she wants to be picked up and cuddled. And when you hold her, she may now intentionally snuggle her face against

your neck, embrace you with her arms or stroke your face. She will even manage to work out what makes you smile and what encourages you to pay attention to her – her smiling at you and uttering sounds such as "ma" or "da".

Smiling and laughter

In fact, she began to smile at you practically from the moment she was born but you didn't recognise the slight changes at the corners of her mouth as a smile. Over the next weeks she "practised" smiling and learned to produce a recognisable smile at around six weeks in reaction to a favourite toy, funny noise or particular action on your part. At around four months, she smiles in response to your smiles – true "social" smiling. When she sees you smiling, she smiles back to tell you that she feels the same way you do.

Soon, your baby will learn to use different types of smile – with closed lips, bared teeth or open mouth – to influence the way you communicate with her. She will laugh if you tickle her or make a pleasing sound. Laughter, like smiling, promotes the ongoing exchanges between you and your baby. It also ensures that whatever made her laugh in the first place is repeated as you will be encouraged to make your baby laugh again.

Pointing

At around six months, your baby will begin pointing to objects out of her reach and you will respond by picking up the toys and giving them to her. By the time she is around a year, she will use pointing not just to indicate a need but also to share an experience with you. She may attract your attention by pointing to another baby she sees in a pram in order to convey that she finds the other baby interesting. Your baby also will use pointing to demonstrate that she knows a word for something. If you ask her "Where are your feet", she will point to them. Even when she begins to speak, she will

Talking to your baby

When talking to babies or young toddlers, parents instinctively adjust their speech to what is generally referred to as "baby-talk" or "motherese". This involves pitching the voice high and using a wide range of intonation patterns, often including a rising tone at the end of each sentence, which is captivating and gives baby-talk its sing-song quality. This speech style also involves frequent use of the baby's name, posing questions, prompting the baby to respond, explanatory hand gestures and regular physical contact. The parent refers only to what can be seen, heard or felt at that moment using short, simple sentences, and the speech is relatively slow and rhythmic, with lots of repetitions. When the baby "says" something, the parent will expand on this in order to make it a two-way exchange and as much like a conversation as possible. When, for example, your toddler points at what you are wearing and says "Mummy's dress", you may reply "Yes, that's Mummy's dress. It's Mummy's party dress. It is red with pretty white flowers. Do you think Mummy's dress looks nice?"

Experiments have demonstrated that only hours after birth, newborns show a preference for baby-talk over normal talk and it is important in your baby's acquisition of language. But baby-talk's real value is not in teaching vocabulary and grammar, it's in improving comprehension and promoting sustained interaction between parent and child so that a baby is encouraged to pay attention to, understand and experiment with speaking. As your baby gets older, you will adjust your speech in relation to her responses, level of comprehension and, ultimately, to her own language production. You will begin to use longer sentences with new structures.

Early pre-speech dialogues between adults and infants share many qualities with later language behaviour and, in fact, lay the foundations for what will later become real dialogues in language. They also give infants a sense of their own capacity to communicate and to be in rhythmic interaction with their parents, particularly if mum or dad responds sensitively to their infant's attempts at turn-taking.

Regardless of the means of "conversing", one participant is active while the other is quiet, then the sequence is reversed. Each participant pays close attention to the other's response and reacts appropriately; with parent-baby interaction, responses are designed to keep the "conversation" going. The baby may slowly build up her responses, crescendo, then go quiet and wait to see what mum or dad will do next. Mum or dad, in turn, will react with more and more enthusiasm, mimic the baby's facial expressions as well as her quiet times, and instigate a new cycle of excited dialogue.

Baby massage

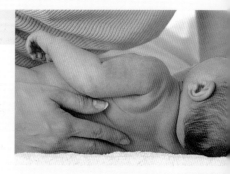

Gentle massage is a great way to bond with your baby. It can be done with your baby laid over your knees or when she is lying flat on a soft, warm towel or mat in a warm, quiet location. You can start off with her clothed if she seems ill at ease. Gently stroke your baby over her back and up and down the length of her spine and limbs. When she is about two months, you can try a full body routine with an appropriate oil (see *Baby Massage* by Peter Walker). Do not massage her, however, if she is tired, hungry or has just been fed.

Back, arms and legs

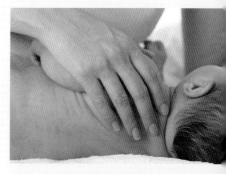

Lay down on your left side, with your baby facing you, lying on her right side. Stroke your baby with the whole of your right hand, from the back of her neck to the base of her spine – in the same way as you would stroke a kitten or a puppy. Continue for about a minute.

Use a circular movement to gently massage around your baby's upper back and then right down the length of her back to the base of her spine. Continue for about a minute.

Next, slowly take the movement to her arm; keep your touch gentle and relaxed as you

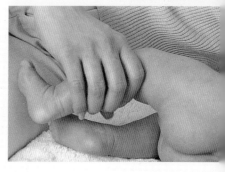

take the stroke from her shoulder to her hand. Continue for about a minute. Repeat with your baby's right arm.

Move your hand to the top of your baby's leg and stroke down from her hip to her foot with your palm. You can give her leg a little gentle shake to loosen it up and help her to relax. Continue for about a minute. Repeat with her right leg.

regularly use pointing to complete a phrase. For instance, your baby may point at her head and say "hat" in order to ask that you put her hat on.

Recognising Mum and Dad

During the first weeks of life, your baby will become increasingly sensitive to the differences in the way you and your partner speak, smell, move and handle her, and the special ways each of you responds when she smiles, coos or kicks her legs. By three months, she will form a very detailed impression of her parents and this influences the way she will interact with each of you and how you, in turn, react to her. For instance, when she sees her mother approach, she may anticipate being fed and make appropriate gestures while if she hears Dad's voice, become excited and kick her legs because she thinks she will be in for a bit of play.

Game playing

From the age of about three months, your baby will begin to recognise the difference between an angry and a pleased tone of voice, and over the next few months she will learn which of her actions will elicit which response. By around eight or nine months old, she is able to remember a whole repertoire of behaviours that will result in the kind of attention she likes best – extra cuddles, praise, smiles and laughter. She even may attempt to mimic the little games you play with her – teasing by holding out a toy and snatching it away just as you are about to take it. or playing her own version of peek-a-boo. Teasing games also form part of learning about giving and sharing. Although these games can begin as early as six months old, it will be some time before your baby will actually happily give you her toy so you can play with it yourself: teasing you does not entail having to give up her possessions. In fact, the toy is largely incidental in this act. Neither is she trying to fool you by making you believe you will get the toy and then withdrawing it from your reach. At this early stage, teasing games are simply imitations of behaviour the baby knows will result in laughter.

Gender-related play

Many studies prove that, however unintentionally, parents often encourage certain gender-linked activities, in other words, dads initiate rougher play with sons but engage in quiet, non-intrusive play with their daughters. Mums, too, tend to show more pleasure when their baby boys play with trucks and blocks rather than dolls and vice versa for baby girls. Both parents may direct their child towards particular "appropriate" toys. As children grow, the attitudes, behaviours and expectations of parents become increasingly gender specific, and this will affect their expectations and values regarding their baby's future.

Although it may not be possible to entirely eliminate gender stereotyping, it is important to be aware that it may limit your baby's potential. If you offer your baby a wide variety of play opportunities and experiences (see Chapters 11), you will support the development of many different skills.

Keeping your baby clean

As well as bathing your baby and washing her hair, you need to teach her to wash her hands after certain activities, particularly before eating and after going to the potty.

Hygiene

Standards of hygiene are individual to each family. Some people believe that the house and children should be kept scrupulously clean to protect against infections; others take the view that a little bit of dirt never did anyone any harm.

It is impossible to protect your baby from every illness and infection and in any case, she will need to build up her immunity against these. However, it is important to keep a balance between under- and over-protection while imparting personal hygiene rules to last her through life.

Children are particularly vulnerable to stomach upsets such as diarrhoea and vomiting, as well as diseases picked up outdoors, so you can help to combat this by teaching her good hygiene habits.

When your child begins feeding herself, get her into the habit of washing her hands before eating or touching food and teach her not to eat any fruit or raw vegetables before these have been washed. She should also learn to wash her hands (or use a hand sanitiser) after going to the toilet, playing outside or with pets. Supervise her hand washing or go over what she has done until you are satisfied she is doing it properly. Make sure your toddler knows which face washer and towel are hers – it is better for hygiene and it may encourage her to use them.

Many toddlers rely on comfort blankets; if your child has one, don't allow her to trail it around and then suck it. Wash it frequently – if necessary when she's asleep and is less likely to miss it.

Try to prevent your child eating dirt, sand or grass and discourage her from sucking dirty fingers. Keep her nails short to minimise dirt getting stuck under them. If you have a sandpit, always keep it covered when not in use. If you are out with your toddler,

carry moist wipes to clean her hands. Toxoplasmosis is an infection caused by a parasite and it is easily picked up by children if they swallow contaminated soil (see box opposite).

Bathing

Instead of the screaming that accompanied baths when your baby was newborn, bath times are probably very pleasurable now. In fact, although getting her to go into the bath is occasionally a struggle, getting her out of it is often the harder of the two. Bath time is a wonderful time for your baby to relax and have fun. She can play with water toys, or learn her body parts and how to wash them, or sit back and listen to you telling her a story. When she is more verbal, it also can be a time to sing songs, talk about all the events of her day, or play word games. Bath time is an opportunity for you to have your baby all to yourself when she is at her best. The many minutes spent together during her bath is real "quality time"

Toxoplasma gondii *are cells found in the faeces of infected animals, such as dogs and cats, and may remain in the ground for two years or more. Toxoplasmosis can cause asthma, stomach upset and listlessness and even sight problems. Treatment includes steroids to relieve symptoms and anti-parasitic drugs. If you are a pet owner, you can lessen the chance of your pet getting toxoplasmosis by having kittens and puppies wormed.*

together. And you can have it every day! If you wish to, you may build this into the evening routine so you can go from bath to pyjamas to bed-time ritual.

However, it is not necessary from a hygienic viewpoint to bathe your baby daily. Giving a bath every two, three or even five days is fine as long as you do bathe her when she gets especially dirty. A quick sponge bath outside the bath is another alternative for days between cleanings in the bath.

Once she can sit up by herself unsupported (about six months of age), you can bathe her in a bath. Safety at bath time is paramount. Don't fill the bath too high – 5–7 cm or waist height is sufficient. Test the water temperature with your elbow before allowing your baby in the water and then place her away from the taps, to prevent any possibility of her touching them and being scalded. To prevent slipping when she stands up in the bath, place a rubber non-slip mat on the floor of the bath or use a plastic infant bath inside the bath. Lift her out of the bath or else hold her hand when she climbs out. As you surely know, never leave your baby unattended in the bath, even for a moment.

Bubble baths are enjoyable and entertaining for children. The material added to your bath water to make the bubbles is non-toxic and washes off easily. Infrequently, exposure to bubble bath is responsible for irritation of the area just outside the vagina in girls or of the urethra in boys, and occasionally this leads to a bladder infection. Obviously, if your child has suffered from one of these effects, avoid bubble baths. Otherwise, you can choose for yourself,

You read in Chapter 2 that newborns are usually washed and shampooed with products specifically targeted at babies, which are supposedly gentler on the skin, while baby shampoos are claimed to sting the eyes less than adult shampoos. The same can be said about the soaps and shampoos you choose for your child when she is older. The main advantage of "baby" products is that they are more enticing to your child – they may have a television or cartoon figure on the label or they

may come in fun colours, shapes or scents. There is no one soap that is better for children than the other soaps, and no shampoo that is better than all the others. Of course, manufacturers would like you to think that their product is the best, but other than unsubstantiated claims, no inter-product comparison studies have been published. If your child has sensitve skin – or even if she doesn't – you may prefer to use a non-soap cleanser (available at pharmacies).

weighing the high chance of enjoyment, but serving no other purpose, with bubble baths. Many paediatricians recommend a non-soap cleanser, which

is less likely to dry out or irritate your child's skin (see box above).

Avoiding problems in the bath

Sometimes, though, bath time is not as wonderful as just depicted. Struggles at bath time, when they happen, usually result from your baby being overtired and grumpy or from a lack of patience on your part. (It is certainly understandable that after a long day of taking care of your baby and your home, or after a hard day at work, that you may feel tired and perhaps stressed.) The way to keep your toddler from becoming overtired is straightforward: insist that she gets to bed on time and that naps are never missed. Techniques to avoid struggles at these times and to learn more about teaching yourself how to be more patient can be found in Chapter 11.

Some young toddlers dislike bath time because they are frightened of being in the water. If your child develops a fear of bath time, try making it more fun by adding a mild bubble bath, soap crayons, a

selection of water toys, or singing appropriate nursery rhymes such as "rub a dub dub, three men in a tub". If your toddler is scared of getting her face wet, show her how to blow bubbles in the water. Taking her swimming or allowing her to play in a small paddle-pool in the backyard (depending on water restrictions) also may help to overcome this fear.

Your child may feel more confident in the water if you join her in the bath. Let her splash you or pour water over your head, then do the same to her. Or, let her bathe with friends – it makes great fun for them. If she is really making a fuss about bathing, let her stand in a bowl of water while you wash her. Or, you can try taking her into the shower with you. If nothing else works, revert to sponge bathing until she feels ready to go back into the water.

Hair washing

While bathing is generally a fun experience for your older baby, shampooing the hair is generally not. Your baby will eventually enjoy lying back in the tub and wetting her hair, but she may initially be afraid to let her head go under water. (Later on she will love doing this!) Scrubbing her scalp is unlikely to provoke protest but pouring water on her head or rinsing out the shampoo is often a scary event. Your baby is afraid of the unpleasant sensation that occurs when soap or shampoo gets in her eyes.

There are a number of solutions to this problem (see box below).

Although products designed specifically for children are really no better than adult products (see box), using a baby shampoo seems a reasonable choice since these shampoos sting less than adult shampoos when they land accidentally in your child's eyes. (But beware they still do sting.)

4 ways to make hair washing easier

1   **Have your baby lie back in the tub, tilting her head backwards;** much of the rinsing then can be done without any discomfort, for the water will fall backwards (away from the eyes).

2   **Hold a dry wash cloth, folded in two, against your baby's eyes and forehead** to shield the eyes from soap and water.

3   **Have your baby wear a shampoo hat/visor** These are available at baby stores or online. Basically, a shampoo hat/ visor consists of only the rim of a hat. The hat goes across the forehead, just over the ears, and around the back of the head. When you pour water on the top of your baby's head, the water will not land in her eyes.

4   **Shampoo as infrequently as possible** Certainly a shampoo is not necessary every day; in fact, you can safely go several days between them if you have to.

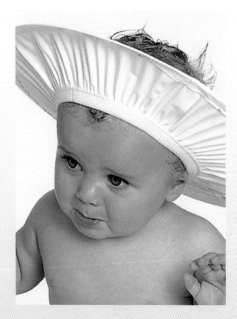

Skin, hair and nail care

The skin of newborns in the first weeks of life is often dry and coarse, and peeling is common. But as a rule, following this initial stage, babies have soft, moist skin – of a kind most adults are jealous. Should a skin condition arise in your baby, it will most often consist of dry or irritated skin.

If your baby was born with a full head of hair, much of the hair, especially on the top of the head, may have fallen out. And, if she spends plenty of time on her back, there may be a bald spot at the back, where she rests her head. But for those babies with little hair and those that lose hair, there is hope: it will grow (or grow back).

So, too will finger and toenails. Luckily, your baby's toenails will grow much slower and require cutting much less often than her finger nails.

Dry skin

You can detect dry skin in your baby if, when gently rubbing your hand over her skin, it feels rough to your touch. Often, if you look closely, you can see fine white flakes or small bumps on the surface of dry skin. You also notice localised areas of dry, rough, slightly raised skin that looks pinker than surrounding skin, called dry patches.

Dry skin has many causes. Some children inherit this tendency from their parents; in others, the dry skin results from lack of moisture in the air of your home (common when the heat is on in the winter) or from being in the water (bath or swimming pool) too long. If skin is chronically dry and itchy, it is called eczema (see page 357).

Treating skin dryness serves two purposes: first, the skin looks much "healthier", which is pleasing to you; second, dry skin can be very uncomfortable and itchy for your baby and treatment reduces or eliminates this.

To remedy your baby's dry skin, give baths a little less often, and when you do bathe her, use a bar of soap containing moisturiser. Immediately after she has been towel dried, apply a moisturising lotion to her skin. Another aid is placing a humidifier in her room to counter dry air.

Irritated skin

This occurs primarily in the nappy area and on the face and is the result of two simultaneous insults to the skin – rubbing and wetness. Nappy rashes are most likely to develop in skin where the wet or dirty nappy comes into direct contact with the skin. Urine and faeces are able to break down the surface barrier of skin and allow irritation. Areas that get wet but do not rub against the nappy, however, such as the thigh creases, are typically spared even though rash occurs in neighbouring areas.

Rashes on the cheeks and chin are also quite common. The irritant for these rashes is usually saliva, but milk, food and material vomited up from the stomach are all quite capable of injuring the

USING MOISTURISER

For dry skin, which moisturiser is best? There are many products advertised for use in infants. They are generally mild, but as a result, they often do not moisturise as well as an adult moisturising lotion. Any adult lotion will do – you can use a generic brand or one of the many widely advertised brand names. There is little difference between brands of lotion when it comes to effectiveness, but there is a huge difference when it comes to price. If you like, you may use whatever brand you use on your own hands for moisturising your baby. Tip: if you have been rubbing on the lotion just after baths or once a day without success, try applying the lotion two or even three times a day.

surface of the skin. Posseting, if it occurs, is likely to begin shortly after birth, and can go on for months. Saliva and drooling also are present from an early age. But at about three months of age, your baby will begin drooling much more than previously. (This is often attributed to teething, but actually, it has little to do with this. Instead, maturation of the salivary glands is responsible.)

To the wetness from the saliva or sick, now add friction from rubbing the face against the sheet of the cot or against your shoulder (when you are holding your baby). A pink-red patch of irritated skin is the result. Sometimes, instead of rubbing, the second force contributing to a skin rash is wind or cold weather.

Yeast rashes also occur in young children. Many nappy rashes become secondarily infected with yeast after an irritant rash has been present a few days. Another area where a yeast skin infection may appear is in the recesses of the neck skin folds. At about two to three months of age, "double" and "triple chins" appear. The depths of the creases of the skin folds between the "chins" are places where drool or excess milk often winds up. The warm, moist environment there is very favourable for the growth of yeast.

Treatment of irritant rashes tries to alleviate the predisposing factors. It isn't realistic to expect your baby to stop posseting or drooling; however, you can provide a barrier to prevent those liquids from getting on the skin surface. Applying a thick ointment (ask at your pharmacy) over the cheek or chin serves this purpose. If wind is the problem, apply the ointment before going outside in cold weather. To prevent wetness in the neck folds, use a bib. (And when a rash is present in the fold, you can also stretch open the neck fold and wipe in that space at nappy changes using a clean wipe.) The ointment overlying the irritated skin also decreases friction between the sheet, blanket or clothing covering your shoulder.

Treatment of nappy rashes and ways to avoid them are discussed in more detail in Chapter 2.

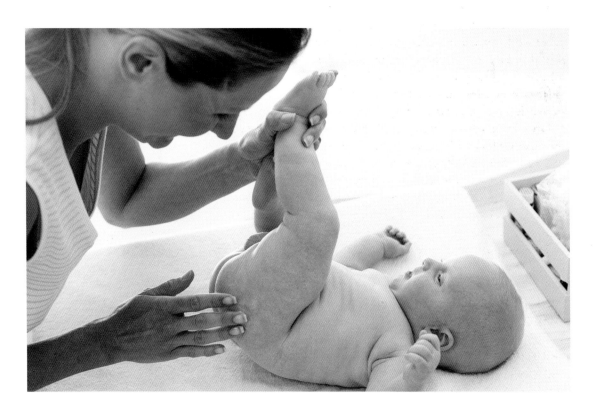

Hair care

The primary purpose of the hair on your baby's head is to keep her scalp warm, which it does not accomplish very well. Hair also has other uses. It provides another visual characteristic to help you distinguish your baby from other infants and it may be a source of fun if you style your baby's hair, especially if you have a girl, and she will look very cute when you finish. But other than these few benefits, hair is more of a nuisance to parents in that you have to wash it, dry it, comb or brush it, and periodically get it cut. If your baby is like most other older infants and toddlers, none of these steps, as with shampooing (see page 193), will be easily accomplished.

Besides scalp hair, your newborn may also have had fine, dark hairs all over her body, especially on her back, forearms and temples. These newborn hairs often disappear gradually over the next months. But in some babies, hair persists or grows on most of the body except the face, neck, hands and feet. Body hairs are most noticeable in children with dark hair, and are normal. Such sparse hairs in children are usually an inherited trait, and often occur in families in which the dad is well endowed with body hairs. Your child's body hairs are best ignored. The one exception to this is in the case of hair in the pubic area. Small, fine hairs in the genital area in your son or daughter also are of no concern; but if the hairs are long, curly, or thick, report this to your paediatrician. It may be a sign of premature puberty, a rare condition.

Haircuts

Cutting your baby's hair can be quite a challenge. Many babies are very uncomfortable and fearful when scissors or clippers are near them. And even under the best conditions, getting your toddler to sit

tips for making hair care easier

1   **Keep hair short.** Shorter hair is much easier to care for than longer hair, so when brushing becomes a battle, organise a haircut.

2   **Distract your baby.** Brushing hair is best done while your baby enjoys a more pleasant activity.

3   **Hair is more easily combed if it is moist or wet,** so comb your baby's hair right after drying at bath time or lightly wet it (with water in a spray bottle) before starting.

4   **Use a detangler.** If your baby has longer hair, strands may become entwined and stuck together. Untangling hair is uncomfortable when brushing. Fortunately, there are spray-on detanglers you can buy that will save the day for you at brushing time.

1 **Cut straight across the top of the nail.** Sculpting a convex nail at the growing end is not necessary and requires a great deal more time and skill.

2 **Cut your baby's nails when she is sleeping** or effectively distracted in a quiet activity.

3 **Have two people do the job.** One person has the responsibility of holding the finger straight and still, while the other cuts the nail.

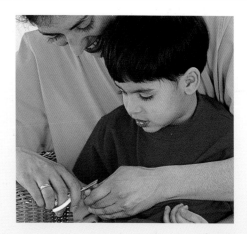

still longer than a few moments may seem impossible. Find a barber or hairdresser who has a lot of patience and plenty of distractions available, or who specialises in cutting children's hair.

Nail care

You will need to cut your older baby's nails less frequently than when she was newborn – every five to six days – but although there are several techniques for doing so, none are easily done or readily accepted by your baby.

Small nail clippers are available for infants and older children. While it is difficult to use these on a young baby without occasionally snipping off a little skin from the finger tip, because it is hard to know exactly where the lower cutting surface is when you cut, by the time your baby is six to nine months old and her fingers are bigger, nail clippers can be used with much greater safety.

You may have used your teeth to cut your newborn's nails. However, now that your baby is older, this method isn't very good at trimming the nails unless her nails are quite long. In addition, there is the risk of introducing infection, with germs from your mouth entering through any small breaks in your child's skin around the nail.

A soft emery board can be used to safely file down your baby's nails, but since much time must be spent on each nail, it is not very practical.

Many paediatricians recommend using baby scissors for nail cutting. Baby scissors are made with one sharp cutting blade and one dull, rounded blade. To use the scissors, place the dull blade facing downward and the sharper blade on top. The dull lower blade will not cut the skin of the finger, while the upper blade can still cut the nail.

Your baby's toenails grow much more slowly and don't need to be kept quite as short as her fingernails nor trimmed so frequently. You will have to check for sharp edges; if these catch on clothing it will be painful.

Any redness, inflammation or hardness around a nail may be an indication of an ingrowing toenail, and these signs should be reported to your doctor.

Tooth care

Taking care of your child's teeth should begin at around six months or when her first tooth appears. The main goal of oral hygiene at this stage is to prevent cavities in her baby teeth. Newly erupted baby teeth have not yet fully developed the toughened outer enamel surface to protect them so are more prone to decay and erosion. Babies of six to twelve months should not be given sugary foods. At this stage, use a clean cloth to wipe your baby's teeth after each meal.

Fluoride

Giving sodium fluoride results in babies and children having stronger teeth and fewer cavities. Researchers have repeatedly shown a 20–40 per cent reduction in the number of cavities in communities that have added fluoride to their water. Fluoride also contributes to stronger bones. In Australia, municipal water systems add tiny amounts of fluoride to drinking water to improve the oral health of all in the community. If your water comes from a rainwater tank, however, you can assume that there is no fluoride in your water. In this situation, consult your local dentist about alternative sources of fluoride.

Ingested fluoride works on teeth as they are formed in the gums, before they have erupted, so the earlier fluoride is begun, the more effective it is in preventing cavities. Although excellent if used properly, fluoride may cause unwanted effects if used excessively (see *Fluorosis*, page 332).

You, therefore, have two tasks as a parent: make sure your baby gets fluoride and ensure that she doesn't get too much. A baby can have too much fluoride if she is getting it from more than one source or is swallowing large amounts of fluoride-containing toothpaste. The latter can be avoided by using only a small, pea-sized dab of toothpaste or using a fluoride-free dentifrice each time she brushes her teeth.

Brushing teeth

Start the lifelong habit of cleaning your baby's teeth as soon as her first tooth erupts. You may use a face washer or a wet gauze pad to wipe off the teeth or a small baby-sized toothbrush with soft bristles. Do not use toothpaste before two years of age.

Most experts recommend that you brush your baby's teeth twice a day, once after breakfast or in the morning, and once in the evening. If your toddler will let

---

MORE **ABOUT** | cavities

Cavities are actually an infectious disease, caused by bacteria living on a child's gums. Under certain circumstances, such as frequent episodes when small pieces of sugary food stick to a tooth, the cavity- causing bacteria can grow to large numbers and begin to digest the surface enamel of a tooth. There are a number of reasons why your efforts to prevent cavities are worthwhile. Cavities, as you know, result in toothaches, and the repair process can be uncomfortable for your baby. Additionally, poor dental hygiene in infancy allows the "bad" bacteria that cause cavities to populate the gums and oral cavity, and "good" bacteria become much less numerous. You might think that cavities in baby teeth aren't very significant, since an affected tooth falls out in a few years and is replaced by a new, adult tooth. However, if the cavity-causing bacteria are present in your child's mouth from dental decay in baby teeth, a grown-up tooth erupting in the same spot will immediately be surrounded by the bad bacteria, and the risk of cavities in the adult tooth is increased.

you floss her teeth, you can add that to your routine.

Most parents prefer to brush before the final feeding because the bedtime feeding is a relaxing part of their bedtime ritual. If the teeth are brushed after this, it may undo the quiet, calm mood your baby has entered. However, they do worry if it is all right to do so. Giving only milk to your baby just before she goes into the cot will not cause cavities. Your baby's saliva will wash away any milk that adheres to the teeth.

One of the important functions of brushing teeth, though, is to remove pieces of solid food that cling to the teeth. Saliva will not wash away such small bits, and the food will remain against the tooth for hours. This permits bacteria to do what they do best: start producing cavities.

If your toddler is permitted lollies and other sweets, brushing her teeth is most important because it is these foods that are most likely to stick to the teeth and to promote cavities. The higher the

DUMMIES AND TEETH

According to the British Dental Health Foundation, using a dummy can result in problems as a baby's teeth grow and develop. The longer your baby uses a dummy, the more chance there is of changes in the shape of the inside of your baby's mouth, which can affect how the baby teeth, and later on the permanent teeth, meet when biting. Therefore, you should try and limit the times when your baby uses a dummy (such as only for going to sleep) and you should try to wean your baby off her dummy when she is about one year old. If your toddler is still using a dummy regularly by the age of two or three, a crossbite (where the upper teeth are behind the lower teeth rather than in front of them), is much more likely to occur.

5 ways your child may receive fluoride

1 **Breastmilk** Fluoride is passed from a mother to her child through breastmilk. However, some mothers produce milk with enough fluoride in it, while other mothers' milk has too small an amount to satisfy a baby's requirement.

2 **Concentrated or powdered formula mixed with fluoridated water** A minority of parents mix formula with bottled water for babies, to which fluoride has been added.

3 **Drinking tap water that is fluoridated** Most commercially available water filter systems (Brita and others) do not remove fluoride from the water.

4 **Toothpastes that contain fluoride.**

5 **Fluoride may also be bought by prescription** – alone or combined with vitamins A, C and D.

Teething

In the strict sense, teething is defined as the discomfort that immediately precedes the eruption of a new tooth. An important part of the definition is that the symptoms must be due only to the appearance of the new tooth. It is quite common to attribute many other events to teething, but most of these are not really caused by the new tooth's arrival.

Teething symptoms

Historically, teething has been said to last for two to three weeks before the arrival of a tooth and quite a few symptoms have been attributed to it. Teething does not

cause the heavy drooling and desire to chomp on hard objects that all babies at about three months of age exhibit as this will occur even if a first tooth does not appear for months. Nor is it responsible when your baby is fussy or sleeps poorly a few nights in a row, but is fine during the day; this is normally the result of bad sleep habits.

High fever, diarrhoea, poor appetite, vomiting, coughing and runny noses are other symptoms seldom caused by teething but may be mistakenly attributed to it. Here is the reason why: there are twenty baby teeth that erupt in the first two to three years of life. There are also many, many illnesses that occur during those years. By chance alone, there will be times when a tooth appears at the same time as a fever or episode of diarrhoea. But because it is human nature to try to find causes for effects, it is easy to assume that the illness is caused by the tooth arriving. While illnesses do at times occur when a tooth erupts, studies of large groups of children have shown that symptoms such as fever, diarrhoea etc. occur just as often in weeks when no tooth appears as in weeks that a tooth does erupt.

For most teeth, eruption occurs without any detectable pain or discomfort. It probably does happen on occasion that an erupting tooth causes some fussiness, drooling and desire to

chomp on a hard object. But if present, these symptoms appear only in the day or two before or after eruption.

When true discomfort results from teething, give your child a hard, safe object to chomp on. A cold object is especially soothing for many infants. Traditionally, a teething rusk is used; but if you try this with your baby, be sure to take it away before it becomes soft and pieces can be broken off. Another popular teething solution is a teething ring that contains liquid within and can be frozen.

If teething pain seems more severe, there are two other options. Medications such as Panadol are excellent and safe pain relievers. The other choice is

a topical anaesthetic such as Bonjela, which contains choline salicylate and cetalkonium chloride. The antiseptic helps prevent the irritated areas from getting infected and so helps them heal. A small amount of the gel should be applied to the sore area of gum with a clean fingertip and rubbed in gently.

Do not use topical anaesthetics with infants below the age of four months, and use only in small amounts and according to manufacturer's instructions with older babies. Some of these products contain benzocaine and carry a risk of methaemoglobinemia – a rare complication of topical benzocaine that occurs if a sufficient amount of the drug is absorbed through the gums into the blood stream.

Infrequently, the eruption of some teeth is preceded by the appearance of a purple, blood-filled cyst, about 6mm in diameter, on the surface of the gum overlying the spot where the tooth will soon erupt. The cyst invariably ruptures as the tooth emerges and a few drops of blood may appear in your baby's mouth. Both an eruption cyst and the small amount of bleeding are normal and harmless.

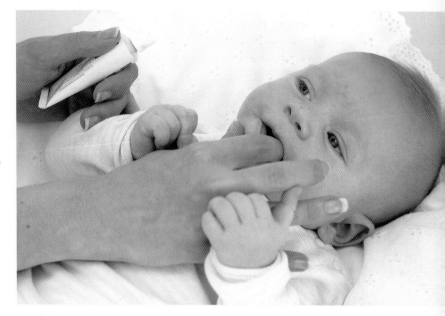

ORDER AND TIME OF ERUPTION OF TEETH

Eruption time varies but by the time your baby is two to three years old, all her primary teeth should be present.

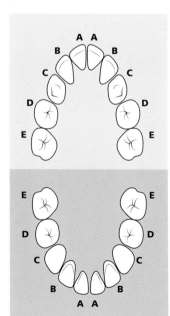

UPPER

A Central Incisors 8-13 months

B Lateral Incisors 8-13 months

C Canines (cuspids) 16-23 months

D First Molars 13-19 months

E Second Molars 25-33 months

LOWER

A Central Incisors 6-10 months

B Lateral Incisors 10-16 months

C Canines (cuspids) 16-23 months

D First Molars 13-19 months

E Second Molars 23-31 months

sugar content of your child's diet, and more importantly, the more often sugar is in her mouth, the greater the opportunity for the bacteria to produce the acids that cause tooth decay. It is certainly preferable that your baby not be allowed to ingest these foods, but such "treats" may occasionally be permitted. You may like to know that cheese is a great acid neutraliser and you should encourage your child to eat it after meals.

The act of brushing your child's teeth may be more challenging than you were expecting. Many children do not like the sensation of the toothbrush rubbing against their teeth and gums. However, they usually do enjoy the taste of the toothpaste! And many toddlers with strong opinions (which is most of them) want to do it by themselves. Of course, they suck on the toothbrush to get the pleasant taste of the toothpaste, but seldom do they actually brush effectively. That must be done by you.

With your child sitting on your lap, allow her to "do it herself"; then take hold of the toothbrush and quickly get in the real brushing. Whether you work up or down, side to side or use a circular motion, the important thing is to clean each tooth thoroughly both front and back. Children's teeth have very deep fissures and extra care should be taken to ensure you clean properly and get into

NURSING BOTTLE CAVITIES

Terrible cavities may develop simultaneously in several teeth if your baby is allowed to sleep with her formula bottle. While saliva will wash away any milk from the last feeding given before placing her in the cot, this is not so if the bottle, left in her mouth for hours overnight, continuously bathes her teeth with milk. If this process continues week after week, multiple cavities will result. This same malady also can strike breastfed babies who spend each night sleeping at your breast. Here, also, continuous exposure to breast milk over weeks and months, can lead to dreadful tooth decay.

those grooves. 90 per cent of all tooth decay in young children happens in the back molars. At first there aren't that many teeth to brush, but new teeth will soon arrive and your job will get harder. Your baby will probably need some help with brushing

until she reaches the age of seven or so.

Be firm and insist on tooth brushing if your baby resists or struggles. Although the milk teeth will eventually be replaced with the permanent set (this begins from the age of around six), it is important that you and your baby take good care of her first teeth. Dental decay can be painful and will require treatment, an unwelcome experience that can easily be avoided. Also, a child may become self-conscious if teeth appear discoloured or contain fillings.

For most toddlers, a stern response will be enough to get them to submit. And, if you brush your teeth together, your baby can copy you and have fun, too. But if a struggle is inevitable, given your child's temperament, it is best to settle for as much as you can accomplish without resorting to battle.

In the most difficult cases you may only get as far as having her brush her teeth by herself, even though you know suboptimal brushing results. Or it

may be necessary to take a few days off from brushing, only to resume your efforts later on.

Thumbsucking and dummies

Many babies suck their thumbs or use dummies because they enjoy the sensation. However, both can lead to problems if the activity is prolonged (see also box, page 199). Getting your baby to stop sucking a dummy is easier than getting her to stop sucking her thumb as the dummy can be gently removed when she sleeps, which helps establish the habit of sleeping without either dummy or thumbsucking. Most children spontaneously stop sucking thumbs or dummies between the ages of two and four, so you should give your baby the opportunity to do so

7 ways to be kind to teeth

1 **Encourage your baby to drink water** as much as possible when she is not having milk. In this way, she will become a water-drinker and will not expect anything else.

2 **Avoid giving your baby sugary drinks,** including fruit drinks.

3 **If she does have juice, dilute it with a large amount of water and give it to her in a cup** rather than a bottle as soon as you can.

4 **Don't leave your baby's bottle in her cot or allow her to use it as a dummy.** If your baby does need a bottle to settle down, fill it with water.

5 **Take your baby away from the breast between feeds**; do not let her use your nipple as a dummy as even breast milk can cause damage if it is in constant contact with the teeth.

6 **Give your baby fruit to end some meals** rather than a dessert. Fruit has a natural sweetness and does not contribute to dental decay as sugary foods do.

7 **If you are offering sweet foods, always do so at the end of meals** rather than as snacks between meals, and before you brush your baby's teeth.

unless changes to the teeth are apparent. Abrupt weaning from the dummy often leads to other negative oral habits such as finger sucking, so you should proceed gently but firmly to encourage separation from the thumb or dummy with good humour. It may take several attempts before the habit is completely broken. Think about using a reward system while your toddler is giving up her dummy; a sticker chart with stars could mark successful days. Alternatively, your toddler may find it easier if you substitute another comfort item. Avoid barter and bribery but always compliment your toddler and tell her how proud you are when she forsakes her thumb or dummy.

Dental check-ups

Your baby's teeth and gums will be checked when your baby is seen by your maternal and child health nurse or GP. Unless there is a problem – your baby chips or injures a tooth, a tooth becomes discoloured or is painful or sensitive when eating hot or cold foods – visits to a dentist only become necessary in the toddler years. At these annual visits, your dentist will check that the teeth have erupted normally and have no problems. Some dentists apply a protective fluoride solutiom to the teeth as extra protection against cavities. However, if it's not time for your annual visit and you suspect a problem with your baby's teeth, don't wait to see the dentist until your child is in pain. She will, in future, associate dental check-ups with pain.

Feeding

From about the age of six months, your baby will be weaned off the breast or bottle as her main source of food and will start to eat solids. Information on this and some recipes to use are in Chapter 10.

Learning to eat with the rest of the family is an important part of your baby's social development. If you normally have your evening meal late, and your baby has already eaten, you could still let her sit with you and give her some finger foods on which to nibble. Also, try to eat breakfast with your baby, or to eat together at weekends.

At mealtimes, much more than food is going into your baby – she is learning social skills such as how to use eating utensils, to communicate and to share and enjoy food. So it is important to make these relaxed and happy occasions. Otherwise, sitting down and eating at a table can be boring to a baby or can turn into a battle of wills between her and her parents. Bear in mind, too, that babies copy adults – if you eat your food with enjoyment, your baby is more likely to do so as well. If she gets bored

at the table, let her get down from her chair and play on the floor.

Be realistic about what to expect from your baby. Some mess is inevitable when she is learning to feed herself. Cover her with a large bib and put some newspaper or plastic covering on the floor. By the time she is 15 to 18 months old she should be able to bring food to her mouth with a spoon without too many spills, although finger feeding may be quicker.

She may also want you to feed her sometimes if she is tired.

Don't worry too much about table manners at this age, but set limits of what you find unacceptable, such as food being thrown on the floor or at someone.

By three years of age your toddler should be able to handle a fork and spoon with some dexterity but will need help with a knife, particularly in cutting up large pieces of food. Build in more time than you think you need for mealtimes as your child learns to

feed herself – and applaud her efforts. Always give small servings; give seconds if she asks. Don't offer bribes for her to finish her meal or reward her if she eats up everything.

Highchairs

When buying a highchair make sure it is sturdy and has both a waist and a crotch strap. It should be secure enough to stop your baby standing up in it and be padded with an easily removable washable fabric. The tray should be large to give support for her arms and have raised edges to catch spills, and should be removable for easy washing. Ones that fold up or can be moved with lockable wheels are good choices when space is limited.

You may prefer to get a feeding table which is lower and more stable than a highchair but it will take up more room and is not as practical if the baby is eating at the family table.

Eating out

If you are going out for the day take plenty of snack foods such as fruits, sandwiches, pieces of cheese and fruit juices, as toddlers get irritable if they don't eat for a long time. Carry wet wipes or cloths to wipe her hands before eating and her mouth afterwards.

It also is a good idea to take your baby to a café or restaurant occasionally as this will teach her to eat in company and to be sociable. Eating away from home also provides an opportunity to experiment with new foods.

Some places, however, may be ill-equipped for babies, which may make the experience stressful for you and no fun for your child. So make sure you try to choose a restaurant that is "family-friendly" and provides highchairs, and always order foods that are quick to prepare. There are, however, a number of easily transportable feeding chairs, which afix to chairs or tables, that are suitable for babies who can sit up independently.

5 ways to minimise the mess

For some children, food is an adventure and they prefer to do everything with it except eat it. Don't worry – this is a transient phase. Just stay calm and patient and avoid making a fuss.

1 **Stand the highchair on a plastic tablecloth or newspaper** to make floor cleaning easier.

2 **Draw a circle on the highchair tray to show your baby where to put her cup.** Or, until she learns to stop tipping her cup upside down, use a cup which has a mouthpiece.

3 **Make a game out of taking her to the sink to wash her hands** if she gets very messy.

4 **Use a plate with deep sides and compartments** so she can get the food up more easily with the fork, without using hr hands.

5 **Use a plastic bib** with a large food-catching compartment.

Clothing and dressing

Buying clothes and dressing your baby can be very enjoyable, but bear in mind that the purpose of clothing is to keep your baby warm and to protect her from the environment not to dress her in stylish, expensive clothing. It is also a good idea to keep in mind that all clothing will get dirty (and will need to be washed often) and that your growing baby will outgrow her garments no matter what size you buy.

Many parents place practicality as their highest priority when choosing clothing. While some garments are relatively easy to get a baby in and out of, others are not. Outfits with press-studs and zippers, for example, are usually more parent friendly than are those with buttons. Since many babies do not like to have T-shirts or jumpers pulled over their heads, you should pick those with wider openings. If your goal is to keep your baby from reaching her hand into her nappy, then buy T-shirts that snap at the bottom. On the other hand, when you are in the midst of toilet training, dress your child in clothes that can quickly allow her to prepare for sitting on the potty, such as trousers with an elasticised waist.

One of the more difficult aspects of dressing your baby, once she reaches nine to ten months of age, is gaining her cooperation. Squirming and resisting efforts to being dressed are quite common for one year olds, while saying "No!" and refusing to get dressed may be a recurrent event when she is two and three years (see *5 techniques for making dressing easier*, page 208). If methods such as distraction, giving choices and being firm are not successful, you have a choice to make. "Which is preferable: getting my way or avoiding the tantrum?" And depending on your answer at that moment, act accordingly. If your toddler wants to go outside in cold weather without a coat, you will feel strongly enough about that you cannot give in and accepting a tantrum would be appropriate. However, if she will put on her coat, but refuses to wear gloves, you may be more comfortable with allowing this. Bring the

gloves along, and in a few minutes, when her hands are cold, ask if she would now like to put her gloves on. Whatever else you do, give yourself plenty of time when getting your toddler dressed. Leaving extra time may require planning on your part and you may even have to get up a few minutes earlier in the morning to avoid having to rush. But if struggles with your toddler over getting dressed are common, it is usually worth it. The worst position you can find yourself in when trying to dress your toddler is to be in a rush. Toddlers seem to know to slow down and resist more when you are rushing and you won't have time to try other methods of persuasion.

5 techniques for making dressing easier

1 Use distraction While your baby or toddler is busy with an interesting toy or book or playing with trucks or dolls, you may find that it is much easier to get her dressed.

2 Be firm If your baby has an easygoing temperament, you will probably be able to overcome her resistance by simply being firm.

3 Give choices If your baby thinks she is getting her way, and you are too – you both win. Offer her a choice of two or three shirts, for example. By letting her make the decision, she feels in control and will be more cooperative. You also come out ahead because your goal, getting her dressed without a struggle, has been accomplished.

4 Leave plenty of time Then you can say to your toddler, "Would you like to get dressed now or in two minutes?" After picking the two-minute option a few times, she may now be ready to get dressed without a fight. Or perhaps you will be able to get on one sock or another piece of clothing each time you broach the subject: eventually she will be fully dressed

5 Humour your toddler Sometimes it pays to let your toddler have her way. If your strong-willed daughter wants to wear the same green T-shirt every day, and will tantrum if not allowed to, wash it daily and grant her request. This is certainly the lesser evil compared with a battle each day. Some girls may only want to wear a dress; so have plenty of dresses that are easy to wash. Perhaps your toddler prefers clothes of a certain colour or fabric. Here, too, if other methods are not succeeding in getting her to put on what you choose for her, it may be easier to let her have her way.

Self-dressing

By the age of 15 months, your toddler will be taking the first steps towards dressing independently. You also may find it difficult to get her to stay still long enough for you to dress her! If your toddler is reluctant to get dressed, try making a game of it, such as hide and seek: "Where's your head gone then? Oh, there it is" when you pull a jumper over her head. If she refuses to put her coat on when going out, take it with you and offer it to her after a few minutes outside. If she is cold, she is likely to accept it.

Singing can also help a reluctant toddler to get dressed. There are songs about dressing or make up your own. Encourage your child to sing along with you. If your child is cranky in the morning, let her have her breakfast before you get her dressed.

At 18 months, your toddler may find it fun to discard her clothes, including her nappy, shoes and socks, having discovered how to do this. But she will also be learning how to cooperate, such as raising her arms for a jumper.

When you dress your young toddler it is a good opportunity to teach her the body parts, what the clothes are, where they go, why you are putting them on and what they do. This will also help her to learn to dress independently. For example "Shirt over vest, trousers over pants, snowsuit keeps you warm and dry, zipper keeps snowsuit zipped, hat goes on head, scarf keeps neck warm, gloves keep your hands warm, boots keep feet dry," and so on.

Very young children don't mind what they wear. But by the age of three, your child may have very definite likes and dislikes and may make a great fuss about certain clothes. As far as practicable, let her choose what to wear and don't criticise her choice. Tact may be needed, however, if she refuses to wear a garment that grandma made!

Helping her self-dress

Although you can do the job more quickly yourself, learning to dress herself is an important step in your toddler learning becoming independent and self-reliant, which you will appreciate in later years. Don't expect too much at first but offer a hand if she wants it. Try not to interfere or laugh if she gets it wrong, otherwise she may become very cranky or discouraged and her pleasure in learning will be taken away. Even if you don't like her choice of colours, do allow her some independence at this stage. To minimise arguments, only put those clothes that you want her to wear in accessible drawers. Don't fight with your toddler about clothes. When she is old enough, let her select what clothes she wants to wear from a suitable range of summer or winter garments.

Lay out the clothes in a way that your toddler can go up to them and put them on easily. For example, if the clothes have a picture on the front, place these downwards so that they are facing away from her when she puts them on. If there are buttons on the back of the garment, place these facing upwards. Lay out trousers with the waist closest and the front upmost.

Put a shirt or jumper down with the head furthest away and teach her how to burrow into these from the bottom.

A "learning to dress" doll can give your toddler practice in doing up buttons, laces and ties, zips and Velcro straps.

Fastenings

When your toddler is learning how to use a zip, teach her to pull this away from the skin and clothes to prevent catching. When she is being toilet trained, buy trousers with elasticated waists that are easy to pull up and down. Velcro fasteners are also easy to manage as are jeans with press-studs, not buttons. When she does learn to use buttons, teach her to button from the bottom upwards – this will help to avoid getting the buttons in the wrong holes.

Shoes

Protecting the feet from sharp objects on the ground and from environmental challenges – cold, heat, snow, water – are the main "jobs" of shoes. While paediatricians and orthopaedic surgeons recommend sturdy but flexible low-cut shoes or trainers, salespeople may try and sell you stiffer, high-cut shoes that they claim "support" a baby's foot.

6 characteristics of recommended footwear

1 **Bendable** You should be able to bend the shoe/trainer with the toe end and heel end both going upward as much as you can bend your own sneakers.

2 **Sturdy** The shoe/trainer should be sturdy, but bendable. Stiff soles are not recommended.

3 **Low cut** Shoes/trainers must be low cut; they should not rise to the level of the ankle.

4 **Contain an arch** There should be an arch inside the shoe/trainer that you can feel with your fingers.

5 **Be well fitting** The shoes/trainers must fit. You should just be able to place your index finger between the tip of your baby's big toe and the end of the shoe/sneaker while she is standing.

Since the role of shoes and trainers is to protect the feet, they need not be worn in your home (unless there is a reason you need to protect your baby's feet). Going barefoot or walking around in socks is fine.

Special event footwear, such as sandals or boots, often do not satisfy the recommended criteria (see box, above), especially in the area of being flexible. However, do your best to find a product that is satisfactory. The advice to wear low-cut shoes does not apply to boots, which by necessity must be above the ankles in inclement weather.

To avoid the hassle of tying shoe laces over and over again, look for trainers and shoes with Velcro fasteners.

Socks

Correct-fitting socks are as important as shoes and should be chosen with the same care. If they are too big, they can ruin a correctly fitted shoe by causing pressure; if they are too small they will scrunch the toes and discourage straight growth. Make sure you check regularly that your baby's socks still fit her.

Socks should always be pure cotton and not acrylic or wool. Cotton enables feet to breathe properly and it minimises the possibility of fungal infections, such as athlete's foot.

Laundry

A baby creates an awful lot of dirty clothes. There is no reason to separate your baby's wash from your own, although this is a widely practised custom in many families. There is also no best laundry product to use as no published scientific studies of different laundry detergents' gentleness and cleansing ability when used with baby clothing have been carried out. In fact, some widely marketed special children's brands remove the protective fire retardant added to infant clothing. As far as is known, one brand is just as good as any other.

Sleeping

From about 12 to 18 months of age your toddler will probably begin to need less sleep. One daytime nap is usually dropped as she starts to find far more exciting activities to do around the house. Night-time sleep problems may also begin as your toddler starts asserting her independence (see *Early waking and other sleep problems*, page 166).

The amount of sleep a toddler needs varies; some toddlers need more and others less. A bad temper and fretfulness can indicate a lack of sleep. Be realistic about how much sleep your own baby needs. If your two-year-old only sleeps 11 hours at night, then it is unreasonable to put her to bed at seven in the evening and expect her to sleep through until eight the next morning. Generally, you can count on: 12 to 14 hours (including naps) for a one-year-old, 12 to 13 hours (including naps) for a two-year-old, and 12 hours for a three-year-old.

Naps

Most toddlers have a nap in the day up to the age of two, and some may need a short sleep up to the age of three or four. A nap will last however long your baby needs to sleep, and usually occurs at a regular time each day. If your baby naps at a time which is not convenient to you or so late in the afternoon that it makes bedtime too late, try to make her naptime 10 to 15 minutes earlier or later each day until she naps when you want her to.

Some toddlers will refuse to nap but may still need to have a rest. If this is the case with your baby, allow her to play quietly with some toys in her bed or put on an audio story or music tape. Or you could use the opportunity to read to her.

To encourage your child to continue taking naps, you could try the following. Ease her away from over-strenuous activity some time before; offer her a soporific snack – milk and biscuits (unsweetened), for example; make sure her room is darkened, and settle her down much as for bedtime. If she's resisting a nap because she doesn't want to lose your company, spend a short time with her reading or just relaxing.

Changing from a cot to a bed

The age you put your toddler into a bed is a matter for personal preference, but once she can climb over

5 things you can include in a bedtime routine

1 **Set a time for your child to go to bed** and make sure she does so regularly. Give her plenty of warning as bedtime approaches.

2 **Bathe your toddler shortly before bedtime** each night; allow her to play a little but don't let her get too excited.

3 **Put her in her night clothes**; give her a milky drink or snack before brushing her teeth.

4 **Don't leave right away** once she's in her bed. Spend some quiet time with her – have a chat about the day's events or read her a story.

5 **Tuck her up** and give her a cuddle and a goodnight kiss. Leave the room before she's asleep.

the top of a cot, you should put her into a bed for safety reasons. She can easily hurt herself if she climbs over her cot's high rail. Most toddlers will not object to changing over to a bed, but the occasional one may be reluctant to leave a familiar environment. If space isn't a problem, keep both the cot and the bed in the room for a few weeks so she can sleep part of the time in each.

Choose a time when your toddler is fairly settled – no new siblings, not getting over an illness or being toilet trained or weaned, and not just before going on holiday.

Your child will probably enjoy helping you to pick out new bedlinen but narrow down her choices in the shop or she'll soon become fractious. Always cover the new bed with plastic sheeting in case of accidents.

Transferring a favourite blanket can help acclimatise a toddler to a new bed, as will a selection of her favourite cot toys although she may prefer a new stuffed animal as a companion for her big bed.

The new bed should be low to the ground to prevent your toddler hurting herself should she fall out. You may also need to put guard rails down the sides or cushions alongside the bed until she gets used to it.

A bedtime routine

Establishing a simple and soothing bedtime routine for your toddler creates security and is the first step in preventing sleep problems (see box). As far as possible, try to keep to the routine, so that your child understands that it leads to going to bed and sleeping.

Out and about

The old adage, "There's no place like home," may well have been coined by a parent just returning from an outing with her child! Travelling to grandma's house may certainly be enjoyable and the image of mum and grandmother standing at the front door, admiring the baby, may come to mind. But complete the image – certainly dad is trailing behind, resembling a fully loaded pack horse, with nappy bag, playpen, buggy, portable cot, and all sorts of toys and paraphernalia in tow. Actually, travelling locally is relatively easy to accomplish, while longer trips and holidays present a host of potential difficulties.

Close to home

There are many reasons why short trips are less complicated than longer ones: the time your baby is limited in her mobility is brief, you need to bring only enough with you for her immediate needs, delays (the time it takes to get your child into the car or wait for a bus or train) are minimal, and you can readily plan your outing around your baby's routines. Moreover, if the trip is not going well, you can just turn around and go home.

Whether you are off to the park or playground or planning a supermarket or museum visit, it pays to be prepared. It's a good idea to keep a small bag packed with a couple of disposable nappies or spare pants (depending on your child's age), baby wipes, tissues, some plastic bags for rubbish, small cartons of juice and a beaker. If she's old enough, let your toddler carry a lightweight backpack with a favourite toy or comfort item (if indispensable), and her own drink and snack.

If your toddler is very active, don't go anywhere where she will be confined to her pram for too long. If you are taking the pram, try to avoid carrying too many other things. A large shoulder bag or a backpack should be sufficient to hold all the essentials for you and your child.

Using a carrier

Once your baby can keep his head up – about 16 to 20 weeks – you can place her face outwards in a carrier. But as she gets heavier, or if you intend to do a lot of walking – particularly in crowded places or on rough lanes – you may want to invest in a back carrier, in which she can sit up and look out with her weight being evenly distributed over your shoulders and across your back. The best ones have sturdy metal frames, adjustable seat heights and stand securely on the floor when you put your baby inside. Backpacks and back carriers are aimed at babies from about six months onwards, when they can support themselves sitting up and their neck muscles are quite strong.

On the bus

Because they don't provide seat belts, safe travel on a bus is difficult. Your choices are to place your child in an infant or car seat on the seat next to you and hold it in place with one hand, or to hold her on your lap the entire trip. If she is in a pram and there is a free designated area, you can travel there making sure the wheels of the pram are locked. However, once she is toddling, she's unlikely to want to stay in the pram for long so it's a good idea, if you travel frequently by bus, to buy a lightweight easily foldable model.

Take your time getting on and off the bus, and beware of automatic doors. Ask other passengers to help, if necessary. Have your ticket ready before you board the bus.

Shopping with a toddler

Shopping for food or other essentials with a lively or bored young child in tow, is an experience many parents would prefer to miss, but can't avoid. You may need to try several strategies to prevent it being a hassle.

- Decide on the rules that suit you, such as never buying sweets in supermarkets, and stick to them.
- Try to go to the supermarket when it's quiet and when both of you are not tired or hungry – or carry a suitable snack such as a bun or banana, which your toddler can eat, if necessary.
- If you can, make it a learning experience by involving your child in choosing food that you are going to buy – for instance, does she want red or green apples, or a particular breakfast cereal. If she picks up unsuitable food, decide whether you

6 ways to ensure a pleasurable trip

1. **Bring distractions** Keep your child busy by taking along books, toys, games, colouring books and crayons. Your child's favourite DVDs, to be used in your car's DVD player, in a portable device, or in the one provided in your hotel room, are very helpful in preventing "boredom".

2. **Bring food** If your child has strong food likes and dislikes (as most toddlers do), make sure her favourites will be available during your trip. Bring a snack or two on board the bus, plane or train, and on daily outings as well. Do not assume your child will like food prepared in restaurants, even though it looks the same as the way you make it, and take along a sandwich or small meal in case this occurs.

3. **Follow routines** As much as you can, keep your child on her typical daily schedule. The happiest children are those who get to bed on time, take their nap, and eat at their usual times throughout the day. (Disruptions in routine often result in your child being cranky and uncooperative.)

4. **Always consider your child's nature** She will be fascinated by a new environment but will be simultaneously be a bit disturbed and less secure without her familiar surroundings.

5. **Carry a first-aid kit** (see box, page 216).

6. **Child-proof any new surroundings** If staying in a hotel or in someone's home, do an inspection as soon as you arrive. Many families travel with a roll of thick tape used to cover power points, hold aside curtain strings, and keep cords from lamps and alarm clocks out of the way. Refer to Chapter 12 about potential hazards outdooors.

are going to explain why you don't want it, or whether it's easier to put it back when she's not looking. If she is old enough, let her for look for items on the shopping list. You could draw pictures of some of these and ask her to remind you what they are.

- If possible, visit stores with the best toilet and changing facilities – and make sure you know where they are!

- Take your child to a small specialist shop such as a butcher's sometimes so that she can see close up how food is cut up or weighed.

- If you have a lot of shopping to do, try to break up the time with a visit to a café or see if a crêche is available.

Local visits

Even everyday outings can be learning experiences for your child. Even before you get to your destination, you will have opportunities to discuss with your child the things you are seeing, such as dogs, buses, or goods in shop windows. While walking, look out for things to collect for later use to make collages or leaf prints, or as a nature display. Horse chestnuts, stones, pebbles, shells, seaweed, driftwood, acorns, feathers, leaves, pine cones or grasses are all collectable.

Once you get to the park or playground, there are fun things to enjoy such as feeding the ducks, playing on equipment or with water or sand, or just running around.

Even if it's raining, you can dress your child in suitable clothes and take her outside for some play or a short walk. Go on a puddle hunt in the rain and let her splash through these in gumboots. Point out the differently shaped clouds and ask her what animals she thinks they look like. Look for her reflection in puddles. If you see a rainbow ask her if she can name any colours. Encourage her to stick her tongue out to taste the rain.

When taking everyday walks, try to vary familiar routes so that your toddler sees new things. Add to her experiences by including interesting places to visit, taking into account her age and personality. If she seems fascinated by dogs, she might welcome a visit to the zoo or a farm. Talk to her about the animals, what they are, the sounds they make and so on. Keep the visits short to avoid boredom. When you get home, look through an animal book and see if your child can spot the animals she saw. If you live near an airport or railway station, your child will enjoy going to look at the planes taking off or

landing, to the station to see the trains or, if you live near the sea or a river, going on a boat trip.

Long-distance travel

Travelling long distances from home with your baby requires a fair amount of time and effort – not only getting to where you are going but once you are there. Time away is bound to be less restful than when you travelled alone, and your daily plans will be strongly influenced by your baby's routines.

If your child frequently gets ear infections or swimmer's ear, you may want to discuss with your paediatrician taking an oral antibiotic or ear drops along with you. If your child has food allergy, diabetes, asthma or other diseases where symptoms may appear suddenly, take emergency medicines – such as adrenaline injections (EpiPen Jr, Twinject and others), insulin and asthma medications – on board an airplane or keep appropriate medicines handy if travelling by other means, so you will be prepared for any disease exacerbation.

TRAVEL FIRST-AID KIT

- Appropriate painkiller.
- Sunblock and a cooling spray or lotion to treat sunburn (if it occurs).
- Insect repellent (if applicable on your trip). Usually the same spray or lotion for relieving sunburn can also relieve the itch of insect bites.
- Prescription medications.
- Band-aids (small and large) are always needed, so bring many. Also, an antibiotic ointment (Savlon, Betradine, others) is useful for cuts and scrapes.
- Antihistamine (promethazine and others) for allergic reactions; car, motion, altitude and sea sickness; and sometimes to use as a cold remedy.
- Vaccination record.

By car

Always ensure your car seat is suitable for your baby and properly installed. Stop every hour or two to change nappies or for your toddler to use the potty and to give her a chance to move around and burn up energy. Try to be on the road during the hours she typically naps. Eat meals at her usual times and allow at least two to three hours for her to wind down before bed time.

By trains and coaches

Train and coach travel can be more difficult than cars. Neither has nappy-changing areas on board or someone to watch your baby while you use the toilet, and stops on coaches to use facilities are limited. As with bus travel, you'll have to place your baby in an infant or car seat on the seat next to you and hold it in place with one hand, or hold her on your lap the entire trip. Also, trains and city buses do not have seat belts so they are less safe. If you are travelling with a toddler, thee is little opportunity for letting him move around and sticking to routines will be harder. If you have the option of picking between several departure times, pick the one that will coincide with nap time or allow you the most compliance with your baby's daily schedule. On a train, you may be able to vary things by taking your toddler to another carriage. Many trains have dining cars, which offer more activity to watch and a place for a treat; some provide electric outlets for computer use. If available, a movie or video pre-loaded onto your laptop or produced on a portable DVD player can capture your child's interest.

By boat

On a small boat, secure your baby on your lap. A life jacket and close supervision are a must. On large boats and cruises, child-proofing your cabin and your typical vigilance are all that is needed. Sea sickness is another form of motion sickness. Scopolamine patches, standard treatment for sea sickness for teenagers and adults, are not recommended for small children. Using an antihistamine (see box) is suggested as an alternative by some experts.

By air

Although most airlines suggest limiting flying until infants are at least a month old, there is no reason for this restriction in modern planes with pressurised cabins. But taking your baby on a flight, no matter what her age, presents a number of challenges:

You need to check whether you have to buy a ticket for your baby or whether it is possible to fly holding her on your lap during the trip; you may need a ticket in any event. It is recommended, wherever possible, to purchase a seat for your baby and have her spend the trip in an approved car seat that is held tightly in place by the plane's seat belt. Now, if there is any sudden turbulence, she will be safely secured.

Getting through security checkpoints is also difficult. Taking off your own shoes, coat and other metallic objects in a short time can be hectic, but it becomes even more complicated if you also have a baby or toddler in tow. This process will go much more smoothly if before entering the queue, you have collected items that must be placed on the conveyor belt and removed as much of yours and your child's clothing as is possible. Folding buggies, which are very handy for travel, must be folded and placed through the x-ray screener.

At the time of writing only liquids in 100ml (or less) containers in a sealed plastic bag can be taken onto a plane. You need to check with your airline about taking expressed breastmilk, formula or juice for your child as well as any prescription medicines.

Exotic travel

Before travel to developing countries, check if vaccinations and malaria prophylaxis are needed with your GP and find out what you need to do to prevent (and treat) traveller's diarrhoea and other possible occurrences (see also page 350). It is best to get travel vaccines at least a month before your departure.

Travel-related conditions

Although most trips will prove uneventful, it's best to be prepared for anything untoward. There are a few conditions that are related to travel in which treatments suitable for adults may need to be

adapted for children. These include car and sea sickness, earache and jet lag.

Car and sea sickness

Motion sickness with associated nausea and vomiting results when the eyes make rapid movements to follow and refocus on moving objects. A good way to avoid it is to position your baby in the middle of the back seat and put blinders – cut from cardboard and taped to the side of the seat – on her car seat to prevent her from looking out the side window. By looking straight ahead, through the front window, the rapid eye movements can be avoided. Some experts also recommend giving an antihistamine such as promethazine (Phenergan) or alimemazine (Vallergan) to prevent motion sickness. It is not clear whether these medications work by an anti-emetic effect or by just make your child sleepy.

Another variety of car sickness is habitual. Some children seem to throw up whenever they are placed in their car seats and the car begins to move. The vomiting typically appears shortly after the trip begins, but will sometimes occur even before there is any motion. If your baby has developed the habit, for whatever reason, of vomiting in this situation, the best thing you can do is to have a plastic bag at the ready as you strap her in her seat and await her throwing up. Try not to show any emotion or disapproval of the vomiting because with many children, your reaction (even though it is a negative one) provides some reinforcement for her behaviour. After one or two episodes of habitual throwing up, the vomiting is usually over and the rest of the trip will be uneventful.

The treatment for sea sickness in young children is rest and Benadryl.

Earache

While there is no doubt that the changes in air pressure associated with the initial ascent and more frequently in the final descent of the aircraft can lead to ear-aches, they are much less common than is generally believed (in one study 6 per cent of children on the ascent and 10 per cent of children on the descent had ear discomfort). The Eustachian tube in the ear is responsible for equalising air pressure in the middle ear with that outside the body. If, however, it becomes "stuck" in a closed position, for example if your baby has a head cold, it won't be able to equalise the pressure and pain may be experienced as the plane ascends and descends. The Eustachian tube, however, will generally open briefly and then close during the act of swallowing and chewing and for this reason, it is recommended that you nurse or give your infant a bottle – or if your child is older, give her something to chew on – during the ascent and descent. When she does this, she is maximising the Eustachian tube's ability to equalise pressures. Yet, although such manoeuvres are helpful, they may not work if your child has a head cold. Carry a suitable painkiller in case an ear-ache does occur. If your child has an existing ear infection, it is not dangerous for her to fly – which may be contrary to what you've heard. Any pus or fluid in the middle ear will have a protective effect on possible pressure changes.

Altitude sickness

Although this will not occur on board an aeroplane with a pressurised cabin, it may appear at your destination if it is several thousand metres higher than what you are accustomed to. Altitude sickness can be recognised as crankiness, decreased appetite, headache and occasionally vomiting or rapid breathing. Often these signs are attributed to jet lag or changes in routine because they, too, may cause the same symptoms in your child. Altitude sickness results because, at very high altitudes, the oxygen level is lower. In a day or two, your child's body will adjust to this change, but symptoms may be troubling until that point is reached. Medications are available to prevent and treat altitude sickness in older individuals, but are usually are not given to infants and toddlers. However, giving your child extra fluids and ensuring adequate sleep before travel and upon arrival at your destination do help, as dehydration and tiredness seem to exacerbate the symptoms of altitude sickness. Some experts recommend giving Benadryl to children with symptoms of altitude sickness, but again, it is unclear if the medication has a direct benefit or just puts a cranky child to sleep.

Jet lag

Where there is a rapid change in time zones and the body's 24-hour rhythms are disrupted, your child may become cranky and complain of tiredness and headaches. Jet lag seldom occurs in a trip with a time zone shift of less than 3–4 hours. Additionally, it is much less likely to occur when you travel from east to west than when going west to east.

To combat jet lag, use common sense. If possible arrange flights to suit yor child's normal sleep patterns. An overnight stop along the way can also help. As with altitude sickness, attention to good hydration is helpful. Also, exposing your child to sunlight at your new destination will help her reset her internal clock.

On brief excursions (less than three days) into a different time zone, it may be best to continue to follow routines staying on the time in your original time zone. But for longer stays, immediately move your routines to the same time of day as before, but according to time in the new time zone.

Toilet training

At birth, bowel movements occur automatically. Newborns have what is called a gastro-colic reflex, which essentially means that when milk enters their stomachs, the lower intestine is stimulated to push out a bowel movement. But by a month or two of age, this reflex is weaker and your infant has to help in pushing out her stool. Shortly before urinating or pooing, your daughter gets the urge and almost immediately begins to urinate or defecate. The earliest sign of physiological readiness for toilet training appears at some point between 18 and 30 months of age: you will observe that your toddler seems to sense a bowel movement coming, at which time she goes to her room, closet, or a "private place" to squat and have the bowel movement.

When to start

To accomplish toilet training, two essential goals must be reached. First, your toddler must sense that she needs to urinate or poo and be able to hold in her excretions until she can get to the potty and second, your toddler also must want to use the potty. Physical readiness is generally accomplished before two and half years of age (particularly in girls); the harder part, by far, is gaining your toddler's consent to be trained.

All doctors and leaders in the field of toileting, no matter what beliefs or philosophical leanings on toilet training are favoured, agree that battling over toilet training is to be avoided. It is clear that a struggle over toilet training is one that you as parent cannot win, unless, of course, your toddler lets you. Toddlers can be quite determined to get their way, and if your child is resolute that she won't go on the potty, there is little you can do to make her urinate or poo outside her nappies. A small number of toddlers who are upset or anxious about toilet training will even show their displeasure with the process by holding in faeces for several days, becoming quite constipated.

It seems reasonable to take early steps in toilet training once your toddler shows an interest (such as sitting on her potty with her clothes on) or is seen to be able to refrain from having a bowel movement until she gets to her private place. Many parents buy a potty when their baby reaches 18 months and display it next to the adult toilet, waiting for signs of interest. You may also wait until you see her capable of delaying a bowel movement.

Choosing a potty

There are dozens of potties available. How is one to choose? And which one or ones is best? The answer is that probably any will do. The colours, decorations, music and other enticements to get your toddler on the potty will probably lose their novelty very quickly.

A more significant choice, though, is between potties and toilet seats. Potties are placed on the ground. They allow your toddler to sit down comfortably, with her feet on the floor. A removable bowl-like receptacle for waste products is taken to the toilet where urine and faeces are dumped and the receptacle can be cleaned. On the other hand, small toilet seats go over the existing toilet seat, allowing your toddler to sit on a seat designed for her size. The central hole is smaller so that your toddler will not fall into the toilet. To get onto the seat, you must place her there yourself or place an appropriate step-stool nearby. Some toilet seats have steps attached. The advantages of the potty are, it is said, that with her feet firmly on the ground, your child will feel more secure and safe. (However, children seem to be quite secure on small toilet seats as well.) The potty can be conveniently placed anywhere your toddler is – you can bring it into your yard while your toddler is outside, so that she

WHY DOESN'T SHE WANT TO GO ON THE POTTY?

There are numerous explanations for why your child doesn't want to be toilet trained. Whether you agree with the psychoanalytical or the behaviouralistic view on this subject, one thing is clear: your child likes her nappy and is very content to continue to use it. Feeling uncomfortable in a wet nappy or being "disgusted" by having a stool against her skin does not seem to bother her in the least. The only motivation that truly drives your child to become trained is her desire to gain your approval. So a kind and gentle approach to toilet training your child is equally if not more likely to succeed that a more stern, demanding style.

will not have far to go if she needs to quickly get to the potty. The main disadvantage of potties is that you must clean the receptacle each time it is used.

Toilet seats do not require cleaning after urination or a bowel movement – flushing the toilet is all that is needed – and they are more portable (they are smaller and lighter than potties and fit into a travel bag readily). On the negative side, though, seats require a toilet. There is also the minor inconvenience of having to remove the seat before you yourself can sit on the toilet. And of course, after you are finished, the seat must be restored to its place in order to be ready for your toddler's next trip to the bathroom. Bottom line: it probably doesn't matter what type you choose. Go with your instincts.

Initiating the process

Once you have your potty, the next step is to lure you toddler into using it. However, don't choose a "bad" time for you – such as when you are about to move or have another baby or during major holidays – as your child will need a lot of your attention.

Some children, out of curiosity or perhaps a desire to imitate you or other household members, will sit on the potty on their own or will do so if you use the toilet at the same time. Others may need asking. Ask especially when you sense (by your toddler's facial expression and behaviour) that she is about to poo. Reinforce potty sitting by praising your child. Then, when at last she wees or poos while sitting, tell her what a big girl she is. Some childcare experts advocate a biscuit or a small sweet as a reward for going to the potty, although many others do not. If you are going to use rewards, offer it right away. Don't expect your child to stay dry for a day or a week before receiving a reward as toddlers have no sense of time. Or you could build up to a bigger treat – a new toy – by using a star chart to reward positive potty action. Once she has earned enough stars, you can proffer the toy but don't

remove any if she has an accident. For some children, the stars on their own are reward enough.

Quite commonly, a child who has shown an initial interest in sitting on the potty may suddenly decide that she no longer wants to sit there. A very good response to this is to drop the matter of toilet training for a short while. Perhaps in another week or two, ask her again if she would like to sit there. As long as her answer is "no" – whether expressed verbally or by your child's actions, back off and try again in the future. Eventually, she will say "yes".

Training boys

Boys are generally slower at being toilet trained than girls and also are messier and more likely to play with their excrement. If the latter happens, simply

toilet training tips

1 **Do not use underpants** (instead of a nappy or pull up) until your toddler hasn't had an accident for several days to ensure she will succeed at staying dry when she is in underwear.

2 **Use the wearing of underwear as a reward** for her progress in learning to use the potty. Do not put underpants on over a nappy if your toddler requests this – by agreeing, you lessen the value of underwear as a reward.

3 **Be prepared for frequent stops** In the first days and weeks after attaining daytime dryness, your toddler will want to go to the potty whenever she feels a small urge to pee or poo, since she wants to avoid accidents. If you are out shopping or at the park, finding a suitable toilet quickly may be challenging so have a plan in hand on how to get her to a toilet when she feels she needs one.

4 **Dress for success** Make sure your toddler is wearing easily manageable clothes – trousers that can be pulled down or a skirt that can be lifted up readily.

NIGHT-TIME DRYNESS

The following strategies are adopted by many parents with some success but don't address the root causes of wetting.

Restrict liquids after dinner The premise behind this recommendation is that if your toddler is given less to drink, she will, as a result, make less urine, and her bladder will fill less during the night. Restricting your toddler's fluid may help a little by delaying the time until her bladder fills but wetting at night, however, is seldom due to a bladder with too small a capacity to hold urine. And while your toddler will produce more urine when she has had a lot to drink, it is not the volume of urine that causes a child to wet but the fact that when her bladder is distended, she is unaware of the signal from her bladder to her brain.

Wake your child before you go to bed and put her on the potty This technique "works" for many families. But although getting your child to empty her bladder after she has been asleep a few hours will delay the refilling of her bladder until she wakes up in the morning, if her bladder is distended, she will not sense it and will have an accident.

Don't use nappies or pull-ups; after your toddler wets herself a few times, she will be discouraged from wetting again This advice is based on the assumption that when your child wets at night, she is doing it with intention or because she is too lazy to get up to go to the bathroom. Typically, however, your child will not become aware she is wet until she awakes the next morning and by dressing your child in pants (instead of a nappy or pull-up) every night, the only result will be a great deal more laundry to do.

clean up the mess and avoid showing disgust. Boys also have a choice as to whether they want to stand up to wee or sit on the potty to do so. Generally boys start to wee by sitting on a potty, so your son will have to be shown how to push his penis down so that the wee goes into the potty. Once he stands, you'll need to show him how to aim into the bowl.

How long will training take?

If you are resolute and unyielding about your child sitting on the potty, and she has an easygoing temperament, it is possible that she can be toilet trained by two and a half years of age. However, if both you and your child are strong-willed, you may very well find yourself in the midst of daily struggles, which should be avoided. Your child should not be forced to be toilet trained. If she is determined not to be persuaded, she may not do so until she is three and a half or older. Although it will take longer, this approach will allow training to be pleasantly completed in just a few days once she agrees to it without having frequent fights (that you will often lose).

Night-time training

Being dry at night is a totally separate talent from being dry in the daytime. It is not a matter of "laziness" but rather a result of your child sleeping deeply and being unaware of the signal from her full bladder to her brain. Not only is she oblivious of urinating, but the wetness does not even wake her.

To remain dry at night, your toddler must sense a full bladder during sleep and respond to the signal by "holding in" urine or waking and going to the bathroom. However, additional neurological maturity is required to detect the signal. Some children are sufficiently mature at the same time that day-time training is accomplished; others may achieve maturity at the age of five, six or even seven. The age at which your child stops night-time wetting, which is also when she starts sensing the signal from her bladder during sleep, is genetically determined. If you or your partner were late to become dry at night when you were young, you may have passed this tendency on to your child.

FEEDING YOUR OLDER BABY

Ready for weaning

Introducing solids to a baby's diet is an exciting stage in your baby's life and a natural part of her development. Bear in mind that the principle of weaning – the process of replacing a baby's total dependence on milk with "solid" foods – is to gradually introduce her to a wide range of tastes and textures until she can eventually enjoy the same meals as the rest of the family. The emphasis is on gradual, so take it easy and enjoy this natural progression.

When should weaning start?

This is one of the most frequently asked questions by new parents. In line with the World Health Organisation's recommendations, current advice is that breast or formula milk meet all of your baby's dietary needs for the first six months and there are no nutritional advantages to weaning before this age. However, there is still an ongoing debate on the ideal weaning age, mainly because all babies are different and have different needs, and many parents continue to wean their babies from four months. The National Health and Medical Research Council (NHMRC) currently recommends that the majority of infants should not be given solids until around six months of age.

In spite of the foregoing, don't feel pressured to start weaning earlier or later than you feel is right for your baby as the guidelines do not fully take into account the wide individual variations in developmental maturity between infants. Having said this, don't leave weaning much later than six months (26 weeks), unless recommended to do so by your health visitor, as by then your baby will need non-milk sources of nourishment to provide sufficient calories, vitamins and minerals. After six months, breast or formula milk no longer meets all your baby's nutritional needs, particularly of iron, and now is the time to introduce "solid" foods to your baby's diet. Requirements for protein, thiamine, niacin, vitamins B6 and B12, magnesium, zinc, sodium and chloride also increase between six and 12 months.

Learning to bite and chew is also important for an infant's speech and language development.

Weaning prior to four months (17 weeks) is not recommended, as your baby's digestive system, notably the gut and kidneys, is too immature to cope with anything more than breast milk or formula. Furthermore, it has been said that early weaning may make your baby fat and increase the likelihood of allergies (although the latter is debatable), while holding off until your baby is six months old may avoid this risk, especially if there is a family history of weight problems and allergies.

Babies who are born pre-term need to be weaned depending on their individual needs and your maternal and child health nurse or dietician will be able to advise on the best time for your baby.

8 signs your baby is ready

1 Seems unsatisfied after a milk feed and hungrier than usual.

2 Shows an interest in your food.

3 Makes chewing motions.

4 Can close her mouth around a spoon.

5 Holds her head up well.

6 Can sit up with support.

7 Can move her tongue back and forth.

8 Is teething.

Introducing solids

While most foods are suitable for your baby from six months (see page 236 for the exceptions), it's advisable to start weaning gradually, especially if there is a family history of allergies. The first step is to simply familiarise your baby with taking food from a spoon; the food should be smooth, semi-liquid in consistency, with a bland flavour. Initially, the quantity eaten is largely immaterial. If your baby is allowed to self feed (see page 229), spoon feeding may develop later.

Choose a time of day when you are not feeling too rushed or your baby too tired to introduce solids; midday often is the preferred time. Bear in mind that eating is a new skill for your baby and don't expect her to get it right from the start. She is using previously unused muscles, so don't be put off if food appears to be "spat" out at first – this is perfectly normal.

Face-to-face interaction is important: talk to your baby through the feed, trying to be both positive and encouraging.

Start gradually – offer some fruit or vegetables (see page 226) on the tip of a plastic spoon or a clean finger. It may be a good idea to give your baby a little milk first to curb any hunger pangs but as feeding becomes more established, start to offer food before milk. Don't expect your baby to eat more than 1–2 teaspoons at this stage – although it could well be more. The first solids you give should be regarded as a supplement to your baby's milk feed, and you will find that her appetite will vary from one feed to another so monitoring how much she is eating is not of paramount importance at this stage. Once she has taken the food or is no longer interested, continue with milk.

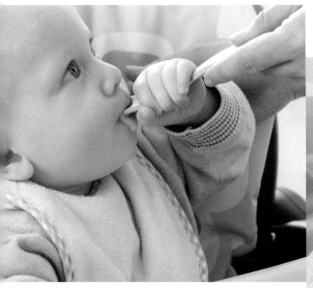

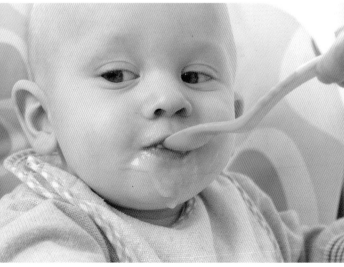

For the first few weeks, offer the same food for around three days at a time to allow your baby to get used to new tastes. It also may be a good idea to keep a food diary to monitor likes and dislikes as well as to gauge if there is any sign of an allergic reaction. Signs that your baby may have an allergy include a rash, diarrhoea, bloated tummy or increased wind.

Don't be surprised when your baby's stools change colour and odour after starting solids. This is perfectly normal. Constipation also is not unusual at this stage – infant rice cereal, for example, lacks fibre or it may be due to dehydration or the fact that the digestive system is getting used to food. If your baby becomes constipated, introduce fruit and vegetables, which are richer in fibre, and consider offering cooled boiled tap water in a beaker (see *Introducing a cup*, page 227).

GETTING EQUIPPED

There is no need to invest in large amounts of equipment but the following are worth considering:

- Bibs – you'll need plenty! There are plenty of types to choose from but the plastic-backed bibs prevent food and drinks soaking through to clothes. The moulded plastic bibs with a trough are more suitable for slightly older babies who have started to feed themselves
- 2–3 shallow plastic feeding spoons
- 2 non-slip plastic bowls
- Sieve or food mincer
- Steamer – while not essential, steaming helps to retain water-soluble nutrients in fruit and vegetables
- Mini food processor or blender – again not essential but these make light work of puréeing and finely chopping meals
- Cup or beaker with lid and two handles

Very first foods

Mild-tasting, single-ingredients purées are a good starting point (see also recipe pages 250-1). Wash or scrub fruit and vegetables thoroughly and peel them, removing any core, seeds or pips. Then roughly chop and place in a saucepan with a small amount of water then cook until tender. Purée in a blender until smooth (see page 230).

Try

- Vegetables such as potato, sweet potato, pumpkin and carrot
- Fruit such as banana, pear and apple
- Dry infant cereal made up with breast or formula milk
- Home-cooked puréed white rice or dry baby rice mixed with breast or formula milk

Milk matters

For the first year, breast or formula milk remains a vital source of nutrients for your baby but you may find that as she eats more solid foods, she naturally takes less milk. Yet, if she drinks too much milk then her appetite for solids could be affected and she may begin to lack sufficient nutrients in her diet. In the early stages of weaning, your baby should still be having at least four bottles of formula or the equivalent number of breastfeeds a day.

Cow's (also sheep's and goat's) milk can be included in cooking from six months of age but is not recommended as a main drink until your baby is one year old. The reason for this is that cow's milk contains too much salt and protein and insufficient iron and other nutrients for your baby's needs. A breastfed baby will take what she needs from the breast; it is not advisable to reduce breastfeeds, as there is no evidence that this will hinder her development.

Give soya-based formula milk only on the advice of your GP or health nurse. Soya formula, which was developed for babies who are allergic to cow's milk, can be prescribed by your doctor, if necessary (see page 85).

Continue to sterilise feeding bottles, as warm milk is an ideal breeding ground for bacteria.

Water

Before six months of age, fully breastfed babies should not require additional fluids including water, unless otherwise recommended. Bottle-fed babies may be given cooled, boiled tap water in hot weather but this should be in addition to milk feeds.

When feeding is more established, your baby may need fluids other than milk. Cooled, boiled tap water is the preferred option; some mineral waters are too rich in minerals for babies and bottled water is not sterile so will still need boiling and cooling beforehand. Avoid concentrated fruit juice, cordials, and syrups as they are high in sugar and can damage teeth, even those that have not yet appeared. At this time, consider replacing the lunchtime milk feed. Start with 15ml of water in a cup and increase the amount gradually as you increase the number of meals a day.

Introducing a cup

It is a good idea to get your baby used to a cup from about six months of age, especially if you are going back to work. If your baby has drunk only from a bottle or breast up until now, changing to a cup may be a challenge since, while some babies happily

accept the change, others take more time and become strongly attached to a bottle. Although lidded and spouted cups are widely available, these encourage frequent sipping and have the potential to damage teeth, interfere with oral muscle development and even may have a detrimental effect on speech. Since the object is for your baby to progress from sucking to drinking, open cups or

New research from the Monell Chemical Senses Centre in Philadelphia suggests that young babies are more likely to be successfully weaned on foods to which they have been previously exposed in the womb, or through the traces that make it into breast milk. Babies even may be more open to the tastes of naturally bitter vegetables like broccoli and cabbage if they are already familiar with them.

Furthermore, babies also are said to be particularly open to new tastes and textures between six to nine months. It has been suggested that parents or carers try providing ingredients individually so infants can taste each one rather than mixing them together into a single mass.

free-flowing feeders are the recommended choices. Lidded cups, too, can harbour bacteria and it's not uncommon for a baby to happen upon a lost cup, hours or even days after it was filled, and suck on a drink that is highly likely to be contaminated. At first, to familiarise your baby with this new method of drinking, try offering some milk in a cup.

Supplements

Breastmilk doesn't contain enought Vitamin D so if you are still breeastfeeding your baby after six months, it may be advisable to introduce a vitamin supplement (ask your maternal and child health nurse for advice).

If your baby is drinking at least 500ml of formula milk or follow-on milk, supplements are unnecessary as these milks are already fortified with these vitamins. However, if your baby is drinking less than 500ml, she may need a supplement.

MEAL IDEAS
from 6 months old

Remember to start weaning slowly by introducing your baby to infant rice or cereal and one type of fruit or vegetable at first. Gradually increase the variety of foods and try combining different ingredients. Many family meals will be suitable but avoid adding any seasoning, and if your baby is sitting in a high chair, then she can start to enjoy the experience of eating together. See also the recipes at the end of the chapter.

- Baby cereal or rice* mixed with fruit or vegetable purées
- Porridge with Apricot Purée*
- Apple, Peach and Banana Purées*
- Carrot and Sweet Potato Purées*
- Pumpkin, Parsnip & Apple Purée*
- Mashed avocado with baby rice
- Lentils mixed with puréed carrot
- Puréed dried apricots* and mashed swede
- Cauliflower, potato and leek purée
- Baked sweet potato with mashed chickpeas and zucchini
- Poached mashed chicken or fish with tomato and rice
- Small pasta shapes (pastina) with mashed squash
- Mashed potato with carrot and parsnip
- Stewed apple and plums with natural yoghurt
- Natural yoghurt with mashed banana

*in recipe section

Baby-led weaning

While current guidelines recommend that weaning begins with puréed food, Gill Rapley, a UK maternal and child health nurse for 25 years, thinks otherwise. She believes feeding babies puréed food is both unnecessary and unnatural and has pioneered what has become known as "Baby-Led Weaning", which primarily centres on babies being in charge of what they eat and how much. The idea is that you present your infant with a variety of healthy finger foods or meals made up of solid pieces of food that can be picked up, rather than starting with purées – providing your baby can sit in a high chair without being propped up.

Rapley believes that spoon-feeding puréed food to children could cause health problems later in life and blames the baby food industry for convincing parents

NO SPECIAL TOOLS
One advantage to feeding your baby "real" food cut into pieces is that you don't need an array of equipment such as blenders, food processors and mashers, nor do you have to make large quantities and freeze them so no need for ice cube trays or containers.

that they need to wean their babies on puréed food first. Offering babies puréed food once they can chew is not only unnecessary, says Rapley, but also could delay chewing skills. In addition, allowing a child to eat as much or as little as she chooses could prevent her from becoming constipated. Constipation can trouble many babies not long after solids are introduced; it's not certain why but it may be down to spoon-fed babies being given more food than they need or with which they can cope.

Ideally, says Rapley, a baby should be fed exclusively breastmilk or formula until six months, and then weaned immediately on to finger food as babies are capable of chewing at this age. She also believes that babies allowed to feed themselves tend to become less picky,

develop better hand control more quickly and appear to avoid foods to which they are intolerant. Another advantage is your baby can eat what you're eating, which eliminates the need for special preparation.

Many paediatricians are interested in her findings but some feel that purées could help some babies make the transition between liquid and solid foods more easily. The general feeling is that all babies are different and the remit that one size fits all is inappropriate.

Increasing the menu

Once your baby is happily eating one "meal" a day (likely to be a few tablespoons), then you can increase the number to two and eventually, over the next few months, to three. Start adding different foods to familiarise your baby with new tastes and flavour combinations and you will definitely reap the benefits since studies have found that children who have been exposed to a variety of foods from an early age are less likely to be fussy eaters later on in life. Researchers have found that between the ages of six and nine months, children are more receptive to new tastes and textures and their experiences during this period are thought to define their palate.

Do bear in mind that all babies are different – some take to weaning readily, happily accepting new foods, while others take longer. Don't panic or rush things; most importantly, try to ensure mealtimes are as happy and relaxed as possible and not occasions for power games.

Cooking for your baby

It is widely believed that good eating habits are formed early, so it's important at this stage to introduce a wider range of fresh foods, including a greater choice of fruit and vegetables along with carbohydrate and protein foods (see page 234). You'll probably find many of your meals, such as shepherd's pie, thick soups, pasta in tomato sauce or vegetables in cheese sauce, are suitable for your baby but avoid adding any seasoning such as salt and hot spices at this stage. Be aware that processed foods may contain sugar, salt, preservatives and milk in various forms such as whey powder.

There are no hard or fast rules as to how much your baby should be eating now but around 1–4 tablespoons per meal is the general guideline. Try to respond to your baby's appetite; if she is still hungry, you can give her a little more but don't force her to eat if she has eaten only a small amount as this is bound to backfire.

At this stage, move on from runny purées to more chunky purées and even mashed or minced foods. If your baby spits out any lumps at first, which is not unusual, don't rush this change but gradually increase the texture of her food, making it lumpier and slightly more of a challenge to eat.

Some babies prefer individual ingredients in their meals to be kept separately so that they can log and identify each taste and texture. This makes sense in many ways but obviously the food has to be presented in a form with which your baby can cope.

It is a good idea to prepare baby meals in bulk and freeze in single portions for future use. If storing meals for later use, cool food as quickly as possible (ideally within 1–2 hours) then place in the fridge. Food can be divided into single portions at this stage then kept in the fridge for up to two days.

If freezing, wrap single portions in freezer cling wrap or food wrap or place in ice-cube trays. Make sure you label and date the food parcels. When you want to use them, remove from the cling wrap or ice-cube tray. The safest way to defrost food is to store frozen food in the fridge overnight or use the defrost setting on a microwave or oven.

Reheat foods thoroughly when defrosted. Once piping hot, stir well to remove any hot spots and allow it to cool until it is the right temperature for your baby to eat. Discard any leftovers immediately; do not reheat, refreeze or re-use under any circumstances, to avoid the risk of food poisoning.

Organic foods

While you may have to pay a bit more for organic food, the benefits are numerous. There is good evidence to suggest a connection between pesticide residues and allergies and hyperactivity in children.

Fresh organic products tends to taste better because it is not intensively grown to absorb excess

KEEP IT CLEAN & SAFE

- Remember to wash your hands with soap before preparing meals and make sure the rest of the family does the same.
- Be meticulous with hygiene and cleanliness and make sure all bowls and spoons are sterilised until weaning is established.
- Avoid keeping any leftover food for future use or reheating food because it could be a breeding ground for bacteria. Any leftover food should be thrown away.
- Give your baby her own utensils and always be near your baby during feeding to avoid any risk of choking.
- If serving food from a jar, ensure that the seal is intact by listening for the popping sound when you open a jar. If the seal has been broken, the food must be thrown away. Spoon out a serving and keep any remainder stored in the fridge for a maximum of 24 hours. If you buy ready-prepared foods, these should be eaten by their use-by date.
- See pages 309–10 for other safety measures.

water and is generally grown in better quality soil and left to ripen for longer. Studies have shown that the lower levels of water in organic produce means that it has higher concentrations of nutrients.

Finger foods

You will probably find your baby loves finger foods; not only do they help to soothe sore gums and make great snacks, but also encourage independence with

The texture of your baby's food should keep pace with her progress. Start by puréeing food to an almost liquid consistency then gradually process for a shorter time in the blender so the food becomes progressively lumpier. From here, you can mash, mince or finely chop the ingredients.

self feeding. Your baby is probably starting to cut a few teeth now and finger foods allow her to practise chewing and will keep her occupied when you are preparing her food or the family meal.

Make sure finger foods are not too small or too fiddly to hold. Ideally, food should be cut into baby fist-sized, chip-shaped pieces, so it is easy to grasp and eat. Remember to remove any core, skin, seeds or pips from fruit. Try to avoid giving sweet biscuits or rusks as these will only serve to encourage a sweet tooth, and do not leave your baby alone when she is feeding to make sure she doesn't choke.

Choose from

- Steamed vegetables such as carrot sticks, snow peas, asparagus, green beans, baby corn and red capsicum strips or chunks of sweet potato or broccoli florets
- Fruit such as peeled wedges of apple or pear or pieces of banana, mango, melon or peach
- Large cooked pasta shapes
- Bread sticks, rice cakes, or fingers of bread, toast or pita bread

Commercial baby foods

In an ideal world we would all feed our babies nothing but home-prepared food but realistically a combination of homemade with the occasional jar of commercially made baby food is more realistic, manageable and practical for most of us. It is, however, important when buying commercial baby foods, to check the label for unwanted additives, sugars (dextrose, sucrose, glucose), artificial sweeteners (aspartame, saccharine), salt and thickeners such as modified starch. There are now

numerous organic baby food companies making both chilled and frozen meals, many of which are close in quality to home-prepared foods.

Milk and drinks

Breast milk, formula or follow-on milk continue to be your baby's main source of nutrients, including iron: around 500-600ml daily is recommended. Continuing to breastfeed ensures that your baby gets milk designed for her needs, so giving other milk may not be needed. If your baby becomes ill and loses her appetite, breastfeeding can keep her well nourished, giving her important antibodies to tackle bugs, as well as comforting her.

However, if you haven't done so already and feeding is established, you now can drop the lunchtime milk feed and provide a cup or beaker of cooled boiled tap water (you may find that your baby naturally becomes less interested in her bottle and is happy to take a cup). At other mealtimes, offer milk afterwards to prevent her becoming too full or preoccupied with the bottle before she has eaten any solid foods. Do not offer cow's, sheep's or goat's milk as a drink until your baby is one year old, but it now can be used in cooking such as in preparing cereals, sauces or desserts.

Vegetarian weaning

With a little planning and attention, a vegetarian diet can provide all the nutrients a baby needs for growth and development. As with any diet, variety is the key. Make sure you provide protein from a variety of sources including dairy products, beans and pulses (including lentils and tofu), seeds, and nuts and eggs (although these latter two are generally not

recommended until your baby is one year old, and you need to be aware of possible allergies). Combine protein sources with vitamin C-rich fruit and vegetables to aid iron absorption. A meat-free diet is naturally high in fibre, too much of which may result in an upset stomach and low energy intake and interference with the absorption of iron, zinc and copper. For these reasons, avoid giving your baby, at least when very young, large quantities of brown rice, wholegrain bread or wholemeal pasta. Try to make pulses and beans a significant part of your baby's diet; they are an important source of iron and also make a great base for many savoury dishes such as soups, stews and dips. Make sure your baby is getting enough B vitamins, and iron and zinc, in particular.

- *B12* Found in eggs, cheese, textured vegetable protein, fortified foods such as breakfast cereals and yeast extract.
- *Iron* Is in beans, lentils, leafy green vegetables, dairy products, fortified breakfast cereals, dried fruit, brown rice and wholegrain bread.
- *Zinc* Found in nuts, seeds, dairy products, beans, lentils, whole grains and yeast extract.

Self-feeding

Lots of babies like to feed themselves from an early age and you may find that your baby tries to grab her feeding spoon from you. This growing sense of independence is no bad thing and also encourages good hand/eye coordination. Let her have her own spoon while you continue feeding with a second one – things may get messy but that's half the fun!

It may take a few months for your baby to become proficient at feeding herself with a spoon and most of the meals may end up on the floor or smeared over the highchair rather than in her mouth. Prepare for the mess by putting a plastic sheet or newspaper on the floor and remaining calm

Colours, flavourings, stabilisers and emulsifiers are added to food, even baby food, to make it more attractive, tasty and long-lasting. It's important to read labels carefully and to be aware of the numbers to ensure your child isn't getting sugar (glucose, fructose and dextrose) or salt (sodium chloride or nitrates such as sodium benzoate (249, 250, 251, 252), under other names, and if you want to raise a vegetarian child, that the additives are not made from animal sources (cochineal and gelatine are not vegetarian). Synthetic food dyes, in particular, have been associated with health, behavioural and learning problems in infants. Ones to be particularly wary of include 102, 104, 107, 110, 122, 123, 124, 127, 129 132, 133, 142, 143, 151, 153, 155, 160b, 173, 174 and 175.

about any mishaps. You can help by offering foods that are easy to scoop up on a spoon like mashed potato, thick cottage cheese, cooked rice and cereal. Finger foods and meals cut into manageable chunks rather than mashed are easier to pick up and may ease any frustration; the more she's allowed to use her hands, the sooner she is likely to become more accomplished with a spoon. This also allows her to take an active part in mealtimes and she'll begin to enjoy being involved.

Three meals a day

At around eight to nine months of age, if your baby is happily eating the meals you are giving her and you have not done so already, you can start to increase the number of solid feeds from two to three. Her daily diet should include 3–4 servings a day of starchy carbohydrates and fruit and vegetables and 2–3 servings of protein foods (see page 234). Introduce new foods gradually and if a new food is rejected, leave it for a few days before offering it again or serve it in a different guise. You will probably find that many family meals are suitable but still avoid chilli, other hot spices and seasoning. Mashed, minced foods or finely chopped foods will encourage your baby to chew.

Statistics show that the number of children with allergies and food intolerances is on the rise. A genuine allergy, which is an immediate immune system response and usually more serious, tends to be far more rare than an intolerance. With an intolerance, the body develops a response to a particular food, and this often takes a period of time – even into adulthood – to manifest itself.

Many food allergies begin in early childhood; the most common allergens are nuts (particularly peanuts), seeds, cow's milk, wheat, gluten, eggs, berries, citrus fruit, tomatoes, sugar and seafood. Allergies can be difficult to detect since symptoms are wide ranging and include colic, upset tummy, rashes, asthma, eczema, breathing difficulties, hyperactivity, swelling of the throat and anaphylactic shock.

You should introduce common allergenic foods gradually and one at a time in order to monitor any possible adverse reactions.

The prevalence of nut allergy has increased threefold over the last 20 years and now affects one in 20 people. Babies at highest risk are those whose immediate family suffer from a nut allergy or other allergic conditions such as asthma, eczema or hay fever. Children who have one parent with an allergy carry a 30 per cent risk of developing a condition but having two such parents pushes the risk up to 70 per cent. Babies at risk should not be given nuts and nut-related products until they are at least three years old; parents must be vigilant when reading food labels as just a small quantity of nuts can cause a severe reaction.

There is no need to avoid nuts if there are no allergies within the family, particularly as they are highly nutritious. However, wait until your child is one year before offering them, and make sure they are ground, very finely chopped or crushed if giving them to young children.

WHAT BABIES NEED

Babies grow a lot in the first year and have high energy requirements for their size. Aim to provide a good balance of especially fresh foods, but at this stage also think about how your baby's diet pans out over a week rather than on a daily basis: eating patterns can be erratic in infants, and after all you are still in the relatively early stages of weaning.

CARBOHYDRATE/STARCHY FOODS
(about 3–4 servings a day)
Listed below are foods that are excellent sources of energy, vitamins, minerals and fibre. Bear in mind, however, that while a diet rich in fibre is perfect for adults, babies find fibre difficult to digest and it can upset their digestive systems. Avoid giving too many high-fibre foods to your baby.
- Sugar-free breakfast cereals and oats
- Pasta and noodles
- Rice
- Bread
- Potatoes

PROTEIN FOODS
(about 2–3 servings a day)
The following provide a good source of protein, essential for growth and repair in the body. Offer a combination of protein foods to get a good mix of essential amino acids.
- Fish
- Tofu
- Meat and poultry
- Meat alternatives
- Well-cooked eggs
- Full-fat cheese (grated or cubed)
- Beans and pulses
- Yoghurt or fromage frais

MILK

Milk provides protein, vitamins and minerals, particularly calcium for strong teeth and bones. Cow's milk can be used in cooking from six months but not as a drink until your child is one year old, when full-fat milk can be introduced. Half-fat milk is suitable from two years, while skimmed milk is not recommended until five years of age, as it does not provide the energy a growing child requires.

FRUIT AND VEGETABLES
(3–4 or more servings a day)

Fresh, frozen, canned and dried fruit and vegetables are an essential part of a baby's diet. They make ideal first foods and provide rich amounts of vitamins, particularly vitamin C, minerals and fibre. Foods containing vitamin C (good for immune system, hair, skin and nails) should be included in meals as they assist the absorption of iron. Try to provide your baby with a variety of fresh produce.The following are all suitable but the list is not exhaustive.

- Peeled apple
- Banana
- Mango
- Apricots
- Peaches and nectarines
- Melon
- Strawberries
- Carrot
- Broccoli
- Green beans
- Peas
- Capsicum
- Snow peas

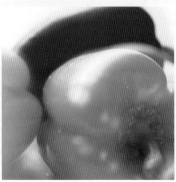

FOODS TO AVOID IN EARLY CHILDHOOD

Whole nuts should not be given to children under five because of the risk of choking. However, all foods containing nuts are to be avoided if there is a history of food allergies within the immediate family. Flaked, finely chopped nuts or peanut butter are suitable from one year if there is no history of allergies.

Sugar Foods made from refined sugar are high in calories, nutritionally poor, will spoil a child's appetite as well as lead to tooth decay and may lead to obesity. Sugary foods often include a fair amount of fat – just think of doughnuts, biscuits and cakes.

Honey is a sugary food and causes similar health problems. It also very occasionally contains a bacterium that has to been known to cause infant botulism. For this reason, honey is not recommended for babies under one year (after this age the intestines are sufficiently mature to prevent the bacteria growing).

Cow's, sheep's or goat's milk are not recommended as a drink for the first year as they do not contain sufficient iron and other nutrients needed by infants (although from six months they can be mixed into food such a cheese sauces or poured over breakfast cereals).

Raw or undercooked eggs Eggs should be cooked until both the white and yolk are solid. Raw or partially cooked eggs may be a source of salmonella, which can cause food poisoning. They can be introduced after one year.

Salt Added salt in food can overwhelm a baby's immature kidneys. Up to seven months of age, babies should have less than 1g salt a day; from seven to 12 months 1g a day is the maximum recommended amount. Between the ages of one to three, children should have no more than 2g salt a day Naturally salty foods such as bacon, cheese, stock, yeast extract also should be limited. Be aware that milk contains salt, so babies are getting some even when not taking many weaning foods.

Shellfish, such as prawns and mussels, due to the slight risk of food poisoning.

Marlin, shark and swordfish have been found to contain significant amounts of mercury and it is recommended that children avoid these types fish as they can affect a child's developing nervous system.

Foods high in saturated fat Avoid giving too many fatty foods such as butter, cheese, margarine, fatty meat and meat products, biscuits, pastry and cakes.

MEAL IDEAS from 8 months old

The following give a suggestion of suitable meals. Try minced, mashed or chopped foods rather than puréed meals at this stage. An asterisk (*) indicates a recipe given at the end of the chapter.

BREAKFAST
- Porridge with Apricot Purée*
- Low-sugar cereal with milk and chopped fruit
- Date & Vanilla Breakfast Yoghurt*
- Fruit muffin and natural yogurt
- Grilled tomatoes with cheese

LUNCH
- Home-made no-salt-or-sugar baked beans and toast fingers
- Chicken with rice noodles
- Baked potato with tuna and sweet corn
- Simple Hummus* with fingers of pita bread and vegetable sticks
- Pea Soup*
- Pasta with pesto and broccoli
- Baby Vegetable Risotto*

DINNER
- Pasta and vegetables in a cheese sauce
- Meat (lamb/pork/beef) and vegetable casserole
- Vegetable Fingers*
- Fishcakes with peas and carrots
- Chicken Balls in Tomato Sauce*
- Ham & Pea Penne*
- Grilled fish with rice and vegetables
- Mackerel (tinned or fresh) with mashed potato and zucchini

PUDDING
- Apple sponge pudding with custard
- Rice pudding
- Natural yoghurt with stewed fruit
- Banana & Maple Yoghurt Ice*

Eating with the family

As your baby approaches her first birthday, she will probably be sitting in a high chair or a baby seat attached to the dining table, enabling her to join in with family meals. She can now enjoy most of the foods as the rest of the family with a few exceptions (see page 236) so there will be fewer occasions when a specially prepared meal is necessary. There's a selection of recipes at the back of the chapter, which both you and your baby will enjoy.

Joining in with family meals is one way to learn good eating habits as these are shaped and honed when young.

When you won't be eating together, consider preparing meals (without seasoning) in bulk and freezing them in baby-sized portions for future use but make sure you defrost and reheat the meals thoroughly before serving. Commercially made baby foods also have their place but don't let them replace homemade meals altogether.

Give your baby food with a fairly stiff consistency in a non-slip plastic bowl. Coarsely mash, finely chop, grate or mince meals, as this will help your baby to practise chewing skills, benefit teeth and aid speech development. It may take a while for your baby to accept foods with a coarser texture but persist, taking things slowly and being as encouraging and positive as possible.

Finger foods are also perfect for practising self-feeding but you may find that all meals are eaten with her hands at first and this is no bad thing. Self-feeding is an important stage in a baby's development as it helps hand/eye coordination and encourages independence.

Meal patterns

Babies thrive on routine and because their energy requirements are high in relation to the size, they require three small meals a day. If convenient, give

SNACKS

- Hard-boiled egg (for children over one year)
- Fingers of bread or toast
- Rice cakes with yeast extract
- Pita bread with hummus
- Cheese sticks or grated cheese
- Vegetable sticks
- Slices or large cubes of fruit
- Pieces of dry, sugar-free cereal
- Yoghurt or fromage frais
- Dried fruit

the main meal of the day at lunchtime when your baby is alert and not feeling too grouchy. If your baby has started to crawl or is going through a growth spurt, she also may need a couple of healthy snacks between meals to keep energy levels sufficiently high. Sugary, salty, high-fat and highly processed snacks are not recommended, as they are low in nutrients and high in calories.

Never force your baby to eat as this will only serve to put her off altogether. If you are worried she is not eating enough, talk to your health nurse who will look at your baby's growth chart and monitor progress – you may well find that your fears are ungrounded and she is continuing to progress well. If she seems active and lively then she is likely to be getting enough energy from what she is eating. Milk is also considered a food rather than a drink so if she is drinking 500–600ml a day then she will be getting a good balance of important nutrients. Some of this milk can now be provided by milky puddings and sauces or from that poured over breakfast cereals.

Other drinks

If you haven't done so by now, try weaning your baby off the bottle by introducing a beaker or trainer cup with two handles, so she can take sips of water or very diluted fresh fruit juice during mealtimes. Drinks from a cup are said to be better

for speech development and for her developing teeth. Tea, coffee, fizzy drinks and sugary fruit drinks, including low-sugar varieties, are not intended for babies and are best avoided.

Trouble-free mealtimes

Your baby is unlikely to love every meal she is given but don't force her to eat if she turns her nose up; avoid giving her the same food or meal for a few days then try offering it again – may be in a different way this time. Teething and general wellbeing can undoubtedly influence a baby's eating habits, which many parents will vouch can frustratingly change on almost a daily basis!

At this stage, many babies also show an increasing desire for independence and may become choosier about what they eat. If you remain calm, the less likely she is going to use eating as a time to test your patience and the more harmonious mealtimes will be; sometimes this may be easier said than done but it's well worth a try!

One year old

Just as you think you have weaning in the bag, it is not uncommon for year-old babies to become more fussy or faddy about food, having happily wolfed down everything that was offered previously. This is perfectly normal and it's good to remember that this is just a stage your baby is going through and it will not have a long-term detrimental effect on health. Stick to your guns and continue to offer as varied a diet as possible, encompassing a wide range of colours, textures and flavours.

The dietary habits of later life are often determined by eating patterns that develop in the early years. If your toddler is picky about her food, as many are, don't be tempted to take the easy option and indulge all her whims. Encourage her to eat as varied a diet as possible

Look at what your child eats over a week rather than on a daily basis, and you may find that overall your child is eating a good varied diet, despite the occasional meal that remains largely uneaten or the day when she only wants to eat peanut butter sandwiches. Most importantly, don't panic if your child goes through periods of not eating well; you'll no doubt find that she is eating what she needs.

Energy requirements increase from years one to three as your toddler continues to grow and becomes more active. Although the need for good quality protein is much the same (two or three servings a day), there is an increased need for all vitamins and minerals. (Vitamin D, of course, is supplied by exposure to sunlight.)

Keep it healthy

The term "balanced diet" can intimidate even the most nutritionally aware parent yet as long as your child eats a good mix of foods on a regular basis then she will get all the nutrients she needs.

A diet high in fibre and low in fat remains unsuitable for children of this age, as they may not be able to obtain all the energy and nutrients they require. Additionally, a diet high in fibre will also

WHAT TODDLERS NEED

CARBOHYDRATE/STARCHY FOODS
4–5 servings a day
Breads, cereals, pasta, noodles, rice and potatoes are excellent sources of energy, fibre, vitamins and minerals. Carbohydrates should form the main part of every meal but bear in mind that toddlers find it difficult to digest large amounts of high-fibre foods such as wholemeal bread and brown rice, so try providing a combination of white and brown carbohydrate foods. If making a fruit crumble, for instance, combine white and wholemeal flour for the topping, and you could also follow this principle if making biscuits, cakes and bread.

Potatoes provide useful amounts of vitamin C, which is found mainly just under the skin so avoid peeling them if you can. Thin-skinned potatoes can simply be scrubbed and jacket potatoes are also a good source of nutrients. Add sweet potato, swede or parsnip to mashed potato to boost its nutritional value.

PROTEIN FOODS
2–3 servings a day
Meat, poultry, fish, eggs and pulses provide rich amounts of vitamins and minerals and are essential for your toddler's growth and development. If she is vegetarian, plan to give her a good mix of protein foods including beans, lentils, tofu, nuts and eggs.

Oily fish is the richest source of omega-3 essential fatty acids, which have been found to benefit the brain, eyes and skin. Research has also shown a correlation between fatty acid levels in children and their intellectual and behavioural performance as youngsters (see box, page 248). You can give boys up to four servings a week of oily fish including tuna (canned is not as rich in omega-3 as fresh), salmon, mackerel, herring, sardines, pilchards and trout, and girls up to two portions. Omega-3 is also found in non-fish sources such as fortified eggs, drinks and cereals, walnuts, linseeds, rapeseed, pumpkin seeds and soya beans.

Red meat and liver are rich in iron, but cut off any excess fat. Lean, good-quality mince can be transformed into homemade burgers and kofta, or used as a base for pastry or potato-topped pies, pasta sauce and in stir-fries.

DAIRY PRODUCTS

Full-fat milk, cheese, yoghurt and fromage frais provide protein for growth and development, calcium for teeth and, together with vitamin D, help make bones and teeth stronger. Childhood is a crucial time for tooth and bone development and continues to influence bone health in adulthood.

Crème fraîche, fromage frais and thick natural yoghurt make useful alternatives to cream in cooking and are also lower in fat; use them in sauces, soups, pies – both sweet and savoury. (See also *Milk and other drinks*, page 243.)

FRUIT AND VEGETABLES
5 servings a day

Whether fresh, frozen, canned, dried or juiced, fruit and vegetables provide a whole host of vitamins and minerals, especially vitamin C, that are vital for good health. A minimum of five portions a day is recommended and a serving for a toddler is one plum, half an apple or banana, five grapes, a floret of broccoli, a dessertspoon of peas or carrots or one tomato. A small glass of fresh fruit juice also counts.

It probably won't come as much of a surprise to find out that most children do not eat enough fresh produce, and the majority of parents will have experienced the struggle to get their children to eat up their greens.

Try presenting fruit and vegetables in different ways. For example, many children turn their nose up at cooked vegetables, but will happily eat them raw, including sticks of cucumber, carrot and red capsicum. Vegetables sticks are good for dunking into dips so serve them with nutritious guacamole or hummus (see page 254) and you'll double the health benefits. Alternatively incorporate vegetables into fritters or rosti, or, if the going gets really tough, disguise puréed vegetables in sauces, stews, soups and pies. A love of fruit is perhaps easier to encourage but again maintain the interest with different types and presenting them in various ways.

... and what they don't

SUGAR AND SWEETS

Most children naturally have a sweet tooth (breast milk and formula milk is sweet, for starters, and babies need this as they feed little and often) but hold off giving your child sugary foods as long as feasible as sugar cravings are hard to break. Foods made from refined sugar are high in calories, nutritionally poor, will spoil a child's appetite as well as lead to tooth decay; what's more, sugary foods often include a fair amount of fat – just think of doughnuts, biscuits and cakes.

Nevertheless, an outright ban can backfire, making sweets even more desirable! It may be preferable to avoid over-processed sugary, artificially coloured confections rather than cutting out sugar altogether. Don't resort to foods that replace sugar with artificial sweeteners, as they have been found to cause digestive problems if eaten in large quantities and in the long term are no better than the refined alternative.

MEAL IDEAS from one year old

BREAKFAST
- No-sugar breakfast cereal
- Banana & Strawberry Smoothie*
- Cinammon French Toast*
- Natural yoghurt with mixed berries
- Boiled egg and toast finger with yeast extract
- Eggy bread with no-sugar-or-salt baked beans

LUNCH
- Chicken and bean stew
- Baked potato with a filling
- Haloumi & Pita Salad*
- Pizza fingers with vegetable sticks
- Thick vegetable and pasta soup
- Toasted tortilla wedges with dips
- Baby Falafel Burgers*
- Pasta with tomato sauce
- Marinated tofu pieces with noodles
- Creamy Guacamole with Dippers*

DINNER
- Spaghetti Bolognese
- Fish with Roasted Tomatoes*
- Tuna & Leek Frittata*
- Cottage pie
- Pork and noodle stir-fry
- Sausage & Potato Roast*
- Turkey Patties with Pineapple Relish*
- Macaroni & Leek Cheese*

PUDDING
- Mixed Fruit Compote*
- Yoghurt ice lollies
- Fruit Swirls*
- Fromage frais with fruit purée
- Carrot Cake Squares*
- Strawberry mousse

*in recipe section

SNACKS
- Hard-boiled egg with toast fingers
- Sticks of cheese with apple slices and oatcake
- Toasted cheese muffin
- Chunks of melon with ham
- Tuna mayonnaise with toasted tortilla triangles
- Hummus and breadsticks
- Rice cake with nut butter
- Mashed banana sandwich
- Pita bread with yeast extract and carrot sticks
- Good-quality meatballs with halved cherry tomatoes
- Dried apple rings
- Toasted fruit muffin or teacake
- Natural yoghurt with mango
- Slice of fruit cake
- Fruit scone
- Chunks of fresh fruit
- Raisins or chopped dried fruit

reduce the amount of minerals absorbed, including valuable iron and calcium. Likewise, children need a certain amount of fat for normal growth and development. Not all fat is bad and it has an important role to play in transporting vitamins A, D, E and K through the body. Unsaturated fat found in vegetables oils, oily fish and soft margarine is an important contributor to good health.

Try to provide on a daily basis a good mix of high-energy, nutrient dense foods based on the recommended food groups (see pages 241–2). Obviously, the range of foods eaten will vary if your toddler is on a special diet, has a food sensitivity or demonstrates eating preferences.

Snacks

Babies have high energy requirements for their size; consequently small, frequent meals, plus two to three healthy snacks, are necessary for children of this age, who do not have large enough stomachs to cope with three large meals a day. You'll probably find that your baby will need a snack mid morning, mid afternoon and maybe pre-bedtime. Some children love to graze; take advantage of this by offering healthy snacks, turning them into mini-meals rather than opting for sugary, salty or fatty processed foods. However, it's also important for children to enjoy main meals and constant snacking can deter them from doing this.

Milk and other drinks

Whole cow's, sheep's or goat's milk can be given to babies over the age of 12 months as a main drink. Your child still requires about 500–600ml milk a day, although some of this can be provided by milky puddings and sauces, or poured over breakfast cereals. Aim for your child to give up a bottle by one year old and to move on to a cup or beaker of milk.. While you may still be breastfeeding, it is no longer necessary to offer formula or follow-on milk, although you can continue to do so if you feel your child is not eating well or you are concerned that she is not getting the range of nutrients needed.

Semi-skimmed can be introduced after your child is two, as long as she is eating well. Skimmed milk is

IRON NEEDS

Iron deficiency is not uncommon in children so try to give a food or drink rich in vitamin C, such as fruit juice or vegetables, at the same time as an iron-rich food as this will help the absorption of this mineral.

Don't give tea and coffee to young children, especially at mealtimes; not only do they contain caffeine but they interfere with the amount of iron absorption.

As iron is more difficult to absorb from non-meat sources, if your child is vegetarian, give her foods containing iron every day such as beans, lentils, green leafy vegetables, dried fruit, particularly apricots, raisins and sultanas, as well as fortified breakfast cereals.

not recommended for children under five years of age, as it does not provide enough energy and vitamin A for a growing child.

Water is always the best drink option for children but diluted fresh fruit juice provides vitamin C and if served alongside a meal containing iron can help absorption of this mineral. However, even fruit juice contains natural sugars, so avoid giving it to your child other than at mealtimes to prevent damage to the teeth since the longer a sugary drink is in contact with teeth the more damage it can do. Fruit squash, fizzy drinks and those containing caffeine are best avoided being high in sugar, a source of empty calories and nutritionally poor. They also fill up children affecting their appetite for meals. Water and milk are the best options between meals.

Supplements

Vitamins and minerals are essential to your child's growth and development. If she is eating a reasonably balanced diet, she should be receiving all that she requires. However, if she is following a vegan diet, or is an especially fussy eater, talk to your maternal and child health nurse about the possible need for supplements.

Two years old and over

As your toddler becomes more active, the more calories she requires to give her the energy needed. Encourage your child to eat a variety of foods so she gets a wide range of nutrients (see *Keep it healthy*, page 240 for guidelines).

Work on establishing a regular eating pattern based on three meals plus two to three snacks a day. Some children continue to dislike lumps in their food so chopping or mincing food may make it more acceptable. Alternatively, finger foods are a great way of encourage your toddler to chew foods and to enjoy those with a coarser texture.

Your toddler may now attend childcare or playgroup and this can come with its own challenges and peer pressure. You may be fortunate to find one that makes its own healthy lunches and snacks; realistically standards can vary so talk to other parents and get some feedback about meals. Some childcare centres are open to parents providing their own packed lunches, drinks and snacks and this may be a welcome option.

Good eating habits

Your child is becoming increasingly aware of the world around her and with this comes a new sense of independence and free will, with both its positive and not so positive side effects, but studies show parents who instil good eating habits from an early age are likely to see the benefits in the long term. Points to consider include:

- Don't get hung up on good eating manners just yet; there's plenty of time for that. Your child will continue to make a mess when they eat – crumbs become a way of life! While ideally you would like her to eat with a fork or spoon, fingers or hands will continue to be much in use.
- While it's not always feasible for the whole family to eat together, you will reap the benefits when you do, even if you manage communal mealtimes only at weekends. Eating together encourages chatter and discussion between parents and children and gets them away from the TV screen. Children also learn good eating habits from their parents so make sure you eat up your greens!
- Be patient and persevere. If you manage to persuade your child to try even a mouthful of food you are making progress, and she may find she likes it after all. Research shows that children acquire a taste for foods over time and it takes an average of 10 "tastes" for a child to accept new foods. The theory is that if parents can persuade their child to eat just one mouthful of carrots on 10 occasions, she will learn to like them.
- Attempts to encourage your child to eat healthy foods can be helped if you make food exciting – this doesn't mean that you have to spend hours making faces out of ingredients but bear in mind different colours, textures and shapes when planning a meal. Interesting or colourful plates, bibs, cutlery and mats can also make a difference as can introducing a theme. Steamed vegetables are brighter in colour than boiled, while fresh vegetables have an appealing crunchy texture.

Imaginative and attractive presentation can usually make the difference between a child eating or refusing a meal.

- Many parents fall into the trap of believing children prefer bland or so-called "children's food". In fact, a study has found that children like stronger flavours than once thought and will happily try curries, stir-fries, chilli and the like.

- Even if you have managed to keep your child away from sugar until now, it becomes increasingly tricky as they become older, interact with other children, and are more aware of children-oriented brands with their brightly coloured cartoon character packaging. Everything in moderation seems to work for most parents but opt for the ones with the least amount of colours, additives and preservatives!

- One of the best ways to get your child interested in food is to teach her to cook or at least become involved in the preparation of a meal, even if it's as simple as a quick stir of a sauce or pouring some cereal into a bowl.

- Similarly, get your child involved in food shopping; allow her to choose from healthy options, weigh fresh produce or unpack the trolley.

Fussy eaters

All children go through stages of picky eating and appetites can be equally unpredictable – a fact confirmed by the majority of parents. But how do you encourage your child to eat what she is given and what do you do if she refuses to eat? Perhaps predictably there are no easy answers but the following tips should help you with those more challenging times:

- Forcing your child to eat is a no-win situation for both of you. Conflict and tension serve only to make the situation more difficult and may lead to your child using mealtimes as a way of seeking attention. It can be very frustrating if your child does not eat a meal that you have lovingly prepared but children are remarkably clever at picking up on the anxieties of their parents and may well tune into your own frustrations about their not eating.

- Gently coax or offer plenty of encouragement to try just a mouthful; sometimes this is enough for her to be persuaded to eat the rest of the meal.

- Praise your child as much as possible, even if she eats just the one mouthful.

- If encouragement and coaxing don't work, take the food away but don't offer an alternative, however hard this may be. It's important that a child gets used to eating what she is given and not to expect endless alternatives if she doesn't like the first option.

- Don't make portions too large as this can be off-putting for a child – you can always give her seconds if a meal is eaten up.

- Peer pressure can work both ways: ask a friend of your child's who you know to be a good eater to come to tea. Children often learn by example and if your child sees her peers eating up, it may well encourage her to do the same.

- Make eating fun: picnics, even if is only a cloth arranged on the floor, or a theme based on a favourite game or book, can be real winners.

- Sticker charts can be unbelievably successful and are a simple way of encouraging children to try new foods, especially unfamiliar fruit and vegetables.

- It may be easier said than done, but don't fall into the trap of bribing your child with a pudding or sweets.

- Compromise is sometimes the only option.

Combine foods you know your child likes with ones previously untried or previously rejected; you may find that new combinations are enough to encourage your child to try new things.

Weight issues

The prevalence of obesity in many parts of the world is rising, and unfortunately children are not immune from what is being called an epidemic.

In Australia, the prevalence of obesity is increasing markedly among both adults and children. According to a year 2000 survey of New South Wales primary school children, obesity was reported a 9.9 per cent of boys and 7.1 per cent of girls. Of the boys surveyed, 26.2 per cent were overweight and of the girls, 28.4 per cent. Many experts put this rise in obesity down to the growing presence of fast-food outlets, advertising and the overwhelming choice of cakes, biscuits, sweets, ice cream, potato chips, fast foods and fizzy drinks in shops. While this hasn't helped the situation, lifestyle also has a role to play. With the ever-increasing popularity of computer DVD games and

television, children are becoming more and more inactive, so are not burning calories consumed.

However, there could be other reasons for being overweight and it may not be as simple as over-eating or inactivity so it's advisable to contact your doctor before putting your child on any type of diet, which could restrict nutritional intake if not handled correctly.

Most fat babies will start to slim down when they start to crawl or walk and become normal weight toddlers, but a few remain overweight. The best way to prevent a child becoming fat is to breastfeed exclusively for six months and to teach good eating habits early on; prevention is much easier than cure. Young children should not be put on weight reduction diets unless advised by a doctor. However, developing a healthy family approach to food and exercise is important in weight management. See *Keep it healthy* on page 240 for guidelines. Try to stick to a routine of three meals a day plus two to three healthy snacks. Many children are grazers but constant nibbling is not ideal and makes them less likely to enjoy a proper meal.

Milk and drinks

If your child eats well and has a varied, balanced diet then it is possible, but not inevitable, to switch to half-fat milk after two years of age. However, skimmed milk is not recommended before five years, as it does not provide sufficient energy and nutrients for your growing child.

Many children don't drink enough and will happily go for hours without drinking anything. Proper hydration helps the brain function as its best, so make sure your child drinks plenty of filtered or bottled water or diluted fresh fruit juice and not dehydrating fizzy sugary drinks. A minimum of six to eight glasses of water per day is the recommended amount for children aged two and over and even more for children who are very active. Dehydration can affect concentration as well as the transportation of nutrients around the body and brain.

DID YOU KNOW...

The influence of diet on behaviour hasn't been proved absolutely but a poor diet, lack of essential fatty acids and food allergies can certainly exacerbate destructive behavour, restlessness, poor concentration, learning difficulties, clumsiness, irritability and poor social skills.

A lack of zinc, calcium and magnesium can case restlessness, poor concentration and learning difficulties. A deficiency of thiamine (vitamin B_1) is linked to aggressive, erratic and impulsive behaviour.

It has been suggested that children with attention deficit hyperactive disorder (ADHD) often have problems metabolising sugar and this may lead to hypoglycaemia (see also page 369), producing aggressive outbursts. Many children with ADHD also have low levels of essential fatty acids.

Depression and mood swings may be a result of omega-3 deficiency.

Some doctors and nutritionists believe that prescribing nutrient supplements such as vitamins B,C D and E, chromium and molybdenum, and omega-3 and 6 fatty acids can improve the behaviour of many disruptive children. A high protein diet and probiotics are other natural ways of improving behaviour through food. Eliminating certain problem foods from the diet such as ready meals and packaged goods, which contain a high level of additives, also has been shown to be efficacious. The Feingold Diet, for example, developed by an American doctor in the 1960s to help hyperactive children, was based on eliminating tartrazine yellow, petroleum-based artificial food dyes, flavourings and preservatives. Young children often become cranky and restless following the consumption of brightly coloured sweets and drinks.

MEAL IDEAS for toddlers

BREAKFAST
- Oat cereal/porridge with mashed banana
- Low-sugar breakfast cereal
- Poached egg with beans and toast
- Ground toasted nuts and seeds with yoghurt and honey
- Porridge with fruit purée
- Pancakes with fruit filling
- Fruit smoothie with toast
- Eggy bread with beans
- Tomato & Egg Scramble*
- Toasted fruit muffin and yoghurt
- Ham & Egg Cups*
- Cinammon French Toast*

LUNCH
- Baked potato with filling
- Haloumi & Pita Salad*
- Baba Ganoush* and Creamy Guacamole* with dippers
- Minestrone soup
- Lentil Dahl*
- Pita pizzas with coleslaw
- Bubble & Squeak Cakes* with sausages/bacon and grilled tomatoes
- Cheese omelette with vegetable sticks
- Vegetable Fingers*
- Easy Sausage Rolls*
- Pasta with creamy ham and pea sauce
- Haddock and sweet corn chowder with garlic bread
- Peach, ham and cheese salad
- Easy Sausage Rolls*
- Rice & Vegetable Fritters*

DINNER

◆ Salmon or haddock fishcakes with peas
◆ Roast meat (or vegetarian alternative) and all the trimmings
◆ Chicken pie with vegetables and mash
◆ Salmon Fingers with Sweet Potato Chips*
◆ Grilled pork or lamb fillet with homemade chips and broccoli
◆ Pasta with tomato sauce and meatballs
◆ Homemade Beef Burgers*
◆ Sausage & Potato Roast*
◆ Chinese Beef with Noodles*
◆ Pork and apple pan-fry
◆ Chicken or vegetable korma with rice
◆ Pesto pasta with peas and pinenuts
◆ Tuna & Leek Frittata*
◆ Creamy Fish Pie*

PUDDINGS

◆ Peach Crumbles*
◆ Ice-cream with fruit compote
◆ Apple pie
◆ Yoghurt and fruit
◆ Fresh fruit jelly
◆ Mango Fool*
◆ Mixed Fruit Compote*
◆ Fresh or dried fruit salad
◆ Pancakes
◆ Carrot Cake Squares*
◆ Fruit yoghurt lollies
◆ Sultana rice pudding
◆ Oat Biscuits*
◆ Baked sponge pudding

*in recipe section

FIRST FOODS... from six months

The recipes on these two pages have been kept very simple to enable your baby to try a "taster" of solids and to become gradually accustomed to eating. The single-ingredient purées can, in time, be combined to make different flavour combinations.

The recipes on the following pages come with an age recommendation, which relates to the suitability of the ingredients used; those containing eggs are from 12 months. However, babies progress at different rates and begin weaning at varying ages, and knowing your baby best, do not offer her something before you think she is ready.

Since the recipes have been created to appeal to babies of different ages, they may not give suggestions for puréeing, mashing, mincing or chopping. Again, use your common sense and serve the dish in the way you know your baby will be able to cope with at her stage of development.

Unless indicated, portions are child sized. You will probably find that your baby will only eat a few teaspoons (if that) at first. Some main meals have been created for a family of two adults and two children to eat together but these often can be frozen if you wish to chill portions for future serving.

BABY RICE

There are commercial versions in the shops but it's easy to make your own. Mix with breast milk or formula milk. Baby rice can also be used as a base to mix with fruit and vegetable purées.

- *4–7 portions*
- * *suitable for freezing*

1 Put **25g white short-grain rice** in a sieve and rinse under cold running water. Transfer to a saucepan and add enough cold water to cover. Bring to the boil, stir, then reduce the heat.
2 Cover the pan with a lid and simmer for 10–15 minutes, or until the water has been absorbed and the grains are very tender.
3 Purée the rice in a blender with sufficient milk to make a smooth, runny purée.

To reheat *Defrost completely then heat through until piping hot to avoid any risk of contamination. Check the temperature before serving.*

BANANA PURÉE

Make sure you use a very ripe banana as this will be much easier on your baby's digestive system.

- *1 portion*

Mash ½ **banana** with a fork until smooth as possible. Add a little boiled water or breast or formula milk to make a thin purée.

APPLE PURÉE

Apple goes well with baby rice and is excellent combined with puréed meat and vegetables.

- *2–3 portions*

1 Wash, peel, core and finely chop **1 dessert apple**. Put the apple in a saucepan with **2 tbsp water** and bring to the boil. Reduce the heat and simmer, half-covered, for 5–8 minutes until tender.
2 Transfer the apple to a blender and purée until smooth, adding a little of the cooking water if necessary.

Variation *Another excellent first food, pear can be prepared in the same way. If the pear is very ripe then simply peel, core and mash it.*

SWEET POTATO PURÉE

Orange-fleshed potatoes are richer in vitamin C and beta carotene than white-fleshed ones.

- 4–6 portions

1 Peel **1 small, orange-fleshed sweet potato** and cut into bite-sized chunks. Cover with water and bring to the boil and cook for 10–15 minutes until tender.
2 Drain the potatoes and transfer to a blender with a little breast or formula milk to make a smooth, creamy purée.

CARROT PURÉE

The colour and sweetness of carrot makes it a popular first food.

- 2–3 portions
- ∗ suitable for freezing

1 Peel **1 carrot** then cut into bite-sized pieces. Put in a saucepan with **2 tbsp water**. Bring to the boil and cook for 10 minutes, or until tender.
2 Put the carrot in a blender with a little of the cooking water and blend until smooth.

Variation *When your baby is happy with carrot, purée it with cooked potato or butternut pumpkin.*

DRIED APRICOT PURÉE

A good source of iron but high in fibre, apricots should only be given in small amounts. Use unsulphured apricots, which have a rich, almost toffee-like flavour for this "dessert" purée.

- 5–8 portions

1 Wash **10 unsulphured ready-to-eat dried apricots** and cut them into small pieces. Put into a saucepan, cover with water and bring to the boil. Reduce the heat and simmer for 20 minutes, or until very soft.
2 Transfer to a blender and blend until puréed, adding a little of the cooking water, if necessary. Leave to cool slightly then mix with **3 tbsp natural yoghurt**.

PEACH PURÉE

A ripe, juicy peach is delicious although nectarines, plums and apricots can be used, too.

- 2 portions
- ∗ suitable for freezing

1 Quarter **1 ripe peach**, removing the central stone then put it in a pan with **2 tbsp water**. Bring to the boil then simmer the fruit for 8–10 minutes.
2 Remove the peach from the water and when cool enough to handle, peel off the skin.
3 Transfer the peach to a blender and purée until smooth; add a little boiled water, if necessary.

PUMPKIN, PARSNIP & APPLE PURÉE

Rich in vitamin C.

- 3–4 portions
- ∗ suitable for freezing

1 Wash, peel and dice **75g butternut pumpkin** (removing any seeds) and **1 small parsnip**. Put in a saucepan and cover with water. Bring to the boil then reduce the heat and simmer for 10 minutes.
2 While the vegetables are cooking, wash, peel, core and dice **1 dessert apple**. Add to the pan and cook for another 5 minutes until tender.
3 Transfer to a blender and process until puréed, adding a little boiled water, if necessary.

BREAKFAST

BANANA & STRAWBERRY SMOOTHIE

This smoothie is full of vital nutrients and provides much needed energy. Serve with toast and a boiled egg.

- ■ *from 6 months*
- ● *1–2 servings*

1 small banana, sliced
3 strawberries, hulled and halved
   if large
2 tbsp thick natural bio yoghurt
4 tbsp milk (breast, formula, cow's
   or alternative)

Put all the ingredients in a blender and whiz until thick, smooth and creamy then pour into cups.

TOMATO & EGG SCRAMBLE

This delicious dish contains iron and B vitamins. The eggs must be well cooked with no sign of runniness. Serve with a glass of diluted fresh orange juice to encourage the absorption of iron.

- ■ *from 12 months*
- ● *1 serving*

15g unsalted butter, plus extra
   to serve
1 medium tomato, seeded and
   diced
2 small free-range eggs
1 tbsp milk (breast, formula, cow's
   or alternative)
½ bagel

1 Heat the butter in a heavy-based medium-sized saucepan. Add the tomatoes and cook for 2 minutes until softened, stirring occasionally.

2 Lightly beat the egg with the milk. Pour the mixture into the pan and using a wooden spoon, stir constantly to ensure the egg doesn't stick to the bottom of the pan. Continue to cook the egg, stirring, until it is cooked and not runny – this should take about 4 minutes.

3 Meanwhile, toast and butter the bagel and cut into wedges. Serve with the scrambled egg.

DATE & VANILLA BREAKFAST YOGHURT

A nourishing and energy-boosting blend of protein and slow-release carbohydrates, which makes an excellent start to the day. Serve with toasted fruit bread fingers for dipping in.

- ■ *from 6 months*
- ● *2 servings*

60g dried ready-to-eat stoned
   dates, roughly chopped
150ml water
60ml thick natural bio yoghurt
½ tsp vanilla extract
4 tbsp milk (breast, formula, cow's
   or alternative)

1 Put the dates and water in a medium-sized saucepan. Bring to the boil then reduce the heat. Put a lid on and simmer for 10 minutes, or until the dates are soft. Leave to cool.

2 Put the dates and any remaining water, yoghurt, vanilla extract and milk in a blender. Whiz until smooth and creamy. Spoon into a bowl.

Storage tip *Store any surplus in an airtight container in the fridge for up to 3 days.*

HAM & EGG CUPS

Eggs provide much needed protein, vitamins D and B and zinc but they must be cooked thoroughly to avoid the slight risk of salmonella. These make great finger food for older babies.

- ■ *from 12 months*
- ● *4 servings*

Olive oil, for greasing
4 slices lean ham
4 free-range eggs

1 Preheat the oven to 200°C (400°F). Lightly grease four holes of a deep muffin tin and arrange a slice of ham in each

CINNAMON FRENCH TOAST

This makes a delicious breakfast or finger food. Serve with a sliced banana, or favourite fresh fruit to add a nutritional boost.

- ■ from 12 months
- ● 1 serving

1 free-range egg, lightly beaten
1 tbsp semi-skimmed milk
Pinch of ground cinnamon
Small knob of butter
1 slice brioche or panettone or
   1 small fruit bun

1 Mix together the egg, milk and cinnamon in a shallow dish. Melt the butter in a non-stick frying pan and swirl it around to coat the base evenly.
2 Dip both sides of the brioche slice in the egg mixture then allow any excess to drip off.
3 Cook for about 2 minutes each side or until the egg is set and light golden.

---

one, overlapping the sides to make it fit and form a "cup" shape.

2 Trim the top of the ham to make it even but make sure it is still slightly above the top of the tin.
3 Crack an egg into each ham-lined muffin hole then bake for 10 minutes, or until the eggs are set.
4 Remove from the oven and leave to cool slightly before removing the pies from the tin.

Storage tip *The ham cups will keep in the fridge for up to 2 days.*

PORRIDGE WITH APRICOT PURÉE

An excellent breakfast for young children, porridge is known to improve concentration. Instead of the apricot purée, try mashed banana or stewed pear or apple.

- ■ from 6 months
- ● 1–4 servings (purée serves 4–6)

FOR THE APRICOT PURÉE
115g ready-to-eat dried apricots
300ml water

FOR THE PORRIDGE
55g porridge oats
125ml milk (breast, formula, cow's
   or alternative) or half water,
   half milk

1 Place the apricots in a saucepan and cover with the water. Bring to the boil, cover the pan, then reduce the heat and simmer for 30 minutes until the apricots are very tender. Place the apricots, along with any water left in the pan, in a blender or food processor and purée until smooth adding more water, if necessary.
2 To make the porridge, put the oats into a saucepan. Add the milk and bring to the boil, stirring occasionally. Reduce the heat and simmer, stirring frequently, for six minutes until smooth and creamy.
3 Pour the porridge into a bowl and stir in a large spoonful of the apricot purée.

LUNCH

DIPS & DIPPERS
Finger foods – bread sticks, tortilla slices, pita bread, toast; lightly-steamed carrot and pepper sticks; cucumber chunks and snow peas – give babies the chance to practise new eating skills and relieve sore gums.

SIMPLE HUMMUS

This delicious dip is made with calcium-rich sesame seed paste . The chickpeas contain valuable iron and B vitamins.

- *from 7–8 months*
- *7 servings*

200g can chickpeas
Juice of ½ lemon
½ clove garlic, crushed
1 tbsp tahini (sesame seed paste)
2 tbsp extra-virgin olive oil
2 tbsp water

1 Drain and rinse the chickpeas and put in a food processor or blender with the lemon juice, garlic, tahini, olive oil and water.
2 Process until puréed – you will have to stir the hummus occasionally during blending to keep the mixture moving. Add extra water if the hummus is too thick.

CREAMY GUACAMOLE

Avocados provide useful amounts of protein, carbohydrate and the highest concentration of vitamin E of any fruit.

- *from 7–8 months*
- *2–4 servings*

1 small ripe avocado, stoned and flesh scooped out
1 tsp mayonnaise
½ clove garlic, crushed (optional)
1 tsp lemon juice

Put the avocado flesh into a bowl and mash with a fork until smooth. Add the mayonnaise, garlic, if using, and lemon juice then mix well until combined.

Storage tip *Guacamole can be kept in the fridge in an airtight container for up to 2 days.*

BABA GANOUSH

Eggplants are rich in vitamins and make surprisingly creamy dips, which often go down better with children than when they are served in other ways.

- *from 8 months*
- *4 servings*

1 small eggplant
1 tbsp olive oil, plus extra for greasing
1 clove garlic, chopped
½ tsp ground cumin
½ tsp ground coriander
Juice of ½ lemon
1 tbsp tahini (sesame seed paste)

1 Preheat the oven to 200°C (400°F). Put the eggplant in an oiled roasting tin. Roast for about 30–35 minutes, or until the flesh is very soft.
2 Leave to cool slightly then cut in half lengthways and scoop out the flesh with a spoon; discard the skin.
3 Put the eggplant into a food processor or blender with the rest of the ingredients and blend until smooth.

Storage tip *The dip will keep in an airtight container in the fridge for up to 1 week.*

HALOUMI & PITA SALAD

This chunky salad is best eaten with the fingers if serving to young children. Edam or Cheddar cubes make good alternatives.

- *from 12 months*
- *1–2 servings*

Small pita bread, split in half
2.5cm piece cucumber
¼ small red capsicum
25g haloumi, rinsed, patted dry and cut into cubes
3 pitted black olives, halved

DRESSING (OPTIONAL)
1 tbsp extra-virgin olive oil, plus extra for frying
½ tsp white wine vinegar

1 Preheat the grill to medium. Open out the pita bread and grill until light golden and slightly crisp; leave to cool. Meanwhile, mix together the ingredients for the dressing, if using.

2 Cut the cucumber lengthways into quarters then remove the seeds and cut into manageable chunks or sticks. Cut the capsicum into manageable chunks or sticks.

3 Put the cucumber and capsicum in a serving bowl then add the olives. Pour the dressing over and toss until combined. Break the crisp pita into pieces large enough to hold and mix into the salad.

4 Heat a little oil in a frying pan and fry the haloumi until beginning to colour. Leave to cool to just warm and mix with the rest of the salad.

BUBBLE & SQUEAK CAKES

These are a perfect way to encourage children to eat cabbage. Delicious served with grilled tomatoes and beans.

- *from 12 months*
- *4–8 servings*

675g potatoes, diced
175g Savoy cabbage, finely shredded

1 tbsp Dijon mustard
2 spring onions, finely chopped (optional)
1 egg, beaten
Flour, for dusting
Vegetable oil, for frying

1 Cook the potatoes in plenty of boiling salted water for 15 minutes, or until tender. Drain well and mash until smooth.

2 Meanwhile, steam the cabbage for 5 minutes, or until tender, then finely chop.

3 Combine the potatoes and cabbage with the mustard, spring onions (if using) and egg in a bowl. Mix well and leave to cool.

4 Shape the potato mixture into 8 cakes using floured hands and dust each cake in flour.

5 Coat the bottom of a heavy-based frying pan with oil. Fry the cakes in batches over a medium heat for 3–4 minutes on each side, until golden.

Variation *Peas, carrots, green beans and onion can be used instead of, or as well as, the cabbage. Grated cheese also can be added.*

MUFFIN PIZZAS

Pizzas make great finger food if cut into strips. A breakfast muffin is used a base for a simple tomato and mozzarella topping.

- *from 8–9 months*
- *2 servings*

2 tbsp passata (smooth tomato sauce) or canned chopped tomatoes
1 tsp tomato pesto
½ tsp olive oil
Pinch of dried oregano (optional)
1 breakfast muffin, halved horizontally
2 slices mozzarella, drained, patted dry

1 Preheat the grill to medium. Mix together the passata (if using canned tomatoes, mash them with a fork until fairly smooth), pesto, olive oil and oregano, if using.
2 Spoon the tomato sauce over the top of each naan bread or muffin until covered.
3 Top with a slice of mozzarella then grill for about 10 minutes, or until the cheese has melted and is slightly golden. Cut into quarters and serve when cool.

BABY FALAFEL BURGERS

These nutritious burgers are made from chickpeas, which are a good source of iron, zinc, folate and vitamin E.

- *from 12 months*
- *3–6 servings*

400g can chickpeas, drained and rinsed
3 spring onions, chopped
2 cloves garlic, crushed
1 tsp ground cumin
1 tsp ground coriander
1 egg, beaten
Flour, for dusting
Vegetable oil, for frying
6 mini bread rolls or pitas

1 Place the chickpeas, spring onions, garlic, cumin and coriander in a food processor and blend. Add the egg and blend again until the mixture forms a coarse paste. Then place the mixture in the refrigerator for one hour.
2 Remove the chickpea paste from the refrigerator and, with floured hands, form into 6 patties, about 6cm in diameter. Roll each one in flour until lightly coated.
3 Heat enough oil to cover the base of a large frying pan. Cook the burgers (in batches and adding more oil, if necessary) for 6 minutes, turning once, until golden.
4 Serve each burger in a mini bread roll or cut into pieces as finger food.

EASY SAUSAGE ROLLS

Use the best sausages that you can find and you won't be filling your children with unwanted additives. If serving to babies, chop the sausages and separate from the tortilla strips, which can be served separately.

- *from 9 months*
- *1–2 servings*

4 good quality cocktail-sized pork sausages or vegetarian alternative
1 small soft flour tortilla, cut into
4 strips
Mayonnaise, tomato sauce, guacamole or hummus, to serve (optional)

1 Preheat the grill to medium-high. Line a grill pan with foil and arrange the sausages on top. Grill the sausages until cooked through and golden.
2 Place the tortilla strips in a dry frying pan and heat until warmed through. Spread a little topping over each strip, if desired and add a sausage. Roll up each strip to encase the sausage.

BABY VEGETABLE RISOTTO

Risotto is very simple to make but does require stirring time, which can be quite therapeutic after a hectic day. Purée or mash depending on your baby's age. Once your baby is 12 months, you can prepare the risotto with low-salt vegetable stock instead of water.

- ■ *from 6 months*
- ● *4 family servings*

2 tbsp olive oil

15g butter

4 baby leeks, sliced

4 baby zucchinis, sliced

1 tsp dried oregano

250g risotto rice

1 litre water

55g baby peas

85g parmesan cheese, grated

1 Heat the oil and butter in a large heavy-based saucepan. Add the leeks and zucchinis and fry for five minutes or until tender. Add the oregano and rice and cook for two minutes, stirring continuously, until the rice is glossy and slightly translucent.

2 Add the water a ladleful at a time, stirring continuously. Wait for the water to be absorbed before adding another ladleful, continue in this way until the rice is tender and creamy but still retains a little bite – it should take about 25 minutes.

3 Add the peas, the last spoonful of water and three-quarters of the parmesan cheese and stir well. Sprinkle with the remaining parmesan just before serving.

PEA SOUP

Soups are a perfect way of encouraging children to eat vegetables. You could also add less water to make a thicker soup or purée. When your baby is older – 12 months or more – you can make the soup with low-salt stock instead of water.

- ■ *from 6 months*
- ● *4 family servings*

1 tbsp vegetable oil

1 leek, finely sliced

1 stick celery, finely chopped

225g potato, diced

1 litre water

280g frozen baby peas

1 Heat the oil in a large, heavy-based saucepan. Add the leek and fry over a medium heat for five minutes or until softened. Add the celery and potato and cook for a further five minutes.

2 Pour the water over the vegetables and bring to the boil. Cover, reduce the heat and simmer the soup for 15 minutes. Add the peas and cook for a further five minutes or until the potato is tender.

3 Using a hand-blender or food processor, blend the soup until smooth. Reheat the soup, if necessary, before serving. For the adult servings, season to taste with salt and pepper.

RICE & VEGETABLE FRITTERS

This recipe is perfect for using up any leftover rice and makes great finger food when cut up. Brown rice is used here because it is a good source of B vitamins and fibre, but white rice is also suitable.

- from 12 months
- 4–8 child-size servings

85g long-grain brown rice, cooked and cooled
2 spring onions, sliced

½ red capsicum, diced
1 clove garlic, crushed
1 small egg, beaten
2 tbsp double cream
2 tbsp plain flour
Sunflower oil, for frying

1 Mix the rice with the spring onions, red capsicum, garlic, egg, cream and flour.
2 Heat enough oil to coat the bottom of a heavy-based frying pan. Place two heaped dessertspoons of the rice mixture per fritter into the hot oil and flatten slightly with the back of a spoon. Cook in batches for three minutes on each side, until golden and drain on kitchen paper.

LENTIL DAHL

Children often like stronger flavours than adults give them credit for, and it's a good idea to familiarise infants with new tastes. The lentil is much underrated but this low-fat, protein-rich pulse provides iron, folic acid and zinc as well as fibre, and its mild flavour combines well with spices. Adults may like to add a chopped fresh chilli.

- from 12 months
- 4 family servings

2 tbsp sunflower
1 large onion, chopped
2 large cloves garlic, crushed
4 cardamom pods, split
2 bay leaves
2 carrots, grated
2 tbsp grated fresh ginger
2 tsp ground coriander

200g red split lentils
500ml water
200ml reduced-fat coconut milk
200ml passata or canned chopped tomatoes
2 tsp garam masala
Juice of 1 lime
4 tbsp chopped fresh coriander (optional)

1 Heat one tablespoon oil in a large, heavy-based saucepan and sauté the onion for 10 minutes, or until softened, stirring frequently. Add the garlic and sauté for another 30 seconds, stirring, followed by the cardamom, bay leaves, carrots, ginger and ground coriander.
2 After one minute, add the lentils, water, coconut milk and passata to the pan, stir, and bring to the boil, then reduce the heat and simmer, covered, for 20 minutes. Stir in the garam masala and lime juice and cook, covered, for another 20 minutes, stirring occasionally.
3 When the lentils are tender, remove the pan from the heat and remove the whole spices then purée with a hand-held blender until smooth. Stir in the chopped coriander, if using.

Storage tip *Lentil Dahl will keep stored in the fridge in an airtight container for up to five days or can be frozen for up to three months.*

DINNER

MACARONI & LEEK CHEESE

A family favourite, macaroni cheese provides calcium for strong teeth and bones.

- *from 6 months*
- *4 family servings*

300g macaroni
50g butter
3 leeks, trimmed and chopped
4 tbsp plain flour
700ml milk (breast, formula, cow's or alternative)
1 heaped tsp English mustard powder
2 tbsp crème fraîche
50g parmesan cheese, finely grated
110g mature cheddar, grated

1 Cook the macaroni in a large saucepan of boiling water following the instructions on the packet.
2 Melt the butter in a medium-sized, heavy-based saucepan, and then add the leeks and sauté for 4 minutes until softened.
3 Stir in the flour and cook for 1 minute, stirring continuously. Gradually add the milk, stirring all the time with a whisk to avoid any lumps. When all of the milk has been added, stir in the mustard. Preheat the grill to high.
4 Bring the white sauce to the boil, then reduce the heat and simmer for 5 minutes, stirring frequently. Stir in the crème fraiche, half of the parmesan and two-thirds of the cheddar and heat through until the cheese has melted.
5 Drain the pasta, reserving 3 tablespoons of the cooking water. Return the pasta and water to the pan and pour in the cheese sauce. Turn until the pasta is coated in the sauce then transfer to a warm ovenproof dish.
6 Sprinkle the remaining parmesan and cheddar over the top and grill for 6–8 minutes until the top is golden.

Variation *In addition to the leeks, you could add steamed broccoli or peas and top the macaroni with slices of tomato.*

Storage tip *Will keep stored in the fridge in an airtight container for up to 3 days or can be frozen for up to 3 months.*

VEGETABLE FINGERS

These vegetarian alternatives to fish fingers are a useful way of disguising vegetables if your child dislikes anything remotely green. Finely chopped broccoli, grated cabbage, finely chopped carrots or green beans can also be used.

- *from 8 months*
- *2–4 servings*

450g potatoes, cut into chunks
55g frozen peas
1 leek, finely chopped
85g canned no-sugar-or-salt sweet corn, drained
55g mature cheddar cheese, grated
Fine polenta or cornmeal, for coating
Vegetable oil, for frying

Continued over page ▷

▶ *Continued from previous page*

1 Cook the potatoes in plenty of boiling water for about 10–15 minutes, or until tender. Add the peas two minutes before the end of the cooking time. Drain the vegetables well and leave to cool.

2 While the potatoes and peas are cooking, steam the leeks for 5–8 minutes, or until tender. Squeeze the leeks to get rid of any excess water and combine with the potatoes and peas. Mash well. Leave to cool completely. When the mixture is cool, stir in the cheese.

3 Sprinkle the polenta on a plate until covered. Take 2 large tablespoonfuls of the mash and, using your hands, form them into a "finger" shape. Roll each finger in the polenta and turn until completely coated. Continue until you have used all the mixture.

4 Heat enough oil to cover the bottom of a heavy-based frying pan. Cook the fingers in batches for 3 minutes on each side, or until heated through and golden.

CREAMY FISH PIE

This complete meal provides a good balance of nutrients such as low-fat protein, C and B-group vitamins, zinc and calcium. Make sure there are no bones.

■ *from 12 months*
● *4 family servings*

2 tbsp vegetable oil
1 onion, finely chopped
1 stick celery, finely chopped
1 carrot, finely chopped
1 bay leaf
700g potatoes, peeled and halved
    or quartered if large
25g butter, plus extra for topping
2 tbsp plain flour
300ml milk
1 tsp Dijon mustard
2 tbsp crème fraîche
250g undyed smoked haddock
    fillet or similar smoked fish,
    skinned and cut into 2.5cm
    pieces
250g haddock fillet or similar firm
    white fish, skinned and cut into
    2.5cm pieces
100g small cooked prawns,
    defrosted if frozen
100g frozen baby peas

1 Heat the oil in a large saucepan and fry the onion, celery and carrot for 10 minutes until softened. Add the bay leaf.

2 Meanwhile, cook the potatoes in plenty of boiling water until tender; drain well. Preheat the oven to 180°C (350°F).

3 Mash the potatoes with the butter until smooth – you want quite a dry mash. Cover the pan with a lid to keep the mash warm and set aside.

4 Stir the flour into the softened onions and cook for 1 minute then gradually add the milk, stirring continuously. When the sauce has thickened, stir in the mustard and crème fraîche and heat through.

5 Add the fish, prawns and peas to the white sauce and stir until combined then spoon the mixture into an ovenproof dish.

6 Top the fish mixture with the mashed potato in an even layer. Dot the top with little knobs of butter then bake for about 25 minutes until golden.

FISH WITH ROASTED TOMATOES

If serving to young babies, peel off the skin after cooking and flake the fish taking care to remove any bones. Mash with the roasted tomatoes. You could use any type of fish in this recipe.

- *from 6 months*
- *4 family servings*

1½ tbsp olive oil, plus extra for frying
20 cherry tomatoes
Handful fresh basil
4 fish fillets
Flour, for dusting
20g unsalted butter
2 tsp lemon juice (optional)

1 Preheat the oven to 200°C (400°F). Heat 1 tablespoon of the oil in a roasting tin and add the tomatoes and basil. Turn the tomatoes in the oil and season with pepper, if using. Roast for 6–10 minutes until tender. Peel off the tomato skins.

2 Dust the fish in seasoned flour. Heat half of the butter and a little of the remaining oil in a frying pan until very hot. Cook the fillets for 4–5 minutes, turning halfway.

3 Place the fish on serving plates with the tomatoes and squeeze over the lemon juice, if using.

SALMON FINGERS WITH SWEET POTATO CHIPS

This healthy version of fish fingers and chips offers plenty of brain-boosting omega-3 fatty acids. Children need essential fatty acids provided by the salmon for their rapidly developing brains and nerves. Peas are a must as an accompaniment.

- *from 12 months*
- *4 family servings*

100g fine cornmeal, polenta or fresh breadcrumbs
3 tbsp freshly grated parmesan
350g salmon fillet, skinned and sliced into 10 chunky fingers
2 eggs, beaten
Sunflower oil, for frying
Pepper, to taste (optional)

FOR THE SWEET POTATO CHIPS
500g sweet potato, scrubbed and cut into wedges
2 tbsp olive oil

1 Preheat the oven to 200°C (400°F). To make the chips, dry the sweet potatoes on a clean tea towel. Spoon the oil into a roasting tin and heat briefly. Toss the potatoes in the warm oil until covered and roast for 30 minutes, turning them half-way through, until tender and golden.

Continued over page ▷

▶ *Continued from previous page*

2 Meanwhile, mix together the cornmeal with the parmesan on a plate. Dip each salmon finger into the beaten egg then roll them in the cornmeal and parmesan mixture until evenly coated.

3 Heat enough oil to cover the base of a large heavy-based frying pan. Carefully arrange the salmon fingers in the pan and cook them for 6 minutes, turning halfway through, until golden. Drain on kitchen paper then serve with the sweet potato chips.

Variation *Try using thick fillets of white fish such as cod, haddock, pollack or hoki in place of the salmon.*

TUNA & LEEK FRITTATA

A protein-rich, nutritious dish, this can be eaten hot or cold and makes a great finger food. You could mix the tortilla with a small amount of milk if puréeing. Delicious served with vegetable sticks and potato wedges.

■ *from 12 months*
● *4 family servings*

1 tbsp olive oil
small knob of butter
1 large leek, finely sliced
200g can tuna in olive oil or spring
    water, drained
6 eggs, beaten

1 Heat the oil and butter in a medium-sized, ovenproof frying pan then fry the leek for 5–7 minutes, or until softened. Stir in the tuna, making sure that there is an even distribution of leek and tuna

and that some chunks of tuna remain.

2 Preheat the grill to medium-high. Pour the eggs evenly over the tuna and leek mixture. Cook over a moderate heat for 5 minutes, or until the eggs are just set and the base of the frittata is golden brown.

3 Place the pan under the grill and cook the top of the frittata for 3 minutes or until set and lightly golden. Serve the frittata warm or cold, cut into wedges or fingers.

Variation *Try adding 200g cooked diced chicken or 4 rashers grilled bacon instead of the tuna. Cooked, sliced sausages (about 4) or 200g diced smoked ham could also be used in place of the tuna.*

CHINESE BEEF WITH NOODLES

Beef is a good source of iron. Serve with a glass of fresh orange juice to enhance its absorption.

■ *from 8–9 months*
● *4 family servings*

2 tbsp sunflower or vegetable oil
500g lean beef, cut into strips
250g medium egg noodles
3 cloves garlic
2 handfuls sugar snap peas,
    trimmed
1 red capsicum, seeds removed and
    cut into 1-cm strips
4 spring onions, sliced diagonally
175ml black bean sauce
2 tbsp reduced salt soy sauce

1 Heat the oil in a wok over a medium-high heat. Add the beef and stir-fry for 2 minutes. Remove the beef using a slotted spoon; set aside.

2 Meanwhile, bring a large saucepan of water to the boil. Add the noodles and stir to separate them. Drain when the noodles are tender and keep them warm.

SAUSAGE & POTATO ROAST

This weekday roast dinner is simple to prepare and cook. When serving to babies, remove the skins from the sausages.

■ *from 12 months*
● *4 family servings*

2 tbsp olive oil
8 good quality pork sausages
4 potatoes, cut into large chunks
300g butternut pumpkin, peeled, deseeded and cut into chunks
2 sprigs fresh rosemary
2 sprigs fresh oregano
10 cherry tomatoes
150 ml hot water
3 tsp cornflour

1 Preheat the oven to 200°C (400°F). Place the oil in a large roasting tin. Add the potatoes and turn to coat in the oil. Roast for 10 minutes.

2 Add the sausages, pumpkin and herbs and stir everything together and return to the oven for 15 minutes. Combine the hot water and cornflour in a jug and pour over the sausage mixture.

3 Cook for a further 10 minutes until the stock has thickened and formed a gravy and the sausages and vegetables are cooked and golden. Remove the herbs and serve.

Variation *For a vegetarian version, use non-meat sausages or alternatively increase the quantity of vegetables. You could use onion, parsnip, celeriac, swede and beetroot.*

HOMEMADE BEEF BURGERS

By using good quality, preferably organic, ingredients, you can have a healthy and delicious burger in next to no time. If you like, serve as baby finger food by cutting the burger and bun into pieces and offering them separately.

■ *from 12 months*
● *4 family servings*

1 tsp dried oregano
1 onion, grated
1 carrot, finely grated
1 garlic clove, crushed
450g lean minced beef
1 small egg, beaten
Pepper to taste (optional)
Flour, for dusting
Sunflower oil, for frying
Burger buns or rolls, to serve

3 Add the garlic, sugar snap peas and spring onions to the wok and stir-fry for 2 minutes then return the beef to the wok with the black bean and soy sauces; stir-fry for another minute, adding a splash of water if the sauce begins to dry out.

4 Divide the noodles between 4 plates then top with the beef stir-fry.

Variation *Chicken or pork and vegetables of your choice also can be used.*

Storage tip *Can be stored in an airtight container in the fridge for up to 2 days. Reheat thoroughly.*

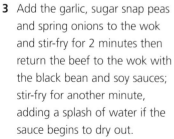

Continued over page ▷

▶ *Continued from previous page*

1 Place the oregano, onion, carrot, garlic, beef and egg in a large bowl. Season with the pepper, if using, and mix with your hands until all the ingredients are combined.

2 Divide the mixture into portions and then, using floured hands, form each portion into a burger shape. Set aside in the refrigerator for 15 minutes.

3 Heat enough oil to lightly cover the base of a large heavy-based frying pan. Place the burgers in the hot oil and fry for three minutes on each side until browned and cooked through.

4 Serve the burgers in buns with relish and tomato sauce.

Storage tip *The burgers can be frozen, uncooked, for up to 3 months. Separate the burgers with a piece of greaseproof paper to prevent them sticking together.*

HAM & PEA PENNE

Good quality ham will give the best flavour but reduced-salt versions are better for babies. Or, serve the salty ham in smaller quantities.

■ *from 6 months*
● *4 family servings*

300g penne
1 tbsp olive oil
2 large cloves garlic, chopped
200ml water
150g frozen baby peas
6 tbsp crème fraîche
4 thick slices of cured ham, cut into
    bite-sized pieces
Pepper, to taste (optional)
Freshly grated parmesan, to serve

1 Cook the pasta in plenty of boiling water, following the packet instructions. Drain, reserving 2 tbsp of the cooking water.

2 Meanwhile, heat the olive oil in a large, heavy-based frying pan and fry the garlic for 30 seconds. Add the water, then the peas and cook over a medium-high heat for 2 minutes, or until the peas are cooked and the liquid has reduced.

3 Add the ham to the pan with the crème fraiche. Cook over a low heat, stirring frequently, until warmed through. Stir in the pasta and the reserved cooking water, if required, and stir gently until combined. Season with pepper, if using, and serve sprinkled with parmesan.

Variation *Replace the ham with 200g canned tuna or salmon. You could also use fresh cooked salmon, flaked into pieces, or cooked, diced chicken.*

CHICKEN BALLS IN TOMATO SAUCE

A great Italian-inspired dish that's delicious with pasta or rice.

■ *from 12 months*
● *4 family servings*

CHICKEN BALLS
500g minced chicken
3 tbsp freshly grated parmesan
50g fresh breadcrumbs
1 small egg, beaten
Flour, for dusting
Olive oil, for frying

TOMATO SAUCE
1 tbsp olive oil
1 large garlic clove, crushed
1 tsp dried oregano
400g can chopped tomatoes
1 tbsp tomato purée

1 Mix together the chicken, parmesan, breadcrumbs and egg. Using floured hands, form into 20 small balls – they don't have to be perfectly round.
2 Heat enough oil to just cover the bottom of a heavy-based frying pan and cook the balls, in batches if necessary, for 6–8 minutes, turning occasionally, until golden and cooked though. Remove from the pan and keep warm.
3 To make the sauce, heat the olive oil in a pan and add the garlic and oregano. Fry for 30 seconds then add the chopped tomatoes and purée. Cook for 4 minutes over a medium-low heat, stirring occasionally.
4 Return the chicken balls to the pan and cook for a further 4 minutes until heated through and the sauce has reduced and thickened.

TURKEY PATTIES WITH PINEAPPLE RELISH

Turkey provides useful amounts of protein and B vitamins and is generally lower in fat than red meat. The pineapple and mint relish is vitamin C-rich.

■ *from 8 months*
● *3–4 servings*

225g free-range lean turkey mince
1 tsp dried oregano
1 large garlic clove, crushed (optional)
Olive oil, for brushing
Mini seeded burger buns or wholewheat rolls

PINEAPPLE RELISH
150g canned or fresh peeled pineapple, finely diced
1 tbsp finely finely chopped fresh mint
4cm piece cucumber, peeled, seeded and finely diced
2 tsp lemon juice

1 Mix together the turkey mince, oregano and garlic, if using, in a mixing bowl. Divide the mixture into portions. Use your hands to roll each portion into a ball then flatten into a burger shape. Put the burgers on a plate, cover with cling wrap and chill for 30 minutes.
2 Preheat the grill to medium-high and line the grill pan with foil. Meanwhile, mix together the ingredients for the relish and set aside to allow the flavours to mingle.
3 Brush the patties with oil then grill them for 3–5 minutes each side, or until cooked through and there is no trace of pink in the centre.
4 To serve, cut the buns in half crossways, add a burger and a spoonful of the relish.

Storage tip *The patties can be frozen, uncooked, for up to 3 months. Separate the burgers with a piece of greaseproof paper to prevent them sticking together.*

PUDDINGS & BAKES

BANANA & MAPLE YOGHURT ICE

This is perfect for soothing sore gums. If the bananas you are using are not too ripe, you may want to add the maple syrup.

- *from 6 months*
- *1 serving*

1 small ripe banana
1 heaped tbsp natural thick
   bio yoghurt
1 tsp maple syrup, optional

1 Peel the banana, wrap it tightly in cling wrap and freeze until firm – at least 3 hours, although it can be stored in the freezer until ready to use
2 Remove the frozen banana from the freezer and unwrap. Leave for 15 minutes to soften slightly then break into chunks.
3 Put the banana in a food processor or blender with the yoghurt and maple syrup, if using, and blend until thick, smooth and creamy. Spoon the ice-cream into a bowl.

Storage tip *This will keep stored in the fridge in an airtight container for up to 2 days but it will defrost after an hour becoming a fruit fool. The banana can be stored in the freezer for up to 3 months.*

FRUIT SWIRLS

Making your own fruit yoghurt means you know exactly what's in it. Frozen fruit – either single fruit or mixed – still counts towards the recommended "5-a-day."

- *from 6 months*
- *2 servings*

4 tbsp mixed red berries,
   defrosted if frozen
1 nectarine, halved, stoned and
   quartered
3–4 tbsp water
Thick natural low-fat bio
   yoghurt, to serve

1 Put the berries, nectarine and water in a saucepan with a lid. Bring up to simmering point then cover the pan and cook for 5–7 minutes or until the berries and plums are soft and beginning to break down.
2 Press the cooked fruit through a sieve to remove any seeds and skin.
3 Spoon a serving of natural yoghurt into a glass or bowl. Add a few spoonfuls of the fruit purée and swirl it into the yoghurt using a spoon handle to give a marbled effect.

CARROT CAKE SQUARES

Your toddler will never guess this light, moist cake contains healthy vegetables.

- ■ *from 12 months*
- ● *about 16*

225g self-raising flour
Pinch of salt
1 tsp ground cinnamon
1 tsp ground mixed spice
225g light muscovado sugar
225g carrots, peeled and grated
3 medium eggs, lightly beaten
175ml sunflower oil

1 Preheat the oven to 180°C (350°F). Lightly grease a 20-cm square cake tin and line the base with greaseproof paper.
2 Sift the flour, salt and spices into a large mixing bowl. Add the sugar and carrots and mix well.
3 Mix together the eggs and oil in a jug, then pour into the flour mixture, stirring with a wooden spoon until combined.
4 Pour the mixture into the cake tin and bake for 50 minutes, or until a skewer inserted into the centre of the cake comes out clean. Leave for 10 minutes, then carefully turn out the cake and leave to cool.

Storage tip *Store in an airtight cake tin for up to 1 week.*

MANGO FOOL

This creamy dessert can be whipped up in a matter of minutes.

- ■ *from 8 months*
- ● *4 family servings*

1 large mango, stoned, peeled and roughly chopped
200ml whipping cream
2 tsp unrefined icing sugar
4 tbsp natural bio yoghurt

1 Place the mango in a food processor or blender, reserving four slices to decorate. Purée the mango until smooth.
2 Add the cream, sugar and yoghurt and blend until combined.
3 Spoon the mixture into 4 glasses and refrigerate for 1 hour to firm up slightly.

Variation *Any soft-fleshed fruit can be used but apples and pears or other firmer fruit will need to be cooked first.*

OAT BISCUITS

These American-style treats are packed with nutritious oats.

- ■ *from 12 months*
- ● *12 biscuits*

120g unsalted butter
75g light muscovado sugar
75g self-raising flour
25g wholemeal self-raising flour
100g whole porridge oats

1 Preheat the oven to 180°C (350°F). Line two baking trays with baking paper.
2 Beat together the butter and sugar in a mixing bowl until light and fluffy. Stir in both types of flour and the oats then mix well to make a soft dough.
3 Divide the dough into 12 pieces. Roll each piece into a ball and arrange on the baking trays, well spaced out to allow room for the dough to spread. Flatten the top of each ball slightly and bake for 15–20 minutes, or until just golden but still soft in the centre.
4 Leave to cool to 5 minutes then transfer to wire racks.

MIXED FRUIT COMPOTE

Many children dislike "bits" which unfortunately can put them off berries. This compote is sieved to remove any offending seeds and skin, resulting in an intensely fruity red sauce. You can buy packets of frozen mixed fruit at the supermarket.

- ■ *from 6 months*
- ● *4-6 servings*

200g mixed red fruit such as strawberries, raspberries and cherries, rinsed, hulled and stoned, and if frozen, defrosted

2 tbsp fresh apple juice

1 tsp cornflour

1 Purée the mixed berries in a food processor or blender. Sieve the purée into a pan to remove any seeds or skin.

2 Add the apple juice and cornflour to the pan and heat gently and briefly, stirring frequently, until thickened..

Variation *This fruit compote is delicious stirred into a live natural bio yoghurt and topped with a sprinkling of granola.*

PEACH CRUMBLES

This variation on the classic crumble uses whole fruits – perfect if you are just cooking for the children since its easier to make small portions.

- ■ *from 8 months*
- ● *2–4 servings*

2 peaches, halved and stones removed

25g plain flour

2 tbsp unsalted butter

1 tbsp porridge oats (optional)

2 tbsp demerara sugar

1 Preheat the oven to 180°C (350°F). Grease an ovenproof dish or baking tin and arrange the peach halves in the dish.

2 Put the flour and butter in a bowl and rub together with your fingertips to form coarse crumbs. Stir in the oats and sugar and mix well.

3 Spoon the crumble mixture over the peaches and add 2 tablespoons of water to the dish. Bake for 25 minutes, or until the peaches are tender and the crumble slightly crisp.

Variation *Plums, apples, pears or nectarines make delicious alternatives to the peaches. If you have any crumble mixture left over, store it in a container or bag in the freezer for future use.*

INTERACTING WITH
YOUR GROWING BABY

Creating a loving relationship

Caring for your baby goes well beyond taking care of his basic needs and ensuring he remains safe and well – all of which is comprehensively covered in this guide. To thrive, all babies need to form a close, loving, emotional attachment with at least one of their parents. Building this relationship begins shortly after birth, when a baby first exhibits responses to his mother's facial expressions and speech, and is vital to his attaining his full potential. But in addition to creating this loving bond, which can help promote the mastery of essential manipulative, locomotive, and communication skills, parents must also ensure that their children become equipped with important social and emotional skills, which will make them "acceptable" members of the community.

Responsiveness

While much of the behaviour that draws an infant closer to his parents is instinctive – when he cries, you will pick him up; when he coos at you, you will coo back – forming a close attachment will be promoted by your being sensitive to your baby's emotional state – some babies are more responsive than others and from an earlier age – and by engaging him according to his developmental stage.

Sensitivity to your baby's emotional state involves knowing when he is alert enough for stimulating play; since all babies are different, they all display different levels of responsiveness between the two extremes – active and passive. An active baby is one who is very expressive and gives out very strong and frequent social signals such as eye contact, reaching, smiling and vocalising. A passive baby exhibits very

few expressions that reveal anything about his inner emotions. Most babies fall somewhere in between.

Young babies are more responsive when they are alert, although simply being awake may not mean your baby is ready for stimulation. Neither is it recommended to stimulate your baby too frequently, as he won't learn to amuse himself, or for you to stimulate him to the point when he becomes fussy and "tunes out". Your baby may be ready for an encounter, however, when he is lying calmly and quietly in his crib but he smiles and moves his arms and legs excitedly as you approach. In any event, you'll soon learn what stimulation works best for your baby – and when. You'll find, for example, that there is no point in showing your young baby a toy while he is feeding, as his concentration is totally focused on eating, whereas when he's older and

eating, a toy can help to distract him while you spoon some food into his mouth. Also, you may find that he is more alert and willing to be engaged early in the day rather than later.

Parental participation

You have a vital role to play in ensuring your baby achieves all that he is capable of achieving. By engaging in appropriate activities, you will help him to make the most of skills as he acquires them. But you will also build your relationship by making it fun for him to practise these skills and praising his efforts, whether he succeeds at what he attempts – or not. Your aim is to provide the encouragement and environment in which to succeed, not to push your baby to learn.

Make sure you spend time every day playing with your baby – and continue to do so as he becomes a toddler and then a child. This will ensure that a close bond develops between you and your baby. Because your baby will take his lead from you in most of the things he tries, be positive and gentle when you are with your baby and try to make his environment a happy place to be. Even from a young age babies pick up on "negative vibes", and harsh voices, even if not directed at him, will upset your baby.

As with other skills (see below), sociability and the emergence of personality have recognisable milestones, though their emergence varies greatly from child to child. It is very important not to typecast your child or impose your own social behaviour on him. Your baby needs to develop his personality and social skills unimpeded by the views or expectations of others.

One of your responsibilities as a parent is to set boundaries for your child so that he comes to understand the difference between right and wrong. Key to this is setting the right example; your child will spend more time with you than with anyone else. You need to show him the correct way to play and interact with others by being polite, sharing things, and showing him how to take turns.

How your baby develops

Your baby is unique and different from all other children, with a physical appearance and a personality unlike any other, but if you look at the "big picture", he shares an enormous number of similarities with most other children. All healthy children, for example, have the same body parts, are born roughly the same size and weight, cry when they are hungry, and trigger a loving response in their parents; they also are remarkably alike in how they mature physically, mentally, and emotionally.

The terms "growth" and "development" refer to the typical patterns that all children go through on their journeys from infancy to adulthood. Growth describes the process of physical enlargement (height, weight and head size), while development denotes the acquisition of body functions, skills (motor, social and language) and the successive stages of psychological maturation.

Physical growth

In the first days after birth, your baby will lose weight. The reason for this is simple: more is going out (urine and bowel movements) than is coming in (milk), but soon everything changes. In the first three to four months of life, your baby will grow remarkably rapidly. After that, the rate of growth slows somewhat for the remainder of the first year and slows down even more between 12 and 24 months. From then on, growth continues at a relatively constant rate until puberty, when there is another huge burst. Growth charts (see pages 380–3), and graphs of height, weight or head circumference as your child ages, reflect these patterns.

Although the criteria given in the "rules of thumb" about growth are often accurate, there are many healthy children who do not grow precisely according

3 "rules of thumb" about growth

1   A child doubles his birth weight by 5 months of age and triples it by 12 months. (Children with lower birth weights double and triple faster; those with higher birth weights take longer than average.)

2   A child reaches half his adult height at 24 months of age. (For greater accuracy the measurement should be taken with the child standing up – and standing still! Boys will typically be about 5cm taller than the 2-year-old height doubled; girls will typically be about 5cm shorter than the doubled height.)

3   Half of a child's head growth occurs in the first year of life; the remainder takes years.

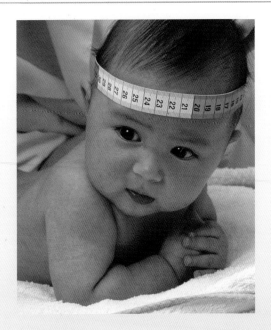

the typical pattern. In other words, while the "rules" are grossly correct, they may not apply specifically to your son or daughter. Many factors are responsible for how big or small your child is. Genetics is a major influence, although no prediction about his ultimate size can be made until he is about two years old.

Charting growth charts

Doctors and health visitors use growth charts to track a child's growth over time. If your baby is growing properly, which is a reflection of good health, he will keep approximately the same percentile value for weight or height as he gets older. So, if you want to be reassured that your baby is growing nicely, check if his height or weight percentile is consistent from visit to visit. It is more important that his measurements follow a curve of the growth chart (of any percentile) than that he is in a percentile with a higher number.

Look, for example, at the two growth charts on page 275. The boy whose weight is plotted on the top is growing consistently along the 25th percentile curve. He is healthy because he is growing as he should. The boy whose weight is plotted on the bottom has a higher percentile value but is not growing properly. He is "falling off the curve" (i.e., successive percentile values are less and less), and there is cause for concern. His doctor will need to find out what is the matter.

Skill acquisition

At birth, there is little about your son that resembles an adult. Besides his small size and appearance, he can't take care of himself, can't walk or talk, and certainly can't follow your commands. However, you can anticipate that, bit by bit, he will acquire new skills, so that eventually he will not only look like, but will also act like, an adult. Although he was born small and helpless, he has the capacity to

While you can understand the reason for charting the growth in your child's height and weight, you may not appreciate why it's important to monitor head circumference regularly. Taking serial measurements of head size is one way of keeping track of brain growth. There are normal values (more accurately, a normal range of values since there isn't just one normal value for each age) for head growth. Your doctor will monitor your son's head growth as well as his developmental skills to make sure he is neurologically normal. If a child's head is not growing well – growing less than expected or not following a percentile curve consistently – this can indicate that the brain is not normal. Conversely, if the head is growing too fast, there may be too much fluid surrounding the brain (hydrocephalus) or other problems.

acquire all the skills of an adult. How he does so depends on his brain and body advancing until both are sufficiently mature. For example, a child typically takes his first steps at about one year of age (though the "normal" range is 10 to 18 months). And while you can stand your baby up and encourage him to walk when he is six, seven, or eight months old, no matter how hard he tries, he just won't be able to walk until, at about one year of age, his brain, nerves, and muscles reach a critical point – the necessary maturation. Sure, practice can help, but only once the basic maturity has occurred.

Your baby will appear to have an innate compulsion to try to develop new skills. He also will practise a new skill over and over again until he can do it well. In a sense, your baby is driven by an internal mechanism, a standard feature in each human being, which tells him, for instance, that he must first learn to walk before being able to climb and run and that he must first utter a few sounds, before learning to say words, and then speaking in complete sentences.

So when it comes to development, all healthy children are alike in that there is a characteristic pattern and timing for the acquisition of new skills. But because children are all different, there is a range of normal ages for developing the ability to perform each new skill. Additionally, there are small variations in the orderly sequence of events; some children even skip a skill, such as rolling over or crawling, before going on to more difficult tasks. (Of course, all children will eventually come back and learn to roll or crawl.)

Your GP or health visitor will carefully observe your baby at surgery or home visits and may ask you questions about new skills he has developed. These newly acquired abilities are referred to as "milestones". As originally used, a milestone was a rock or stone placed every mile along the road. Counting milestones allowed a person to know how far he had come, and with each passing milestone, the traveller knew he was getting closer and closer to his destination. Although milestones in child development are not as equally spaced out as the stones along a road, they are markers you can use to chart out your child's progress (in gaining skills) as he makes his journey to adulthood.

Set out on pages 278–9 is the usual order in which your baby will gain new skills and the common timing that skills appear. In addition to the average age, it is very important to pay attention to the range of ages that are normal for any new achievement. For each task, your child may succeed at the average age or may be earlier or later. As long as the new skill occurs in the interval reflecting the range of normal, it is normal. Bear in mind that your healthcare provider won't judge your baby's developmental progress on the basis of a single skill. If he is late on just one (for example, clapping his hands) but completely normal on other related skills, there is little reason for concern.

Each of the body's systems and normal functions mature at different times and at different paces. However, as examples for understanding generally how they all develop, you can see below how vision, teeth, and speech evolve. These examples demonstrate that there is a blueprint for the maturation of function of every part of the body and for every developmental skill and milestone. Since every child will accomplish some tasks early, some at an average pace, and others a bit slower than average, each child's development is different from every other's. On the other hand, the similarity in the way each child grows and acquires skills is remarkable. So, all children are very much the same, while at the same time, your child is unique!

Vision

In the first month of life, your newborn sees clearly only objects that are quite close to his face; everything else seems hazy. By about one month of age, he will enjoy focusing on people's faces and will be able to distinguish your face from the faces of others. While you will take pleasure in being the object of your son's gaze, be aware that you will encounter stiff competition for his attention from a light bulb, window or television screen. Bright lights seem to fascinate him. While he can see near objects clearly, he still has difficulty seeing far objects. By six months of age, he will see you well if you stand one to two metres away, but his vision is probably only 20/100. (These numbers rate his vision compared to the average, normal adult. The first number refers to how far the subject being tested is from the eye chart; the second number is how far away an adult with

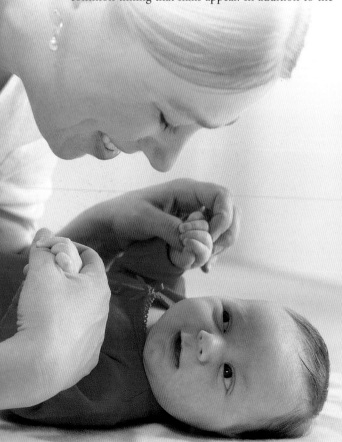

Growth charts

Growth charts are created by measuring a large number of healthy children of all ages (the "reference group"). Among these children, there is a range of weights (or heights) for each age. The percentile value given to a child's weight or height is a way of seeing where that weight fits in among all the other boys or girls in the reference group.

If a baby is on the 10th percentile for height and weight it means that 90 per cent of babies are taller and heavier then he is. Similarly, a baby on the 90th percentile is taller and heavier than 90 per cent of other babies. Although these two babies are very different in size and at different ends of the percentile range, both are within the "normal" range.

Unfortunately, however, parents often use the information given by percentiles incorrectly. Those whose children measure less than the 50th percentile ask, "Why isn't he bigger (or heavier)?" while parents whose children are in a higher percentile somehow feel quite proud. Growth is not a contest to see who can be the tallest or heaviest, and a higher percentile is not better than a lower one. A child can be healthy and growing well even if his percentile value for height or weight is below average; keep in mind that half of all children are at or below the 50th percentile.

Charts for for boys' and girls' lengths and weights for the first three years can be found on pages 380–3).

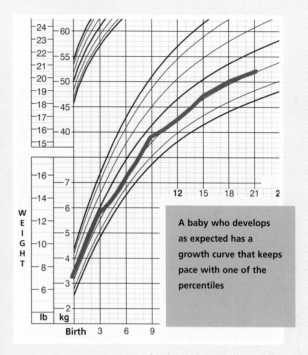

A baby who develops as expected has a growth curve that keeps pace with one of the percentiles

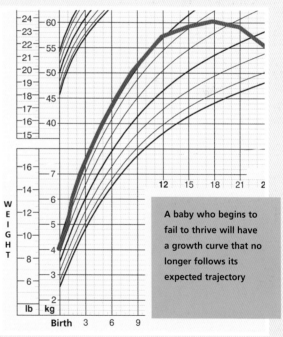

A baby who begins to fail to thrive will have a growth curve that no longer follows its expected trajectory

Denver developmental screen

Many doctors use the above test as a tool for assessing your child's progress in reaching new milestones; it contains normal ranges established for children of the same age. By using this chart, your doctor is following your baby's development as he/she tracks growth on a growth chart. Instead of height, weight and head circumference, however, skills in four categories (gross motor, fine motor, language and personal-social [shown below]) are plotted and compared to the normal range of ages for acquiring them.

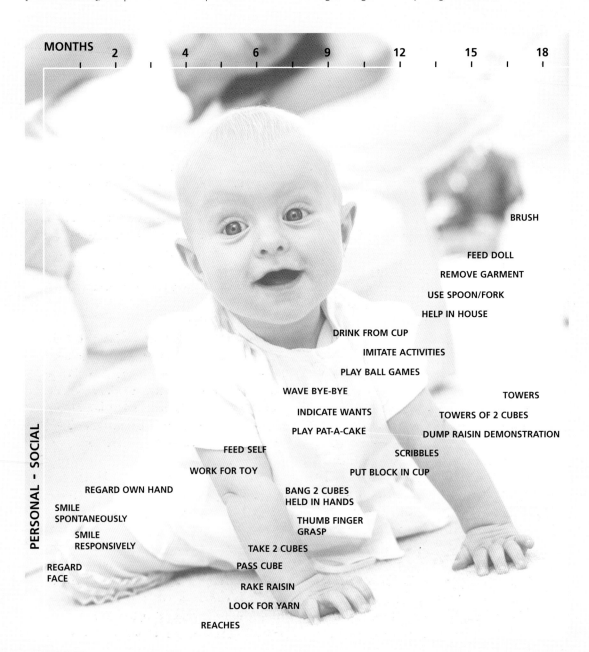

MONTHS 2 4 6 9 12 15 18

PERSONAL - SOCIAL

BRUSH

FEED DOLL

REMOVE GARMENT

USE SPOON/FORK

HELP IN HOUSE

DRINK FROM CUP

IMITATE ACTIVITIES

PLAY BALL GAMES

WAVE BYE-BYE

INDICATE WANTS   TOWERS

TOWERS OF 2 CUBES

PLAY PAT-A-CAKE   DUMP RAISIN DEMONSTRATION

FEED SELF   SCRIBBLES

WORK FOR TOY   PUT BLOCK IN CUP

REGARD OWN HAND   BANG 2 CUBES HELD IN HANDS

SMILE SPONTANEOUSLY

SMILE RESPONSIVELY   THUMB FINGER GRASP

TAKE 2 CUBES

REGARD FACE   PASS CUBE

RAKE RAISIN

LOOK FOR YARN

REACHES

THE ACQUISITION OF LANGUAGE SKILLS

	Average age	Early talkers	Late talkers
Babbling (single syllables)	7–8 months	6 months	9–10 months
First words	12–15 months	10 months	16–18 months
2 words sentence	20–24 months	18–20 months	24–30 months
3 words sentence	24–26 months	21–24 months	up to 36 months
Follows a command (without you pointing)	15 months	12–14 months	16–17 months
Name parts of body	15 months	12–14 months	16–18 months
Counts to 10	26–30 months	24–26 months	30–36 months

"normal" vision would have to stand to see the chart exactly as clearly as the subject does. In other words, if your baby has a visual acuity of 20/100, his vision when he is six metres from an object is equivalent to the vision of an adult standing 30 metres from the same object. (Normal adult vision is 20/20.) By age three or four, your child's vision will improve to about 20/40; by age five to six, it will be 20/30; and by age seven, it will reach 20/20. His eyesight will then be as good as (or better) than yours.

Teeth

On average, your child will cut his first tooth at approximately six months of age. However, as in all aspects of development, there is great variation between children. Although uncommon, some children are born already having an erupted tooth, while at the other extreme, a number of children get a first tooth at 12 months or later. There is clearly a genetic effect on how and when teeth erupt; often a child with late erupting teeth comes from a family where one of his parents also was late in getting teeth.

The first two teeth to arrive are usually the bottom central incisors. After that, the top four incisors erupt, followed by the lateral incisors on the bottom. The next teeth to come in are typically the first molars, at about 18 months of age. When the molar erupts, there is a space between the lateral incisors and the first molar, because the canine, or "eye" tooth, comes in after the first molar. The last of the 20 baby teeth are the second molars, which arrive to the outer side of the first molars at about two and a half years of age (see also page 201).

Although many children's teeth do come in at about these ages and in the "usual" order, there are many variations, which are also normal.

Speech

A young child's brain is better equipped than an adult's brain to absorb language. A child possesses not only the built-in equipment for acquiring the ability to communicate using speech but also a compelling drive to do so. Like so many other areas in growth and development, there is an orderly sequence of steps that lead from no language to fluent speech.

In order to attain the skills, an baby must simultaneously master three processes – input, "central processing" and output. He must be able to recognise the difference between speech and other sounds, and must learn to discriminate between the numerous combinations of sounds that constitute speech. Additionally, he must somehow learn the particular combinations of sounds that represent words, and by intuition, decipher the meaning implied by the speaking person. And finally, once he

Key developmental milestones

0–3 months

- Lifts head when held at shoulder
- Arm and leg motions
- Growing ability to follow objects and focus
- Vocalises sounds (coos)
- Smiles spontaneously and responsively
- Likes to be held and rocked

6–9 months

- Rolls from back to stomach
- On back, can lift head up
- Climbs stairs
- Learns to crawl
- Feeds self
- Reaches for a toy that is dropped
- Curious, puts everything in mouth
- Responds to name
- Speaks single consonants (da-da, ba-ba)
- Imitates sounds
- May cry when strangers approach
- May cry when parent leaves the room

3–6 months

- Rolls over from stomach to back
- Lifts up knees
- Reaches for objects
- Sits with support
- Looks at objects in hand
- Grasps with both hands
- Follows a moving object with eyes
- Coos/gurgles
- Chuckles/squeals
- Smiles responsively
- Laughs aloud
- Has expressive noises
- Recognises primary caregiver
- Anticipates food on sight

9–12 months

- Crawls well
- Stands holding on to furniture with hands
- Learns to grasp with thumb and finger
- Puts things in and out of containers
- Interest in pictures
- Drops objects on purpose
- Understands "No"
- Uses "Mama" or "Dada"
- Knows meaning of 1–3 words
- Cooperates in games
- Plays peek-a-boo and pat-a-cake
- Waves bye-bye

12–18 months

- Creeps up stairs
- Walks well alone
- Can stoop to recover an object
- Seats self on chair
- Interest in self-feeding
- Looks at pictures in book
- Scribbles spontaneously
- Uses spoon
- Holds own cup and drinks from it
- Follows one or two directions
- Has 3-5 words
- Will point to one body part
- Will point to at least one picture
- Uses jargon
- Points or vocalises to make desires known
- Cooperates in dressing

18–24 months

- Runs and jumps
- Uses fingers with skill
- Turns pages of a book
- Walks backwards
- Can point to 2–3 body parts
- Has at least 20 words
- Combines 2 words into phrases
- Verbalises desires with words
- Uses spoon
- Handles a cup well
- Imitates housework
- Removes one piece of clothing

2–3 years

- Ready for toilet training
- Highly mobile – skills are refined
- Uses spoon to feed self
- Throws and kicks a ball
- Disassembles simple objects and puts them back together
- Can do simple puzzles, string beads and stack toys
- Capable of thinking before acting
- Loves to pretend and to imitate the actions of people seen
- Engages in creative activities such as block building and art
- Uses plurals
- Names at least one picture
- 100–300 words
- 2–4 word phrases
- Identifies over 5 body parts of own body
- Has great difficulty sharing
- Has strong urges and desires at same time, developing ability to exert self control.
- Wants to please parents but sometimes has difficulty containing impulses
- Displays affection – especially for caregiver
- Imitates own play activity and occupies self
- Interest in peers beginning

The words for mother and father are remarkably similar in different languages. In English, children call their parents daddy and mummy, and depending on the family, grandparents may be addressed as grandpa or papa and grandma or nanna. In French, Italian and Spanish, the same names are commonly used so it is logical to think that this can be explained by the relatedness of the languages. However, in Swahili, mother is also mah-mah; in Indonesian dialects, father is bah-pah, and in Hebrew, mother and father are ah-bah and ee-mah. It is as if the words for parents derive from the first sounds (repetitive syllables) made by children. Children usually say da-da before they say ma-ma, because the da-da sound is easier for a child to produce.

knows what he wants to say, he must be able to direct his mouth, lips, tongue and breathing to produce the appropriate sounds.

It may seem an easy task to figure out that "mama" means "mother". However, if the loving person who cares for him is "mama", does mama mean "mother", "woman", "adult", "caring person" or "tall person with long hair?". Deciphering the meaning of abstract notions such as colours, shorter and taller, or good and bad, is even more challenging. Yet all healthy children do it. Then there are more complicated issues: sentence structure, grammar, tenses, plurals, pronouns and tasks such as discriminating between different meanings of the same word or words that sound alike but have different meanings.

The beginnings of speech

Your child will initially study you (and the faces of other adults) as you talk and try to imitate the oral movements that produce the sounds. He will experiment with sounds in the first months of his life and will be very pleased with himself each time he discovers and succeeds in making new sounds and noises. At five to six months of age, he will make sounds known as "raspberries" ("PLLLLLLLLLLL") and may discover how to make screaming or shrieking cries. At seven to eight months, he may begin saying a syllable repetitively – "da-da-da-da" or "na-na-na-na" (see box). Soon words begin to appear. However, more than for nearly any other development accomplishment, the range of what is normal for acquiring speech is incredibly wide.

Babies who are unusually early talkers say many words well before their first birthdays and speak in full sentences before the age of two. "Late bloomers", who often have a parent or close relative who was also late to speak, may only have a handful of words at 18 months and may not form complicated sentences until older than three years of age (see box page 277).

Playing with your baby

Playing with your baby is important for many reasons. First and foremost, it strengthens the bond of love between the two of you. When you smile adoringly at your baby, his face fills with joy. He senses your deep devotion and concern for him. This is essential to his emotional wellbeing; for feeling loved is a major prerequisite for the growth of his confidence and sense of self-worth.

Besides being fun, play is also educational. When the two of you play peek-a-boo or when your baby throws objects to the floor and then looks to see where they land, he is learning about the permanence of objects (people and objects continue to exist even when they are out his sight). Rolling a ball or passing a small object back and forth to each other allows your baby to practise taking turns. The goal of naming games (as is reading) is to teach your baby the meaning of words – "Where is your nose?", "Where is the dog (in the picture book)?"

3 types of toys to avoid

1 **Toys that are noisy** A toy drum or xylophone, or one that makes a loud noise, may at times give you a headache.

2 **Toys that have many small pieces** In addition to any safety risk, pieces of toys often get lost, limiting how the toy can be used or enjoyed.

3 **Toys that require batteries** In addition to frequent battery replacement, electronic circuits may easily become damaged and the toy will no longer work.

Play also allows your child to practise social skills. Towards the end of your baby's first year, play becomes more interactive. Waving bye-bye to each other, blowing kisses or making silly faces are games that require two people to be played as well as further lessons in the art of social intercourse.

Sharing or taking turns is difficult for your baby to accept, since he (along with all other children) is born with a relatively self-centred and selfish nature. Yet these concepts are central to successfully participate in play. Sharing, although often reluctantly, is typically mastered by age two to three.

Your toddler will also enjoy games in which he uses imagination, such as role-playing that enables him to practise social interactions (your baby can be a chef and you the restaurant customer; when you order food, he pretends to cook it and serves it to you). Games also enable him to channel the frustration and anger he keeps within (after being denied having his own way many times each day). If he plays the role of mum or of another person who has complete control over his environment, he might order you around exactly as he perceives he is ordered around. The more often your baby can express his negative feelings through play, the less severe and frequent his temper tantrums will be.

Play also enables your child to hone locomotive and manipulative skills and to benefit from exercise. Your baby or toddler probably doesn't need to be told to go and exercise; instead, he has a natural desire to "be on the go". This intrinsic drive is satisfied only by physical activity. If your child is "full of energy", take him out to the playground or garden; if you have a designated play space in your home, this also will do. Now his desire to move around can be satisfied in a safe and convenient environment. Let him run around. He will enjoy the slide, swings and climbing equipment at the playground; when he is ready to sit still he can join in the fun in the sandpit.

Toys

A toy is age-appropriate for your baby if it is safe (see page 318) and he finds it fun. An enormous number of toys bought for babies are never played with because, while a toy looks exciting to us, children don't agree. In fact, you will probably be surprised at which toys your baby finds most interesting. Often, the simplest toys or common household objects are favourites because his imagination can dream up multiple uses.

Young babies don't need many toys and even toddlers can make do with a small number of inexpensive ones. Paper and drawing materials can

RECOMMENDED TOYS

Age	Toys
2–4 months	Rattles, mobiles, brightly coloured board books with bold colours
4–7 months	Textured toys that make sounds; baby mirror; baby books with board or vinyl pages.
8–12 months	Stacking toys; bath toys; large building blocks; push-pull toys; "busy boxes" that push, open and squeak.
13–18 months	Lift-out puzzles; digging toys; cars, trucks, and trains; board books; shape sorters; dolls; crayons.
19 months–2 years	Hammering toy; simple puzzles; toy telephone; musical toys.
2–3½ years	Construction toys; dress-up clothes; paints; toy tools and safe household items (for example, dustpan and brush).

engage your child from around 15 months and throughout his life, while pots and pans can be used to make noise and fill with and carry all sorts of interesting things. Toys that leave more to the imagination – puzzles, building blocks, and shape sorters – are generally more popular than those that are full of realistic details. While your son will enjoy playing with toy cars, trucks and trains, your daughter will likely gravitate towards dolls and playing house. However, it's important not to force gender-specific toys on your baby or be unhappy if your baby prefers those of the opposite sex.

Activities

There are many activities you can do with your baby at home that he will find fun. Between the ages of nine and 18 months, he will happily sit in front of a low-level cabinet in the kitchen and play with pots and pans. In the bath, he will enjoy pouring water into cups, blowing bubbles and floating boats.

After 18 months of age, your toddler will want to help with the housework. He can wipe off the table or, with your help, he can also put the clothes in the washing machine or add the laundry liquid (which you have measured out) or pick up his toys.

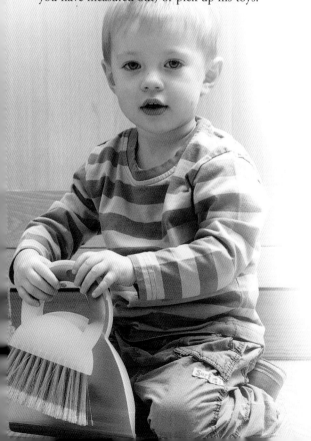

TODDLER CLASSES/PLAYGROUP

The main benefits of these classes are:
- ◆ It is an activity you can do together.
- ◆ There may be some equipment available there that you wouldn't have at home (trampoline, swimming pool, musical instruments, for example).
- ◆ It is a great way for you to meet other mothers and fathers with children about the same age as your own.

The downsides of infant and toddler classes are:
- ◆ The money spent on tuition.
- ◆ The increased risk of your child getting sick from germs spread child-to-child or via toys, tambourines, etc.
- ◆ Your child may have trouble sitting still for long (if he is by nature a "busy" child).

Two activities that are nearly universally engrossing to children are baking and art. When you bake biscuits together, he can shape the dough with his hands or use a cutter, and decorate them with sprinkles or chocolate bits. Painting at an easel with poster paint, drawing with crayons and working with clay also are loads of fun.

Other ways you and your child can enjoy yourselves are to play with balloons, dance to music, and dressing him up in your old clothes and shoes.

There also are many activities available outside the home. Worthwhile (and some free) outings include going to the park, zoo, fire station or a children's museum. Use the time getting there to point out things or talk with your baby about what you see en route. Recent research has shown that babies interact more with their parents and are less emotionally stressed if they are transported in face-to-face buggies compared with babies wheeled in front-facing buggies.

Ways to play

People, particularly parents, rather than inanimate toys, are the best and most effective playmates for babies. By playing with your baby, you not only amuse him but will teach him things as well, like language and how things work. Through play, you can help your baby develop all the skills he needs – physical, intellectual, emotional and psychosocial. However, you'll be most successful if you interact with him in ways that keep pace with his development. Playing peek-a-boo, for example, will be much more fun for both of you when your baby is around eight or nine months old and begins to realise that even when you are hidden from him, you'll soon reappear.

One month
You can start to play simple games with your baby now. Put him on your lap, with his face close to yours (no more than about 20–30 cm away). Lean towards him and talk happily. Pause, and give him a chance to react – smile, gurgle, wriggle or move his mouth back at you. Try doing these things one at a time: smile, stick out your tongue, open and close your mouth widely, or giggle. Your baby may start to imitate you!

Two months
Your baby will still enjoy responding to your expressions but now you can try looking together in a mirror. Change the angle of the mirror but allow your baby plenty of time to watch the reflections. He will like it when you sing songs and move his arms and legs in time.

Three months
Coming into contact with brightly coloured or differently textured materials will be fun for your baby. Stroke his hands with toys or objects – scarves, teething rings, feathers – that are hard and soft, warm and cool, furry and smooth. Shake a rattle holding it close to his face; roll him over a beach ball and play gentle rolling and rocking games.

Four months
Encourage your baby to reach for objects by holding a brightly coloured toy or rattle just in front of him. Sing songs or recite

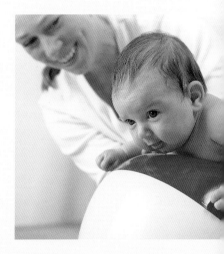

nursery rhymes and accompany by gently raising your baby from a lying to supported standing position.

Five months
As you go about your activities, carry your baby around your home and point out familiar items, letting him touch flowers, cushions, rough surfaces and

wooden tables to gain a sense of their different feelings to touch. He will enjoy studying faces and objects – and also looking at pictures in a book, so this is a good time to start "reading" board books with large pictures.

Six months
Your baby will enjoy dancing – that is, being held in your arms and moved to a rhythm. He will also make greater efforts to reach a toy placed out of his grasp.

Seven months
Continue to read, sing and talk to your baby as much as possible. Now would be a good time to introduce soft baby blocks and help him "build" with them while he sits on the floor.

Eight months
It will be hard to keep your baby in one place now but you can try to do so and at the same time make it more interesting by stacking differently sized cushions on the floor and letting him navigate this "obstacle course" in search of some soft balls or rattles. He'll also like peek-a-boo and uncovering hidden items.

Nine months
Your baby exhibits great curiosity and you can stimulate his hearing by playing music and encouraging him to produce noise – even by banging pots and pans. Introduce him to different textures – helping

him to "walk" over carpet, hard floors and upholstered chairs, and encourage water and sand play. Let him smell flowers and show him brightly coloured pictures.

Ten months
Your baby will enjoy physical play and will like to climb over you. He will like to experiment with objects – putting things into and out of each other – so put together a box with socks, and a variety of "safe" objects such as soft balls, cotton reels and blocks and under your observation, let him practise filling and emptying.

11 months
Reading together will be more fun. Your baby will copy the expression on your face, repeat

more of the words that he hears and will enjoy linking sounds to pictures. You should, therefore, enliven your sessions by making appropriate noises such as

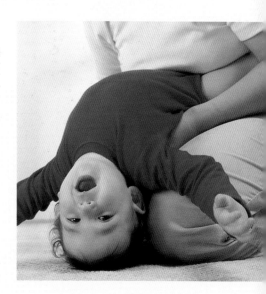

"oinking" when there is a picture of a pig or explaining that water goes "splash". Whatever you do together – giving him a bath, feeding and dressing him – can be turned into a game and he'll reward you with laughter.

12 months
Your baby will particularly like toys that allow him to do things that you do – toy telephones and tea sets, for example. If you can interact with him using them – exchanging calls or feeding teddy together – you'll both enjoy it and if you talk about what you're doing, you are building language skills.

13 months
You may find that your baby starts taking the lead in play, telling you what to do, so games become more him throwing

things, and you fetching them. Messy play will be particularly enjoyable and you can introduce your baby to finger paints now.

14 months
Your baby will love putting small things into and taking bigger things and kitchen items out of yoghurt pots, plastic beakers and juice cans. He can start to build and you can encourage this using bricks and join in at his level. Build a tower and then knock it down, and make a bridge for a car to go underneath.

15 months
Your baby will be more and more into chasing games such as hide and seek in which he can initiate the play and "order" you about. It's a good time to engage in activities with commands or actions – "Touch your nose" –

that your baby has to follow or to recite rhymes with gestures, such as "The Incy Wincey Spider". Your toddler may find that finger puppets will increase his enjoyment of storytelling and develop his manipulation skills.

16 months
Help your baby learn how the world works by exposing him to different play materials – sand, earth and water. Work on simple jigsaw puzzles together, asking him to show you the various pieces – "Where is the pig?" – before he attempts to replace them. Now is a good time to begin simple ball games.

17 months
Encourage him to collect interesting "finds" when you are out – stones, shells, leaves, etc. – and build on this interest by keeping these "treasures" in a special place and by using them to describe the times you had in the past in collecting them or incorporate them into his artworks or a scrapbook.

18 months
Your baby will be much more accurate at stacking and sorting, at fitting shapes through holes, and at using blocks for building. Making things with play dough is fun and you can ask that he make certain things for you such as a "biscuit".

20 months
Your baby will be interested in identifying and classifying items –

animals, household objects and vehicles. Using models, blocks, pictures cut from magazines or puzzle pieces, ask your toddler to sort things into groups – two horses, kitchen equipment, things to ride in.

22 months

Singing and dancing together will be great fun for your baby. He will enjoy reading and may want to hear the same story over and over. Dressing up will a fun thing to do and you can help by playing along – inviting Mr X to tea, for example. Painting his face and pointing out people's reactions is another activity to do together.

24 months

Your baby has become much better working with building blocks and may engage in imaginative play with them – building a fort or other enclosure or tower. He should join you in singing songs and repeating nursery rhymes and will particularly like those with actions, such as "Ring-a-rosy".

26 months

Your baby will be interested in pretend play – taking care of his sick teddy or putting his baby to bed – but may ask you to help, too. Although he won't play with other children, he may enjoy sharing activities with you at a toddler gym or swimming class

28 months

Pretend games are great fun and can be endlessly developed, from being the postman delivering letters to setting up shop with some mini provisions. You can help by constructing a special place for him to practise imaginative play like putting a cloth over a table so that he can "camp out" underneath or letting him use a large cardboard box as a fire truck or car. When you tell him stories, have him or someone he knows appear in them. Ask him questions about the story.

30 months

Your baby will be more adept with his hands and will want to help join in the housework (which he sees as fun, not a chore). Baking and simple jobs involving water, like sponging down his highchair or watering some plants, will be the most fun for him. You can also involve him in simple artwork projects – asking him to help decorate Christmas cards by colouring or adding glitter or stickers.

32 months

Your baby will be interested in drawing and in colours and can use crayons and paint and making a mess with this will be endlessly attractive. You may be able to interest him in other projects – like making prints with a potato and poster paints, or creating a sticker book.

34 months

Your baby will enjoy doing jobs which are simple and easy. He can join in with baking – mixing flour, adding raisins, bringing a box

from the pantry, or putting the spoons away. He may enjoy a simple treasure hunt; show him a picture from a magazine or a book, for example, and ask him to find one similar. Now is the time to introduce books with a proper story and you can allow him to choose what book he wants for a bedtime story.

36 months

Although your baby will enjoy playing with others now, anything he does with you will still be the greatest fun. Making music together, dancing, playing catch, helping with putting groceries or the laundry away, baking and creating artworks are all opportunities to engage with your child and teach him valuable lessons at the same time.

You also may choose from dozens of classes – gym, swimming, massage, art, music, dance, etc. Or, you may want to take your baby along to a local playgroup where he will be exposed to a number of different activities. Playgroup and toddler classes can be fun for your baby starting at 10–12 months of age, but there is nothing that goes on in classes that he can't also learn or be exposed to at home.

Reading

One of the most important activities you and your baby can do together is to read. Listening to your voice as you read helps your infant gain language skills. He hears and learns not only the sounds and meanings of words, but also the way to phrase sentences and the rhythm of speaking. When he is older, beyond 15 to18 months, he can understand the content of what is being read and can get pleasure from the story.

For toddlers and older children, reading holds the key to imagination and is a wonderful educational source. The enjoyment of reading and the habit of doing it regularly will continue as your child begins to read by himself. It is well known that the ability to read and reading frequently have a strong correlation with later school success.

Television and DVD watching

Watching television should not be an important activity for your baby. While there may be some benefits to television, there are also some consistent disadvantages (see box). Current recommendations are that children under two years watch very little, if any television. For preschoolers (between two and five years), a maximum of an hour a day (of programs made specifically for preschoolers) is recommended. However, rather than adhering to a time limit, it may be better simply to place television viewing low on the list of daily activities. If your toddler has played outside, used his imagination, been read to, participated in other activities (drawing, building with blocks, etc.) and played with toys, then – and only then – should you consider permitting any screen time.

TELEVISION

Advantages

- Educational videos or television shows (such as *Sesame Street*) have been shown to help early language development and pre-reading skills in children.
- At times, you may need a brief rest after an exhausting day of running after your child. Or he may just need time to calm down. Watching television, if the content is good, may provide the break you need. There are many high-quality DVDs for children that he will love. However, keep tabs on how much TV watching occurs and limit the amount of "screen time" your child is allowed. Also be warned that he may enjoy seeing the same video over and over again.

Disadvantages

- Watching too much television means there is less time for physical activities and reading, which are far more important.
- Many of the cartoons and programs on television contain violence and material inappropriate for children. Obviously, you should avoid these.
- Sometimes nightmares result from scary scenes seen on TV.
- The more television your child watches, the higher the chance he will become obese. Instead of sitting on the couch, he should be outside running around.

Discipline

Children, at birth, are completely unaware of the "right" way to behave. It will take at least eighteen years before your child learns to act and think like an adult although some of this progress is made in his first years. Discipline refers to the enforcement of rules of conduct, and as such, has a negative connotation. When we think of what comprises discipline, what usually comes to mind is a parent raising his or her voice at a child or punishing him. This, however, is a false image; much of your baby's socialisation will be accomplished without using such undesirable techniques. When you play with your baby – sharing things with him and taking turns – you are imparting valuable lessons about being with others. He will certainly emulate much of your behaviour and there are other ways to teach a child proper behaviour that do not involve disciplining him. Positive reinforcement for desirable behaviour is as good, if not far better, than punishment for bad.

Although it is unrealistic to expect that you will never have to enforce your baby's obedience, your goal as a parent will be to educate him as to what constitutes acceptable behaviour with the minimum amount of confrontation or penalisation. Whether it is a human trait or just part of our culture, adults tend to focus on and criticise a child's behaviour far more often than we think to use praise. Some may say that this seemingly overabundance of telling our children not to do undesirable acts results simply from the fact that children misbehave quite frequently. Yet this is not the case. If you look carefully, there will be numerous times a day when your baby does the right thing, but these moments seem to slip by without notice. Let's take meal times as an example. On some occasions, your baby is certain to throw food on the floor. You could tell him "We don't throw food," at the time he does it but a more positive thing to try is to tell him how pleased you are with him for eating nicely when he does not throw his food. Your praise and

reinforcement of positive behaviour is highly effective and has the added bonus of increasing your baby's feelings of self-worth. While too much praise also can be harmful (a child will start to feel you are not being truthful if you are happy with all his behaviour), this is seldom a danger for most parents. It may take time, but with a little practice you can find many moments a day when your baby's behaviour is worthy of praise.

You and other adults in your baby's life have the important job of shaping the kind of person he will become. However, it's important to bear in mind that social and emotional skills, like the many other processes in his growth and development, are achieved via a programed and orderly sequence. While it may seem that imparting the rules of behaviour is an ongoing, seemingly never-ending, day-to-day process, there is only so much your baby is capable of mastering at any given age. But the environment in which he grows up does have a major influence on how he will act.

Since no parent is perfect, it is likely you, too, will at times make mistakes, say the wrong thing, lose your temper, or handle a situation badly. Everybody does. Luckily, your baby will forgive your missteps; what matters most is that he feels loved and treasured. Still, you will no doubt want to be the best parent you can, and that is one who educates with the minimal need for discipline.

Why children behave as they do

Based on social norms and personal experiences, adults have a series of expectations concerning the behaviour of other adults – partner, relatives, friends and co-workers. In particular, we regularly anticipate that others will both consider our needs and understand the consequence of their actions. When told what to do or not to do, we rightly expect that another adult will comply with the directive from that point on.

Children, however, do not behave as adults and it is wrong to apply adult standards of behaviour to their actions. The consequences of ignoring this fact, as most "normal" parents do from time to time, are that if your child neglects to consider how his deeds make you feel, you may feel that he is selfish. Should he repeatedly commit the same "misdemeanour", you may feel he is stubborn and purposefully ignoring you. You may even feel that he is challenging your authority or that he misbehaves just to upset you. These feelings of being angry with your child, however, do not help to teach him to behave better. Often, in fact, an anger-driven response will "hurt" rather than "help" the situation, and certainly it will trigger guilt in you.

Progressively, and not until after he has reached the end of his first year of life, your baby will learn what he is and what he is allowed to do. But even when he knows intellectually what he cannot do – touch the knobs on the television, run into the street, or hit and bite – it does not automatically follow that he can stop himself from doing these deeds. Although what Sigmund Freud called the "super ego", the voice inside each of us that tells us what is wrong or right, is present in toddlers, it is weak and incompletely formed. Therefore, until your toddler is quite a bit older, there is a basic imbalance between the strong urge to do the undesirable act and the voice of restraint. When, for example, your toddler is upset or excited, he may have a very strong urge to strike out. However, unlike in an adult, the restraining voice telling him not to do so is very faint, and no match for the intense desire commanding him to go ahead and hit you. Even though when calm he may be able to verbalise the rule that hitting is wrong, when full of overwhelming emotions, he just can't stop himself

MORE **ABOUT** | emotional immaturity

While cherished members of the family, young children possess a number of characteristics that you will on occasion find undesirable. Between the ages of one and three years, your child may at times be stubborn and entirely self-centred. He only knows what he wants, and he wants it NOW! Patience, which is a very handy trait for a parent, is in short supply at this stage of life. Your child's ability to see a situation from your perspective or to consider how his actions make you feel is limited. He has very little insight into why he does what he does or why he wants the things he does. Nor does he have much impulse control, so it may seem that at times he acts first and thinks about it only afterwards. When he is having trouble getting you to understand what he wants or he can't have it, a temper tantrum may result. Your efforts to reason with him are often doomed to fail, since looking at a problem rationally (instead of emotionally) is not within his capabilities.

A true story: A father brought his son, John, to the doctor's surgery for a routine check-up. As is typical of young children, John was afraid. He screamed the minute he was brought into the room. He refused to stand on the scale and cried and struggled when the nurse attempted to see how tall he was. His father repeatedly told John to do what he was told to do. John continued not to cooperate. His father's voice became louder and louder: "Your behaviour is atrocious!" his father yelled. To this, John only screamed louder and fought harder. Then his father said, "Stop it! You're acting like a two year old!" Not surprising as John was only two years old and he acted in the only way of which he was capable. The one in this example who has to change his behaviour is the father, who needs to learn that his son is not an adult and cannot be expected to behave as if he were one. Patience, realistic expectations and realising that the parent's role is to help his child through a difficult event (not scream at him to behave) are all more helpful than anger when dealing with a youngster.

Steps to becoming more patient

1 Recognise when you have lost patience
Each time you are unhappy with your own response to your child's actions, take a moment (once you have calmed down) to reflect on the scene in which you just took part. Write down in a notebook answers to these three questions: A) What happened? B) What clues were there to alert you of the impending loss of patience? C) What factors may have shaped your undesirable response? Were you in a hurry to get somewhere? Were you highly stressed from events in other spheres of your life (perhaps a tough day at work, an argument with your partner, a million things to do, financial stresses at home, etc.). Were you ill and not feeling well? Were you tired from lack of sleep?

2 Analyse the event Later in the day, perhaps after your child is asleep, look at your notes and think. How could you have changed your actions so that if allowed to replay the scene, you would now get it right? The answer may be relatively simple:
- I was in a rush to get to the birthday party; next time I'll leave myself more time.
- I wasn't in a good mood myself (I was tired; I was stressed, etc.). If I had recognised this, I may have made allowances for my bad mood. I could have remained silent instead of yelling when he did not listen to me.
- He is a very strong-willed child. I'll have to get used to the fact that this is just the way he is. Next time I'll expect him to say "No!" when I ask him to do something.

3 Notice the pattern Until we effect a change in our behaviour, we tend to repeat the same mistakes over and over. As you analyse more and more examples of your behaviour, you will start recognising right after one of your "bad moments" that this scene is like one that occurred before. ("Last week, I lost my temper when I was in a rush and he wouldn't move

quickly. It just happened again.") When you check your notebook that night and review today's event, focus especially on what happened early in the scene. Identify clues you can use to warn you that you are about to act badly. Think of a different approach, one that would have avoided the struggle.

4 Change the way you respond Eventually you will come to the point when, before it happens, you see that you are about to lose patience. If you can see it coming, you can act differently.

from lashing out in similar situations. You can tell him over and over again that hitting is wrong, but until he develops a stronger super ego, he will continue to disobey you. The same sequence occurs whenever he has a strong desire to have or to do something else. Noticeable progress will be made by the time he is two to three years old, but it will take several more years to gain adult-like self-control.

You may find it challenging to constantly keep in mind that you are dealing with a child and not an adult. The goal, of course, is to be comfortable shifting gears from expectations you have for adults to expectations that are more realistic for your child. Demands for appropriate behaviour ideally should be tailored to his age and level of development. When he is between one and two years old, it is unlikely that he will be able to follow many of the rules you would like him to, and he may not listen to your instructions. At this age, discipline consists of keeping him out of danger and somehow getting him through the day, accomplishing what you need to, with the minimum number of struggles. Simply taking him away from a "No" object or keeping the

object out of sight in the future is all that is necessary. Distraction often works, too. Instead of raising your voice if your toddler has picked up something you don't want him to have, quickly give him a favourite toy and take back the other. Or, if he is getting into mischief in the kitchen, divert him to another, more acceptable, activity.

How your child will learn to behave and the ways you will practise the art of parenting depend on a number of factors.

Your child's temperament

Philosophers have compared the innocence of a child to a blank slate or to a pile of moist clay. Accordingly, he can be moulded into any type of person his parents want him to be. But surely, the concept of species similarity (all children are alike) and individual variation (all children are different) applies here as well. While your child may be susceptible to shaping by you, every child starts off with a slightly different temperament (see page 138).

Your baby's temperament determines where the "shaping" process begins. If he is normally shy and

clingy, you can encourage him to be more outgoing. However, it is unlikely he will ever be as gregarious as a child who was more outgoing from birth (assuming, of course, this other child is raised in an environment where gregariousness is valued and encouraged).

Your child's innate personality traits will also determine how he learns and how best to teach him. For example, if your child is easygoing, it may only take some firmness on your part to quell his protests about brushing his teeth. But if he is determined and stubborn, this approach may be totally unsuccessful. You must discover which style of parenting will work best, given your child's unique temperament (see also page 139). Teaching your child is a learning process for you as well as for him; you will try certain approaches that succeed and many that will fail. When one technique fails, you will try another, and another, until you find the ones that are most effective for your child.

Parenting factors

Your baby is not the only one in your family to have a unique temperament; you also have one and so does your spouse. Are you calm and easygoing, or will you get upset easily with your child?

Parents vary tremendously in one aspect of temperament that is central in raising a child: how much patience they have. Let's face it, children are wonderful but they are guaranteed daily to try one's patience. In his first months of life, your baby may cry for hours, despite your best efforts to calm him; he may posset all over his new outfit just as you put it on; and invariably his nappy will need changing just as you have him ready to go out. Later on, he may throw his food on the floor, create havoc in your handbag or your CD collection, refuse to go to sleep at night, say "No!" to getting dressed, have a tantrum when you won't buy him sweets at the checkout counter, etc. (Do bear in mind that there will also be many moments when he is adorable, sweet, well-behaved and a perfect angel!) No parent is a saint. Not one of us can put up with the constant mischief and rule-challenging that our children dish out every day without sometimes

WHEN TO EXPECT BAD BEHAVIOUR

- Your child is tired.
- You are tired.
- Your child doesn't feel well.
- You don't feel well.
- You try to rush him.
- Your life is full of stress.
- Your child is hungry.
- Everyone needs you at once.
- Daily routines are disrupted.
- You could use just a few minutes to calm down.
- At the end of a long day.
- It's important that he behaves well.
- Everyone is watching.

getting angry or losing our tempers. However, each of us varies in how much we can take before reaching breaking point.

When you lose your temper, you may very well say or do things you later wish you had not. You may yell and scream at your child. You may call him names or label him with very negative epithets ("You're a trouble-maker!"). You even may strike him. Sadly, parents' actions at these moments are seldom effective ways to get children to behave better. The most likely outcome will be that you feel bad about your behaviour and wish you hadn't lost control. The more patience you have as a parent, the less often such episodes will occur and the better a parent you will be.

Your own upbringing

Once upon a time, you were a child and your parents had to teach you to become a civilised adult. How they did this has a huge effect on how you parent your own child. Mysteriously, people usually respond to their children's behaviour exactly as their parents did to theirs. It is as if, as children, we incorporated our parents' parenting approach into our brain and adopted it as our own so that now we are set by default to imitate their techniques. This can have a very beneficial effect on you; if your parents were patient and loving in their dealings with you, you will probably, without much effort, be patient and loving with your child. But if your parents treated you in ways you promised yourself you would never repeat with your own child – yelling at and occasionally hitting you – you may be upset with yourself when you find, without thinking, that you have acted exactly as your parents did many years ago. In this case, you will need to make a concerted effort to act otherwise. Teaching yourself to be more patient takes time. It is unlikely that you will change your temperament if you just tell yourself to be more patient. You will have to work at it over months. The box on page 291 will give you some tips on becoming more patient.

Parenting strategies

In Chapter 6, you read about styles of parenting. Child-oriented parents believe that the best way to raise their baby is to respond immediately to his emotional and physical needs. If he is hungry, feed him now; if he is upset, pick him up and calm him. Schedule-based parents hold that routine is good for their baby. They want him to fit into family routines and therefore only allow feeding and sleeping at predetermined times. A better style, however, is believed to be a mixture of these two approaches – the flexible parent. Flexible parents acknowledge that household routines and guidelines for behaviour are good for children, but they also agree that a loving environment, with occasional exceptions made to the rules, is also important.

These same profiles can be used to describe approaches to raising older children. Child-oriented parents will continue to place the highest priority on soothing their upset or frustrated baby immediately; schedule-based (though at this age a better term might be rule-based) parents will expect their baby to obey behaviour guidelines set for everyone in the family; flexible parents, the preferred style of many experts, will take the best from each. They will impose structure and rules while carefully attending to the emotional needs of their baby.

Many parents, especially those whose parenting style leans toward that of the schedule/rule-based style, conceive of discipline as a very heavily front-loaded process. Such parents believe it is important to be strict in a child's first years. To them, bad behaviours must be expunged soon after they appear, for if not dealt with swiftly, these will, by repetition, become permanently embedded in a child's behavioural repertoire. Additionally, schedule/rule-based parents feel that if a child is allowed to get his own way frequently (i.e., the child-oriented approach), he will become "spoiled". As logical as this all may sound to you, there are a number of problems with this approach to discipline. For starters, unless your toddler is very mild-mannered and lacks the stubbornness typical for this age, this method seldom works out as well in practice as in theory. A parent who believes in this theory has unrealistic expectations about what his/her son is capable of achieving (see also *Why children behave as they do*, page 289). Also, the strictness required by parents disciplining according to this style is bound to result in numerous daily struggles. Parenting, in this scenario, is not much fun; instead, it has potential to become a daily nightmare.

An alternative way of viewing discipline, the flexible parent, accepts the fact that your child's capacity to act as an adult is very limited in his first years. As he gets older, he will develop the ability to be less self-centred and to accept the many rules that infringe on his unfettered freedom. He doesn't have to and can't be expected to obey all the rules beginning at an early age.

Using this approach, the goal of each day is to get your toddler to do what has to be done with a minimum of struggling. Sometimes this will include invoking the rules and being firm; at other times it may mean using another strategy. As your toddler gets older, his behaviour will be shaped gradually, in step with his psychological development. When he becomes more capable of more mature behaviour, your level of expectation will also rise. You have twenty years to accomplish the feat of moulding him into an adult. So if his behaviour improves by only five per cent per year, you will ultimately get there!

When to be strict

There are only a handful of situations in which you as parent must surely get your way. Obviously, your child's safety is paramount; if he is about to do something that may result in him injuring himself, you must stop him immediately. Similarly, if he is hurting another person, this must cease right away. Destroying your home and valued property is also absolutely unacceptable.

In addition to the above it is also crucial that your child goes to bed on time and that naps are enforced. Tired children (like tired adults) are cranky and easily upset. So if you let your toddler skip a nap or allow him to stay up beyond bedtime, his behaviour is certain to be much worse than usual the next day.

There may also be one or two other rules that you and your partner, by mutual agreement, hold dear and want to elevate to non-negotiable. But for the majority of behavioural offences, winning absolutely and immediately is unnecessary.

Setting limits

Children, in general, feel most secure and behave best when they know there are limits to their behaviour. But where should you set the limits? If the boundaries are set too strictly, the number of struggles you will face will increase markedly. On the other hand, if boundaries are set too leniently, your child will have no reason to behave better. The ideal solution: adjust the limits to a point that usually allows your child to comply with your expectations. Keep these boundaries at this point and as he gets older, gradually increase what is expected of him. Since he will reach higher levels in the development of his ability to conform to rules, re-adjust the limits to accommodate his new capabilities.

From experience, you will discover which rules your child will follow and which will usually result in a struggle. If your toddler typically brushes his teeth when told to do so, it is reasonable for you to make this a behavioural boundary. Should he ever baulk at brushing, be firm and insist he do it. (This is keeping the limit where it has been.) Firmness, when it is likely to be successful, can be a useful tool. However, there still will be other occasions when firmness and refusing to accept "No!" from your child are unlikely to succeed. So, to summarise: there will be times when you must always win the battle (matters of safety, harming others, destruction of property, going to bed on time) and times when being firm will usually work. For all the rest, there is room to manoeuvre.

How to get positive results

Use distraction Most toddlers will easily allow their attention to shift from one object to another, more interesting one. If your toddler has hold of something he shouldn't have, prevent a struggle by quickly giving him something else with which he can safely play while you take away, and remove from sight, the other.

Alternatively, physically remove your child from "the scene of the crime" to a place where there is less temptation.

The countdown This technique is especially helpful if your child has difficulty in moving from one activity to the other. He may become quite upset, for example, if he suddenly has to leave the playground, get out of the bath, go to bed, or stop playing with his toys. Try, therefore, to give him a warning before the change in activity. Start the process of leaving the playground long before you actually want to leave (see *Plan ahead*, page 297). Every few minutes announce, "It's almost time to go home."

Another variation is to ask him, "Do you want to go home now or do you want to stay another minute?" No doubt he will choose the latter, but after you repeat this process a few more times, he just may be willing to leave without a fight. Your child will feel that he got what he wanted (to stay longer) and you get to leave on time!

You may also want to try the "countdown" technique using numbers with older toddlers. Start by announcing, "It will be bedtime in five minutes" (hold up five fingers). A few minutes later (your child's sense of time is not as well-tuned as yours), tell him that bedtime will be in four minutes. Then three, two, and one minute. At the conclusion of the countdown he will have had several minutes to get used to the impending change.

Make it a game Try to get your child to do what he should by making it seem like fun. For example, to interest him in tidying up, try "Let's see who can put away the most toys. Ready, set, go!" Or you can have a race from the living room to the bathroom to see who will arrive first for tooth-brushing.

Give choices Let your child feel he is in control of what happens to him (while still ending up with something agreeable to you) by allowing him to choose amongst acceptable alternatives. "Which shirt would you like to wear today – the red one, the blue one or the one with the panda on it?" Assuming that you offer only shirts acceptable to you, your child wins by getting to pick for himself, while you win by avoiding a potential struggle. Other variations: "Which do you want to do first: brush your teeth or get into your pyjamas?" "Do you want to get out of the bath now or in another minute?" (see *The countdown*, above).

The tickle monster This is a fun alternative to threatening a punishment ("If you don't start getting dressed now, you won't be allowed to go to Tim's house to play"). Tell your child that he must start getting dressed by the count of three or the tickle monster will appear. Actually, you are the monster.

One of two outcomes will follow. Your child may run to his room and start getting dressed to avoid being tickled. Or he may stay and let you tickle him. (When the tickling is over, he is much more likely to be inclined to go along with your request.) It's a successful outcome either way. Even if you "have to" tickle him, you win because you avoid raising your voice or punishing. You turn what could be an unpleasant situation into fun for both of you.

Plan ahead Thinking things out beforehand can go a long way towards preventing struggles. If you make allowances for predictable problem behaviour, many battles can be avoided. Here are two examples:

- Every time you are at the supermarket checkout, your toddler wants a chocolate bar. If you say "No", a tantrum follows. Solutions: A) Don't take him shopping with you. B) Decide it is okay to let him have the chocolate if it saves a miserable scene.
- It's impossible to get your child dressed in the morning and you're frequently late for work. Solutions: A) Get up a few minutes earlier so that you have more time and don't need to rush things. B) Have him pick out his clothes the night before. C) Have your partner help you. D) Change your work hours so you start a little later.

Avoid rushing Do everything possible to build in extra time for each step of the way, just in case your child decides to resist at any point. You will find that at times when you need to leave home straightaway, your toddler will refuse to let you put on his coat; children just seem to know to slow down when parents are in a hurry. If you steamroll ahead, the usual result will be a tantrum. You may not always have the luxury of having added time to set aside for your child's refusals but if you can make this part of the schedule, the time you spend together will be more enjoyable.

Think outside the box Is there some other solution besides the usual ones? For instance, for a toddler who is slow to get dressed in the morning, another solution is to let him sleep in his clothes instead of pyjamas. When he wakes up, he is already dressed! Or, for a toddler who refuses to put his hat on before going out in winter weather, letting him go out without his hat on but taking it along may save stress. In a few minutes, when his ears are red, he will probably put his hat on if asked to do so.

Be firm With some children, simply not giving in and telling your child he has to do as he is told can also work and is another way of avoiding struggles. But if tantrums and yelling or screaming are the result, try to avoid that particular situation in the future or use another technique.

Give in Sometimes acquiescing is a good choice, but only do so if no harm will result. Don't give in while your child is in the middle of a tantrum. (See also box, page 298.)

GIVE IN

Letting your child have his way is an option when
- There is very little consequence if he prevails.
- The consequences of not giving in (a tantrum) are much greater than those of giving in.
- Distraction or other techniques to avoid a struggle don't work.

Only give in at the beginning of a potential struggle, never during the heat of it.

DON'T GIVE IN

Preventing your child having his way is important when
- It's a matter of safety, hurting others, ruining valuable possessions.
- A little firmness is likely to work.
- Distraction or other techniques to avoid a struggle will work.
- A tantrum has already begun.

When to give in

The myth that children must ALWAYS listen to adults is widely believed, but not very realistic. For this reason, in any given situation, one option you have is to give in to your child's wishes. Giving in may be one component of dealing with your child when the boundary of your expectations must, by necessity, be set low. Other techniques for these occasions include avoiding such situations (before they happen) and the parental art of distraction (see page 296).

If you think that in giving in to a tantrum, your toddler will learn that yelling, kicking and falling to the floor will get him what he wants, you are correct. Letting him have his way at this time reinforces the undesirable behaviour and makes it more likely that he will use this approach in the future. That's why the time to give in is before the struggle begins. Giving in at the first sign of his resistance, before the scene turns into a struggle, will not be perceived by your child as a reward for his misbehaviour (since he hasn't misbehaved yet).

Giving in, however, is an option when there is very little consequence to doing so. For example, your child wants to hold your keys, but you are afraid that if he has them he may lose them. You have already tried distracting him but he is clinging to the idea of holding the keys. You sense that, unless you can find a solution, your toddler may soon completely wind himself up. This is a situation when giving in is a reasonable choice. If you watch him carefully, it is unlikely that he will lose your keys or damage them in any way. In fact, he is quite likely to lose interest in them fairly quickly at which time you easily can retrieve them. You give up very little by letting him have his way here and you gain a happy moment instead of a difficult one.

Vary your approach

It is surprising how often parents continue to use a method that hasn't been working. If you try one approach (see pages 296–7) and it doesn't give you the results you are seeking, the next time the situation arises, try handling it in a different way. Bear in mind that no technique is always successful but one thing is certain: repeatedly using a failing technique will continue to be unsuccessful. Also, it is a given that whatever struggle you are having will be many times worse if your child is overtired. That's why naps and bedtime should not be negotiable.

It is vitally important that any approach you do try is consistent. Children are most comfortable when they know there are boundaries to their behaviour and they also do best when they feel that a specific action on their part will result in a known response from you. You can imagine how confusing it must be for a child if one day his mother praises him for helping to set the table and the next day screams at him when he tries to do so again.

Another problem arises when parents don't agree on what should or should not be allowed or on how to handle misbehaviour. Actually, it is very normal for a mother and father to have different notions of how to best teach their child. However, it is necessary for parents to discuss areas of disagreement and come up with a mutually acceptable compromise. This should include supporting your partner's actions and decisions involving your child, even if you would have acted in another way. Toddlers are quite talented at detecting differences between what each parent will permit, and are happy to exploit these differences. If you tell your child he can't go to the park, he may go straight to his other parent and ask again, hoping for a more favourable response, or he may learn that he is more likely to get what he wants by asking one parent rather than the other. As your parenting skills increase, the problem of inconsistency should arise much less often.

Tantrums

All kids engage in tantrums to release strong feelings of anger and resentment although the severity of the tantrum often has no correlation with the enormity of what is denied. (There is, however, a correlation between severity and lack of sleep: tired children tantrum more often and the tantrums are much more intense and harder to stop.) When not allowed to have his way, a child may suddenly start screaming. Some children lie down on the floor and beat their fists and feet against the ground. Others may bang their heads repeatedly against the wall, start throwing objects around the room, or begin hitting or biting.

The best way to deal with a tantrum is to prevent it from ever occurring. Once started, however, it is too late to give in or try other techniques. At this point, the most effective way to end the tantrum is to ignore your child, conveying the attitude that "You can do this all you want, but I'm not going to be upset by it. In fact, I couldn't care less." If at home, ignoring your child includes walking away from him, not looking at him, singing a song, and/or not responding to his pleas. Some parents will put their child in his cot for the duration of an outburst. If you are concerned that your child may hurt himself, pick him up and convey him to a safer place but try hard not to look at or respond to him.

If a tantrum occurs in a public place, pick your toddler up and immediately head for home. While it is common to imagine that all the spectators to the event believe you are a terrible or mean parent, the truth is that many of them have had a similar experience with their own children. Instead of condemning you, they are thinking to themselves, "I feel so sorry for that mother/father. I remember how embarrassed I felt when my son did this."

Punishment

As you now know, the preferred option is to avoid struggles and help your child get through difficult moments. In the first 18–24 months of life, traditional punishment (see page 300) is not necessary, and if pursued, is usually ineffective at changing your baby's behaviour.

Under a year of age, there is no reason to punish your baby at all; between one and three years, your toddler is unlikely to do anything that will merit more than minor punishment. If you do feel the need to punish, here are some things you must bear in mind:

- To be effective, the punishment must occur soon after the offence is committed. In other words, if you choose to punish your toddler when he misbehaves, the punishment should be immediate. If you postpone the punishment, the connection between the misdeed and the consequence of that behaviour will be lost on a young child.
- The severity of the punishment must be in proportion to the infraction.
- Never, ever, threaten to leave your child and walk away. Not only is this extremely distressing to a child but you will almost certainly have to eat your words!

Ways to punish

Withholding affection Although not a punishment in the strict sense, briefly withholding your affection is the most effective consequence for misbehaviour. Your child, like all children, desperately wants your love and approval. Because of this, he will become quite unhappy if you sternly reprimand him. For a short time, perhaps 30–60 seconds, show him you are disappointed with him (even if you need to pretend to). You might, for example, ignore him for that brief interval. Don't give a long explanation; just state in one sentence why you are upset ("We don't hit other people."). Try not to be personal or critical in your message (avoid saying things like "You're a terrible child"); instead, focus on the rule broken ("Biting is not allowed").

Raising your voice or shouting These should be used sparingly as they are very powerful tools that will often bring your baby to tears. However, they will lose potency if used too frequently. After being stern or raising your voice, try not to remain angry. While it may be natural for you to continue to be upset with your toddler, it serves very little purpose. Your child will return to his normal state of mind in a few minutes, and you should strive to do so as well. This is when having more patience is very helpful.

Taking away privileges or toys With this method, first tell your toddler that he must stop misbehaving. Then announce what the punishment will be. ("If you don't stop throwing your food, there will be no dessert.) An alternative response that tries to avoid punishment might be, "We don't throw food in this family. Dinner is over."

One good place to use the "taking away" technique is when your child isn't sharing with another. ("Since you can't share that toy, neither one of you can have it." Then take away the toy.

It's important to only make "threats" you intend to keep. If the behaviour you are requesting does not materialise, enforce the consequence. If you do not do so, your child may learn that you won't follow through with punishments, leading him to misbehave more often.

Try not to escalate. Avoid this type of parental reaction: "If you don't stop that, there will be no going to the park today". Your child doesn't stop. "Okay, stop now or you won't go to the park tomorrow as well". Your child still doesn't stop, and the punishment continues to escalate until it is way out of proportion to the misdeed (you are up to weeks of missing park visits!). Later on, you will probably not want to impose such a huge consequence.

Time-outs This technique works best after two years of age. Start with a warning that any bad behaviour will result in a time-out. When something occurs, your child has to immediately sit in a certain chair or on the "naughty step" or go to his room.

The time-out should be brief and connected to some action. Say, "You can come back to play when you have calmed down," not "Stay in your room for an hour." An arbitrary time period is less effective because the time-out is no longer connected to its purpose (calming down).

A time-out accomplishes many useful objectives. It stops bad behaviour (your child is removed from the "crime" scene), shows that you disapprove of it, and gives your toddler time to return to his normal state of mind. Like raising your voice, however, this technique loses its strength if used too often.

Spanking A gentle smack on the bottom is no longer recommended by paediatricians, since the other techniques listed above are more effective and avoid modelling the use of violence as a means of controlling minor misdemeanours.

Encouraging independence and sociability

One prime long-term goal of every parent is to educate and enable his/her child to become a functioning adult, capable of living independently, and able to interact comfortably with other individuals. This is a far cry from the needy newborn that is totally reliant on you for his care and nourishment or from the self-centred, strong-willed toddler who doesn't want to follow rules of behaviour. Achievements such as your baby feeling secure when he is out of your sight, learning to take turns and playing according to the rules come only after much effort. It is quite amazing that your baby will actually come to see that he is not the centre of the universe; that he is a member of a social network and therefore must behave according to its norms

and values; and that there are times when he must place another person's needs above his own. This startling transformation occurs gradually and predictably as your child reaches stage after stage of social and emotional development.

Independence

Beginning at about 10–12 months of age, your baby will begin trying to take more and more control of his life. It may start with him wanting to hold his own cup or bottle, or feed himself. When, for the first time, he accomplishes one of these tasks without your assistance, he will certainly be very proud. Clearly, it is quicker, easier and less messy for you to pour the juice, put your child's sock on or

3 things to do when you have to leave your baby

1 **Do not sneak out** as this will increase your baby's anxiety that you will sneak out again and will make him worry even more about this possibility whenever he can't see you. Tell him you are going out before going away.

2 **Leave quickly** Don't linger trying to calm him down. If you are like many parents, you will be feeling quite guilty about upsetting your baby so much, but it is highly unlikely that a few more minutes of hugging or explaining to him that you are coming back soon will allay his worries.

3 **Remember that the crying typically stops a few minutes after you leave** and will resume when you return (now he is "punishing" you for leaving). To prove this to yourself, the next time you go out leaving behind a screaming baby, stand outside the closed door to your home. You may think his crying will continue indefinitely, but surprisingly, the crying will stop in just a few moments.

put the key in the door than to let a one- or two-year-old do it; however, within reason, it is good to give your child a chance. His own sense of accomplishment, coupled with words of praise from you, help instill a sense of confidence and will reinforce a positive self-image.

Paradoxically, at the same time that your one-to-three year old seeks more independence, he also may be more inclined to cling to you. Being away from you and more on his own (more independence) is wonderful until suddenly it becomes scary; now he needs to be close to you. In this instance, it is also good, within reason, to accommodate him. So while you need to encourage independence, be prepared to provide additional reassurances for moments when your baby needs to be close to you.

Dealing with a clinging baby

It is flattering when your baby gets upset when he isn't near you. You are the most important people in his life: he only wants you to hold him or to change his nappy. But it certainly can become quite taxing at times. Here is a good piece of advice on how to respond to your clingy child: if you can conveniently humour his wishes involving dependency on you, do so; if you can't, then don't.

Humouring his wishes

As discussed in *When to give in* (see page 298), if picking your baby up or being the one to give him a bath is easier than the alternative (your baby screaming), then feel free to do it. You are not spoiling him. (It would be spoiling if he had a greater capacity to be independent and you continue to cater to him.) Unfortunately, always humouring his wishes in this regard can be exhausting.

When you can't accommodate him

There surely will be times when your arms ache from holding your baby or when you must leave your home without him. After all, you are entitled to take a shower, go to work or have a few minutes to yourself. And certainly you can't cook meals with a baby in one arm. In these situations, it is appropriate to put him down in a safe place (a playpen or cot or into the care another caregiver) and not give in to his wishes. Your refusal most likely will result in him crying and being very upset, but no harm will come to him. Ironically, as with most tantrums, the better you are at ignoring him at this time, the sooner the crying will end.

Comfort Items

From a toddler's point of view, life can be very difficult. First of all, a toddler feels he is constantly being told what to do (and what not to do). In the space of a few hours he can be frustrated that he can't get his way, angry at you for not meeting his needs immediately, confused about the conflict between your rules and his urges, guilty when you show disapproval and anxious about separation when you are momentarily out of his sight. No wonder your child will require a way to calm himself and engender a feeling of safety. His relief may come through an attachment to a teddy bear, a blanket or some other object.

As an alternative to a security object, your child may be comforted when he twirls his hair, sucks his thumb or wears the same shirt every day. These are also ways he can help himself feel better and generally should not be discouraged.

You also provide a great deal of comfort to your child by hugging, smiling at and praising him.

Feeling loved by you is the greatest comfort he has. Give out your approval and affection liberally.

Soothing fears

At the age of about two or three, your baby may suddenly become fearful of dogs, clowns or the dark. He may also suffer more from nightmares and night terrors (see pages 167–8).

It is best to acknowledge the reality of your toddler's fear ("I know you're afraid. That can be very scary") and let him hear you say that you will protect him from harm. Trying to use logic with your toddler will not lessen his fears. He will not be able to think about them rationally until he is much older. With time, however, such fears go away, but for the present, avoid placing your child in situations that are scary (avoid dogs, don't go to the circus, use a night light).

Sociability

Learning to share and to play "nicely" with other children is a sentinel achievement. Before the age of 30–36 months, however, your child's concept of

sharing is likely to be able to play with another child's toy (but not allowing others to use his own toys), and playing together is merely two children sitting next to each other, each playing by himself. True sharing, albeit sometimes begrudgingly, typically happens after two and a half years of age, and over the next few years, such social skills get better and better. Your child will be able to take turns and abide by a game's rules before he enters primary school. Even at this age, he may very well get upset, though, when he doesn't win the game.

Much work is involved in convincing your toddler to accept these social demands. Sometimes the easiest way to deal with children who aren't playing well together is to take your child home. Or you can take away a toy not being shared. Along the way, though, there will be times when you will have to cajole and encourage your toddler to share and follow the rules of games. There will also be occasions when being firm or else scolding him will be needed. Yet when he behaves in the desired way, your praise will be invaluable for making the behaviour appear again.

How difficult is it to teach a child to take on these social skills? It takes years to refine these abilities and there are plenty of grown-ups who still don't like to share and who get upset when they don't win the game!

Being with others

There are two good reasons for your child to go to childcare: both parents may need to go out to work or may want to provide their child with a day full of fun and games. Although a childcare centre will offer your child many opportunities to learn both socially and academically, having a good time with friends in a safe environment should be the main goal. Acquiring any formal academic knowledge must be secondary. Children who do not go to childcare are not at a disadvantage. All skills learned there can be accomplished at home by a stay-at-home parent or a good babysitter. Instead of playing with other children at childcare, your toddler can go to the park or play over at the neighbours. And certainly the academic gains of childcare, if not already mastered at home, can be achieved in a very short time when your child starts kindergarten.

Separation difficulties

When beginning childcare, the major issue facing you and your child is the difficulty of separation. While two and three year olds typically do not cope well with being apart from their mother (or father), some parents also find it very hard to be away from their children. Needless to say, if your reaction is like this, it is better to at least pretend to be calm about the separation. If your child sees you are getting upset, it will increase his anxiety even more.

As with other aspects of a child's temperament, your toddler's tendency to become anxious at being apart from his primary caregiver may range from mild to severe. Children who have already had numerous experiences with being apart from their mothers or fathers tend to have less difficulty with separation at childcare. However, there is no benefit to intentionally imposing separation events solely to prepare. There will be time to overcome these fears at the beginning of kindergarten.

Most childcare centres have some type of separation program that helps children to get accustomed to being there without their parents. For the first days or weeks, parents typically are asked first to sit at the side of the room. After a number of days, you may sit just outside the room. If your child is upset at your absence and cannot be calmed by the teachers, you will be asked to return to the room. If goodbyes are still tearful after many days at the centre, be firm and leave quickly and when you are instructed to. If you're worried that your child is having a very difficult time being away from you, ask the staff; generally, you will find that like most children, yours will make a fuss initially but happily settle down within a few minutes. In some cases, it may be less traumatic for your child if someone besides his mother or father drops him off at school.

CHILD CARE

CHILDCARE CENTRE
Advantages
- Staffing is more reliable, regular hours, most are licensed.
- Your child will have lots of playmates and be exposed to many different activities.

Disadvantages
- Your child will catch more colds and infections at a younger age.

LIVE-IN HELP
Advantages
- The only child being cared for is yours; you can determine what you want to happen.
- The helper can perform other useful functions: errands, cooking, etc.
- You can tailor your helper's working hours to meet your needs.

Disadvantages
- If your helper becomes ill, you are stuck scrambling to make other plans.
- Cost is quite variable and should be considered when deciding.
- A helper may not have the same standards of safety and child-rearing techniques that you expect.

LICENSED CHILDMINDER
Advantages
- Fewer children are being cared for so your child may still have playmates but a reduced chance of becoming ill.
- Costs are generally cheaper and hours flexible.

Disadvantages
- If she becomes ill or is late in arriving, you will have to make other arrangements.

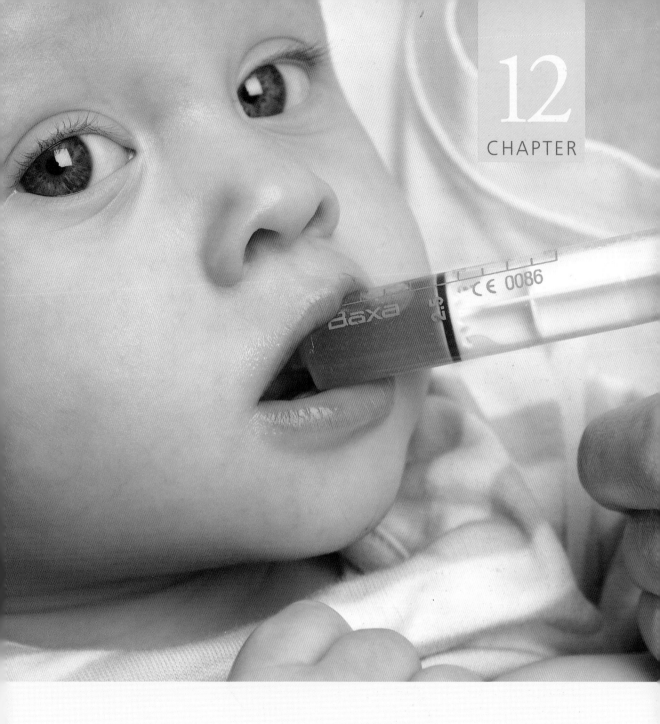

KEEPING YOUR
BABY HEALTHY

Parental priorities

Guaranteeing the health and wellbeing of your baby means creating a safe environment for her, taking her for check-ups to monitor her development, ensuring she is immunised against disease, making sure she has good dental care, and recognising when she is ill or hurt and providing the appropriate care – all this in addition to daily displays of love and attention so that she thrives emotionally, too.

Providing a safe environment

Most of the changes that are needed to childproof your home and garden are easy to make. It's a good idea to look at your home "through your baby's eyes", so you can spot changes that will need to be made to keep pace with her developmental achievements. Childproofing your home also protects any other small child who may visit.

As well as taking measures to protect your child, you will also have to make her aware of dangers in and around your home – teaching her about water, electricity and medicines and other hazardous substances that may be ingested. As with so many other things in her life, your baby will learn about safety from your example. Hazards should not be ignored. Show your baby how you draw away from something hot and say "Ouch, hot!" or something sharp and say "Ouch, sharp!" If you constantly use distraction to deal with potential dangers, your baby will never learn about safety. You need to explain the reason for the danger first and then interest your child in something else. It is important that your baby sees you do the right things; for example that you always check the road both ways before crossing, always wear your seat belt in the car and always put on your helmet when riding your bike.

Try to achieve the correct balance between protecting your baby from the hazards around her and allowing her to learn by exploring and trying new things. Although she needs to be watched at all times, you should give her some space for her own adventures.

Over time and with your example and simple explanations, your child will learn how to avoid dangers (see box). Bear in mind that it is important to be specific. Warning a young child to simply "be careful" without explaining why will not help her learn to avoid hazards.

Ensuring your child stays well

A team of healthcare professionals is at hand to monitor your child's health and to support you

POTENTIAL DANGERS

- **Roads and traffic** Narrate what is happening as you cross the road, even when your baby is still in her pram. Explain about the green and red man at the crossing and when she is old enough, ask her to tell you when the green man appears and you can cross. Make sure that, once walking, she holds your hand as you cross the road and joins you in looking both ways to check that the road is clear.

- **Strangers** Many outgoing toddlers are happy to talk to anyone. Of course, at this age your baby should be with you constantly when you are out but at the same time it is worth encouraging her to be cautious of strangers. Teach her to check with you first before talking to someone. However, don't make her afraid; you are looking for a balanced approach.

- **Foods and medicines** Your baby needs to learn that she must only eat food and drink that a grown-up she knows has given her as well as to understand that medicines are not sweets and that she must only take them from you.

should problems arise. Weight and growth records, as well as the timing of developmental achievements, give an indication of your baby's wellbeing.

You can reduce the risk of health problems in the future, by nurturing your child's health as well as you can. One example of this is good dental care. Making sure your child's teeth are brushed regularly will not only reduce the risk of cavities in the short term, but also, hopefully, will make it more likely that she will care for her teeth later in life.

To prevent your child becoming overweight, you need to ensure that she eats healthily (see Chapter 10) and gets plenty of exercise. Eating and exercise patterns set in childhood are likely to be followed in adulthood.

Childhood vaccinations also are important. The national immunisation schedule (see page 337) prevents illnesses that may be serious and even life threatening.

Managing an ill child

Most children will be unwell at some time or another. There are a wide variety of conditions that tend to affect children, from ear infections to head lice. Some illnesses are particularly common in childhood while others, like gastroenteritis, affect all ages but small children are particularly vulnerable to their effects. The information on common illnesses will give you an understanding of the cause of a

particular condition and also the likely outcome should your child be affected.

As a parent, you need to be able to recognise when you should seek medical advice and to know what to do to care for your child when she is unwell. It can sometimes be difficult to tell how ill a child is and particularly a baby, whose symptoms often may be less specific than those of older children and adults. Knowing what to look for as well as a familiarity with your baby's individual personality and habits will enable you to decide when medical help is needed.

Once you understand what is going on with your child, you will need to take the appropriate measures to control her symptoms and keep her comfortable. As well as cuddles and reassurance, you must ensure she has the fluids she needs and, if necessary, medicines to bring down her temperature or ease any discomfort.

You will also need to know how to deal with simple cuts and grazes, bites and other commonly occurring incidents and, ideally, you also should familiarise yourself with the first aid measures needed should a more serious accident occur (see also pages 41–3). Attending a first aid course that includes resuscitation techniques for babies and children will give you confidence in your ability to cope in emergency situations.

Safety

Babies are naturally inquisitive and once on the move, they become increasingly fascinated by everything both in and outside the home. While it isn't possible to make every situation childproof, you can take some simple measures to keep your child's environment as safe as possible.

It's also important to revisit the changes you make to your home and garden to take account of new skills your baby will acquire. For example, at around eight months, your baby will learn to crawl and then pull herself up. This opens up a whole new world to her, and you will have to put objects higher up to ensure they stay out of her reach. You will also need to lower the base of her cot to make sure she doesn't climb or topple out.

On the other hand, with time, some hazards will become less of a concern. Babies tend to put objects into their mouths in order to experience things they encounter and learn about them, so you will need to keep a careful look-out for any small objects that may present a risk of choking. However, from about three years or so, this should no longer be such a problem. Do bear in mind that children are individuals in terms both of their personalities and their development. While some children never become interested in putting small objects in their mouths – or in pushing them up their noses or into their ears for that matter – others continue to put things in their mouths way past the age of three. Some children will test the boundaries more than others and be more adventurous in their exploring. Because children reach their milestones at varying ages and also are unpredictable in that they can suddenly acquire a new skill, like walking, safety measures need to be tailored accordingly. By far the safest approach is to be prepared well in advance for your child's exploits.

Constant supervision

As well as following the simple measures outlined below, there are other ways to keep your child safe – the key one being to ensure that your child is watched over at all times. No matter what changes you make, your home will never be completely hazard-free, so keeping your child under constant supervision remains the single most important thing you can do to make sure she stays out of danger. In addition to this, it is advisable to familiarise yourself with first aid measures (see pages 41-3) so you are prepared if accidents do happen.

Keeping clean

Another important aspect of keeping your child healthy and safe is to have a reasonable approach to cleanliness – not to be over-anxious, but rather to take reasonable measures to protect your child from food poisoning and other infections. That being said, children build up their immunity when they encounter bacteria and viruses, so it is not desirable, nor is it possible, to prevent them from encountering all infections.

Food safety and hygiene

Some general measures worth taking to reduce the risk of food poisoning relate to how you store and prepare food, as well as the way you keep your kitchen clean (see also page 231).

Food storage

Foods like rice and pasta, which can be stored in cupboards, should be kept in sealed packets. Meat and ready-to-eat foods should be stored in the fridge to help prevent bacteria from breeding in them. Raw meat should be wrapped well in cling wrap or placed in a covered container and stored on the bottom shelf of fridge; this will ensure that juices from the meat do not drip onto other foods stored below. It should also be kept separate from other foods during preparation.

Food should also not be left lying around. If you cook a dish to serve later, let it cool down (wait until steam has stopped rising from the food) and then put it straight into the fridge. To cool the food as quickly as possible, put into a shallow dish or cut into smaller portions.

Leftovers can usually be kept in the fridge for up to two days. If you use part of a tin of food, keep the remainder in a covered bowl in the fridge rather

USING THE MICROWAVE

If you heat up your child's meals with a microwave, some areas of the food will be much hotter than others. Also, food keeps cooking after the microwave stops. To avoid burning your baby's mouth, stir the food and then allow it to cool before dabbing it on your wrist or sampling it with a spoon.

than leaving it in the tin. Bought food must be frozen by its use-by date and ideally on the day of purchase. If you prepare food to be eaten later, freeze it in portions within 24 hours of preparation. Thaw frozen food according to the manufacturer's instructions. Otherwise, the ideal is to allow it to defrost in the fridge over 24 hours. You can defrost frozen food in the microwave if you intend to cook it straightaway. When cooking defrosted food, ensure that it is piping hot all the way through. Avoid refreezing thawed food. Food poisoning bacteria can grow in frozen food while it is thawing, and if the food is frozen a second time, the bacteria do not die so the food is likely to have higher levels of food poisoning bacteria.

Food preparation

Wash your hands thoroughly before you start to prepare food. It is a good idea to have separate chopping boards for raw fish, meat and poultry and cooked foods and vegetables. Work surfaces and chopping boards should be cleaned and wiped down with a sterilising fluid. Keep separate cloths for wiping down the highchair and for using in food preparation areas.

It is important to wash utensils and chopping boards as well as your hands after handling chicken and other raw meats, raw fish and eggs. You also need to dry your hands carefully as bacteria breed more rapidly in wet or damp environments.

When opening a jar, wipe the top before you unscrew it. This applies to the tops of tins, too. Keep

your tin opener clean, washing it regularly in the dishwasher or by hand. Any uncontaminated baby food can be stored in the fridge for up to 48 hours.

Reheated food needs to be heated thoroughly and should be piping hot through to the centre before allowing it to cool down. You can check that the temperature is right for your baby by dabbing the food on the inside of your wrist. Food should not be reheated more than once, so any leftover reheated food should be discarded.

Bacteria can also multiply in cuts so you should cover a cut with a plaster when you are preparing food.

Keeping the kitchen clean

Wash the kitchen surfaces down before and after food preparation. Kitchen cleaning cloths should be washed frequently – damp cloths are good breeding grounds for bacteria. Tea towels also should be washed regularly; if you use them to dry your hands they will quickly become a breeding ground for bacteria so use paper towels, which can be discarded immediately after use and do not harbour bacteria.

Hygiene around the home

Making a safe home for your child does not mean scrubbing it from top to bottom. If you continue your usual cleaning routine, you will not go far wrong. Children play happily on the floor at home and this includes picking objects up off the floor and putting them straight into their mouths. This does not cause problems – as long as the floor is kept reasonably clean there will not be too many bugs around.

You will wash your hands after changing your baby's nappy and once she is out of nappies you will show your child how to wash her hands after using the potty. If you have a girl, you also will show her how to wipe properly – from front to back – in order to prevent bacteria from the anus transferring to her urinary tract. These normal habits of cleanliness will be perfectly adequate to prevent infections.

Childproofing your home

Accidents in the home are very common and the under fours are particularly at risk. Young children learn the skills they need to get around, but do not know how to avoid the dangers they encounter. It is your job, as a parent, to protect your baby from as many hazards as possible, but at the same time to teach her about them so she acquires the knowledge to keep herself safe when she is older.

When childproofing your home, you need to consider what may be in your baby's reach – not only from the floor, but also from furniture once she is able to climb. Looking around each room from your baby's viewpoint will enable you to spot potential hazards.

General measures

As well as those that are specific to particular rooms, there are some safety measures that apply to all areas of the home.

Doors

It is so easy for tiny fingers to be trapped as a door closes. This can be avoided by positioning stoppers so that doors don't close fully or attaching protectors to doors that stop them slamming.

Stairs

Always leave the stairs free of items that may cause you or your child to trip.

Position stair gates at the top of the stairs and three steps up from the bottom. This gives your toddler the opportunity to learn how to climb stairs without running the risk of a nasty fall.

When buying stair gates, make sure they are fairly easy for you to open and close. If they are difficult to use, it becomes tempting to leave them open when popping back and forth through them. Some gates are permanently attached to the wall; others are held in place by fittings that allow them to be moved. Travel gates are also available that can be packed and installed in holiday accommodation.

PLAYPENS

Although not all parents will favour the use of a playpen, they do give the opportunity to have a minute's peace. Playpens are more attractive and child-friendly than they were years ago. Some can also be used as travel cots. They can be a great help when babies start to crawl (around six months) and some toddlers will happily go in their playpen up to the age of two. It is worth keeping a few special toys in the playpen that will keep your baby amused for a while.

Stair gates should meet Australian safety standards. (See the Australian Competition & Consumer Commission's website for a useful booklet entitled "Keeping Baby Safe".) The individual poles of banisters should not be more than 10 cm apart. If they are, a barrier is needed.

Windows

Guards can be fitted to prevent children from climbing out of windows. Window locks also can be used that only allow windows to open a certain amount (should be no more than 10 cm). In addition to these measures, it is important to make sure children keep away from open windows. Also, furniture should not be positioned near windows as it may help children to climb out.

Cords on blinds may present a risk of strangulation. They should be tied out of reach.

Attaching stickers to large areas of glass like French windows will draw attention to them and help reduce the risk of accidents.

Furniture and ornaments

It is important that all furniture is stable. Look out for pieces that your toddler could pull over onto

5 principles for keeping your baby safe

1. **Keep your baby under constant supervision** Nothing can replace the need for this. An accident can happen in a second so a baby must never be left unattended, wherever she is. You may consider buying a playpen for those times when you need to leave her for a few moments. Babies should never be left alone in a car. They should also never be left with pets or other small children. Both are unpredictable.

2. **Never let yourself be distracted** It is very easy to be lose concentration mid-task and to leave hazardous objects like scissors within your baby's reach. Even when you are busy or under pressure, make sure you keep in mind the actions needed to ensure your baby's safety, like locking stair gates securely and storing potentially dangerous items when not in use.

3. **Keep things out of reach** Clearly some objects, such as knives, scissors and medicines, must be kept well away from little hands. Some parents chose to leave some ornaments around the home and to teach their children that they must not touch them. However, putting ornaments and other treasures out of reach keeps the stress levels down and cuts down the number of times parents need to say "Don't" in a day.

4. **Protect against potential dangers** Safety equipment like stair gates, window guards and power point covers are all vital in keeping your baby as safe as possible at home.

5. **Teach about dangers** It is never too early to pass on information regarding safety. At first, your baby will not take your advice in, but eventually she will come to understand the dangers around her.

herself. This can easily happen when a baby pulls herself up to standing using furniture as her support. Where possible, attach such furniture items to the wall or otherwise put them away. Make sure drawers cannot be pulled out completely. If they can, attach safety latches so that your toddler cannot pull them out onto herself. Keep your television on a low piece of furniture and fix a guard to the DVD player to prevent items being pushed inside. Make sure heavy lamps cannot be pulled over.

Carpets and rugs

These should be fastened down securely. Non-slip pads should be placed under rugs unless they have a non-slip undersurface.

Fires and radiators

Guards must be placed in front of fires and ideally around radiators, too. Objects should not be put on the mantelpiece as they may tempt children to try to climb up to reach them.

Bins

It is important to think when placing items in the bin. Anything potentially hazardous, like razor blades or a detergent bottle, should be sealed in a bag and put in the bin outside. Small children will be fascinated by the contents of a bin, no matter how unpleasant. Put your bin in a cupboard that is out of your baby's reach or has a safety latch that means she cannot open it.

Plants

Plants should be kept out of reach; they can be pulled over and may be poisonous. Poisonous houseplants include amaryllis, cyclamen and English ivy. You also need to watch out for pebbles in plant pots, which may present a choking hazard. For more information on poisonous plants see page 321.

Choking and suffocation hazards

These include anything with a diameter of less than 3.5 cm, toys that have small parts or toys that have small pieces that may break off (remember the toys of older siblings may present a choking risk), pens and pencils, coins, batteries (whether new or dead, these can release dangerous substances into the child's gut when ingested), anything magnetic that may be swallowed, jewellery and balloons. Keep plastic bags well out of reach, but also tie a knot in them for added safety.

Injury hazards

Sharp, fragile and heavy items can cause injuries. Sharp household objects include knives, scissors, needles and pins. China, glassware and light bulbs are easily breakable and may cause injuries if broken. Tools can also have sharp edges or be heavy and lead to injuries, as can heavy furniture or ornaments that can be toppled.

If your baby wants to use a pencil or pen, make sure you watch over her carefully and take it away from her when she has finished. Otherwise give her wax crayons or chubby felt pens.

Fire and poison hazards

Matches and lighters are fire hazards. Alcohol, cleaning fluids, medicines, mothballs, make-up, perfumes and mouth-wash are all potentially

BASIC SAFETY EQUIPMENT

The following simple equipment will help you to make your house a safer place for your child:

- Stair gates
- Door stoppers/guards
- Window locks/guards
- Power point covers
- Corner guards for sharp corners on furniture
- Locks for drawers and cupboards – also for the oven and the fridge
- Stove guards – to protect from pans on the stovetop – and stove knob guards
- Covers for bath taps – to prevent your child from banging her head and also to protect her from burning herself on the hot tap.

poisonous and must be stored out of reach (see also page 315).

Electrical hazards

Electric power points can be fascinating for small children and they are often positioned within easy reach. It is all too easy for babies to poke things into the pinholes, making them at risk of electric shocks. This is easily avoided by putting special covers on all unused points. Instead of waiting until your baby is on the move, fit them early so that you are prepared. Also, it is important to leave switches in the off position when points are not in use.

Keep hairdryers, toasters and all other electrical equipment well away from your child. Don't put lamps near curtains as this presents a fire hazard.

Flexes need to be kept away from small children as much as possible. As well as presenting a choking hazard when long, they can enable children to pull electrical equipment onto themselves or within their reach. Lead tidies can be used to keep a collection of

SAFETY**FIRST**	out of reach

As your baby grows and goes from crawling to standing and walking, you will have to position objects higher to keep them out of reach. Be vigilant for signs of climbing; once this is achieved, nothing on tables, sideboards or work surfaces will be safe any more. At first your child will climb onto furniture in position, but later she will learn to push chairs and other items to form a stepping-stone to reach whatever has caught her interest.

leads together. Put leads in inaccessible places behind furniture as much as you can. Keep them in place with flex holders.

Water safety

The dangers of water for children are well known, but a number of babies still drown every year. Babies must never be left unsupervised with water, even if it is very shallow. Always empty your bucket straightaway after mopping the floor, for example; likewise, empty the bath immediately. Never leave your baby alone in the bath, even for a second.

Purchase a seat lock for the toilet so that it can be kept securely closed when not in use.

Fire safety

There are a number of measures you should take to protect your family. It is an essential to fit smoke alarms that comply with safety regulations. Fit at least one alarm on every floor; ideally, there should be one on the landing and one on the hall ceiling. Position an alarm near the kitchen rather than in it, where it is likely to be set off accidentally.

Smoke alarm batteries should be checked every week and changed as the manufacturer recommends. It is also worth keeping fire extinguishers in the house (out of children's reach). They must be regularly serviced and replaced when out of date.

All clothes should be flame retardant and any upholstered furniture should have the permanent fire-resistant label.

Candles must be positioned out of reach and never left unattended when you leave the room.

5 ways to prevent falls

1   **Use lighting** Keep areas like stairs and the path to the bathroom lit at night.

2   **Avoid leaving objects lying around.**

3   **Secure floor coverings** Make sure rugs have non-slip backing and that carpets are held down securely.

4   **Dress your child in proper footwear** Have her wear non-slip socks or slippers or go bare footed.

5   **Clean up messes** Wipe up spilled drinks and remove dropped food.

Keep a guard in front of all fires and any coal, matches and lighters out of reach.

Take special care with cigarettes. It is strongly recommended that no one should smoke in the home but if you or another family member does, ensure that lit cigarettes are never left unattended and that they are always completely extinguished.

The heating system should be checked regularly.

It is recommended that every homeowner should work out a route for leaving the house in case a fire starts. In most homes, the best route to follow will be the usual one taken through the front or back door. However, an alternative is needed in case the chosen route is blocked. Tell babysitters and other caregivers who come to your home about the planned route. Make sure keys for doors and windows are near to hand.

Local fire officers are happy to advise on minimising the risk of a fire. They give information on the best detectors and extinguishers for use in the home as well as an appropriate escape route.

Poisons safety

Babies and toddlers often explore the world around them by putting objects they encounter into their mouths. This can be dangerous because of choking risks and because many substances around the home, even seemingly harmless ones, are poisonous. Take particular care if you have a workshop or garage; not only will there be tools that should be kept away from children, there probably will also be a variety of toxic substances.

To reduce your child's risk of ingesting toxic substances:

◆ Ensure all poisonous substances are kept well out of reach in lockable cupboards. Even quite small children can find ways of climbing up to high cupboards if they are determined enough.
◆ Keep medicines in a locked cupboard.
◆ Never leave hazardous substances unattended or within reach of your baby. It is so easy to leave a job half-done when distracted (for example, if the phone goes or the doorbell rings).
◆ Don't keep medicines in your handbag and if you have make-up or other potentially hazardous

items there, make sure you put it somewhere out of reach. It is a good idea to get into the habit of putting your handbag – and those of visitors – out of reach just in case.
◆ When buying any hazardous substances, avoid colourful containers that may catch your baby's interest.
◆ Go for the least dangerous options available when choosing household cleaners and other substances for use around the home.
◆ Buy bottles with childproof tops. However, remember they are not absolutely childproof and so still need to be kept out of reach.
◆ Don't store hazardous substances in food containers, such as an ice-cream container. Keep all substances in their own containers and ensure they are clearly labelled as poisonous.
◆ If hazardous substances are not to be used, put the container in a sealed bag in the rubbish bin rather than in your kitchen bin.
◆ Be vigilant when visiting others to make sure

nothing hazardous is within your child's reach.

♦ Don't make taking medicine seem like a treat. Children need to understand that medicines are given to make them feel better when they are ill and are only to be taken if parents administer them.

Dangerous substances

The following are found in most homes. Some, such as mouth-wash (often contains alcohol), may surprise you. If in doubt, shut or lock the substance away.

♦ Alcohol
♦ Antifreeze
♦ Bleach and other cleaning materials like dishwasher, toilet and oven cleaner
♦ Decorating agents (e.g. paint remover and thinner)
♦ Dishwasher detergents and washing tabs
♦ Furniture and metal polish
♦ Glues
♦ Insect repellants and poisons

♦ Make-up and perfume (also nail polish and remover)
♦ Mothballs
♦ Medicines, including aspirin, paracetamol, and iron pills
♦ Mouth-wash
♦ Petrol and paraffin
♦ Weed killer

Kitchen safety

The kitchen will hold great fascination for your baby – there are so many things to explore – but it also can be dangerous. As with all areas of the house, never leave your baby alone in the kitchen even for a moment. She will quickly find her way into all sorts of hazardous places.

Hot foods

Never carry your baby around when you are cooking or holding a hot drink. Hot foods and drinks can easily spill and splash. Anything hot must be placed towards the back of work surfaces and away from the edges of tables to ensure it is well out of reach.

Cupboards, drawers and work surfaces

Special latches and locks will help to protect your baby but only fit types that you can open without too much trouble; otherwise you will be tempted to leave drawers and cupboards open to avoid a

Why not keep one kitchen cupboard for your child? Put in utensils that are safe but will keep her amused, like a wooden spoon, a pan and a plastic bowl. This will let her have fun with you in the kitchen without taking risks.

struggle when their contents are needed. Don't restrict latches and locks to floor level. For added security, make sure that any hazardous items are kept in cupboards that are well out of reach:

- *Cleaning items* – all detergents and washing materials are potentially toxic.
- *Cling wrap* and other dispenser boxes with serrated edges may cause cuts.
- *Plastic bags* may cause suffocation.
- *Fridge magnets* may be swallowed. Small magnets present a choking hazard and are particularly dangerous when swallowed; ingesting more than one magnet may lead to serious bowel damage.

Do not allow your child to sit on work surfaces in the kitchen. Not only may she fall off, but this will also bring all sorts of hazards into her reach.

Appliances

Use the rings at the back of the stovetop in preference to the front and make sure handles are always turned towards the back of the stove. Stove guards are available that shield children from pans on the stovetop. If knobs are within reach your baby's reach, it is worth applying knob covers. Clean the stove, grill and toaster often, and empty the crumb drawer frequently – grease and crumbs can easily set alight. Keep tea towels away from them. Use spark devices rather than matches to light a gas stove. Keep a fire blanket in the kitchen.

Fit a lock to the fridge so that your child cannot get her hands on unsuitable food such as raw meat.

Make sure dishwasher and washing machine doors are kept securely closed at all times; children can easily get hold of sharp and breakable items in the dishwasher or the detergent inside the machines. They also can climb into washing machines and pull the doors closed behind them.

Smaller kitchen appliances, such as a toaster, should be positioned well away from the edge of work surfaces and have no trailing leads that your baby can use to pull them into her reach or down on top of her.

Bathroom safety

The bathroom is another dangerous place for babies but with your vigilance and by following the measures described you can minimise the main risks of drowning, scalding and falling.

The bath

Put a non-slip mat in the bottom of the bath and another on the floor. Great care must be taken to avoid scalding. Set your water heater so that the temperature of the water cannot go above 49°C (120°F). Test the bath water with your wrist or use a water thermometer (the temperature should be no more than about 37°C or 100° F). If possible, when in the bath, position your baby away from the taps as children can easily bump their heads on them or burn themselves. Guards also are available that will protect them from these hazards. Bath water need only be deep enough to cover your baby's legs to give her a good clean. From the age of around six months your baby will be able to sit in a seat in the bath. This will free up your hands to wash her. However, never leave a baby unattended in the bath until the age of at least five years. Always empty the bath as soon as you have finished with it.

The toilet

Buy a toilet seat lock so you can keep the lid secured down when the toilet is not in use.

Dangerous items

A number of items normally kept in the bathroom must be stored out of reach. These include:

- *Cleaning materials* including toilet detergents.
- *Electrical appliances* – ideally don't use these in the bathroom and keep them well away from water.
- *Medicines;* these should be kept in a locked medicine cabinet positioned high on the wall.
- *Make-up* and other beauty products.
- *Mouth-wash* as it is toxic to babies if swallowed.
- *Sharp objects* such as razors and scissors.
- *Choking hazards.*
- *Hazardous rubbish,* for example used razors and empty mouth-wash and detergent bottles.

It is worth keeping the door locked securely when the bathroom is not in use. This will act as an extra safeguard. Stick a note on the door as a reminder.

Bedroom safety

The safety precautions needed here will change as your baby grows and develops.

The cot

Choose your cot with care to ensure it meets safety standards with correctly positioned bars and a firm, tight-fitting mattress. Pillows, duvets and bumpers are not appropriate for babies as they present a risk of suffocation. The side of the cot should be locked in the up position when you leave your baby alone. Never let your baby sleep with toys that may cause choking or suffocation.

As soon as your baby can kneel and then stand you will need to lower the base so that the rail reaches her chest. Once the cot bar is lower than her chest, it will be time for her to move to a bed. Most babies can stay in their cots until the age of around two years. Once your baby can kneel or stand, mobiles should be removed from above the cot.

Part of making sure your baby is safe when she sleeps is ensuring that she remains at the right temperature. Many parents are concerned about their babies getting too cold and they wrap them up accordingly. However, over-heating is also a risk for babies and so it is important to keep your baby's room at the right temperature and to position the cot away from heaters as well as to use appropriate nightwear and bedding for her. Bear in mind that babies cannot kick or throw their bedding off if they are too hot. For more information on safe sleeping, see pages 156–9.

Changing area

It is all too easy for a baby to roll off a change table and so, as with any raised surface, you must not turn away from your baby, even for a moment. A safety strap will add to your baby's safety.

Alternatively, you can place the change mat on the floor. Make sure the toiletries are kept out of your baby's reach.

Toy safety

Always choose age-appropriate toys for your baby. Be guided not only by the age range given on the packaging, but also by your baby's own development. Although toys with smaller parts tend to be labelled as unsuitable for the under threes, your baby may continue to put objects in her mouth beyond this age, in which case such toys will continue to be unsuitable. Bear in mind that older children's toys may present a hazard for babies and toddlers. Keep an eye out for small pieces left lying around.

Toys for the under threes should be chunky with large pieces. They should be well made and well maintained to make sure small pieces, such as eyes, can't come away and cause a choking hazard. Look out for sharp edges and avoid heavy toys that could fall on your child and injure her. Strings on toys should be no longer than 30 cm, to avoid the risk of strangulation. When buying soft toys look for ones that are washable so they can be cleaned every so often.

If you are in doubt about the safety of a toy, don't buy it, or throw it away. It is great to be given second-hand toys, but make sure they are in good condition before giving them to your baby.

When storing toys, toy chests are neither the most efficient n or safest ways. The entire contents often need pulling out to retrieve one at the bottom

SAFETY**FIRST**	children's clothes

There are a number of features to look for when buying baby and toddler clothes that will mean they are unlikely to cause an accident. Clothes including nightwear should be fire retardant, the correct size and have no drawstrings (such as are found on hoodies) or ribbons attached that are more than 15 cm long as these present a risk of strangulation.

and many have heavy lids that can trap small fingers. There is also the risk that small children can climb in and become trapped. Unless you choose a toybox with a light lid and mechanism to protect fingers and ventilation holes, use shelves for storing toys.

Pets

Many pets are child-friendly and cope with the antics of babies well but even the most docile pets can be unpredictable when provoked so it is important that children and pets are supervised at all times. As well as injuries, there also are hygiene risks associated with pets, so it is not a good idea to buy a pet for a young child. If you already have a cat or dog you will need to take appropriate measures.

Children under the age of four are most at risk of dog bites as with time children learn how to behave with animals. It is worth showing your baby how to treat animals early on but it will take time before she will understand your advice and act accordingly. You need to teach your child to:

- Be calm and gentle with pets.
- Never disturb a dog or cat when it is asleep or eating.
- Stand still when a dog comes up to her.
- Never go up to a dog she doesn't know.
- Never touch dog or cat excrement.
- Wash her hands after playing with a pet.

Some pets can become jealous when a new baby joins the family and this may affect behaviour; you may need to give your pet some special attention while it gets used to this new family member.

It is worth bearing the following in mind:

- A net attached over a baby's pram will give some protection against cats. As well as the risk of scratching, there is also the risk that a cat may suffocate a baby if it jumps into her pram (or cot). Remember to keep an even closer eye than usual on your baby if she is sleeping in the garden and there may be cats around.
- Keep pets out of your baby's bedroom.
- Make sure your baby keeps away from the cat litter tray.
- Remove all dog excrement from the garden.

BABY WALKERS

The use of baby walkers is controversial. If you let your child use one, make sure you watch her very closely. Babies can move really fast in a baby walker, which means they can easily topple over or hit furniture and hurt themselves. As well as this, babies in walkers are higher than they would normally be so they can get hold of objects that would usually be too high to reach.

Walkers not only do not help babies to learn to walk, they may actually retard it as they reduce the time babies spend moving around the floor by natural means like crawling. The Child Acccident Prevention Foundation of Australia says that "use of a baby walker has been known to delay the development of a child's gross motor skills".

- Make sure your pets are fully wormed.
- Consider making a fenced dog run in your garden to ensure there is no dog excrement in your child's play area and to help you keep track of your dog when outdoors.

Safety outside the home

Various safety measures should be taken in and around the garden as well as remembering that children should never be left alone there.

In the garden

Your garden should be a secure environment and this means ensuring that the fence or hedge around it is well maintained with no gaps. All garden equipment should be locked away securely when not in use. This applies to potentially toxic substances, too (see *Dangerous substances* page 316).

Try to avoid using dangerous equipment like power tools and shredders when your child is anywhere around; wait until she is safe and secure inside. If you must use these types of machinery, make sure a second person is around at all times to watch your baby while you are at work.

Play equipment

When purchasing, check that the equipment meets approved safety standards. Look for the official Standards Australia logo but you should also carefully check the equipment; it must be sturdy, well made with no sharp edges and appropriate to the age and development of your baby.

If you are putting the equipment together yourself, follow the instructions carefully. Position it well away from walls and fences and on a soft place for landing. Wood bark, wood chips, and rubber blocks or mats are recommended.

Children must be carefully monitored when using outdoor play equipment and the equipment must be well maintained and checked regularly.

Ride-on toys

Make sure you purchase the correct size; buying your toddler one to grow into will only put her at greater risk of accidents.

Ensure she always wears her helmet when she rides a tricycle – even if she's in your garden. The helmet will reduce the risk of a serious head injury if she falls and at the same time she will be learning good habits for her bike-riding days later on.

Pools and ponds

Great care must be taken around water and children must be supervised closely at all times when they have access to it.

A swimming pool needs to be fenced off with a self-closing and self-locking gate. The fence should be designed and constucted so as to be non-climbable by young children (refer to Australian Standard 1926, "Fencing for swimming pools"). Bear in mind, however, that a fence does not provide complete protection – the gate may be left open or may not be closed properly and come open. Pool owners need to remain vigilant at all times. Ideally ponds should be filled with sand. Otherwise they can be covered with a rigid grille or mesh. This should be positioned above the surface of the water, secured all the way round the pond, and strong enough to bear a child's weight without sagging. It must also be well maintained. Again, a fence around a pond should be non-climbable.

Paddling pools should be emptied whenever they are not in use. They should then be put away or turned upside down so that rain cannot collect in them and present a drowning hazard. Don't leave water containers like buckets out in the garden. Water will collect in them and make them a hazard. Remember, there is a risk of drowning in any collection of water even if it is very shallow.

Poisonous plants

Many garden plants are potentially harmful: some can cause skin or eye irritation; others are classed as poisonous and may result in serious effects if eaten. It is important to teach your child that she should not play with plants or put plants or berries in her mouth. However, it will take her a while to take this in, hence the need for constant supervision in the garden. The safest course of action is to remove all poisonous plants from your garden. If you are not sure whether a plant is poisonous, try taking a clipping to your local garden centre for identification. If your baby does put poisonous leaves or berries into her mouth, remove as much as possible and seek immediate medical attention. If you are unsure whether the plant is harmful, seek advice, taking a piece with you.

In the drive

Make sure your child is carefully supervised if you are driving in or out. Check under your car as well as around it before moving it.

Out and about

You and your child will have great fun together as you explore the world around you. At the same time you want to ensure her safety. Key to this is making sure she holds your hand at all times or is securely strapped into her pram.

In the car

To keep your child as safe as possible in the car it is important to remember the following:

- Choose the seat that is appropriate for your baby's age, height and weight and make sure it is installed securely in the correct position. The seat should face the rear of the car until your baby is at least one year old and 9 kg. Ensure she stays in the car seat at all times.
- Buy a car seat that carries the Standards Australia AS/NZS 1754 logo.
- Do not let your baby play with window locks or door handles.
- If there is an airbag for her seat, switch it off.
- Switch on the child locks.
- Do not allow yourself to be distracted by your baby so that you take your eyes off the road. If your child needs you, pull in at the first safe opportunity.

- Remove items from the ledge behind the seats; they can easily slip off and hit someone when you slow down or stop suddenly.

At the shops

Keep your child right next to you at all times. If she is riding in the shopping trolley ensure that you keep the belt securely fastened.

In the playground

Make sure you are always close by and that you do not take your eyes off your child for a second. Teach her how to play safely. Your child should not twist swings around as they may untwist and hit he,r or walk in front of or behind a swing for the same reason. Make sure your child plays carefully on roundabouts and waits until they have stopped before she climbs on or off. She also needs to learn that she should never climb up the front of a slide and that she must wait until the child in front of her slides off at the bottom before she goes down.

In the sun

Try to keep your baby in the shade as much as you can, particularly around midday. If less than 12 months, she should be kept out of the sun altogether. She should wear loose, cool clothes that cover as much of her as possible and a hat. When in the water, she should wear sunglasses and a protective swimsuit that covers her arms and legs.

Apply factor 30+ sunscreen regularly; babies can be burned even when out of the sun. Some products will show clearly where you have applied the cream.

Protecting your baby's skin is very important; frequent sun exposure and sunburn in childhood increase the risk of melanomas in adulthood. Babies are particularly at risk of burning because their skin is thinner and more sensitive.

While travelling

Visiting new places is a wonderful experience for children and safety measures will ensure all goes well while journeying. It is important to ask your GP about any vaccinations needed for your destination. Once abroad, you may need to take special precautions to reduce the risk of food poisoning, which can cause your baby to become very unwell.

Plane travel

Under the age of two, babies sit on a parent's knee. Alternatively a carrycot or special infant seat may be used, if available.

Bulkhead seats at the front of the plane offer more leg room. Also, they often have extra oxygen bags for baboes who do not have their own seats. However, there is no storage under the seat in front so you may spend quite a bit time getting up and down to get what you need from the overhead locker.

Many airlines allow babies up to the age of three to sit in their car seats (as long as they conform with approved safety standards) placed in a normal seat. It is worth finding out about this in advance.

Train travel

Encourage your baby to sit on your knee or by the window; this way, she is less likely to dash off. Don't let her run up and down the aisle; a sudden jolt of the train may throw her off balance and she may also present a hazard to other passengers. Take her to explore if you wish – after all train journeys hold great excitement for small children – but make sure she holds your hand at all times.

HEALTH**FIRST**	upset tummy

Sometimes just a change of diet can affect your child's bowel habits for a while but there is also a risk of infection from food eaten when abroad. To minimise the risks:

- *If you think the water may be unsafe for drinking, boil it or use bottled water.*
- *Only give your child pasteurised dairy products.*
- *Wash fruit with water that is fit to drink and then peel it.*
- *Give your child bottled fruit juice rather than freshly squeezed.*
- *As at home, make sure that all meat and fish is cooked thoroughly.*

Serious first aid situations

Even with your best endeavours it may not be possible to prevent all accidents. You should be able to deal with grazes, cuts and bites (see pages 340–3), while being able to recognise when urgent medical help is required. In each of the following instances, you should either ring 000 for an ambulance or seek urgent medical attention.

Having the necessary supplies at hand will make treating injuries easier, see page 343.

Poisoning

If your child ingests something harmful or you suspect that she has, or a potential poison has come in contact with her skin and eyes, call 000 for an ambulance immediately.

Try and find out what she took, how much and how long ago, so that you can inform the doctor or paramedics.

Keep a sample of any vomit she produces – but don't try and make her sick. You can give her sips of water but not large amounts to drink.

If your child is breathing but unconscious, put her in the recovery position.

Bleeding

Your main aim is to stem the flow of blood. If you have disposable gloves available, use them to reduce the risk of cross-infection. Check whether there is an object embedded in the wound.

If there is nothing embedded, press on the wound with your hand, ideally over a clean pad, and secure with a bandage. If the wound is on an arm or leg raise the injured limb above the level of the heart.

If you suspect there is something embedded, take care not to press on the object. Instead press firmly on either side of the object and build up padding around it before bandaging to avoid putting pressure on the object itself.

Burns and scalds

Babies with burns, even small or superficial ones, should have urgent medical attention.

Cool the burn as quickly as possible by placing the affected area under cold running water for at least ten minutes.

Cover the injury using a sterile non-sticky dressing such as a clean handkerchief or other clean covering such as cling wrap. Hold the dressing in place with a loose bandage. Do not apply any creams that may introduce infection. Raise the limb to reduce swelling.

Drowning

If you find your baby in water, lift her out immediately and hold her so her head is lower than her body. This will help prevent water, or vomit if she throws up, getting into her lungs. If she is unconscious but still breathing,

put her in the recovery position, while you call 000 for the emergency services. If she is not breathing, begin resuscitation. Water in the lungs will mean you will have to breathe more firmly than usual to get the lungs inflated.

Electrocution

Call 000 for an ambulance immediately.

Break the contact between your baby and the electrical supply by switching off the current at the mains, if it can be reached easily.

If you cannot reach the mains to protect yourself, stand on some dry insulation material, such as a telephone directory. Using something made of a non-conductive material (e.g. a wooden broom), push your baby away from the electrical source or push the source away from your baby.

If at any time your baby becomes unconscious, stops breathing or is choking, see pages 41–3 for emergency resuscitation techniques.

Health monitoring

It is important that your baby's health is monitored during her early years so that any potential problems can be picked up early. Your baby will have her first medical assessment during her first day or two and will continue to be cared for by a health care team thereafter. However, you are key in overseeing her wellbeing. As the person who is with her every day, you will observe her at close hand and be the first to pick up if things are not as they should be.

The child health team
Potential key members of the team include a number of different specialists trained in looking after babies.

Paediatrician
Some paediatricians cover all aspects of child medicine; others focus on one particular area, such as heart disorders. If your GP has any concerns about your child's health that need further assessment or specialist treatment, a hospital referral will be made. In addition to hospital-based paediatric consultants, there are community paediatricians. These doctors have a special interest in child development and childcare away from the hospital environment. If you do see a paediatrician, a letter will be sent to your GP giving the diagnosis made and what treatment has been initiated if any. In this way the GP surgery keeps a full record of your child's medical history. You will only be entitled to receive copies of any letters.

General practitioner
GPs treat many of the ailments that crop up in early childhood. They will also advise on the measures needed to ease the symptoms of illness. It's a good idea to find out which of the GPs in your practice has a particular interest in caring for children and to take your baby to see the same doctor on every visit. In this way you build up a rapport and the doctor comes to know your child.

Maternal and child health nurse
In the early days of your baby's life, you will both be cared for by a midwife. From then on your baby will be looked after by a health nurse, who will be able to give you advice on all aspects of baby care and will monitor your child's progress. If you have any worries about your child's development or behaviour, your health nurse will probably be your first port of call. She can also help if you are feeling low, if your baby cries all the time, or if she won't feed or is not gaining weight. Most are very experienced and also can put you in touch with local services for babies and young children.

Dentist
Your dentist will advise on the best dental care for your child and check that all is well. Again, it is worth looking for a dentist who specialises in looking after children. Positive experiences at the dental surgery in early childhood are very important in setting the stage for a lifetime of good dental care.

Checking development

Formal screening checks are performed during early childhood as part of the child health surveillance program. Some aspects of physical health, including weight gain and growth, are also assessed. In addition to seeing children at the scheduled check-ups, doctors and health nurses assess children informally at appointments made for other reasons, such as illness or vaccinations.

Every child will develop at her own rate, which is determined by the genes she inherits and the environment in which she is raised. Because of this individuality, you should not become too concerned about the exact timing of every developmental milestone but it's worth being aware of the usual age range for achieving key milestones (see page 278) and keeping a record of when your child acquires these skills (see page 326).

All aspects of development – posture and movement (gross motor), vision and manual skills (fine motor), hearing and speech, and social behaviour and interaction – will be reviewed at the developmental check-ups. However, the emphasis may change to take account of the way young children acquire skills. For example, in the first 18 months, gross motor skills are learned at an amazing rate and so these will be a key focus when assessing young babies.

Physical health

Development and physical health are closely related. For example, learning to crawl and later walk depends on the correct working of muscles and coordination, which both rely on a healthy nervous system. Therefore problems with development may alert

healthcare professionals to the presence of a medical disorder. Some medical conditions are usually picked up during physical examinations. An example of this would be murmurs (see page 328), which may be detected when the doctor listens to a child's heart with the stethoscope. In addition to examinations, blood tests may reveal certain conditions.

Routine assessments

After six weeks of age, early childhood assessments are carried out at regular inervals with a maternal and child health nurse. As well as assessing development, your doctor or health nurse may take these opportunities to make certain physical checks, including whether the hips move normally and whether any heart murmurs are present when listening to the heart sounds. Measurements will be taken to assess weight gain and growth.

MORE **ABOUT** | congenital hip dislocation

In some young babies the socket that holds the ball-shaped head of the femur is too shallow, so that the head can move out of the correct position. It may slip in and out when the baby is examined or, less commonly, stay outside the socket. The latter is a relatively uncommon congenital condition (one that is present at birth) known as congenital hip dislocation. Early diagnosis and treatment are of great importance so that a child can learn to walk properly. Without treatment, walking is likely to be delayed and an affected baby may limp and sway from side to side when she walks. The affected leg may appear shorter and the range of movements of the hip on that side will also be restricted.

Your baby's hips will be examined at her newborn check and at 6–8 weeks. If a problem is suspected, she will be referred for ultrasound hip scanning and to an orthopaedic surgeon.

The treatment depends on the severity of the condition. In some cases monitoring will be all that is needed and the condition will right itself with time as the socket develops. Other children will be fitted into a splinting device that keeps the hips turned out and allows them to develop normally over a period of months. Sometimes a period of traction followed by further splinting is needed and occasionally surgery is required.

KEEPING YOUR OWN DEVELOPMENT RECORD

A development record is an invaluable source of information to help monitor your baby's development. Every baby in Australia is issued with a personal child health record at birth. Your GP or health nurse will fill this out at regular intervals and use this to put your child's current stage of development in context by looking at the timing of the milestones she has already achieved. They will be able to see whether her development is continuing at the expected rate or whether one or more aspects of development have slowed, which may indicate a problem. However, you may wish to record certain key milestones and have them as a wonderful keepsake to return to in later years.

First smile _____

Stands with support _____

Sits without support _____

Feeds herself finger foods _____

First words _____

Crawls _____

Says "mama" and "dada" _____

Waves bye-bye _____

Claps _____

Points _____

Takes first steps _____

Drinks from cup with two hands _____

Walking steadily _____

Climbs into a chair _____

Throws a ball _____

Runs _____

Walks upstairs _____

Feeds herself with a spoon _____

Kicks a ball _____

Stays dry during day _____

Walks up and down stairs confidently _____

You will be asked various questions about your baby's progress at each assessment, including whether you think there are any problems with her hearing and vision. You'll also have the opportunity to ask questions about her health and development as well as to voice any concerns you may have. However, you can contact your GP or health nurse at any time to do this.

New baby check

Within the first 24 hours or so of her birth, your baby will have a physical examination. The doctor will first check her appearance, including her fingers and toes and back to check her spine looks normal. The doctor will shine a light in your baby's eyes to detect signs of a cataract (see page 333) and check the roof of her mouth for palate irregularities. The doctor will listen to the heart and examine the hips for evidence of a congenital dislocation (see page 325). If your baby is a boy, the doctor will also check that the testes are in the scrotum. Hearing tests are also carried out (see page330).

The developmental assessment is limited at this early age and physical checks are the main focus, but at later checks (for example, from six months onwards), development will predominate.

Sometime during the first week of life, the midwife will ask to take blood from your baby's heel to test for a number of important disorders including hypothyroidism (underactivity of the thyroid gland), which can have a number of serious effects including learning difficulties if it is not picked up early.

2, 4 and 8 week checks

During these check-ups, all the key aspects of development will be assessed. You may be asked whether your baby has started smiling yet, when she cries, and how she reacts to sounds (factors important in social development, language and hearing).

Simple observation of your baby's muscle tone and early head control is a check for gross motor development. Watching whether your baby follows an object with her eyes when it is moved across her field of vision is a way of assessing her eyesight.

The doctor will carry out some physical checks, too, including examining the hips, listening to the

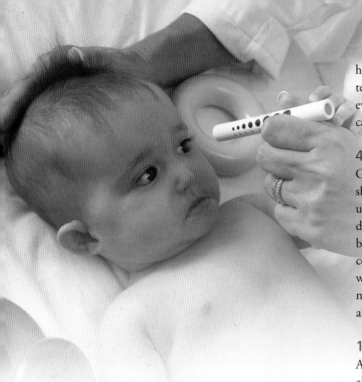

heart sounds and re-checking the position of the testes in boys. He may also check the eyes for evidence of cataracts and other eye conditions that can affect young babies.

4 month check

Gross motor skills are coming on now – your baby should be able to hold her head steady when upright, roll over, reach for an object and turn in the direction of a voice (especially her mother's. She may be able to say "ah goo" or similar vowel- consonant combinations, blow a raspberry and even bear some weight on her legs when held upright. Your health nurse will assess all of these milestones and ask about fine motor skills, as well as speech.

12 month check

Again, your maternal and child health nurse will ask about several key developmental milestones. By this age your baby may be really on the move, perhaps cruising (walking with the support of furniture) and even taking early steps. At around 10 months she may start to hold small items between her finger and thumb (known as the pincer grip). From around 12 months she may call "mama" and "dada". She may use a few other words too. Socially, she may be starting to eat with a spoon and to hold a cup using both hands.

Subsequent checks usually occur at 18 months, two years and older or as recommended by the health nurse.

18–24 month check

Many skills have been acquired by the age of two years in all areas of development. Your health nurse will be able to engage your child in activities and see the great progress that has been made. Your

MORE **ABOUT** | heart murmurs

In addition to the normal sounds heard when listening to the heart with a stethoscope, other sounds such as those caused by turbulent blood flow in the heart may be heard. These can indicate a problem with one of the heart valves or another heart abnormality. Some heart problems are found during antenatal scans, but others are not picked up until after birth.

Some congenital heart abnormalities are caused by a problem with the development of the heart during pregnancy. Others occur when the changes in the baby's circulatory system that normally take place at or around birth do not occur as they should.

If a murmur is heard, an appointment with a paediatric cardiologist and an echocardiogram, a special ultrasound scan that looks at the heart's structure and functioning, will be arranged.

Some murmurs of early childhood are considered to be normal. These are described as innocent murmurs, which require no treatment and usually disappear during the first few years of life. However, in some cases, surgery will be needed to treat an underlying abnormality.

During a boy's development in the uterus, the testes follow a path of descent from the abdomen where they are formed down into the scrotum. Sometimes this descent stops before the testes reach the scrotum and one or both testes remain in the abdomen (known as undescended testes). This is quite a common condition, with about five per cent of boys being affected at birth. It is more common in premature babies as the testes move down into the scrotum during the last months of pregnancy.

In some of these boys the condition will resolve on its own when the testes descend into the scrotum during the first few months of life. Otherwise treatment will be needed for two main reasons. First, fertility will be affected in later life, as the temperature inside the body is too high for the production of sperm; the lower temperature in the scrotum is ideal.

There is also an increased risk of malignancy for testes that remain inside the abdomen. In addition, the testes should be brought down for reasons of appearance.

Checking that the testes are in the scrotum is an important part of a baby boy's early check-ups. (In a few cases, the testes cannot be felt in the scrotum because they have not developed.)

Sometimes one or both testes will pop up into the groin area during the examination. This is caused by a muscle reflex and the testes are described as being retractile; in this situation the testes can be guided back into the scrotum by the examiner. A retractile testis is regarded as normal and requires no treatment, just monitoring to ensure it eventually stays in the scrotum.

In most cases, surgery will be carried out to bring the testis down and fix it in the scrotum. [Occasionally, a normal testis can move up out of the scrotum later on in childhood and this will also require treatment.]

---

baby will probably be a confident walker now. She may hold a pencil and scribble and build a tower of three to six bricks.

As far as language is concerned, she will be able to communicate some of his needs and wishes with short phrases like ' Want milk'. He will probably feed himself well with a spoon by now.

Vision and hearing assessments

Normal vision and hearing are crucial to development and parents may notice problems when engaged in everyday activities with their babies. However, to be absolutely sure that all is well, certain tests may be carried out routinely at the developmental checks; others are used when problems are suspected.

Vision checks

In the newborn, the doctor will be checking mainly for abnormalities of the eye itself, such as cataracts. By the 6–8 week check the examiner can test to see whether a baby follows an object moved across in front of her face.

In the early months, visual assessment is very simple – at six months the examiner will check whether your child reaches out for toys. By two years, more formal checks can be carried out, like asking children to pick out small objects on pictures and then at three years by asking children to match letters on charts (a letter is held up across the room and your child is asked to point to it on her chart). Should any problems be identified by these simple tests your baby will be referred to the hospital or a specialist for review.

Hearing checks

A number of hearing tests may be arranged during early childhood. In addition, you can monitor your baby's hearing (see box); you will be aware of your child's responses to sounds and to your voice.

Newborn tests

The following tests can be used to check hearing in newborn babies:

- *Evoked otoacoustic emission* Earphones placed over the babies ears emit clicking sounds into each ear in turn. Earpieces in the ears should pick up vibrations in the cochlea if it is functioning normally.
- *Auditory brainstem response audiometry* Again, earphones placed over the ears emit clicks. These noises trigger impulses in the ear that are carried to the brain where they trigger electrical responses. These responses are recorded and analysed by a computer.

If the results of these tests are not normal, a baby is referred for further assessment by an audiometrist.

Other tests include:

- *Distraction testing* (from around 7 to 9 months). The tester sits opposite the child and keeps his attention while an assistant makes sounds of high and low frequency just outside the child's field of vision. The child should turn to the noises.
- *Speech discrimination test* (from around 18 months). The tester sits opposite a child and names toys quietly with a hand placed in front of the mouth. The tester asks the child to point to each toy on the table between them.

Although these simple tests are not always accurate they do give a good indication as to whether a child has a hearing problem or not.

4 times to check your baby's hearing

1   **In the first weeks,** does she react to sudden noises?

2   **At four months,** does she turn to your voice?

3   **At seven months,** does she turn to quiet noises?

4   **At around nine months,** has she started making babbling sounds?

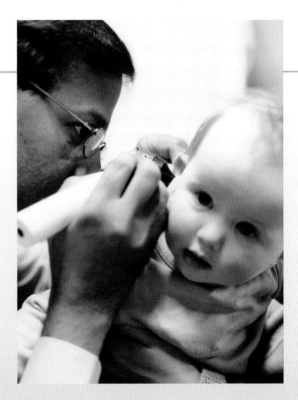

Developmental concerns

As parents, you will often be the first to suspect if your child's development is not as it should be. While the timing of milestones varies from baby to baby as well as the way they are reached (see page 273), you should approach your health nurse or GP if you suspect your baby has any developmental issues at all. The likelihood is that your baby's development will be normal and there is no underlying problem but there is no point in waiting and worrying. It is better to seek a professional opinion so your baby can have the appropriate assessment and treatment if there is a problem.

A multidisciplinary team of professionals is available to support and give help with developmental issues. Your child may be referred on to a paediatrician (hospital- or community-based), a speech therapist or a physiotherapist. Other members of the child development team include psychologists, play specialists, and occupational therapists. The paediatrician will often be the first point of referral as he or she will be able to consider any problems in the context of both physical and developmental health, as well as having access to the appropriate therapists.

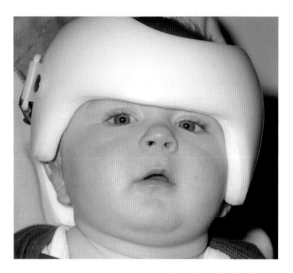

Common developmental problems

Developmental delay may affect one particular area or may be more general (known as global delay). Chapter 13 covers in more detail many of the longer-lasting problems.

Plagiocephaly

Skull misshaping is caused by a baby constantly holding her head turned to one side when lying down. Where a head-turning preference persists, it is likely that the muscles on the side of her neck will adjust to the situation. The muscles controlling head position will become shorter and tighter on one side. This adds to the problem, since in addition to being undesirable, it will now be uncomfortable for your child to turn to the non-preferred direction.

Your doctor may demonstrate some exercises to do with your child to lessen the muscle tightness, or he or she may refer you to a physiotherapist to do the muscle stretching. Studies show that if left alone, the shape of a baby's head will improve as he gets older and spends less of his time flat on his back. Growing a full head of hair will also contribute much towards making a baby's head look quite round.

In rare cases, a moulding helmet will be prescribed. A helmet will restrict skull growth in certain directions and encourages rounding out of flattened areas. Helmets need to be changed as your child's head grows, are expensive (and sometimes not covered by insurance), and need to be worn around the clock for months.

Fluorosis

Fluorosis is the effect of too much fluoride on teeth. Ever since fluoride has been added to community water systems, the number of children with cavities has declined dramatically. But the incidence of fluorosis has also inched upwards. Fortunately, the vast majority of cases of fluorosis are mild, unnoticeable, and of no dental significance. However, moderate cases can lead to white spots on teeth and less strong enamel. Severe fluorosis can damage teeth, but neither moderate nor severe fluorosis is likely to occur if simple precautions are observed:

- Discuss fluoride with your paediatrician or dentist. If your water comes from rainwater tanks and fluoride is prescribed for your baby, this is supposed to be the only way she gets it.
- Do not allow your child to get fluoride from multiple sources. For example, if she drinks fluoridated water or takes a fluoride supplement, use a toothpaste without fluoride.
- When a supplement is given, do not give more than directed. Although for many nutrients, more is better, this is not true for fluoride. Too much is to be avoided.
- Count fluoride from swallowed toothpaste when determining how much fluoride your child is getting. Even if fluoridated toothpaste is the sole source of fluoride for your child, never give more than a small dab of toothpaste at each brushing session. He may frequently ask for extra toothpaste, since it is very good tasting; however, resist the temptation to give him more.

Motor development issues

These often arise in the first 18 months when babies tend to make major advances in gross motor development. If a problem is suspected, your baby will be referred to a specialist paediatrician and a physiotherapist for a full assessment. Rarely, an underlying muscle disorder such as hypotonia (see box) or another problem will be discovered. However, in most cases, parents will be reassured and advised on measures to encourage progress, such as physiotherapy.

Speech and language issues

Speech development may be delayed for various reasons. Often, there is no cause for concern and normal speech will develop, just later than it does in most children. Speech delay may run in the family. A hearing impairment is another possible cause.

Sometimes language will be delayed as part of a more general developmental problem and if this is suspected, a general assessment will be needed. Another important cause is lack of stimulation; this is where a baby is raised in an environment that does not encourage talking or language learning.

Some children have speech disorders that affect comprehension and/or expressiont. There may be problems with pronunciation of words. For a few children, the speech disorder will be part of a problem affecting communication and social interaction (see *Autism*, page 378).

Assessment by a speech therapist and possibly a developmental paediatrician will be needed. If a hearing impairment is suspected as the cause, hearing tests will be carried out.

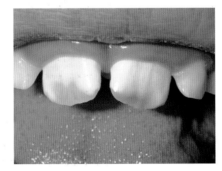

The effect of fluorosis on teeth.

Problems with social development and interaction

As with all other areas of development, children will vary in when they develop social skills and how well they communicate at a particular age. For some children, communication problems relate to delays in speech and language development. In a few cases, problems with communication and social skills will be part of a more generalised disorder, the autistic spectrum disorder (see *Autism*, page 378).

Concerns about vision and hearing

Development, in particular fine motor and language development, relies heavily on normal visual and hearing skills, so it is imperative that problems in these areas are picked up early and treated appropriately. Testing in the early years can pick up a number of eye disorders and visual problems, as well as the two main types of hearing impairment.

Cataract

This is a clouding in the lens of the eye that can impair vision. Although more common in the elderly, cataracts also may be present at birth (congenital cataracts) or develop during childhood. One or both eyes may be affected. If a baby has a cataract in one eye, her vision is likely to be fine in the other, so no problem may be noticed.

The effect cataracts have on vision depends on their size and position in the lens. If they are large and central, their effects will be more noticeable than if they are small and lie away from the centre.

If you suspect your baby has visual problems or you notice her eyes jerking quickly from side to side (a condition known as nystagmus that may be associated with cataracts), seek advice from your doctor who will arrange an appointment with an ophthalmologist. Surgery may be performed to remove the cloudy lens and an artificial lens may be inserted in the eye to replace it.

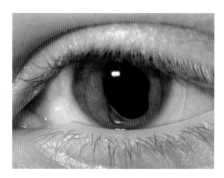

This child was left with a distorted pupil after surgery for a congential cataract.

The timing of surgery will depend on the degree of cloudiness and visual impairment. If the cataract is only moderately severe, surgery may be delayed until your baby is older when vision is easier to assess. Surgery may be followed by more treatment in the form of glasses and sometimes patching if one eye is weaker than the other. Patching the stronger eye will encourage the weaker eye to work harder and reduce the chance of lazy eye developing (see page 334).

Long-sightedness (hypermetropia)

A common condition whereby children are able to see things better far away than close up. It may be picked up at routine assessments or by parents. If you have any concerns that your child is having problems looking at picture books, or if she has a squint or complains of her eyes or head hurting, get in touch with your GP. A review with an optometrist will be arranged and glasses may be recommended. Many children grow out of hypermetropia by the time they are adults.

Short-sightedness (myopia)

Not as common as long-sightedness, but some young children are able to see things better close up than far away. Diagnosis of the condition requires an assessment by an optometrist, who will prescribe glasses, if required.

Squint (strabismus)

This is when the eyes are not aligned correctly and so appear to be looking in different directions. Often the squint will come and go. Squints may have various causes; often one eye is not working as well as the other, perhaps as a result of hypermetropia or a cataract. Squints are common in new babies, but if they have not disappeared by the

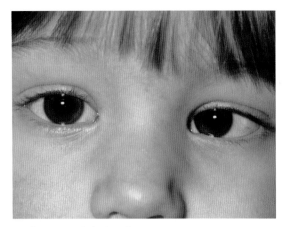
Toddler with ambylopia or lazy eye.

age of two months, a specialist review by an ophthalmologist is needed. Treatment will depend on the underlying cause, but glasses or less commonly surgery may be recommended.

Astigmatism

The cornea at the front of the eye has a smooth curve that helps bend the light rays from objects in the field of vision to meet on the retina at the back of the eye and form an image. If the curve of the cornea is not the correct shape, the light rays will not meet on the retina as they should and the image formed will be blurred. If impaired vision is picked up at a routine assessment or suspected by parents a review by an optometrist will be arranged. Astigmatism is common in young children and often resolves as they get older. In the meantime, glasses may be recommended to help with vision.

Lazy eye (amblyopia)

This condition can develop if the light rays that enter the eye are not focused as they should be on the retina at the back of the eye, as occurs in long-sightedness or astigmatism. The part of the brain that forms images by making sense of the way the light rays meet on the retina cannot learn to do its job properly. Early treatment of the underlying condition with glasses and patching of the good eye so that the weaker eye has to work harder should help to prevent amblyopia from developing.

Conductive hearing impairment

This is caused by problems in the ear canal or middle ear, where the tiny bones called ossicles lie. The commonest cause is otitis media with an effusion, or so-called glue ear (see page 345). In such cases, the hearing impairment may come and go. However, if the fluid in the middle ear persists, the hearing impairment may continue for months. Eventually speech development will be affected. If hearing is impaired, the function of the middle ear will be assessed. Glue ear may clear up without treatment, but in some cases medicines or surgery will be required.

Sensorineural hearing impairment

This results from a problem in the cochlea or with the auditory nerve that carries messages from the ear to the brain. This type of hearing loss is uncommon and is present at birth or develops during the first weeks of life. The impairment is permanent.

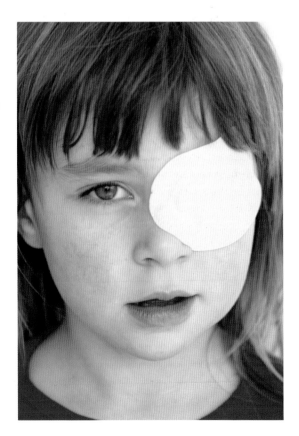

Treatment is with hearing aids or, if these do not help sufficiently, a cochlear implant. Children with sensorineural hearing loss may need help at school from specialist teachers. They may be able to learn to speak, but this is likely to be delayed. Simple signing in the early years will often be a great help in learning to communicate.

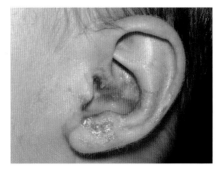

This baby is suffering from otitis media – a middle ear infection – with associated redness and discharge. Recurrent episodes may lead to glue ear and subsequent hearing loss.

Growth and weight gain problems

The rate at which young children grow and gain weight is another very important indicator of their wellbeing (see also page 273).

Your maternal and child health nurse or GP will provide a personal health record for your baby which you will need to take to all her check-ups and when she is vaccinated. In this book, you will find charts for weight, length, head circumference and height. The charts differ for boys and girls (see pages 380-3).

Weight gain may occasionally falter, perhaps as a result of a short illness, but overall it should continue to rise steadily. If the rate at which weight increases tails off significantly, the condition may be described as growth faltering. In rare cases this may be caused by an underlying medical condition but more often it results from an insufficient intake of food, perhaps because an effective feeding routine has not been established.

If there are problems with weight gain, a thorough assessment of diet and feeding routines, developmental progress and physical health will be needed to identify the cause. If there are feeding difficulties, a health nurse and possibly a nutritionist will advise. If a medical condition is suspected, tests will be arranged to confirm the diagnosis so that appropriate treatment can be arranged.

If you have any concerns about your child's growth, see your health nurse straightaway. She will take a series of accurate measurements and assess them in the context of your child's previous growth and weight gain.

As well as identifying babies with impaired growth and weight gain, monitoring weight will also pick up children who may be gaining weight too rapidly. Obesity is a growing problem in all age groups of the population, including young children. Heavy infants (those who have a high body mass index) and those who gain weight rapidly during the first and second year of life, are more likely than other infants to be obese at all stages of their lives.

Health maintenance

Visits to the dentist

It is usually recommended that children start seeing the dentist at the age of around three years but it's a good idea to take your child along with you to check-ups before so that she gets used to visiting the dental surgery.

At the early appointments, the dentist will spend time putting your child at her ease and will check that tooth brushing is done correctly, for signs of tooth decay and that new teeth will erupt in the correct position. Unless there are any problems, your child will probably be asked to visit the surgery twice a year.

Immunisations

A schedule of immunisations is recommended for early childhood to protect against various childhood infections. When you see your doctor for these, he or she will ask you a few questions about your child's health and possibly about her development. Doctors and health nurses often see these appointments as opportunities to catch up on developmental progress and wellbeing.

Why vaccinate your baby?

There are two key reasons: to protect your baby from potentially serious diseases, and to protect other children around you.

It is important that as many children as possible have their childhood vaccinations, although, for medical reasons, a small number of children cannot be vaccinated. If a high enough percentage of the population is vaccinated, these few vulnerable children are largely protected, as not enough unvaccinated children are left to pass the infection round. This is know as herd immunity. Once vaccination uptake falls, more children are left unprotected and infection can be passed around more easily so the incidence of the disease rises. If you choose not to have your child vaccinated, you are relying on all the parents around you to have their children vaccinated.

What do these immunisations protect against?

Tuberculosis

This bacterial infection is still a problem in developing countries. However, it does occur in developed parts of the world too, with those at particular risk being individuals who live in an area where there is a high incidence of the disease or whose parents or grandparents were born in a country where TB is still a problem. The TB vaccination is offered to newborn babies in these groups. The infection, which is passed on when people with the disease cough, tends to start in the lungs, but can also affect other parts of the body. Effective treatments are available, but without treatment the disease can cause persistent symptoms and can be life threatening in some cases.

Diphtheria

Now rare in developed countries, this bacterial infection affects the throat and can cause breathing problems. It is transmitted when infected people cough or sneeze. The infection may also spread in the blood to cause potentially life-threatening problems, including heart failure.

Tetanus

The symptoms of tetanus occur when a particular bacterium infects a wound and releases a toxic substance into the bloodstream. This toxin affects nerves that control muscles, resulting in severe muscle spasms. Sometimes the muscles of the throat and chest are involved, which will affect swallowing and breathing. The jaw may also be affected, hence the other name lock-jaw. Tetanus can be life threatening.

Pertussis

This bacterial illness, also known as whooping cough, causes severe bouts of coughing. The disease, which can be potentially life threatening in the very young, has decreased in incidence with the introduction of the vaccine.

THE SCHEDULE

Newborn	Hepatitis B
2 months	Diptheria Tetanus Pertussis/Whooping Cough, Hepatitis B (DTPa/HepB), Haemophilis Influenzae type B (Hib), Polio, Pneumococcal disease, Rotavirus
4 months	DTPa/HepB, Hib, Polio, Pneumococcal disease, Rotavirus
6 months	DTPa/HepB*, Hib, Polio Pneumococcal disease, Rotavirus
12 months	Hib, Measles Mumps Rubella (MMR), Meningococcal C, HepB*
18 months	Chickenpox (varicella)
4 years	DTPa, Polio, MMR

*HepB may be given at 6 or 12 months

Poliomyelitis

Now rare in developed countries thanks to the immunisation program, the effects of polio can vary from mild to very severe problems affecting the nervous system, even paralysis. The virus is passed on by contact with infected faeces, often through contaminated water or food. Polio is still a problem in some developing countries.

Haemophilus influenzae type b (Hib)

This bacterium can serious diseases including meningitis and septicaemia (infection in the blood). It can also cause epiglottitis, inflammation of the flap of cartilage that lies behind the tongue, which is a life-threatening condition (see page 349).

Meningococcus C

This bacterium can also cause the life-threatening conditions meningitis (see page 348) and septicaemia.

Measles

Measles causes a rash and cold-type symptoms. In some cases it can cause serious and potentially life-threatening complications, including encephilitis or brain infection (see page 354).

Mumps

Characterised usually by swelling of the salivary glands in front of the ears or around the neck, there can be various possible complications (see page 355).

Rubella (German measles)

The symptoms of rubella tend to be mild, but there can be serious complications, including damage to the unborn child (see also page 355).

Pneumococcus

This bacterium can cause serious illnesses including pneumonia (see *Lung infecions*, page 347)and meningitis (see page 348).

Rotavirus

This virus is the most common cause of severe gastroenteritis in infants and young children in Australia. Almost every child will suffer at least one infection by the age of three years.

Why babies are not vaccinated

There are only a few reasons why vaccinations are not given and these are if a baby:

- Is unwell and has a raised temperature (colds and coughs with no fever are not reasons for postponing immunisations)
- Has reduced immunity (being treated for cancer, taking immuno-suppressant drugs, or suffering from HIV).

Possible side effects

In the vast majority of cases, any problems will be minor; serious complications such as severe allergic reactions are very rare. There may be slight swelling or redness at the site of the injection and a slight fever. A mild form of the illness may develop after certain vaccinations such as measles and rubella.

Use the usual measures to treat a fever (see page 339). In some cases, a high fever may be associated with a fit, known as a febrile convulsion (see page 341). You should get medical attention straightaway if:

- Your baby's temperature is 39°C or more.
- Your baby has a fit.
- You think your baby has had a severe reaction. Remember, the risk of serious complications following immunisations is far lower than the risks associated with the diseases they protect against.

Travel vaccinations

Children may need vaccinations when travelling abroad, particularly to developing countries, but some vaccinations are not recommended below certain ages. It is important that you seek specialist advice about the protection needed for your child. Ideally, find out before booking so that you can use this information to make a final decision on your destination. Otherwise, you need to attend your GP surgery or a travel clinic at least two months before you travel to allow time for a course of immunisations if they are required.

MORE **ABOUT** | mmr vaccination

There have been concerns amongst parents about possible complications associated with the measles, mumps and rubella vaccine, in particular autism (see page 378) and inflammatory bowel disease. These links were suggested in a paper published in 1998, which looked at only 12 children with autism and inflammatory bowel disease. Following this publication, the uptake of the MMR vaccine fell; some parents chose single vaccines for their children; others chose not to vaccinate them at all. The single vaccines were mainly available privately and actually had been studied (and used) far less than the triple vaccine. The incidence of measles rose, which is very worrying in the light of the serious and potentially life threatening complications it can cause.

It is understandable that as a parent you may have concerns. However, it is worth remembering that the MMR vaccine has been given to millions of children around the world. Also, studies of very large numbers of children have shown no evidence whatsoever of the links suggested by Dr Wakefield in 1998. The triple vaccine is recommended by most experts, who believe that the protection it offers against three potentially serious and, in some cases, life-threatening illnesses is of major benefit to children.

When your baby is unwell

It can be a worrying when your baby is ill, particularly if she is unable to explain what it wrong. Familiarising yourself with the signs of common childhood illnesses and the simple measures needed to relieve the symptoms they cause will give you confidence to care for your baby when she is unwell and to know when medical help is needed.

Fevers

The normal body temperature in childhood is 36.5°C to 37.8°C. Above this, a temperature is considered to be raised.

A raised temperature or fever is a sign that the immune system is working to get rid of an infection. However, high temperatures need treating as they cause children to feel unwell and can be associated with febrile convulsions (see page 353).

Measuring body temperature

There are two main types of thermometer recommended for children. The digital thermometer can be placed in the mouth (better for toddlers and older children) or in the armpit (better for babies); sensor thermometers are used in the ear but are inappropriate for children who have a known ear infection or who have earache.

Treating a fever

Fevers are often associated with shivering, headaches and dehydration. They are common during childhood and usually short-lived. If your baby has a fever she may be flushed and will feel hot to the touch. Check her temperature: then,

- Make sure she drinks plenty of cold drinks
- Use a tepid, not cold, sponge to cool her down
- Don't use too many blankets or clothes; although your baby may be shivering, too many covers and clothes will only increase her body temperature and make her feel worse
- Don't overheat the room. Be guided by whether you feel comfortable in normal indoor clothing
- Give a fever-reducing medication (see box).

After you have followed these measures for around half an hour, retake your baby's temperature. If it is persistently raised for more than 24 hours or if you are worried about any of your baby's symptoms, seek medical advice straightaway.

Giving medicines

Most parents will be called upon to give medication at some time so it is important to know how to give the various types correctly in order to cause the minimum of distress to your baby as well as ensure the medication's efficacy. Babies generally are not at their most amenable when on the receiving end of medicine, in which case time and patience are also needed. It is often easier to give medicines with a helper who can help hold the baby.

Oral medicines

These can be given with a syringe or on a spoon. Prop your baby up or have her sit so that her head is raised higher than her body. Have a favourite

---

MORE **ABOUT**   children's medications

To treat fever and pain in children, doctors will usually prescribe children's preparations of paracetamol and ibuprofen (which can be bought over the counter). As with all medication, it is vital to read the label carefully and stick to the recommended dosages. Children under the age of 12 should not be given drugs containing aspirin as there is a small but significant risk of Reye's syndrome developing, a serious condition which affects the brain and liver.

drink ready for afterwards – but never mix the medicine in with a drink as you won't know whether she has had the full dose. If it fits in with instructions, it is a good idea to give oral medicines before a feed when the baby is hungry.

Ear drops

Sit or lay your baby next to you with her head resting on its side on your knee. Pull her ear upwards and back slightly to straighten the ear canal and allow the drops to fall straight in. Keep her head on its side for 30 seconds or so to prevent the drops from trickling out again.

Eye drops

Lay your baby across your knee on her back and support her head in the crook of your arm. The bottom eyelid should be pulled down gently so that the drops can fall as they should

HEALTH**FIRST**	seeking medical advice

You know your child better than anyone. So if you are worried, this is reason enough to seek medical advice. Ask yourself: does your baby seem her usual self? Does she smile at you? Is she responsive? These are all indicators of how well she is. However, you should see the doctor if your baby:

- *Seems more sleepy than normal and does not have her usual times when she is alert and active*
- *Seems more floppy than she usually does*
- *Is crying more than usual*
- *Has a cry that sounds different from her usual cry*
- *Is eating or drinking less than usual*
- *Is passing less urine than usual*
- *Is vomiting*
- *Is passing blood in her stools*
- *Has a high temperature that remains high (over 39°C) despite measures to bring it down (see page 339) or persists for more than 24 hours*
- *Has a severe or persistent cough or one that brings up phlegm when she coughs (a productive cough)*
- *Seems to be having problems with her breathing*
- *Has one or more purplish-red spots (For more about meningitis and septicaemia, see pages 348–9.)*

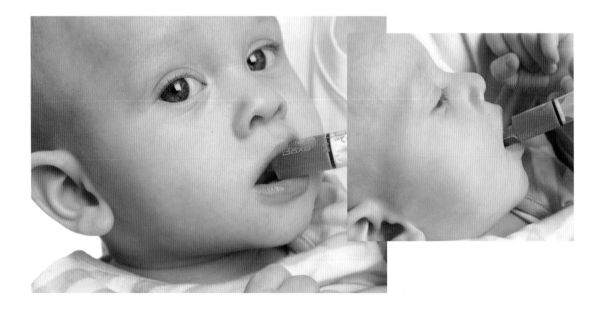

between the eyeball and the lower lid. You will probably need a helper so that you can hold your baby still in the correct position and open up the eye or wrap her up in a blanket to keep her arms out of the way.

Cuts and grazes

The aim is to stop any bleeding and prevent infection from entering the wound. Ideally you should wear disposable gloves when you are cleaning the wound – if these are not available ensure you wash your hands thoroughly before you start.

Rinse the wound under cold running water to get rid of any dirt. Then clean it with wipes or swabs, using a new one every time you wipe across the area. Start with the wound itself and then work on the skin around so that you do not introduce baceria from the surrounding skin into the wound. Use a piece of clean gauze to dry the area. Apply a plaster to small wounds or a dressing kept in place by tape or a bandage to larger wounds.

Bruises

Caused when small blood vessels are damaged and allow blood to leak out into the surrounding tissues, bruises are treated by controlling any swelling and relieving discomfort following the injury.

Bruising may develop quickly in which case it is worth applying a cold compress which will help to reduce any swelling. Make the compress by soaking a flannel or other cloth in cold water then wringing it out. Hold the compress firmly over the area for five to ten minutes. Sometimes bruises appear gradually over a period of days if the blood leaks out of the blood vessels slowly.

Dog bites

Wash the bite carefully with soap and water. Pat it dry with clean swabs. Cover the bite with a sterile dressing or a plaster.

MORE **ABOUT** | febrile convulsions

Relatively common in childhood, fits can occur when body temperature rises rapidly. Around three in 100 children are affected between the age of six months and five years. Febrile convulsions can run in families. The main features are stiffening and then jerking of the body.

If your baby has these symptoms, you should:

- ◆ *Lay her on her side, ideally with her head at a lower level than the rest of her body*
- ◆ *Not try to hold her still but let the fit take its course*
- ◆ *Call 000 if the fit continues for more than 5 minutes. Otherwise, you should seek urgent medical advice once the fit has stopped. The doctor will check your child over and look for the underlying cause of the raised temperature. This assessment may include blood and urine tests as well as an examination of the ears, throat and chest.*

In most cases, febrile convulsions are caused by a viral illness that requires no treatment other than those recommended for bringing down a fever (see page 339). However, sometimes the cause is a bacterial infection that needs to be treated with antibiotics.

Your doctor will give you advice on dealing with a fever and with the symptoms of a fit should they occur again. (Up to 40 per cent of children affected will have another fit.) Some children have prolonged febrile convulsions and medication may be prescribed to treat these when they arise.

The problem generally settles as the child gets older. However, the few children who have prolonged, more severe fits and convulsions that occur more than once during the same illness may be more likely to develop epilepsy.

See your doctor as antibiotics or a tetanus booster may be needed.

If the area is bleeding, apply firm pressure with a clean cloth or sterile dressing and raise the limb. If the wound is deep or large or the bleeding continues take the child to your local casualty department immediately.

Cat scratches

These should be washed carefully and disinfectant applied.

Sunburn

If your child does become sunburned in spite of your best efforts (see page 322), you should dab cold water onto the area using a towel. You can then apply calamine or other soothing creams.

If a large area is affected or the area is blistered you should seek medical advice.

Your child may be dehydrated if she has been out in the sun, so it is important to make sure she drinks cool fluids.

Stings

The aims are to remove the sting if possible, relieve pain, and control swelling. Often it is possible to remove the sting by scraping across the area with a credit card. An icepack, bag of frozen peas wrapped in a towel or a wrapped bag of ice will help to relieve any discomfort and swelling.

Splinters

You may be able to remove the splinter if it is protruding from the skin, but if it is embedded and there is no end to get hold of, you should seek medical attention. Poking around will only cause pain and may cause the splinter to become more deeply embedded.

MORE **ABOUT** | anaphylactic shock

This is a severe allergic reaction following an insect sting or in response to eating a particular food, such as nuts. Such reactions are fortunately relatively uncommon, but should they occur, urgent action is required as they may be life threatening. The symptoms of these severe reactions may include: breathing difficulties and wheeziness; swelling of the face, neck and around the eyes; and redness of the skin. The child may become unconscious (see pages 41–3 for emergency first aid). If you think your child may be having an anaphylactic reaction you should call 000. In the meantime, sit her up to help her *breathing. Talk to her reassuringly to calm her as much as possible.*

Children known to have these severe reactions are given medication to be administered as necessary. A special pen device is used to deliver the drug adrenaline into the body. If your child has these reactions you must be taught how to administer the drug and make sure anyone else who cares for your child knows about the condition and how to deliver the medication.

First run cold water over the area to remove any dirt. If the end of the splinter is sticking out of the skin, get hold of it with a pair of tweezers and pull it out firmly but gently in the same direction as it entered the skin. The ends of the tweezers should be sterilised by holding them in the flame of a match for a second. Let the tweezers cool down before removing the splinter. You should wear disposable gloves for the procedure if possible, to reduce the risk of introducing infection into the wound.

Foreign objects

Young children are curious by nature and if they get hold of small objects they are likely to ingest them or put them in their ears or up their noses.

If your baby swallows an object, it is worth seeking medical advice on the right course of action. In many cases it is appropriate to let nature take its course and allow the object to be passed in the stool. In other cases, however, X-rays may be needed to monitor the progress of the object through the gut or a treatment may be needed to remove the object.

If your baby pokes something into her ear, look in her ear to check whether the object is visible and tilt her head on one side to see whether it falls out. If it remains lodged, seek medical attention. You should not try to remove it yourself, as it is very easy to damage the delicate structures inside the ear and to push the object further into the ear.

As well as picking their noses, many babies like to stick things up there. If an object does become lodged in your baby's nostril, you should seek medical help so that it can be removed.

If a drug is prescribed for your child it is important that you know the following. Your doctor or pharmacist will be happy to advise you.

- *What is the drug for?*
- *How much should be given and how often?*
- *When should it be taken, e.g. before or after meals?*
- *What are the possible side effects?*

If your child has any long-term illnesses or is taking any other medicines, make sure the prescriber is aware.

When you come to give and store medicines, always

- *Look at the label carefully – check the name of the drug, the dosage and the use-by date*
- *Measure the medication out carefully as directed by your doctor*
- *Antibiotics are usually prescribed for a certain number of days and these courses of treatment must be completed.*
- *Keep them in a cool, dry place out of sunlight unless advised to keep them refrigerated.*

YOUR FIRST-AID BOX

You can buy a ready-made kit and add to it, or start your own. Make sure the container fastens securely and remember some of your medical supplies will need to be locked away safely. Basic contents for your child first-aid kit are:

- Thermometer
- Paracetamol or other painkiller for children
- Calamine for itching
- Ointment for insect bites
- Antibacterial cream
- Scissors
- Plasters and bandages, dressings and a compress
- Adhesive tape
- Sterile gauze
- Syringe and spoon for giving medicine to children

Childhood illnesses

Most of the illnesses described below are common conditions of childhood. Some, such as meningitis and epiglottitis, are fortunately uncommon, but nevertheless need to be discussed so that you are aware of the all-important signs that mean urgent medical attention is required.

Colds

Viral infections causing colds and snuffles are very common in early childhood. Many viruses are known to cause these upper respiratory infections. A toddler becomes vulnerable to picking them up when she starts to come into contact with infections that her immune system has not encountered before. This often happens when she goes to childcare. Cold viruses are often passed on in the coughs and sneezes of those affected. They may also be transmitted when a child wipes her hand across her nose and then touches another child. Colds are not caused by going out without a coat or with wet hair.

Symptoms

A runny or blocked nose, sneezing and sometimes a raised temperature. Other symptoms may include a

sore throat, a cough that is often worse at night, poor feeding, lethargy and tiredness.

Children with colds may go on to develop other infective illnesses, such as chest infections and ear infections. These may result from so-called secondary bacterial infections. Even a simple cold may be associated with a high temperature in children and this may in turn go on to cause a febrile convulsion (see page 341).

Colds usually last for a week or so.

Treatment

You need to relieve the symptoms and keep your child comfortable, which will mean ensuring an adequate fluid intake and possibly giving medication to bring down a high fever (see page 339). However, you should see the doctor if she:

- Has a very high temperature that cannot be brought down by the measures described
- Is very lethargic
- Is not eating or drinking
- Has a persistent cough or is bringing up sputum
- Is having breathing difficulties or is wheezy
- Is pulling on her ear.

Of course, you should seek medical attention if you have any other concerns.

Ear infections

Acute infections of the middle ear (otitis media) are common and can be caused by both bacterial and viral infections. Many children have recurrent episodes because, in children, the Eustachian tube that connects the outer ear to the middle ear is short and positioned horizontally rather than at an angle. This means that the secretions that are present in colds cannot drain away easily and infections are prone to develop.

Symptoms

Cold-type symptoms (including a runny nose, snuffles and a cough) and maybe a fever to begin with. Your baby may pull on her ear, which will usually be painful. She may be off her food. Young children may not be able to describe ear pain and will just be generally miserable.

If the eardrum becomes very inflamed, it may perforate (pressure causes a hole to develop), allowing fluid to drain to the outside. The perforation should eventually heal.

Recurrent episodes of otitis media can cause a chronic condition known as glue ear (see box) to develop. Other complications such as meningitis (inflammation of the layers that cover the brain and spinal cord) and mastoiditis (inflammation of one of the bones of the skull) are now uncommon.

MORE **ABOUT** | glue ear

Recurrent episodes of acute otitis media may go on to cause a condition known as chronic otitis media, or glue ear, so-called because of the thick, sticky fluid that builds up in the middle ear. This can cause hearing impairment at a time when good hearing is needed for speech development and other aspects of learning.

Often glue ear will clear up without any treatment. However, if hearing loss is persistent and may be interfering with learning, insertion of grommets may be recommended, possibly with removal of the adenoids. In this operation, tiny tubes (grommets) are inserted in the eardrum to let the fluid drain out of the middle ear and then afterwards to allow air to circulate in the middle ear so that fluid doesn't build up again.

Diagnosis and treatment

The doctor will examine your baby's ears with an auroscope (viewing instrument) to look for the redness and swelling of the eardrum that is characteristic of the condition.

Medication will be recommended for the pain and also to bring down the fever. Antibiotics may also be prescribed for the infection. In most cases the condition clears without specific treatment.

Bronchiolitis

An inflammation of the small airways in the lungs (the bronchioles), bronchiolitis is caused by a virus, in most cases the respiratory syncytial virus. The disease mainly occurs in the first year of life and in most cases is mild. However, it may cause breathing problems and require admission to hospital.

Symptoms

Cold symptoms usually develop first and these may be followed 2–3 days later by a dry cough. The baby may be short of breath and wheezy. Sometimes, feeding becomes a problem due to the shortness of breath. If your baby develops breathing difficulties, seek medical advice.

Diagnosis and treatment

The doctor will examine your baby by listening to her chest and will probably take a sample of the nasal secretions with a swab to look for evidence of the virus. A chest X-ray may also be arranged.

Babies with mild symptoms usually can be cared for by their parents at home. Care will include medication, such as paracetamol to bring down the temperature, and fluids. Humidifying the air with a bowl of water placed next to a radiator also may help relieve the symptoms.

Those infants that need hospital admission are often treated with oxygen and are sometimes given drugs that widen the airways and help breathing. These bronchodilator drugs are given through a nebuliser, which delivers the drug through a mask. They also may be given fluids through a drip or a tube passed through the nose and down into the stomach. Small babies in particular may need ventilation to help their breathing.

Most children affected will recover within a couple of weeks although some will have further bouts of coughing and wheezing.

Tonsillitis

Inflammation of the tonsils that lie on either side of the back of the mouth due to a bacterial or more commonly a viral infection.

Symptoms

A sore throat (older children will complain of this), lethargy, fever, headache, tummy ache and swollen glands.

Treatment

Antibiotics may be prescribed if a bacterial cause is suspected. Otherwise, treatment involves treating the fever and discomfort with the appropriate medication and fluids.

Tonsillitis usually settles within a few days. Removal of the tonsils may be recommended for those children who have frequent bouts of tonsillitis.

Croup

In this common condition, a viral infection affects the larynx (the voice box) and the trachea (windpipe). Croup may be caused by a number of viruses and is particularly common in autumn. It affects children between the ages of six months and six years, but it is those aged one to two years that are most likely to be affected.

Symptoms

The illness will often start with a fever and cold-type symptoms, such as a runny nose and snuffles. The main symptoms will then develop – a barking cough, noisy breathing (particularly when breathing in) and hoarseness. These symptoms tend to be worse during the night. The inflammation and swelling of the lining may, if severe, cause narrowing of the trachea and breathing difficulties.

Treatment

If the symptoms are mild, you may be happy to care for your baby at home, ensuring she has enough fluids and giving her medication for her fever. You may also find placing a bowl of water over a radiator and allowing her to breathe the air eases the symptoms. However, if you have any worries, seek

medical attention, particularly if your child continues to breathe noisily or draws her chest in when she breathes. Once in hospital, a child with croup may be given medicines by mouth and through a mask to reduce the inflammation and widen the airways. Oxygen may also be needed. Ventilation may be used when breathing difficulties are severe. However, with current treatments the prognosis is good and ventilation is rarely needed.

Influenza

More often known as flu, this viral illness is highly infectious, being easily passed on in the secretions of those affected.

Symptoms

The symptoms develop within a couple of days of contact with the influenza virus. They are similar to those of a cold but more severe.

The illness causes a fever that often goes above 38°C. An affected child has the shivers and may have a runny nose, dry cough and sometimes sneezing. She may complain of a sore throat and have swollen glands. She also will probably be off her food.

Flu may be complicated by a bacterial infection, often affecting the lungs or sometimes the ears. Babies and young children are particularly vulnerable to these so-called secondary infections.

Treatment

An affected child may need medication to bring down her temperature and relieve any related aches and pains. Remove most of your baby's clothing and try sponging her with tepid water if her temperature is very high. It is important to allow her to rest and to ensure that she has plenty of fluids to keep her well hydrated.

In most cases, the symptoms will settle over a few days. However, you should seek medical advice if you have a young baby with a fever. You also should see the doctor if the symptoms described persist for more than a few days and if the fever is very high (over 39°C). Medical advice is also needed if your baby has breathing difficulties or wheezing, earache

Around one in 10 children snore. A few of these will find their normal breathing patterns disturbed as they sleep and will stop breathing for short periods. In most cases this is due to the presence of very enlarged tonsils and adenoids that are limiting the flow of air at the back of the nose and *throat. Children with OSA may be tired and out of sorts during the day as they are not getting a night of good quality sleep. However, others with the condition can be overactive. The treatment for OSA is surgery to remove the enlarged tonsils and adenoids.*

or discharge from the ear, a very sore throat, a persistent cough, or a cough that brings up phlegm (a productive cough). These are symptoms that suggest another illness, which may need specific treatment.

Lung infections

This term can cover a number of conditions, from bronchitis in which the upper airways of the lungs become inflamed to pneumonia in which the tissue deep within the lungs is affected.

Bronchitis can be caused by both bacterial and viral infections and children of any age can be affected. The infections are passed on in the coughs and sneezes of those with the illness.

Pneumonia is a more serious condition and the inflammation may have a variety of infective causes as well as some other causes including inhalation of chemicals. Pneumonia can occur at any age, but very young children and those with long-term illnesses are particularly at risk.

Symptoms

Cold-type symptoms will usually be a feature of bronchitis. Your baby also may have a fever and a cough, which may be worse during the night. Sometimes she may vomit after a bout of coughing, which may produce discoloured sputum. She also may be wheezing.

Children with pneumonia often will start with a cold and then become increasingly unwell. Those with infective pneumonia (the commonest type) will have a fever, as well as a cough, which may bring up

discoloured sputum. They may breathe rapidly and wheeze. The skin may be bluish, reflecting a lack of oxygen in the blood due to the breathing difficulties.

If your baby has a persistent or severe cough, or breathing difficulties, or there are any other worrying signs like a high fever (over 39°C), seek medical attention. Infections affecting the upper airways may spread down into the tissue of the lungs. Pneumonia can be a serious condition and potentially life threatening in some cases.

Diagnosis and treatment

Lung infections are usually diagnosed through listening to the chest through a stethoscope. Sometimes, a chest X-ray is arranged to help make the diagnosis. Antibiotics may be given, intravenously if a child is very unwell. At home, you may need to give your baby medication to bring her temperature down and soothe her cough, as well as ensuring she drinks enough fluids.

Pneumonia will probably need hospital treatment, which may include chest physiotherapy to help clear the infective secretions from the lungs.

If your baby has bronchitis, the fever will usually settle over a few days, but the cough may persist for a couple of weeks. Pneumonia is a more serious condition, but with the appropriate treatment it should start to settle within a few days. Children with impaired immunity, such as those receiving chemotherapy, will be more likely to have problems recovering from pneumonia and will be more likely to go on to have complications. Both bronchitis and pneumonia can recur.

Whooping cough

This is a form of bronchitis (see *Lung infections*, page 347) caused by the bacterium Bordetella pertussis. The infection of the airways may go on to affect the tissue of the lungs (pneumonia). Fits can also occur in some cases. Although most children make a good recovery, whooping cough can be lifethreatening in some cases, particularly to infants and small children.

The whooping cough immunisation does not give 100 per cent protection, but it does reduce the risk and also make the disease less severe if an immunised child does get the disease.

Symptoms

The illness starts with a week of cold-type symptoms before children develop the characteristic cough, which occurs in bouts with whooping noises on breathing in at the end. The episodes of coughing tend to be particularly bad during the night.

The child's face may go red during a bout of coughing and there may be vomiting and sometimes nose bleeds. The force of the coughing may cause little blood vessels in the conjunctiva (the whites of the eyes) to burst so that red spots appear. Small children may stop breathing for short periods (known as apnoeic episodes) and in such children the whoop may not be present.

Bouts of coughing can go on for up to six weeks and coughing may continue for some months.

Treatment

Many children can be cared for at home, but children who become very unwell with severe coughing bouts, and babies who have apnoeic episodes, will need to be admitted to hospital for treatment and monitoring.

Swabs may be taken from the nose to be tested for the presence of the bacteria.

The antibiotic erythromycin may help reduce the severity of the symptoms if given early on in the disease. Those who come into contact with an affected child should therefore be given erythromycin.

Meningitis

This condition involves inflammation of the membranes that surround the brain and spinal cord (the meninges).

It may have a number of causes, the commonest being viral and bacterial infections. Viral meningitis tends to be milder. In bacterial meningitis, the symptoms are more severe and come on rapidly. In addition, the bacterial infection can be carried in the bloodstream – this is called septicaemia.

Symptoms

Affected babies may exhibit
- Fever
- Vomiting
- Being less alert than usual
- Poor feeding
- Being floppy and drowsy
- Fits and loss of consciousness.

If able to vocalise their symptoms, older children may complain of a headache, neck stiffness and an aversion to light. They will also be lethargic.

If bacterial septicaemia develops, a rash may develop, first as tiny purplish spots, which join to form purplish-red patches (see box page 349).

If you suspect meningitis for any reason or if there is even one suspicious spot, seek urgent medical attention.

Children with viral meningitis tend to recover over a few days. However, meningitis is a potentially life-threatening condition requiring urgent treatment. Some children make a full recovery while others will sustain long-term problems, such as hearing loss or epilepsy.

Diagnosis

The doctor will probably carry out a lumbar puncture in which fluid is removed from the space between the meninges surrounding the spinal cord. Blood tests and possibly a throat swab will also be taken to help identify a bacterial infection.

The signs of meningitis can be vague and difficult to identify in babies so it important to be on the alert for any signs that your child may be unwell. (See the symptoms of meningitis above.) The rash can develop late on in the disease and so do not be reassured if it is not present.

To check a rash, press a glass firmly over any pin-prick red spots or large purple marks to see if they fade or turn white under pressure. If the spots and rash are still visible through the glass, seek urgent medical attention.

However, whatever the appearance of a rash, you should seek advice immediately if you have any concerns. No one will blame you for being cautious if there is any chance at all that your child has meningitis.

Treatment

Bacterial meningitis requires immediate treatment with intravenous antibiotics. Intravenous fluids and other supportive measures may be needed while the child is very unwell.

Children with viral meningitis are likely to need only simple measures to relieve their symptoms.

Epiglottitis

This is a very serious condition in which the epiglottis, the flap of tissue that hangs down at the back of the tongue, becomes inflamed and swollen due to infection with the H. influenzae type b bacterium. Epiglottitis has become much less common since the introduction of the Hib vaccine, which is given as part of the childhood immunisation program (see page 337).

The swelling of the epiglottitis and the surrounding tissues limits the flow of air into the trachea and down into the lungs. The infection also passes into the bloodstream (this is called septicaemia), causing the affected child to be very unwell.

Children between the ages of one and six years are particularly at risk.

Symptoms

Your baby will have a high temperature and feel unwell. The throat is very painful, making it impossible for her to swallow so that she drools. Her breathing may be noisy and very soon she will have great difficulty breathing. She will keep her mouth open in an effort to breathe and will sit very still. If your baby has features of epiglottitis she must receive urgent medical attention.

Treatment

If a doctor suspects the diagnosis, he will not examine your baby's throat, but will start treatment immediately. This involves putting a tube through the mouth and down into the airway under a general anaesthetic. Once this procedure called intubation has been completed, intravenous antibiotics will be given.

Once the treatment has been started, affected children tend to recover fully within a few days. Close contacts are given an oral antibiotic to prevent them from getting the condition.

Conjunctivitis and sticky eyes

Inflammation of the conjunctiva (the tissue that covers the eyeball and lines the eyelid) is common, particularly in the first week or two after birth.

Conjunctivitis may have a number of causes, including bacterial infections. However, it often settles without medication.

Symptoms

There will be redness of the conjunctiva and this may be accompanied by stickiness.

Treatment

The stickiness will often clear by wiping the eyes with cotton wool and water. (Use a fresh piece of cotton wool for each eye.)

If redness and stickiness persist despite simple cleaning measures, medical advice should be sought. A doctor may take a swab of the discharge for testing before prescribing antibiotic treatment in the form of drops or ointment.

Infective conjunctivitis is easily passed on to others, so children who attend childcare may be asked to stay at home until the stickiness clears up. In addition, a child with conjunctivitis should not share her towel as this is a possible means of transmission.

Gastroenteritis and food poisoning

Stomach upsets are common in all age groups, but babies and young children are particularly at risk from

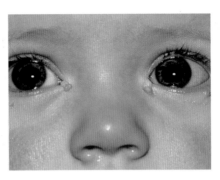

the effects as they can quickly become dehydrated. Gastroenteritis may result from a variety of bacteria and viruses, some of which are transmitted as a result of poor hygiene techniques when handling food (see pages 231 and 309–10).

The commonest cause of infective gastroenteritis in children is the rotavirus infection. It is particularly common in the winter. Gastroenteritis is much less often the result of bacterial infections.

Symptoms

There will be diarrhoea and often vomiting. Your baby may have a fever and be listless. There may also be signs of dehydration (see box).

There may be blood in the stools – this is usually suggestive of a bacterial infection. An affected child also may complain of abdominal pain. Some bacterial infections can cause very high fevers, which may be associated with febrile convulsions (see page 341).

Treatment

Medication may be given to bring down the fever, but the key focus of treatment is to ensure an adequate fluid intake. Oral rehydration solutions will be recommended by your doctor or pharmacist. These fluids should be continued until the symptoms of diarrhoea and vomiting settle, when you can return to your baby's normal milk and food. There is no need to omit milk from the diet or to give it in a watered-down form.

You should contact your doctor if:
- The vomiting or diarrhoea persist for more than 24 hours
- Your baby has any signs of dehydration
- There is blood in the stool
- Your baby has a very high fever.

Your baby may need hospital admission for intravenous fluids. Stool samples may be collected and sent to the laboratory for analysis. Antibiotics

---

RECOGNISING DEHYDRATION

Young children in particular can easily become dehydrated when they are unwell. The signs of dehydration are:
- Passing urine less than usual
- Sunken eyes
- Dry skin
- Lining of the mouth becomes dry
- Lethargy
- Breathing more rapidly than usual
- Less alert than usual and may be drowsy

may be prescribed if a bacterial cause is identified. Drugs are not given to prevent the diarrhoea of gastroenteritis as this may prolong the illness.

Don't wait for the signs of dehydration. If your baby has a tummy upset ensure she has plenty of fluids straightaway.

Urinary tract infections

Relatively common in childhood, urinary tract infections may affect the bladder (cystitis) or the kidneys (pyelonephritis); it is very important that infections are investigated and treated appropriately. Some affected children have an underlying problem in the urinary tract that makes them more prone to get infections (see *Vesicoureteric reflux,* below). It is also crucial that kidney infections are cleared up as soon as possible to prevent them from causing damage to the kidney tissue.

Symptoms

In cystitis, the symptoms tend to be milder with a slightly elevated or normal temperature. Pyelonephritis causes children to be more unwell with a high fever.

In general, the symptoms tend to vary according to the age of the child. Babies will not be able to describe specific symptoms and so parents will tend to find they are generally unwell, with a fever and possibly a tummy ache. The fever, if high (over 39°C), may be associated with febrile convulsions (see page 341). Affected babies also may vomit and have diarrhoea, as well as problems with feeding and will need careful watching as it is very easy for young children to become dehydrated (see page 350). Babies also may be jaundiced in which there is yellowing of the skin and whites of the eyes.

Older children will have the non-specific symptoms of an

COLLECTING URINE SAMPLES

With a young child, the main methods include catching a specimen in a clean pot when the nappy is taken off or using a "clean-catch" plastic bag that is attached around the area with adhesive tape until the child passes urine. The area should first be cleaned carefully to remove as many contaminants as possible. If a young child is very ill, the doctor may withdraw urine from the bladder into a syringe using a needle inserted through the skin of the lower abdomen.

Older children can be asked to give a midstream sample of urine.

MORE **ABOUT** | vesicoureteric reflux (vur)

VUR results from an abnormality in the development of the urinary tract. Usually, the ureters (the tubes that lead from the kidneys to the bladder) meet the bladder at a particular angle. This positioning acts as a valve, preventing backflow of urine up the ureters. However, in vesicoureteric reflux this angle is absent and the ureters go straight into the bladder. The condition often runs in families. It may be very mild with urine flowing up into the lower part of the ureters when the bladder contracts to expel urine, or it may be severe and cause urine to flow all the way back into the kidneys, even when the bladder is not contracting. In such cases, problems may develop when cystitis occurs and infected urine enters the kidney and causes damage. This may in severe cases lead to chronic kidney disease and high blood pressure.

VUR will usually decrease with age, but it is important that the kidneys are protected from infections in the meantime.

Children with a proven urinary tract infection need further investigations to look for evidence of reflux. These may include an ultrasound scan and special X-rays. Various measures are needed for children with VUR to keep the risk of infection as low as possible. Long-term antibiotics may be recommended in some cases to prevent infections from developing.

infective illness – fever, lethargy, a poor appetite, vomiting and diarrhoea – but they also may describe more specific symptoms, such as passing urine more frequently than usual, pain on passing urine, abdominal pain, and pain in the small of the back. Older children also may start to wet the bed again after a period of being dry at night.

Diagnosis and treatment

A urinary tract infection requires prompt treatment with antibiotics, first with an antibiotic that covers the commonest infective causes of urinary tract infections in childhood. Once the specific bacterium has been identified by testing the urine, the antibiotic may need to be changed.

A urine sample istaken – this can be tested on the spot for evidence of an infection, but it is also sent for laboratory testing so that the specific bacterial cause can be identified.

Constipation

Babies vary in their frequency of passing stools; some pass motions every day; others, including breastfed infants, may not pass a motion for a few days. If, however, your baby passes hard stools infrequently and this is accompanied by discomfort or pain, she is constipated.

Short-lived bouts of constipation may follow an infective illness such as a cold. Sometimes if a child has a small tear in the skin near the anus caused by passing a large or hard stool, she will tend to avoid passing motions as this can cause further pain. In these cases, her normal bowel habits are likely to be resumed in a few days when the tear has healed. Occasionally, however, constipation may become a persistent problem and there are a variety of possible causes for this, including worries to do with potty training or problems in the home or at childcare.

In a few cases there will be an underlying medical condition, such as an underactive thyroid gland or a muscle deficiency at the lower end of the child's bowel.

Symptoms

A constipated child may experience pain when trying to pass a stool. She also may complain of tummy pain prior to opening her bowels. Within a few days, the rectum can become overfull so that the wall is stretched. Eventually, the child may lose the urge to pass motions and may pass stools involuntarily so that she soils herself.

Diagnosis and treatment

If your baby appears to be constipated, seek medical advice promptly so that the problem can be addressed early on. The doctor may examine your baby's abdomen before recommending a course of action to restore normal bowel habits.

For mild constipation the simple measures of increasing fluids and fibre in the diet may be recommended. Sometimes a laxative that draws fluid into the bowel and softens the stool may be prescribed or a mild stimulant laxative that increases the contractions of the bowel wall, so helping to move its contents along.

More severe constipation will require a more intensive treatment regimen, which may include stool softening laxatives, stimulant laxatives, and special fluids to increase the water content of the stools. Laxatives may be continued for some time

MORE **ABOUT**

shingles

This tends to affect adults but can also occur in children. The virus that causes chickenpox may lie dormant in nerve cells and then be reactivated to cause a group of blisters that always appears in one particular area, often on the back.

The rash may be preceded by tingling and discomfort in the affected area. Early treatment with antiviral drugs should help reduce the severity of the symptoms and shorten the duration of the illness.

until a regular pattern of defecation is achieved and maintained. Dietary advice will also be given with the aim of avoiding further episodes of constipation. This will include following the five-a-day regimen of fruit and vegetables and increasing the amount of fluids taken.

In mild cases, constipation tends to settle over a few days or a week or two. Once constipation is long-standing and the rectum has been distended for some time, it is likely to take a while for the rectum to return to its usual size and for the urge to pass motions to return. Chronic constipation and soiling can be very upsetting for children who will need plenty of encouragement and support while the problem is treated.

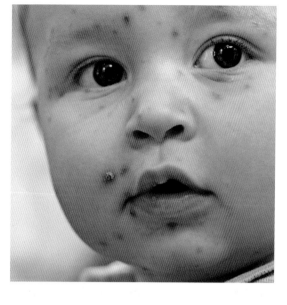

Chickenpox

In this common illness, the varicella zoster virus spreads around the body to cause a characteristic rash.

Symptoms

The red spots, which soon develop into small blisters, tend to appear first on the head and trunk before spreading out to the arms and legs. A mild fever is also present. The spots take up to five days to appear and then over the next few days crust over. Sometimes there are only a few spots.

For most babies, the main problem is itchiness of the spots. Spots in the mouth may cause sore areas. However, in a few cases, complications may develop, such as a bacterial infection of the spots. Other uncommon complications include encephalitis (inflammation of the brain tissue).

Diagnosis and treatment

The diagnosis is usually clear from the appearance of the rash. In most cases, treatment consists of calamine and other anti-itching creams as well as medication to treat the fever. Those with impaired immunity are particularly at risk from chickenpox and they will usually be given an intravenous

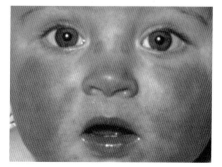

antiviral drug. This drug is also given when the symptoms of the disease are severe, which tends to be the case in young babies, adolescents and adults with the condition. Small babies and those with impaired immunity should see the doctor, as should those children who seem unwell.

Most children with chickenpox will be over the worst within 10-14 days. Infection with the virus gives protection against further attacks of chickenpox, but the virus can collect in nerve cells in an area of the body like the back and cause episodes of shingles (see box, page 352).

The illness is no longer contagious when all the lesions have crusted over.

Fifth disease

Caused by a type of parvovirus, this condition can occur at any time of the year, but is particularly common in the spring. The virus is often passed in the secretions of those affected. The illness can occur at any age.

Symptoms

The illness begins with a fever and headache. Redness of the cheeks (its other name is "slapped cheek disease") develops a week or so later. There may be a very slight fever or none at all. A rash then appears on the trunk, arms and thighs, which may be itchy, and persists for up to six weeks.

Complications are rare in children, but may include joint pains and inflammation.

Treatment
No specific treatment is required as the symptoms are very mild.

Hand, foot and mouth disease
The main symptoms of this common viral illness are blisters in the mouth (including on the tongue) and on the hands and feet. These blisters are painful, but settle within a week or so. The illness can occur at any age, but children under the age of 10 years are most commonly affected. It is not the same condition as foot and mouth disease in cattle.

Symptoms
Affected children tend to start by feeling generally off colour, possibly with a fever, for a day or two. These features are followed by a sore throat and then small spots in the mouth. These spots soon develop into painful ulcers. Within a day or two spots develop on the hands and feet, as well as the legs and buttocks and other areas of the body in some cases. The spots look similar to those that occur in chickenpox, but are smaller in size. They tend to be sore rather than itchy as the spots are in chickenpox.

Serious complications are very rare – inflammation of the heart (myocarditis) or brain (encephalitis) occasionally can occur.

Treatment
Measures are recommended to relieve the symptoms – children's paracetamol and similar drugs may be given to bring down a fever and relieve the discomfort in the mouth. Cool drinks and foods can also help to ease the soreness as can ice lollies. It is important to keep encouraging your baby to drink even though she may find it uncomfortable for a few days.
The disease is infectious, particularly while the spots and ulcers are present. However, even after this, the

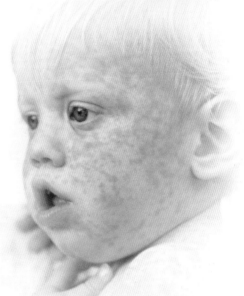

virus may be passed in the faeces and so good hygiene measures, in particular hand washing after going to the toilet and before eating, are very important to minimise the spread.

This tends to be a relatively mild illness with the blisters settling within a week or so. The biggest problem for children with the disease tends to be the sore mouth, which can cause discomfort when eating and swallowing.

Measles
Caused by a virus, this infectious disease of childhood has become less common thanks to the measles vaccination. However, it still occurs, and is currently on the rise due particularly to the fall in uptake of the MMR vaccine (see page 338).

Measles is a potentially very serious illness. It causes children to feel miserable and unwell, but can also cause life-threatening complications in a small but significant number of those affected – in about 1 in 5000 cases, there is inflammation of the brain tissue (encephalitis), a life-threatening complication. Other possible problems include diarrhoea and hepatitis (inflammation of the liver). Children with impaired immunity, such as those being treated for cancer, are particularly at risk.

Symptoms

The illness starts with a fever and cold-type symptoms, including snuffles, a cough and sometimes conjunctivitis.

After three days or so, the rash appears, first on the face, then behind the ears and then moving down the rest of the body. The rash begins as groups of spots, but after three days or so the spots join together to form a blotchy rash. Ear infections and pneumonia can develop.

Treatment

For most children with measles, bringing down the fever and ensuring adequate fluids are the principal measures. Antibiotics may be needed if an ear infection or pneumonia develops.

A child with measles is infectious from before the rash appears until day five of the rash.

Mumps

Mumps tends to be a mild illness during which children may have no particular symptoms, or they may have a fever lasting three days or so and the characteristic inflammation and swelling of the parotid glands that lie in front of the ears. Occasionally complications occur; there may be problems with hearing after mumps, but this is usually on one side and temporary.

In a few children, the mumps virus causes meningitis (inflammation of the membranes covering the brain and spinal cord [see page 348]) and infection of the brain itself (encephalitis). Inflammation of the testes may occur, but this tends to affect teenage boys and adults rather than younger children. The inflammation usually only occurs on one side and fertility problems following this are rare. Inflammation of the joints (arthritis) may also occur.

The incidence of this viral illness fell with the use of the MMR vaccination. However, more unimmunised children have once again been affected by mumps in the wake of the fall in uptake of the triple vaccine (see page 338). Mumps tends to occur in winter and spring. It is spread through the secretions of those affected.

Symptoms

Swelling of the glands beneath the ears may begin on one side, but in most cases the other side will also be swollen within a few days. The swollen glands may be painful and there may be discomfort on swallowing and earache. The swelling lasts for 5-10 days. The disease is infectious for a week after the swelling of the parotid glands develops.

Treatment

If swallowing is painful, feed your child plenty of fluids and soft foods. A children's pain medication can help relieve pain and bring down any fever. You should notify your doctor that your child has mumps but contact him or her urgently if your child becomes seriously ill, has a headache with a stiff neck, swollen testicles, abdominal pain or persistent earache.

Roseola infantum

This common viral illness causes a rash and a high fever. It is particularly common between the ages of six months and two years.

Symptoms

The following tend to develop first: a high fever, a dry cough, earache, and swollen glands in the neck. Some children will have mild diarrhoea. After a few days, a rash of tiny spots develops on the face and trunk.

Treatment

No specific measures are needed. A high fever may be associated with febrile convulsions, so it is worth taking measures to bring down your child's temperature (see page 339), ensure adequate fluids, and give medication for any discomfort. The condition settles on its own within a week or so.

Rubella

Also known as German measles, this viral illness is usually mild in those affected and may pass unnoticed. However, the major concern about rubella is the damage it can do to the unborn baby during pregnancy. The infection is passed in the secretions of those affected.

Symptoms

A rash of tiny pink spots develops on the face and trunk before moving down the body. This rash lasts for up to five days. There may be swelling of the lymph glands and a mild fever, but otherwise no particular signs of the illness. Inflammation of the joints (arthritis) and brain (encephalitis) may occur, but these are rare.

Treatment

No specific treatment is required other than to reduce any fever or discomfort using a child's medication.

Threadworms

This infestation is common in childhood and particularly in preschool children. The worms live in the gut and then during the night the females work their way down to the end of the bowel and lay their eggs in the area around the anus. The eggs are picked up on the fingers when scratching and then are passed on to others and ingested, starting the cycle over again.

Threadworms can be spread easily and strict hygiene measures are needed to eradicate them permanently.

Symptoms

The worms can cause intense itching around the anus and sometimes in the genital area. There may also be pain. However, in some children the worms cause no symptoms at all and may go unnoticed for some time. The tiny worms may be visible in the anal area.

Treatment

Nails should be cut short to prevent scratching and, if possible, children should not suck their thumb or bite their nails. Cotton gloves may help prevent itching, but some children will not wear them.

Frequent and thorough hand washing is crucial to getting rid of threadworms and also to preventing them from coming back. Underwear should be changed in the morning. More eggs may be laid during the night so it is important to wash the area

carefully. Towels should not be shared so that the worms are not passed on to other members of the family. They should also be washed frequently. The hygiene measures should be continued for six weeks, as this is how long threadworms live.

A number of different medications may be prescribed. These do not kill off the eggs so hygiene measures need to be continued for two weeks. Every member of the family should be treated.

Even with medication and hygiene measures, they may sometimes persist. If this is the case, the doctor will give advice on additional medication and further hygiene methods to help clear the problem, including frequent vacuuming and washing of nightwear and bedding.

Head lice

This is common in childhood when close contact in childcare centres and schools encourages the transmission of the head lice from one child to another.

Symptoms

The scalp may be intensely itchy. You may see lice on the scalp or the empty eggs on the hairs. These eggs are known as nits. They stick to the hair and so move away from the scalp as the hairs grow.

Treatment

Precise treatment recommendations vary as lice can become resistant to certain drugs. However, all involve the application of a lotion or hair rinse and often the use of a fine tooth comb to comb out the lice. If your child has a head lice infestation it is worth seeking advice from your surgery or local chemist on the best treatment to use.

As well as through close contact, head lice can be transmitted by brushes, combs, towels and clothes.

Impetigo

This common skin condition is caused by a bacterial infection and is passed on very easily. Impetigo is particularly common in early childhood and tends to develop in areas of skin that are already damaged, for example by eczema (see below).

Symptoms

Affected areas – common sites are the face and hands with additional patches soon developing on other areas of skin – become reddened and small blisters quickly develop. The contents of the blisters leak out leaving crusted areas, which are typically honey-coloured.

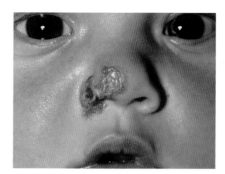

Diagnosis and treatment

The diagnosis is usually made from looking at the affected areas although swabs sometimes may be taken for analysis to identify the bacteria. Treatment is with antibiotics, sometimes in the form of ointments for mild cases, but usually as oral drugs. As the condition is highly contagious, children should be kept away from childcare until the areas have dried completely.

Eczema

Eczema is a chronic illness that may need specialist medical attention. It is a common condition in which there is reddening and itching of the skin. Fortunately, the symptoms usually can be relieved to a great extent by the measures described below and the condition tends to decrease in severity as affected children get older.

Up to one-fifth of children are affected by atopic eczema (eczema that is associated with allergies). The condition often begins during the first year of life. Often, other family members of affected children also have eczema or another allergic condition, such as asthma or hay fever, to which children with atopic eczema are at increased risk. Some affected children are found to have allergies to a particular food or a constituent in food.

Atopic eczema tends to improve with increasing age, with around half of affected children no longer having the condition by the time they reach their teenage years.

Symptoms

Reddening and itching of the skin, which can be intense and become distressing, causing those worst affected to have problems sleeping at night. A hot environment can make the itching worse. The areas children scratch will be weepy and form crusts. Repeated scratching may lead to thickening of the skin. The skin tends to be dry all over and needs frequent applications of moisturiser.

The areas of the body affected by the eczema rash tend to change as an affected child gets older. For infants, it tends to be found particularly on the face and neck, and sometimes the scalp, whereas older children tend to have patches at the creases of joints.

Sometimes patches of eczema will become infected when bacteria enter the damaged skin. Viral infections, such as herpes, also may cause skin

---

MORE **ABOUT** | seborrhoeic dermatitis

This form of skin inflammation tends to begin on the scalp and may then move to face and areas of the body where there are creases in the skin (behind the ears, the neck, the armpits, and the groin area extending out across the creases at the tops of the legs.) Seborrhoeic dermatitis affects young babies, but does not cause any itching or distress. Cradle cap is used to describe the thick yellow crusts that are present on the scalp; there is reddening of the skin in other areas of the body.

Various treatments are used, including special moisturisers and creams that combat bacterial and fungal infections (such infections may perpetuate the condition). The scales on the scalp may be removed with the help of special ointments that have a loosening effect when left on the scalp for a few hours.

infections in those with eczema. Some children find their condition worsens when they are stressed.

Treatment

A number of measures may be used to try to control the eczema. The nails should be kept short. and substances that can irritate the skin, like soap, must be avoided. Clothing made from man-made fibres should be avoided.

Emollients are used frequently to moisturise the skin. Soap substitutes also are recommended. Various ointments may be applied, including steroids, which should be used sparingly and according to the doctor's instructions. Oral drugs may be given, such as antihistamines to relieve itching and medication to treat bacterial and viral infections should they arise.

Sometimes, if the condition is severe, the affected areas are wrapped in bandages containing special pastes. This treatment aims to calm the inflammation and relieve the itching. Occasionally, eczema requires treatment in hospital.

SEEING THE DOCTOR

Short-term illness

Even when a child is not seriously ill it can be difficult to take on board all that the doctor says to you during your appointment. It is worth having a checklist of questions so you can make the most of the time you spend with the doctor. These may include:

- What is the diagnosis?
- How long is the illness likely to last?
- What is the prescribed treatment and what can I do to alleviate the symptoms?
- When shall I come back, e.g. if it doesn't settle in 48 hours?

A long-term illness

If you are seeing the doctor when your child has an acute illness such as a viral infection, the diagnosis and treatment will usually be easily understood. However, if your child has a chronic illness the explanation from the doctor may be more complex and more difficult to take in. In these circumstances it is a good idea to take a friend or relative with you to the hospital to help you to remember the information you are given.

It is also worth thinking about what is worrying you in particular and taking a list of questions to the appointment. It can be very frustrating to come away from a long-awaited appointment only to recall particular concerns that have not been addressed.

During your visit to the hospital it is also worth noting down the name of the doctor you have seen and any contact details. Ask what the follow-up arrangements will be and when your GP is likely to receive the information. You should receive a copy of any letters sent to your GP and you should request copies if you don't.

If you have had worrying news and need to discuss it further, there may be counsellors or nurse specialists available who will be able to give you support and additional information so ask what support is available. Importantly, ask your doctor to write down the name of the condition your child has. The specialist may also draw you a diagram to help you understand the condition.

Caring for your child in hospital

Few events are as terrifying to a parent as their child being diagnosed with a serious illness. Illness that is treated in your doctor's surgery may seem severe enough, but admitting your child to hospital signals a higher degree of concern on your doctor's part, and thus in your own level of fear and worry. Fortunately, the majority of hospitalised children are not critically ill but hospitalisation may be necessary because:

- Outpatient treatment has not been successful;
- The necessary treatment requires special equipment, personnel or supervision;
- There is a chance that your child could get worse and observation for such complications is best done in the medical setting;
- Your child could be cared for as an outpatient, but the effort required is far too great for a single pair of parents.

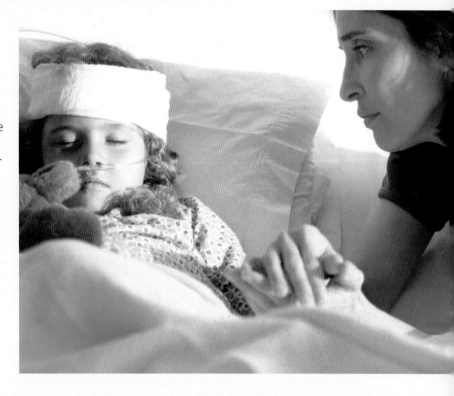

The most common reasons that young children are admitted to hospital are set out below. In many of these cases, discharge from the hospital is achieved in only two or three days.

Occasionally a more severe problem prompts admission to the hospital – accidents or trauma, surgical emergencies, cancer – and the length of admission will be much longer. But such conditions are far less common.

Regardless of the reason for your child's hospitalisation, you will be very worried and fearful of some real or imagined poor outcome. You will feel that you have little control over your child's illness and over what is happening to her in the hospital. Very likely, the hospital is a new and strange world for you. You are asked to trust nurses, aides, technicians and doctors you have never before met. And usually

REASONS FOR HOSPITALISATION

- Respiratory illnesses (such as moderate or severe cases of asthma, croup, bronchiolitis and pneumonia). In these cases, oxygen, intravenous medications, fluids and close observation may be needed.
- Dehydration from a stomach virus; intravenous fluids needed.
- Moderate or severe infections; intravenous antibiotics and observation are required.
- A convulsion, which is not rapiidly followed by complete recovery.

you have very little knowledge to judge if what they are recommending is correct and necessary.

Your child, too is likely to be feeling fearful upon entering the hospital. (She also may be feeling quite ill.) She lacks the security of familiar surroundings and separation from you for whatever reason (X-ray or another procedure) is also quite terrifying. She certainly will be aware of how anxious and apprehensive you are, and this can further upset her. Moreover, strange people keep examining and treating her, and some of what they do is scary and unpleasant. Just being examined may be a torture, plus there is also the pain of blood tests, intravenous insertion and other medical procedures. Even placing a mask over her face for oxygen or inhaled respiratory treatments may make her feel she is being smothered.

What you can do to help your child

Although you may feel powerless to help your child get well sooner, there is much important work for you to do. You are your child's tie to what is familiar and constant. Just by being there with her, you are providing tremendous support. If at all possible, a parent or other well-known adult should be with your child at all times, including during painful procedures, and be able to stay overnight. Your role is to comfort your child and reassure her that

she will soon get well. Here are some tips:

◆ Try not to show your child how worried you are. Obviously, your effectiveness as a soother and calmer will be quite limited when you are visibly upset.

◆ Hold her and try to distract and comfort her during painful procedures.

◆ Let the doctors and nurses do their jobs. Cooperate as much as you can.

◆ You know your child the best. If you have an idea on how to make her more comfortable, let the hospital staff know. Your suggestions will be very helpful, but remember that your doctor and nurses have had much more experience in dealing with sick children than most parents.

◆ Educate yourself about your child's illness and the plan of treatment. Ask questions of your doctors and nurses until you understand what is occurring. Have them "translate" any unfamiliar terms that you hear. It may be tempting to go on the internet to research your child's disease; however, it is usually best to avoid this (see page 66).

◆ Bring in some of the objects from home that may comfort your child: her blanket or teddy bear; her favourite book or DVD. If she is allowed to eat, also have her favourite foods from home on hand.

◆ If your child is well enough, keep her occupied with activities such as colouring,

simple games or puzzles, or read to her.

◆ As much as is possible, try to stick to your child's daily routines.

◆ Reassure her often that she will be well soon and can then go home.

◆ When discharged, give your toddler a chance to "come to grips" with her hospital experience. One way to accomplish this is to get a toy doctor kit and pretend she is the doctor and you or a teddy bear are the patient. Ask her how the patient feels about being sick. Another technique is to have her draw pictures of what it was like to be in the hospital. You also can read a book about going to the doctor or the hospital. Or you can tell her a story about a make-believe child who was sick enough to go the hospital and experienced trials and tribulations similar to what she did. Of course, end the story happily with the child getting all better and going home, where her parents loved her for ever and ever!

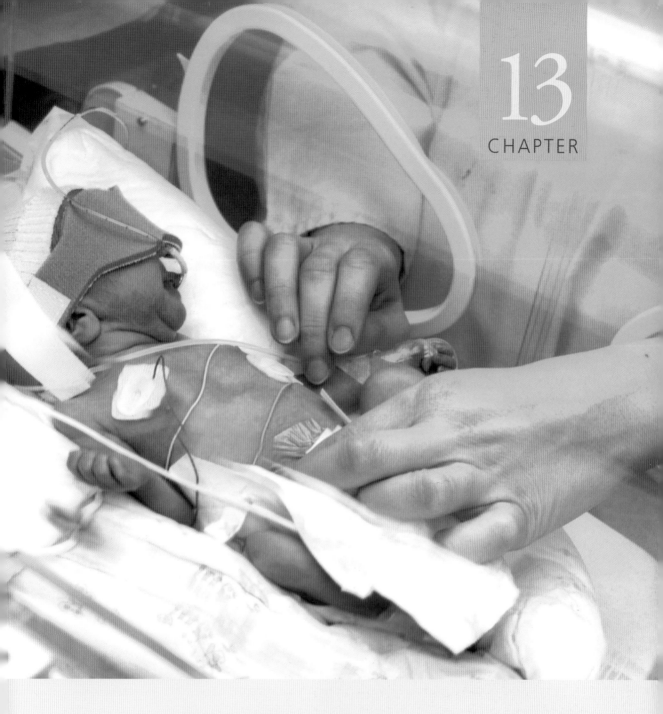

CARING FOR YOUR SPECIAL NEEDS BABY

Special challenges

Very few parents are prepared for anything but a perfect delivery and a perfect newborn. Perhaps this is so because we are a species of optimists; more likely though, we avoid considering all the possible things that can go wrong to save ourselves from perpetual worries. So if you do learn of a problem with your baby, it can be devastating. The shock of discovering that your baby may be in trouble, coupled with the intense emotionality that childbirth brings, can provoke a very strong reaction – even if the difficulty is not so serious.

Sometimes the method of delivery results in injuries or short-lived medical conditions. Rarely, a deformity or more serious problem may be present at birth. Of these, many don't require any special long-term care. However, there are other conditions that not only will affect your child his entire life but also how you parent him. For an explanation of common injuries and conditions, see pages 380-91.

In addition to the already exhausting tasks other parents face, as a parent of a special needs child, you also may have medications to give, equipment to use and monitor, extra visits to medical specialists, and frequent physical, occupational and speech therapy sessions to get to. You need to stay in touch with therapists, pester your doctor or local education authority to obtain the services your child needs, and continually research the latest therapies available. There also may be much physical work for you if your toddler is not mobile and requires carrying and lifting or if he continues to need you to meet his basic needs.

Internally, you will probably experience mixed emotions. You will certainly have frequent strong positive feelings about your child. But you may, if you are like most parents, have occasional moments when you resent him and his disability. It also would not be surprising if at times you felt any of the following: sadness, anger and guilt.

Sadness may surface when you think about the child your son could have been, had not his current disability appeared. Or it may arise when you reflect that you didn't get the life you wanted; you are prone to feel sorry for yourself once in a while.

When caring for him is difficult and frustrating, you may feel anger towards your child; perhaps you will find out that you hold within anger directed towards the world in general or with the God you believe in for burdening you with this undesirable fate. You may ask: "Why me? What did I do to deserve this?"

Then, right after considering such thoughts, you are further bothered by guilt. You tell yourself you must be a bad person to resent your child or the life his disability mandates. Your stress level varies but often it is high; you and your partner may fight about what to do next or how to raise your child.

Medical care

Look for physicians to care for your child who are kind, caring and familiar with his problem. Knowledgeable specialists are an important part of your child's medical team, but bear in mind that

specialists tend to look at only one part of a child. Your paediatrician or GP also has a prominent role to play. Besides attending to general medical needs (from vaccines to head colds), he/she can coordinate your child's care, being the one doctor who is responsible for his total body care and everything that is going on with him. Make sure you keep your doctor abreast of decisions made and treatments suggested by specialists, and feel free to ask questions such as "Do you agree with the plan? What do you think should be done next? Should we get another opinion?"

But the most valuable member of the team is you. No one will know as much about your child's history, ongoing care and future needs as you do. Stay organised to be most effective. Many parents use a calendar or a computerised hand-held equivalent to keep track of appointments and provide reminders of future needs.

If certain care or supplies are denied by your local health authority, work with your doctor to get the decision reversed. Sometimes further documentation of need or a letter from a caregiver will result in a reversal.

Education

All children, including those with disabilities and special needs, are entitled to necessary services and educational opportunities. Although there are small variations between states, special educational services are quite similar throughout Australia. Early intervention programs offer services to special needs children and their families, including information and parent education; assessment of the individual

DOES EARLY INTERVENTION WORK?

Early intervention programs are a relatively recent phenomenon. They are now considered worthwhile because studies in animals have clearly shown that large gains in brain function can occur when young animals are given extra "teaching" and stimulation. The ability of the brains of young animals (and presumably infants as well) to show such increments is called "plasticity". This quality, with its enhanced ability to learn, is present in much lower amounts in older children and adults.

It is hoped, thus, that stimulation at this time of unprecedented learning potential will be able to negate or minimise deficits already present. The most widely studied early intervention program is the Head Start Programme for disadvantaged (not disabled) pre-school children in the USA. Researchers have demonstrated substantial gains in cognitive and social skills compared with similar children not involved in the program when the children reach kindergarten. The difference between groups was less pronounced several years later, though. Early intervention has also proved

successful in improving outcomes in children with autism and with hearing loss. Furthermore, modestly improved developmental outcomes have been realised in premature infants after early intervention. However, the evidence that extra practice in motor, language and cognitive skills is equally worthwhile in children with other deficits is sparse. In children with disabilities resulting from cerebral palsy or developmental delay not due to prematurity, the preliminary data does seem to favour the early intervention, but improvements are not as dramatic as one would hope for, and seem to occur most often in less severely affected infants. Unfortunately we still need answers to questions such as: "Which groups of children do and which do not benefit from early intervention programs? How substantial are the gains? Are achievements made just short-term gains or are they still apparent years later?" The final word on early intervention has not yet been written; clearly, further studies are required to be able to say without doubt that these programs work.

Daily care aids

There are a wide range of products available that can help make looking after a special needs baby easier. Some may be provided by statutory services and others may be covered by insurance.

Bath supports
Overlays and hoists can all help to reduce back strain for parents as bathing even small children in the bottom of a standard bath can be difficult and uncomfortable.

Special potties
Ones with integral backrests, trainer seats and toilet support seats and frames can provide additional support for a child. Mobile potty chairs can be wheeled over a toilet or used with a separate commode are particularly good where space in the bathroom is limited.

Cots
Those with adjustable heights and drop-down sides make it easier to place children in bed while anti-suffocation mattresses and pillows create air cavities even when supporting the weight of a baby's head.

Special clothing
Choose garments with large, front fastenings, elasticated waist-bands, stretchy fabrics and loose styles.Buy Velcro-fastening shoes and trainers.

Prams
Ones with adjustable seats, supportive seating, and a backrest with head support are available. Specially adapted double prams also are manufactured.

Play equipment
Toys that can cater to specific needs such as helping children improve their sense of balance or manipulation and co-ordination skills, or can provide additional support or soft play are available. It also is possible to buy toys with adapted switches or special joysticks.

Child restraints
Those with special restraints, swivel mechanisms and head and foot supports can help make transferring and transporting your child easier. It is also possible to find special car seats for children suffering from hip displacement.

needs of the child and family; assistance in coordinating services; education and therapy programs; assistance with the move to school; and respite care.

Sleep

Children with developmental delay, cerebral palsy (CP) and a number of other disabilities have a higher occurrence of sleep problems than other children. There are probably many reasons to explain this observation, but some factors are within our power to change.

A big part of the problem in many families is that the child has developed bad sleep habits. Children sleep best if there is a set bedtime each night, preceded by a constant calming routine for preparing for going to bed. Ideally, a child should fall asleep in a quiet, dark room without accompanying music or associated aids such as rocking him to sleep or letting him fall asleep while taking the bottle. It is difficult for many parents to upset their child by being firm about the bedtime routine, but if you can do this, the results are impressive.

Gastro-oesophogeal reflux (see page 171), more common in children with CP and similar disorders, can cause discomfort and interfere with sleep. This and other medical issues should be considered as possible causes for poor sleeping before concluding that the root of the problem is just bad sleep habits.

Discipline

The "rules" of disciplining special needs children are no different from those used in other children (see pages 289–90) – the developmental level of the child and his temperament are the key determinants of how much a parent can expect of him. Just as it is not appropriate to demand that a two year old be as well behaved as a much older child, it is similarly unfair to demand more of a special needs child than he is developmentally capable. Avoiding frequent struggles is also desirable with such children. Below are some special points to consider.

Guilt

Whenever you upset your child by denying him what he wants, feelings of guilt are likely to arise in you. Even though stopping him from misbehaving or keeping him out of danger is the right response, when he cries you may feel bad. It is simply human nature at moments like these to question your decision and actions. No one wants to upset his/her child. If you were angry or raised your voice, if you lost your patience, or simply if you said, "No," his unhappiness, although likely momentary, may break your heart.

Feelings of guilt at such times do not appear only in you – all parents feel the same way. However, as a parent of a developmentally delayed or special needs child, you many feel particularly bad. In a flash, long-held feelings of sadness for your child's misfortune can appear. Being strict and displeasing your child, who has so much more to deal with than most other children, may be difficult for you to do because you do not want to add to his many burdens. Emotionally you may doubt yourself, but your child, like all other children, needs to be taught how to behave appropriately for his level of development. And while disappointing him may be hard to do, the alternative, not asking him to become what he is capable of, shortchanges him and "spoils" him.

Giving in

Again, the guiding principles of when to give in (see page 298) are the same for your developmentally challenged child as for every other child. What may be different, though, are the added behaviours that are not negotiable. The paradigm for disciplining children with disabilities is no different than that for other children. For important items, you must win. Your child may not do anything that may result in harm befalling him, he may not hurt others, he may not deface or destroy valuable objects. and he must take naps and go to bed on time. He must also take medicines and participate in therapeutic and medical events.

While you have to prevail in all these issues, you certainly may try to do so in the least confrontational way. It may be fairly easy to make your child take medications, but what do you do if he refuses to cooperate at speech therapy? The answer is complex, but no different for your child than for a child without disability. There are many possible solutions: be stern, make it a game, give a time out, use rewards, or admit that this session just isn't going to work out and go home. And always make sure your child gets to bed on time and has his nap, for like everyone else, when he is tired, his behaviour deteriorates. But if his resistance occurs regularly, work with the therapist to try a different, more enjoyable, approach to therapy.

For all other matters of discipline, two guidelines apply:

- If in the past your child has cooperated with your requests for good behaviour in particular situations, continue to expect him to do so whenever these situations again arise. At times when he is not behaving, be firm and insist that he do as instructed.
- For situations where being firm has repeatedly failed, think of something else. Perhaps you need to lower your expectations for his behaviour or try another approach (see pages 296–7).

The broad category of special needs children encompasses children of very diverse developmental capabilities. Severely challenged children may have only the capacity of an infant, while others with more limited disability (e.g. hearing or visual loss) may function as other children their age in nearly all spheres. For the former, appropriate discipline is the same as it is for infants (none or very minor), with limited expectations of what level of obedience is possible; for the latter children, discipline appropriate for their age is indicated. In all children, discipline tailored to the developmental level of the child is needed.

Independence

As the parent of a child with disability, it would not be surprising to find out that you are very protective. Your child has been through so much in his short life, so you don't want any more trouble befalling him; because he already has some deficits, you worry that an injury or accident may further impair him. And you are afraid his self-confidence will be harmed by repeated failure when he attempts to do what other children can do and thus you want to shield him from this possible outcome. The result may be that you discourage him from taking risks or participating in activities with even a drop of danger. You may not let him go on the swing for fear of him falling off or you may not let him try tricycle riding due to his clumsiness. And you may avoid letting him try an activity or task because you fear he won't succeed.

You may be used to providing much of the daily care your child requires. You have become accustomed to your everyday routines and perhaps helping your child with feeding or doing up his trainers is something you enjoy doing. But while it is easier and quicker for you to do everything for him, your child needs to be given the chance to do some of these tasks for himself.

A child with a disability possesses many of the same innate psychological strivings as other children; he, too, has a natural need to take control of the world around him. Whenever your child first succeeds in accomplishing something by himself, he is delighted. He will feel even better about himself when you add to this your own praise of his achievement. Failure is not unique to a special needs child: all children, in their efforts to do more and acquire new skills, will frequently not succeed. But even at those moments you can make this into a positive experience with comforting words such as, "I know that __(blank)__ is so difficult to do. And you tried so hard. I'm proud of you!" By giving your child a chance to try new activities and do more for himself, you are also giving him a chance to succeed and to feel good about himself. Even if there is special equipment needed or if extra precautions are taken, he will still enjoy trike riding as much, or perhaps more, than anyone else. It is important that he be given chances to enjoy life and to accomplish personal growth – all according to his ability. Encourage your child to become involved in activities that other children do by modifying the rules of the game or providing extra safety precautions. Your child will be happier and feel much better about himself if he is treated as much as is reasonably possible like a non-disabled child.

Love

You weren't planning on having a child with a disability when you imagined your future life. But your child is a special person and you will love him as every other parent loves his/her child. Your love for your child will not cure his disability. But it will make all you do for him seem worthwhile. No matter what his limitations, he is unique; he is wonderful, and he is your precious child.

6 ways you help you cope

1 **Rally your supports** Your family can be an enormous help. They can assist you physically (by taking care of your baby) and emotionally (validating your many opposing feelings and showing you that they care about you and your child). Some families find great comfort through prayer or attending religious services.

2 **Have personal time** Give yourself a break by letting another trusted person look after your baby while you do something for you – taking a nap, going to a movie, working out at the gym, or just getting out of the house. It is human nature to be grouchy and more prone to anger and frustration when you are tired and stressed. A little time away, on a regular basis, is refreshing and when you return to duty, your patience level will be much higher and life will seem much better.

3 **Work on your relationship with your partner** It is almost always the case with a special needs baby that the bulk of both partners' energy is directed at his care. With all the other time-consuming things to do, tending to your relationship is often at the bottom of the priority list. Make an effort to spend some time alone with each other frequently. Sharing your worries and feelings about your baby will strengthen the bond between you. Your lives will be much more pleasant if you both work together in caring for your baby. Listening empathetically to your partner's feelings is a wonderful source of support for him/her. And, of course, when your partner understands your emotions and stresses, you also will feel better.

4 **Contact organisations** Finding other parents who have similar concerns and experiences also will aid you. No matter what disability or medical problem your baby has, there is likely a national organisation that provides educational information, offers advice and prepares you for what you will face in the future. Chat rooms and other sites for parents to make contact are often available.

5 **Investigate** Learn as much as you can about your baby's condition. This allows you to begin to take charge of your child's care. Knowing what you are going to do and how you will do it will silence many of your self-doubts.

6 **Counselling** For some parents, help in dealing with emotional health is vital. Look for support groups in your community. Other alternatives include professional counselling or seeking guidance from religious leaders.

Birth injuries

Most injuries occur during a vaginal delivery but Caesarean deliveries are not without their risks as well.

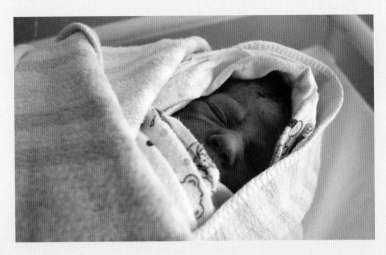

Cephalhaematoma

During a vaginal delivery, uterine contractions can force a baby's head against his mother's pelvic bones, resulting in a raised, soft lump (which is caused by blood collecting in the soft tissues) and bruising within the skin of the scalp. Usually, cephalhaematomas occur on one or both sides in the back of the head but do not cross the midline. They are rarely more than a temporary issue, as they gradually become smaller and harder but may contribute to jaundice (see page 369) as the haematoma is full of red blood cells that need to be destroyed. Most completely disappear, but occasionally you will still be able to feel a remnant – a small hard bump on your baby's skull.

Clavicle fracture

During a vaginal delivery, a very large baby is more at risk of a fractured collarbone; often this is diagnosed the day after delivery when the skin overlying the clavicle appears swollen or bruised. This injury is usually harmless and heals without any treatment, but a newborn with a clavicle fracture may be hesitant to raise his arms above his head, although otherwise moves them

normally. More unusually and during a difficult delivery, nerves from a baby's spinal cord to his upper arm can be injured as they pass from the area beneath the clavicle to the upper arm. An affected infant will not be able to move his arm or shoulder well, and his arm may lie limply at his side. Luckily, many such injuries resolve in a matter of weeks.

Deviated septum

When large amounts of downward pressure are exerted on a baby's nose in utero or during delivery, the nasal septum, which divides the right from the left side of the nose, can be pushed off its track. At birth, the nose looks crooked (the alignment of the bottom part of the nose is off centre) and the nostrils are differently sized (one is large and the other is small). If detected, a deviated septum can be put back on its track relatively easily by an

ENT (ears, nose and throat) doctor while the baby is still in the hospital.

Forceps marks

After a forceps delivery, bruising occurs in the facial skin directly underlying the place where the instruments were applied. These curvilinear black-and-blue marks gradually fade and disappear in a few days. However, at about one week of age, and after the forceps marks are gone, you may feel a peanut-sized hard lump just below the skin surface of your newborn's cheek. This is an injury caused by the forceps to the fatty layer of skin that will slowly shrink and go away. Once in a while, however, the pressure of the forceps injures the facial nerve controlling the mouth muscles so that when a baby cries, the shape of his mouth will be uneven. The majority of such injuries resolve over the following few weeks.

Minor problems at birth

Either the delivery or the maturity of a baby can result in a condition that is generally short lived.

Polycythaemia and hypoglycaemia

Both a high red blood cell count and low blood sugar occur primarily in very large infants (especially those whose mothers had gestational diabetes), and very small ones.

Polycythaemia, which will be suspected if the baby's skin colour is very ruddy, is confirmed by a blood test revealing an elevated haemoglobin or haematocrit (measures of the volume of red blood cells). Your doctor may encourage your baby to take fluids, draw off blood and replace it with IV fluids, or do nothing – allowing the condition to "right" itself.

Hypoglycaemia symptoms are shakiness, pale colour, rapid breathing and lethargy. In most hospitals, a blood sugar level can be quickly obtained by pricking a baby's heel, placing 1–2 drops of blood on a reagent strip and reading the value either manually or using a glucose meter.

Specific treatment for hypoglycaemia varies according to your baby's gestational sage, the extent of the disease etc. If breastfeedng your baby as soon as possible does not increase her blood sugar enough, she may be given a glucose-water mixture or formula to help. Once feedings are established, most hypoglycaemic infants will maintain their blood sugar normally.

Transient tachypnoea

Shortly after birth, a number of babies develop short-lived rapid breathing, which is caused by their failure to completely clear away amniotic fluid from within their lungs. Infants born by Caesarean section, because they have little time to prepare for their births, are most commonly affected. Most infants with transient tachypnoea require only close observation and will resolve the problem on their own in a day or so.

Jaundice

If in the first few days of life, your infant displays yellowing of his skin and of the whites of his eyes, this is known as neonatal jaundice. Jaundice occurs when there is a high blood level of bilirubin, a waste product from the degradation of haemoglobin.

In all of us, bilirubin is made each day as a small percentage of our old red blood cells are destroyed and replaced with new ones. In adults and older children, bilirubin is efficiently removed from the bloodstream by the liver and secreted into the bile; in utero, bilirubin is transported across the placenta and removed by the mother's liver. In many full-term newborns, the liver's removal function does not mature until three to four days of life, and with premmie babies, takes even longer to become efficient.

In the three to four days from birth to liver maturation, bilirubin accumulates in the bloodstream and, if a high enough level is present, jaundice may result.

Jaundice is most common in newborns with cephalhaematomas (see page 368) or other bruises incurred during delivery, in those whose blood type is different from their mother's (see box on *Maternal antibodies*, page 95), and in those born prematurely.

Most often, jaundice does not need to be treated. Harm can come from bilirubin only if its concentration is very, very high, but usually your paediatrician will just monitor the level until it reaches a safe value. (Since bilirubin reaches its highest point on days three to four after birth, your baby's doctor may advise a surgery visit at the time if you have already been discharged from hospital.)

Phototherapy (see page 370) is used when treatment is indicated.

Phototherapy

Exposure to light therapy was introduced into modern medicine long before we learned why it was effective. Its use resulted from the observation of a very good nurse who noted that babies placed in cots near the window were much less likely to become jaundiced than those who did not receive exposure to sunlight. Phototherapy lights were designed to artificially emit the same frequencies of light as sunlight.

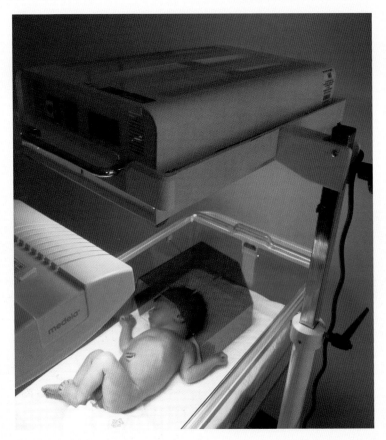

We now know that phototherapy works by imparting energy to bilirubin molecules in the skin and superficial blood vessels. This extra energy causes a small structural change in the bilirubin molecule, allowing it to be easily excreted in urine. Phototherapy does not cure jaundice, but it does keep the bilirubin level in the safe range until liver maturation is reached.

Phototherapy is effective only if the light rays reach the skin; for maximum advantage, as large a surface area of skin as possible should be exposed to the light. This is why a baby is undressed (except for a nappy and possibly a hat) and placed in a heated incubator to keep warm. An infant's eyes are traditionally protected from the light by being covered by soft patches, even though the eyes are shut most of the time. Research has shown that in some experimental animals, sustained use of phototherapy can injure an animal's eyes but so far there have been no reports of an eye injury in a human infant from the light rays.

While a baby is under phototherapy, it is not possible to visually judge how jaundiced he is. The phototherapy results in removal of bilirubin where the light rays strike, so a baby will look much less jaundiced (on the outside) even if the level of bilirubin is still high in his bloodstream (on the inside).

The more time a newborn is under the phototherapy lamps, the better it will work. Thus if your newborn is affected, the medical staff may want you to limit the time you have him out of the incubator for holding and feeding. However, you can sit next to the incubator, with hands inserted through the port holes, and touch and talk to your baby while he is being treated.

Abnormalities at birth

Given the complexity of our bodies' structure and functions, the complicated process of going from a one-cell fertilised egg to an organism with billions of cells, and the hundreds of errors that can occur along the way, it is remarkable how many babies are "normal". Fortunately, when physical abnormalities are present at birth, they are usually minor ones. More serious defects do occur, but they are much less common. Here are some of the ones seen most frequently.

Finger and toe problems

Most abnormalities of fingers and toes are inherited. Examples of these include second toe taller than the big toe, the fifth toe curves in, two toes joined together at their bases (but separated further toward the ends), and extra fingers or toes.

Extra digits range in complexity from a small (1–2cms long) bullet-shaped object with no nail or internal bones, hanging from the side of the fifth digit (pinky or little toe) by a very thin stalk, to a fully developed sixth finger or toe.

Many parents elect to have the extra digit removed for cosmetic reasons, but they constitute no health issue. Those on a thin stalk can be tied off with suture material or removed by a surgeon in the hospital or later at his/her clinic. More complete extra fingers or toes, if removed, require removal in the hospital.

Skin tags

Pimple-sized areas of extra skin, skin tags most often appear near the "button" of the ear lobe, but can occur anywhere. Usually, the only concern is for appearance. Rarely, they are a clue to an underlying problem (if located over the lower spine or if they occur in association with an abnormal ear lobe).

Hip dislocation

Clicks and clunks detected by a paediatrician while examining a newborn may signify an immaturity in the development of the hip socket (see *Congenital hip dislocation*, page 325).

Club foot

This foot deformity may affect one or both feet. At birth, the affected foot is held straight (flexed downward) at the ankle, turned in (the long axis of the foot points about 45 degrees towards the midline, instead of straight ahead), and everted (the foot is tilted sideways so that the big toe side of the foot is raised and the little toe side is down). A baby's risk of having a club foot is significantly greater if a parent or sibling also had one.

In many cases, a cause for this deformity remains unknown, but occasionally it results from the foot being held fixed in this position in the womb, without room to move to another position. Club feet may also result in rare diseases of the muscles or nerves, which affect other joints as well as the ankle and foot.

Treatment of a club foot begins shortly after birth. Conservative treatment can be very effective, and consists of placing the foot as close to normal position as can be done gently and holding it there in a plaster cast. A week later, the cast is removed and a second cast is applied after the foot again is manipulated a little closer to normal position. The process is repeated weekly and by about three months of age, the final position is reached. One more cast is now used to hold the foot in its final orientation for another two to three months.

Surgery is also an option for those infants whose feet are not adequately helped by casting and in more difficult-to-treat cases. The prognosis for full function with a pleasing appearance of that foot, whether treated by casts or surgery, is excellent.

Undescended testis

If at birth one testis is undescended (not present in scrotal sac), there is little concern for it will usually arrive in its normal position within a few months. For additional information see box on *Testicular descent*, page 329.

If both testes are not detected, which is very unusual (except in small premature babies), there is cause for further tests. Quite rarely, this may suggest that a child is a female with masculinised external genitalia. A blood test for analysing the chromosomes will give a definitive answer as to whether the child is a male or female.

Hydrocele

This is a small amount of tissue fluid surrounding one or both testes. If present, one testes will seem larger than the other (the larger one is the one surrounded by fluid). Most small and medium-sized hydroceles resolve in the first months of life. Those that do not disappear or are large may persist because they are associated with an inguinal hernia (see page 101). If so, minor surgery is recommended.

Heart murmurs

A heart murmur is a noise your doctor hears with his/her stethoscope when listening to your baby's heart. Murmurs occur when blood flow through an area within the heart or a major blood vessel is more turbulent (not as smooth) than usual. Murmurs detected on the first day of life are often transient, gone the next day, and are a normal variation. Some heart murmurs, however, are indicative of a structural problem in the formation of the heart. The most common cause of a

significant murmur is a VSD (ventriculoseptal defect). Instead of the right and left ventricles being separated completely by a muscular wall (septum), there is a small area, often smaller than a five-cent piece, where the wall is incomplete and blood from the left ventricle can enter the right ventricle. This murmur typically is noted after two or three days of age. The majority of VSDs fully close as the heart grows (see also page 328).

Other heart problems

There are a variety of less common heart malformations, some of which are serious. Clues to a heart problem include blueness of the lips (not the hands and feet – they are normally purplish-blue in healthy newborns), rapid breathing, paleness and poor feeding. When a structural cardiac defect is suspected, your doctor will investigate further, possibly using tests – an ECG (electro-cardiogram), echocardiogram (sonogram of the heart) and chest X-ray – or request a consultation from a paediatric cardiologist.

Cleft palate

This is an opening in the roof of the mouth (palate) allowing communication between the oral and nasal cavities. In the newborn period, this defect can make feeding difficult for a baby, since the cleft prevents generation of the negative pressure needed for successful sucking. A temporary solution is to give bottle feeds

using a very large teat. A plastic device, like the plate often used in children being treated by orthodontists, can be made that artificially closes off the opening. Surgical repair of the cleft palate is usually recommended before a year of age with excellent results.

In severe cases, a cleft palate can be accompanied by a split upper lip (hare lip). More extensive surgery is needed in such cases, again producing a pleasing result. In general, children with repaired cleft palate are prone to ear infections, often require speech therapy and have nasal-sounding voices

Sacral dimples

These are small puckerings of the skin over the lower spine, appearing in the upper quarter of the natal cleft (buttocks crease). If the bottom (base) of the dimple is skin-covered and there is no opening to deeper tissues, a sacral dimple is considered a normal variation. If that area has a small tuft of hair or skin tag, or if the bottom of the dimple cannot be seen well, a connection downward to the area of the spinal cord may be present and the possibility of a range of abnormalities called spina bifida (see also page 386).

An opening or sinus tract that leads from the skin to the area surrounding the spine may result in bacteria from the skin causing serious spinal infection. Other potential problems with spina bifida include benign fatty tumours (whose danger lies in pressing on the spinal cord) and injury to the lower spinal cord and nerves leaving the cord on their way to the pelvic area and legs. Although sacral dimples are common and spina bifida or sinus tracts are relatively rare, your paediatrician will recommend a study (sonogram or MRI) to further clarify this issue in the event there is any suspicion.

Hydrocephalus

Normally, the brain and spinal cord are surrounded by a protective, water-like liquid called spinal fluid, which is produced in a small number of large cavities within the brain, called ventricles, and travels via anatomical passageways to the area between the brain and skull and between the spinal cord and surrounding vertebrae. Spinal fluid is constantly produced and an exactly equal amount is removed by cells lining the outer brain, so that the volume of spinal fluid remains constant. A blockage in any of the passageways within the brain will result in fluid accumulating in the ventricles upstream from the blockage. As the ventricles become distended with excess fluid, the pressure of the fluid against the surrounding brain tissues increases, and if high enough, will cause symptoms.

Hydrocephalus is the name for conditions in which there are excessive amounts of spinal fluid and elevated pressure exerted upon the brain by the fluid.

Hydrocephalus due to the blockage of spinal fluid circulation can occur in ill premature infants when bleeding within the ventricles takes place: blood clots may block the path used by spinal fluid to exit the affected ventricle. Hydrocephalus may also be the result of an error in the formation of the ventricles or passageways during gestation, scarring following a brain infection occurring in utero, or a tumour in the brain compressing the ventricle or spinal fluid passageways.

Hydrocephalus can also develop by a second mechanism. Failure to properly reabsorb spinal fluid, which can be the result of injury to the cells lining the brain following meningitis (see page 348), results in an imbalance between production and removal of the fluid. An elevated volume of fluid and increased pressure in the ventricles may result.

As hydrocephalus develops, the increased volume of spinal fluid leads to rapid enlargement of the skull. An abnormally large head circumference (see also page 273) may signal the presence of hydrocephalus. If the skull cannot expand fast enough and the pressure within the skull rises further, the anterior fontanel may bulge upwards and vomiting and lethargy will develop. Another sign of increased pressure, called sun setting, consists of the eyes remaining fixed in a looking down position. Since only part of the iris (the coloured part of the eye) is visible above the lower eyelid, it resembles the setting sun as it drops below the horizon. If hydrocephalus is slowly developing and symptoms are not severe, spinal fluid can be removed by lumbar puncture (spinal tap) to lower the pressure. Repeated taps are often done on premature infants with hydrocephalus from bleeding within the cerebral ventricles to temporise while the blood clots blocking the spinal fluid flow are reabsorbed by the body. In other cases, a shunt is inserted to divert spinal fluid. A shunt is a long plastic tube inserted into one of the ventricles, which upon leaving the skull passes under the skin and ends within the abdominal cavity. In some models, a pressure sensitive valve is incorporated into the shunt so that fluid will leave the ventricle only when fluid pressure there is elevated. When spinal fluid reaches the abdominal cavity, it is readily absorbed into the circulation.

Shunts can be plagued by a number of complications, but the most significant ones are failure and infection. In recent years, some centres have stopped using shunts and instead perform a procedure to greatly enlarge the exit from which fluid from within the brain flows to the area surrounding it. It remains to be seen whether this procedure will become preferable to shunt insertion.

Lifelong conditions

It is not possible to cover all the many illnesses and diseases with major ramifications for the life of an infant. Thankfully, most of these are quite rare. Instead, we will focus on a few of the more common ones, some of the broad categories of disability, and finally, a discussion on living with and helping your special needs child.

Down's syndrome

Caused by an error in cell division early in the life of the tiny foetus, the typical facial and physical characteristics and associated medical problems all derive from an extra copy of chromosome 21 in each cell.

A number of mothers are aware during the second or third trimester that they will deliver an affected infant. Often, however, parents don't learn of the diagnosis until after delivery. Newborns with Down's syndrome do not yet have the typical facial appearance, so it may be difficult for a diagnosis to be suspected. However, there are two clues that suggest Down's syndrome – very floppy muscle tone and a "scruffy" neck (excessive, loose skin at the back of the neck).

Children with Down's syndrome may have a host of medical problems. In the newborn period, congenital heart defects (which may require surgery) and intestinal blockage may occur. In childhood, there is an increased risk of ear infections and hypothyroidism (under active thyroid). An affected child should also be examined for instability of the upper spine before playing vigorous sports activities.

Although intellectual disability and delay in reaching milestones are also prominent features, there is a wide variety of outcomes. Characteristically, children are sweet and happy. It is very easy to love a child who has Down's syndrome.

Cerebral palsy (CP)

This is a disorder of motor skills caused by damage to the brain areas controlling these functions, occasionally accompanied by intellectual disability, although there are many bright, fully-functioning children whose only deficit is with muscles and muscle control. CP can result from complications of prematurity, difficulties during labour and delivery that result in oxygen deprivation to the baby's brain, meningitis (see page 348) or head trauma. However, many times there is no clear cause for the motor abnormality.

The signs of CP are usually not present in the neonatal period, but become apparent at five to six months of age or later. Delays in reaching motor milestones and tight muscle tone are often the first signs. A number of patterns of CP exist:

hemiplegic (both the arm and leg on one side of the body are affected); diplegic (both legs are involved) and dystonic (posturing of the body, including head held to the side, wrist held in the bent position).

Medical problems can include muscle stiffness and weakness, gastro-oesophogeal reflux (see page 171), swallowing and feeding difficulties, clumsiness and seizures. Associated neurological difficulties, such as intellectual disability and learning disabilities, can also be present.

The injury to the nervous system that resulted in CP is not reversible, but on the other hand, the damage done is finite and does not progress or increase in severity. Treatment involves minimising symptoms of reflux, ensuring adequate nutrition and maximising motor performance (physical therapy and occasionally injections of botox [botulinum toxin] to relieve muscle tightness and orthopaedic devices such as braces to improve walking skills).

Spina bifida

This condition encompasses a continuum of abnormalities in the formation of the posterior part of the spinal column (the bones or vertebrae which surround and protect the spinal cord) and overlying skin and soft tissues. Most often the abnormality is located at the lower end of the spine. The mildest cases, called spina bifida occulta, may be diagnosed only when an X-ray of the abdomen or pelvis is taken for unrelated reasons and the lower spine is seen to have no posterior closure of the vertebrae.

The most severe cases, known as meningomyelocele, involve, in addition to the abnormality of the vertebrae, the lack of a skin covering over the lower spine. Without skin, soft tissues and vertebra to protect the spinal cord, the cord's lower end protrudes through the resulting defect. In meningomyelocele, damage to the nerves leaving the lower spinal cord for the lower extremities, bladder, anus and genital area is common and may result in leg weakness and incontinence. Also, a significant proportion of cases have associated hydrocephalus (see page 373). Variations with severity in between spina bifida occulta and meningomyelocele also occur. A sinus tract connecting the spine to the skin is such an example.

A clue to spina bifida not readily apparent at birth is the presence of other skin defects overlying the sacrum (lower part of the spinal column). Sacral dimples (see page 372), tufts of hair or skin tags in this area may signal an abnormality of deeper tissues and vertebrae.

Spina bifida occulta requires no treatment. Sinus tracts and other soft tissue abnormalities near the lower end of the spinal

cord are corrected surgically as soon as they are detected. In the case of meningomyelocele, a radiological study is first done to see whether or not hydrocephalus is present. Then surgery to close the spinal defect, and to also treat the hydrocephalus if present, is done in the newborn period.

Spina bifida occulta typically has no complications, while in repaired defects of intermediate severity, some damage to nerves may occur. Nerve damage is almost universally present in meningomyelocele. Injury to nerves exiting the lower spinal cord can result in leg weakness, loss of sensation below the waist, and in males, impotency. Nerve injury may also affect the lower intestinal tract (incontinence of stool, chronic constipation) and urinary system (incontinence and poor bladder emptying). Incomplete emptying of the bladder following urination can result in urinary tract infections and occasionally may lead to damage to the kidneys.

Heart disease

Heart disease can be either congenital or acquired. Congenital defects are due to errors in formation of the heart structures during foetal development; acquired disease may be the consequence of infection – viral infection of the heart muscle (myocarditis), bacterial infection of the heart valves (endocarditis), rheumatic fever (a complication of strep throat), inherited diseases of

metabolism or connective tissue (Marfan's syndrome), poisons and toxins, or diseases of unknown etiology (Kawasaki's disease).

Many of the congenital defects can be improved or even cured with surgery. Children who cannot be helped fully by surgery and those with acquired disease can suffer ongoing disability. The major problem for children with chronic heart disease is the inability – whether due to poor pumping ability, failure to bring sufficient blood to the lungs for oxygenation, or inadequate delivery of oxygenated blood to the rest of the body – to meet the body's need for oxygen. Many children do fine when they are at rest, but when demands for additional delivery of oxygen are made, during exercise for example, they become winded and exhausted. For small infants, the work of sucking on a bottle or the breast to obtain a feed can be overly taxing, resulting in sweating, shortness of breath and the feed ending before satiety. Older children have a limited ability to perform the usual activities of childhood.

Surgery may benefit some structural defects. In severe cases, cardiac transplantation may be recommended. Medication to increase the heart's efficiency can be given when the heart's pumping function is suboptimal. Antibiotics may be suggested before dental work for children with a small number of specific abnormalities to prevent heart valve infection. Attention to nutrition is always important. Infants with severe degrees of disability may qualify for palivizumab (see page 96) to prevent infections with RSV (respiratory syncytial virus).

Cystic fibrosis (CF)

This is an inherited disease that affects primarily the lungs and gastrointestinal tract. All manifestations of this disease are the consequence of abnormally thick mucus secretions in the lung, pancreas and other organs. In the lungs, the thick secretions clog the small air conduits (bronchioles), leading to repeated cycles of infection and inflammation. With time, the cumulative damage to the lungs becomes severe, and lung function declines. When the thick secretions block pancreatic ducts, digestive enzymes cannot reach the intestines and digestion is impaired. The trapped enzymes also cause damage to the pancreatic cells.

The initial appearance of CF may take many forms. In the neonatal period, vomiting and intestinal obstruction from a mass of faeces (meconium) and thick mucus may signal CF. This syndrome, called meconium ileus, is unique to CF, but is not a frequent presentation of the illness. More commonly, a previously healthy infant or toddler has recurrent episodes of pneumonia and wheezing, prompting suspicion of CF. For some children, poor weight gain and diarrhoea, due to poor

digestive function, are the signs that point to the diagnosis. And recently, with the implementation of newborn screening for CF, a number of children with CF are being diagnosed shortly after birth, before any disease manifestations have occurred.

The presence of CF can be confirmed by either a sweat test or a blood test. The sweat test is based on the observation that mothers found that sweat from their CF afflicted children tasted salty. The sweat test is performed by collecting sweat from the child and measuring the concentration of sodium chloride (salt). In the last decade, a blood test has been introduced that looks for the specific gene mutations that result in CF. Neither test is perfect: an inaccurate sweat test result can be obtained if an insufficient amount of sweat is collected; the blood test can identify only 80 per cent of CF cases since there are many subtle variations in the exact CF mutation.

CF is a chronic, progressive disease. Over the years of childhood, gradual worsening of lung function occurs. Although pulmonary disease causes the most difficulty for children with CF, a number of other complications can result from the abnormal secretions. Multiple episodes of sinusitis (due to thick mucus clogging sinus openings) and nasal polyps are common and the high salt losses in the sweat can lead to dehydration in infancy. Injury to the pancreas also can result in destruction of

cells that produce insulin and thus diabetes may complicate this already unremitting illness. Thick secretions in liver ducts can lead to liver damage.

CF should be suspected in children having any of the following: meconium ileus, recurrent episodes of lung disease (chronic cough, pneumonia, wheezing), poor growth, persistent diarrhoea, nasal polyps and multiple sinus infections. Some of these manifestations, such as wheezing, sinus infections and nasal polyps, are also common in healthy children without CF.

Treatment of CF is a multidisciplinary endeavour and usually takes place in regional CF centres located at large hospitals. To slow pulmonary decline, pneumonias are treated aggressively with antibiotics. On a day-to-day basis, rigorous chest physiotherapy – exercises consisting of placing the child's body in various positions and not so gentle chest pounding – are needed to help unclog air passageways. Inhaled medication for the same purpose is used in some centres. To enable better digestion of foods, pills containing pancreatic enzymes are taken every day.

With advances in treatment and better nutrition, the lives of children with CF have improved markedly, but daily routines are vigorous, and numerous hospitalisations and gradually worsening exercise capacity can be expected.

Developmental delay

This is a category of disability that encompasses a wide variety of conditions. All have in common a similar end result: deficits in reaching milestones. Temporary developmental delays, caused by environmental factors or illness, are generally considered a variation of normal (see also page 325). Developmental delay, as used here, refers to persistent delays in at least two, if not all, of the four spheres of development (gross motor, fine motor, personal-social and language).

A closely related term, intellectual disability, is used by some experts as a synonym for developmental delay, but this is more precisely defined as having an IQ (intelligence quotient) less than 70, with the average being 100, and having significant difficulty with daily living skills including communicating.

If the delays are primarily those of motor skills, than the term cerebral palsy can be used (see page 374).

The list of causes for developmental delay is long, but includes inherited conditions, disorders of brain formation and growth, congenital infections, environmental toxins, injuries to the brain, oxygen deprivation, meningitis and others. In addition, in many cases a reason for the delays cannot be found. Obviously, developmental delay is suspected as a child progresses in age but is significantly behind expectations for reaching milestones. Other clues may include a small head circumference at birth, poor head growth, and seizures or abnormalities on neurological exam. However, some children with developmental delay display none of these.

Very few causes of developmental delay have specific treatments. One notable exception is the case of children raised in orphanages or other non-stimulating environments; when the social isolation is ended, many (if not all) deficits will improve. In cases with other causes, treatment consists of love and providing education and activities to maximise further developmental gains.

Hearing impairment

Like heart disease, hearing impairment can be present at birth (congenital) or develop later in childhood (acquired). Premature infants have a higher incidence of hearing problems. Causes of congenital loss include in utero viral infections and inherited forms of hearing loss. Acquired hearing deficits can be the result of prematurity and its complications, medications, meningitis and uncommon diseases of the middle and inner ear. Early detection and intervention – hearing aids, speech and language therapy, programs designed for hearing-challenged children and, for some children, cochlear implants – have greatly improved the speech and language outcomes of infants with hearing loss (see also page 334).

Visual impairment

Visual deficits in children result from numerous diseases and injuries. These include inherited diseases of the eye, congenital cataracts (see page 333), glaucoma, amblyopia (see page 334), damage to the area of the brain responsible for interpreting visual input, trauma and prematurity.

Two peculiarities of the way our eyes and brain cooperate are important in understanding acquired visual loss in children. First, there is a critical period for vision in the first one to two months of life; if an eye is not exposed to visual stimuli in this period – say due to a congenital cataract – the brain area which converts signals from that eye to visual images will not develop fully and vision from that eye may be poor for life. A second "illogical" property of the infant visual system is its response to what we call blurred vision. If, as in amblyopia, eyes are not aligned properly and the brain ignores the image from one of the eyes, permanent brain-based visual loss can result in the suppressed eye if the blurring is allowed to continue.

Glaucoma

Increased pressure in the fluid in the eyeball in an infant can be detected by the combination of a large iris (the coloured part of the front of the eye) compared to the other eye, tearing in that eye, and accompanying redness of the white of the eye. Fussy behaviour is often reported as well. (Note that the most common cause of increased tears in an eye is a benign condition, a blocked tear duct. This can be distinguished by the absence of the other findings.) Glaucoma, if sufficiently severe, can cause visual loss as the increased pressure present gradually damages the optic nerve.

Treatment is occasionally with medicated eye drops and often involves surgery to lower the pressure within the eye.

Autism

A form of developmental delay in which primarily language and social interactions are impaired, children with autism lack the ability to form bonds and interact with other people in the usual way. They also have difficulty with verbal communication, and have speech delays and deficiencies in skills required for holding interactive conversations.

Autistic disorders are referred to as pervasive developmental disorders (also known as PDD), but this term may be misleading in that children with autism often have few, if any, delays in gross and fine motor skills, and many are quite intelligent.

Our knowledge of what causes autism is rudimentary. Autism may well be a final common pathway of several disorders. We do know that there are some genetic predispositions to its occurrence and that, at least in many cases, the process leading to autism has begun before a child's

birth or shortly thereafter. Despite popular belief, autism is not caused by vaccinations (see box page 379).

It is difficult to diagnose autism in young infants because sophisticated interpersonal interactions and language are not normally demonstrated until a child reaches 15–18 months of age or more. A diagnosis of autism is based on a deficit in these skills, so autism is only able to be diagnosed after this age. Since that is about the time when the MMR vaccine is given (typically at 13–15 months of age), you can see why, by coincidence alone, cases can be diagnosed at about the same time that the vaccine is given.

The social and communication deficiencies of autistic children can be improved with early diagnosis and intense individual behavioural therapy.

Peanut allergy

You may not think of an allergy to peanuts (or other food capable of severe allergic reactions) as making your baby a special needs child. However, if your baby has such an allergy, because of the ever-present possibility of accidental exposure and a life-threatening allergic reaction, called anaphylaxis, both your life and that of your child's will be changed forever.

The number of children with peanut allergy has increased markedly in the last two decades, though exactly why is unknown. One popular hypothesis – that

the higher number of affected children is the result of introducing peanuts into the diet earlier in life – has led to delaying the time children are given peanut products until they are two or three years old. However, studies to provide the hoped-for proof have so far been unconvincing.

Anaphylaxis may occur moments after accidental ingestion of a peanut-containing product, and consists of any combination of swelling of the mouth, lips and throat; shortness of breath; wheezing; abdominal pain and vomiting; rash (hives); pale appearance; and low blood pressure (shock).

Anaphylaxis can be treated with injections of adrenaline and chlorpheniramine (Piriton), but the bulk of the "treatment" of nut allergy is prevention. This is no small task with a young child. The easy part is carefully reading food product labels to ensure no peanut is present. And even here, products with no declared peanut can be contaminated with small amounts of peanut from other products manufactured at the same plant. Also, manufacturers of products you know to be safe can, without warning, change the ingredients to include peanuts. Eating out is also problematic. You must carefully question the waiter or waitress about the use of peanuts in foods, sauces and cooking oil. A remnant of peanut may remain on the scoop that serves your child his peanut-free ice cream if it had just been used to provide another child with a flavour dangerous to your baby. You will worry that your child might unknowingly ingest some peanuts during lunch at play group if he eats what another child has brought in. Treats doled out at a birthday party may contain peanuts. A play date at a friend's house may turn disastrous if the friend's mother forgets or isn't careful to check a product's label. The ever-present fear that an accidental ingestion will occur may make it hard to let your child out of your sight, and surely can turn even a calm parent into a very anxious one.

Children with peanut allergy should have injectable adrenaline with them at all times. A written emergency plan and adrenaline will be required for your child's school. Constant checking, asking and reminding will be part of your life.

3 myths about autism

1   **Autism has increased in the last decades** There are more children with autism now than thirty years ago. Studies have shown much of the apparent increase is due to doctors' heightened familiarity with the disease (and thus recognising it more often) and a broadened definition of what is considered autism. In the past, only "classic" or "full blown" cases of autism were diagnosed to be this condition, while now we talk of an autistic spectrum of disease in which variations and milder cases are included. A recent study demonstrated that as the number of diagnoses of autism steadily increased in the last two decades, the number of diagnoses made of other, somewhat similar, conditions decreased. In other words, children who in the past were given a different diagnosis are now counted as having autism.

2   **The MMR vaccine causes autism** In 1998, Dr Andrew Wakefield published an "Early Report" in the *Lancet*, which started an international uproar – the misinformation heard round the world. Dr Wakefield stated in his conclusions, "We did not prove an association between measles, mumps and rubella vaccine and the syndrome described... Further investigations are needed to examine this syndrome and its possible relation to this vaccine". Since then, over fifteen scientific studies examined the connection between autism and MMR; all have shown that there is no relationship between MMR and autism. It is clear that when autism is diagnosed soon after the vaccine it is a coincidence, not a cause–effect relationship. However, many children are not being vaccinated and the cases of childhood diseases are increasing in frequency. Some parents feel that autism is caused by the combination of three individual vaccines in the MMR and therefore want to give each of the three separately (see also page 338). Since MMR combined does not cause autism, separating the vaccine into its three components will not prevent autism. However, as the rate of measles vaccination falls, the chance of your child contracting the disease (with its potentially serious effects [see page 354]) increases.

3   **Thimerosol (ethyl mercury) in vaccines causes autism** Although no evidence has ever been presented that the mercury preservative in vaccines has harmed children, it was removed from all vaccines given to infants in 2001. No decrease in diagnoses of autism has occurred.

GROWTH CHARTS – BOYS

LENGTH-FOR-AGE PERCENTILES: BOYS, BIRTH TO 36 MONTHS

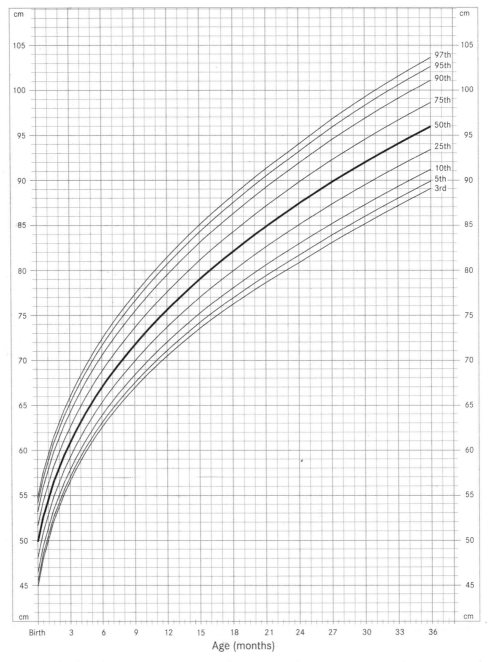

SOURCE: Developed by the National Center for Health Statistics in collaboration with the National Center for Chronic Disease Prevention and Health Promotion (2000).

WEIGHT-FOR-AGE PERCENTILES: BOYS, BIRTH TO 36 MONTHS

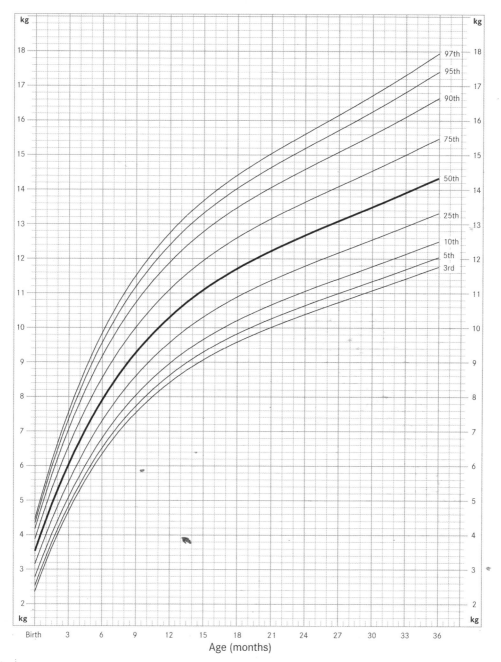

SOURCE: Developed by the National Center for Health Statistics in collaboration with the National Center for Chronic Disease Prevention and Health Promotion (2000).

GROWTH CHARTS – GIRLS

LENGTH-FOR-AGE PERCENTILES: GIRLS, BIRTH TO 36 MONTHS

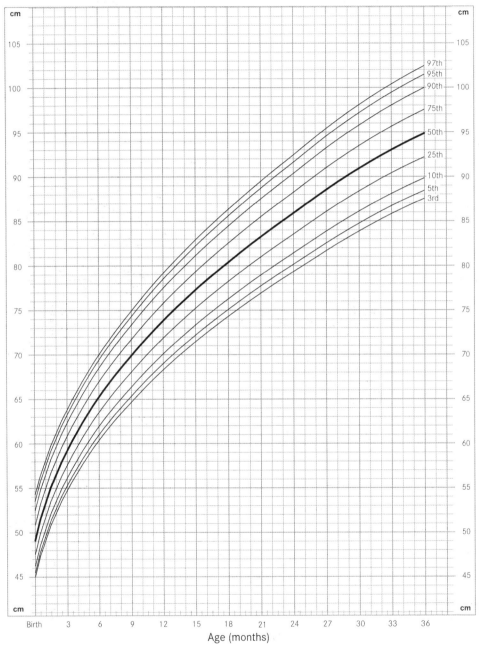

SOURCE: Developed by the National Center for Health Statistics in collaboration with the National Center for Chronic Disease Prevention and Health Promotion (2000).

WEIGHT-FOR-AGE PERCENTILES: GIRLS, BIRTH TO 36 MONTHS

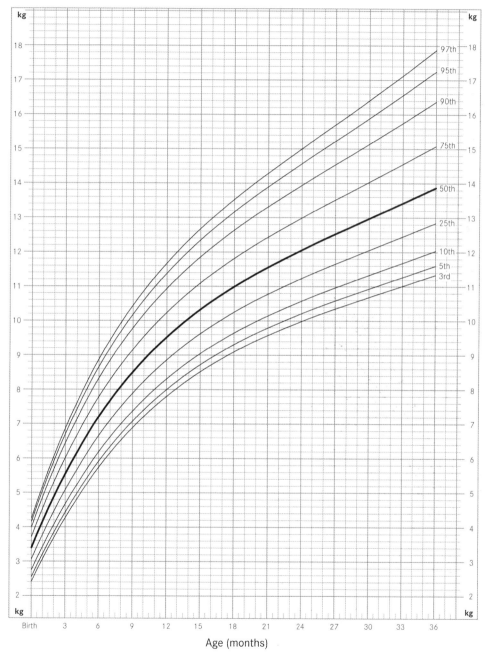

SOURCE: Developed by the National Center for Health Statistics in collaboration with the National Center for Chronic Disease Prevention and Health Promotion (2000).

Index

Useful addresses

Breastfeeding

- Australian Breastfeeding Association (1800 686 2 686)
  breastfeeding.asn.au (see website for contact details in each state)
- La Leche League (laleche.org)
- breastfeeding.com

Bottle-feeding

- betterhealth.vic.gov.au (advice on bottle-feeding with formula)
- newbornbaby.com.au/bottle-feeding-tips.html

Twins

- Australian Multiple Birth Association (amba.org.au)

Special needs babies

- Each state government provides its own information and services
- Raising Children Network (raisingchildren.net.au)
- Children, Youth and Women's Health Service (cyh.com)

Acknowledgements

Carroll & Brown would like to thank:

Proofreader: Brackley Proofreading Services
Make-up: Jeseama Owen

Picture credits

Front Jacket: Camera Press/Eltern
p9 Photolibrary.com; p10 Mothercare; p12-15
Mothercare; p16 Photolibrary.com; p21
Photolibrary.com; p25 Photolibrary.com; p27 (top
left) Scott Camazine/Science Photo Library; (top
right) Lea Paterson/Science Photo Library; (bottom
left) Dr P. Marazzi/Science Photo Library; (bottom
right) Science Photo Library; p46 Photolibrary.com;
p48 image courtesy of JoJo Maman Bebe; p56
Photolibrary.com; p58 Photolibrary.com; p60
BabyBjorn; p61 Photolibrary.com; p65
Photolibrary.com; p67 Photolibrary.com; p72
Photolibrary.com; p74-75 Angela Spain/Mother &
Baby Picture Library; p76 Indira Flack/Mother &
Baby Picture Library; p79 Photolibrary.com; p87
Photolibrary.com; p89 Photolibrary.com; p94
Photolibrary.com; p97 Tiny Traveller image courtesy
of Bettacare Ltd; p98 Tracy Dominey/Science Photo
Library; p118 Photolibrary.com; p119
Photolibrary.com; p121 Photolibrary.com; p124
Photolibrary.com; p126 Photolibrary.com; p128
Photolibrary.com; p130 Photolibrary.com; p155
Photolibrary.com; p161 (left and right)
Photolibrary.com; p163 Photolibrary.com; p168
Photolibrary.com; p169 Photolibrary.com; p172
Photolibrary.com; p176 Leigh Schindler; p179
Photolibrary.com; p130 Photolibrary.com; p196
Photolibrary.com; p201 Photolibrary.com; p210
Photolibrary.com; p211 Photolibrary.com; p213
Photolibrary.com; p215 Photolibrary.com; p219
BabyBjorn; p220 BabyBjorn; p221
Photolibrary.com; p229 Photolibrary.com; p238
Photolibrary.com; p239 Photolibrary.com; p272
BSIP, Villareal/Science Photo Library; p280
Photolibrary.com; p281 Photolibrary.com; p286
Photolibrary.com; p287 Photolibrary.com; p292
Photolibrary.com; p295 Photolibrary.com; p296
Photolibrary.com; p303 Photolibrary.com; p312
Photolibrary.com; p319 Photolibrary.com; p321
Photolibrary.com; p324 Ian Hooton/Science Photo
Library; p328 Photolibrary.com; p330 Annabella
Bluesky/Science Photo Library; p331 Dr P.
Marazzi/Science Photo Library; p332 Dr P.
Marazzi/Science Photo Library; p333 Dr P.
Marazzi/Science Photo Library; p334 (top) Dr P.
Marazzi/Science Photo Library; (bottom) Paul
Whitehill/Science Photo Library; p335 Dr P.
Marazzi/Science Photo Library; p337 Ian
Hooton/Science Photo Library; p349
Gustoimages/Science Photo Library; p350 Dr P.
Marazzi/Science Photo Library; p353 (top) Chris
Knapton/Science Photo Library; (bottom) Dr
H.C.Robinson/Science Photo Library; p354 Lowell
Georgia/Science Photo Library; p357 Dr P.
Marazzi/Science Photo Library; p361 AJ
Photo/Science Photo Library; p362 LA LA/Science
Photo Library; p364 (top) Bath Support image
courtesy of Homecraft Rolyan Ltd; (middle) Buggie
image courtesy of Amilly International Ltd;
(bottom) Photolibrary.com; p368 Photolibrary.com;
p370 Gustoimages/Science Photo Library.

Illustration: Amanda Williams